Charm of Favor

A true story of the rise of the Clinton Crime Syndicate

By Brooks A. Agnew

2nd Edition (new content)

"Because destiny does not ask twice."

Copyright 2017: All rights reserved. No copies or excerpts, electronic, printed, or broadcast will be permitted without written permission from the author.

The AUDIO VERSION is a free bonus directly from the author if you send a copy of your receipt to brooks@CharmOfFavor.com. Contact the author by email to request an interview.

Table of Contents

Prologue 1
Foreword 1
Chapter 1 10
Chapter 2 16
Chapter 3 23
Chapter 4 37
Chapter 5 52
Chapter 6 60
Chapter 7 72
Chapter 8 87
Chapter 9 95
Chapter 10 109
Chapter 11 118
Chapter 12 148
Chapter 13 158
Chapter 14 170
Chapter 15 192
Chapter 16 216
Chapter 17 226
Chapter 18 242
Chapter 19 248
Chapter 20 266
Chapter 21 276
Chapter 22 285
Chapter 23 293

Chapter 24	310
Chapter 25	330
Chapter 26	342
Chapter 27	352
Chapter 28	362
Chapter 29	374
Chapter 30	394
Chapter 31	419
Epilogue	430

Prologue

This book is based upon true events taken from actual accounts, news articles, personal testimonies, and court findings. I place my fictional characters into the story to carry you along at the ground level, behind the scenes, so you can smell the smoke, and feel the love and the fear in the fight for America against a dark and nefarious Syndicate. The other names have not been changed, so that the reader understands the portent of what has happened, and what may happen.

For thousands of years, the world was ruled by a handful of men from wooden ships. In 1776, a small group of colonialists gathered together and debated into existence a new government based upon liberty and freedom, two concepts the world had never imagined before. In 1787, a convention produced a concise constitution that has become the oldest and most respected form of government in history.

But prophecy made no mention of this government. No prophet, no seer, no revelator saw the creation and existence of the richest, most powerful government the world has ever known. Why? Because, I believe, these men saw that future written down for them and chose a new one. They believed, as I do, that they were empowered to do so by God, and that along with this came a set of unalienable rights.

Barely 60 years later, the men who had ruled the world for millennia cause a corporation to be formed that would be dedicated to removing that balance between the powers of government that keeps us free men. That corporation was founded with one purpose in mind; to see that America was ruled by one man, and that man would be of their choice and under their control. The true seizure of power leaped forward in 1933, and again in 2001. America may not survive this next surge.

All the wars fought by America have been between that power and the free citizens of this country. For all but just a few years, they have ruled America and slowly eroded her down to a shadow of her original glory. They almost won it all in 2016, but America rose up and saved it at the last minute; against all odds and in defiance of all the pollsters.

This book is the story of the rise of the world's richest, most powerful and bloodthirsty crime syndicate the world has ever known. It has used laws and oaths and covenants to build an empire worth trillions by selling the powers of war to America's enemies, so that one day they can deliver the richest treasury on earth into the hands of the original power of evil on this world.

Will they accomplish their evil design? Will you wake up in time to stop them? Not, I dare say, until you read this book.

Foreword

Less than 61 years after the original 1787 Constitutional Convention, Washington D.C. was already well on its way to becoming the central control power the founding fathers feared. Politicians arguing and positioning over access to power, and to the treasury, debated to prevent any one man from acquiring a throne like that of mother England. Far from it. It was designed to act like a Republic, where everyone in the country had representation in the halls of a government that served the people and did not rule over them. The original 13 States had already grown to 30 with the addition of Wisconsin on May 28th of 1848.

Just days before, on May 22nd, the Democratic National Committee was formed, and almost immediately began asserting itself to seizing control of the government. Previously known as the *anti-federalists,* the Democrats highly favored a country run solely by the President. Formerly known as the *Whigs,* the Republicans thought the nation would best adhere to the Constitution by letting Congress take the lead.

Within 24 months, however, elected officials began abusing their power, as they supposed, to levy the Tariff of Abominations against the Southern States. It was crafted to extract money from the South's agrarian prosperity and foreign trade to subsidize their industrial political supporters in the North. The Democrat's lust for power left those States—most of which were slave owning Democrats—no choice but to secede from the Union by listing the same grievances against the Federal government as the original 13 colonies had filed against King George. After all, the Union was new, and it was not working for every State equally.

After countless impassioned pleas on the floor of Congress for more than ten years, thirteen Southern States, led by South Carolina began filing Declarations of Causes as reasons to secede from the Union. The result of the filing of those 1861 grievances was exactly the same as the colony's 1774 submission, except that the 13

States could not withstand the military industrial supply chain of the North coupled with their scorched earth battle tactics. The Southern States were forced back into the Union through unconditional surrender and by signing a writ of Reconstruction. Only Texas refused to sign as they reentered the Union.

Still, it was a Republican President Lincoln who tried his best to bring the nation back together, but his lack of diplomacy led the country into the bloodiest war in US history, costing three quarters of a million Americans their lives and injuring at least that many more. History does not widely report that Lincoln acquired many enemies, which included a central banking cartel determined, by any means necessary, to gain control over this new nation's money supply. He also had not pleased the Democrat powers of the North, which drew into it the Southern States, from whom they were leeching the capital required to expand their profits.

His real opponent was never the States of the South, but rather a cadre of secret powers operating inside the American government who would never allow a Republican President to take credit or control of what could already arguably be considered the greatest economic potential the world had ever known, so they conspired to have him assassinated. Then, as now, the ones responsible for unspeakable crimes and espionage were never brought to justice. Almost as soon as Lincoln stopped breathing, the United States signed the Rothschild central bank charter.

The history of men is not like the concentric rings in a tree stump. It is not an academic or predictable record like the decay of a nuclide, or even a geometric proof. Most people would agree it is not even a legitimate attempt at the truth, but rather is crafted and polished by the victors. In some cases, it was scraped together out of ashes by the survivors; scattered and forgotten victims of wars so terrible and brutal that the officers lost their minds in endless nightmares or took their own lives to stop the pain.

In still other cases there was a concerted and presumably successful attempt to fabricate the past so that a future of choice could be charted. Once the ships of time sailed from the shores of that past, the frothy trail left in the sea of potentialities was the only truth men would know from that time forward, if time does indeed only go forward. But when humans begin to reconstruct things upon which future generations would reflect, like assembling the pieces of a crashed passenger airliner, the reconstruction begins to tell a different story. The true purpose of history cannot be withheld from the universe. It can be forgotten by men. It can be corrupted. It can even be denied, but the truth can never be erased from the universe.

Everything we do will eventually affect the universe, and effects cannot exist without first there must be a cause. Just as a rounded pebble is proof there was once a moving body of water that made it, there are spots of blood, or threads of uniforms, or documents, or bullets, or screams laying in the soil that record what really happened. There is always fear in the dust of history. There is the fear that the victims will remain nameless. There is a fear that justice lies docile beneath a beautifully manicured lawn. For some it is a fear that justice will never be served, and for others it is that it will.

When evil makes its grand and terrible designs, the planning can take centuries. The roots that feed the design must remain obscured so that in war and peace, they can nourish the organism that will choke off the light from everything else around it.

Crime syndicates are like twisted, hard, and mercilessly dark wood so relentless and strong that they can break apart solid stone. A member of that syndicate would no more betray it than a root or a leaf would betray the tree organism it serves.

The early churches were excoriated by Jesus for placing all value upon their genealogy. It was vital to be a child of Abraham, and if you could actually recite your lineage all the way to Adam, it provided you a rite of passage, an unmitigated authority over the tribe, as it were. The denial of a birthright throughout the scriptures has been the cause of every evil uprising. Cain and Abel, Esau and Jacob, Lamon and Nephi, Lucifer and Adam all tell the same story.

To evil, the birthright is paramount. To righteousness, the purity of the soul's intent attracts the blessing of inheritance. Perhaps nowhere is it expressed more clearly than in the Book of Luke.

> Jesus said, "Bring forth therefore fruits worthy of repentance, and begin not to say within yourselves, We have Abraham to our father: for I say unto you, That God is able of these stones to raise up children unto Abraham." KJV Luke 3:8

Crime syndicates gain their power through inheritance. The name and the lineage is the key to all power. It is a type and a shadow of how powers function on earth. A man without a family heritage is an outsider, and may win an election from time to time. But they will never be handed the keys of power, because those keys are held by principalities that adhere to these ancient ways of magic and darkness.

Just such a genealogical pathway was crafted where none existed in 1945, while William Jefferson Blythe, Jr. was U.S. Army active duty serving in Italy. He is listed by most accounts of history to be the biological father of William Jefferson Blythe Clinton, the 42nd President of the United States.

The biological problem with this claim to lineage, is that Virginia Dell Kelley Cassidy, Bill Clinton's mother, was already three months pregnant with him when Blythe returned from Italy. Reports that Virginia gave birth at 6 months of pregnancy due to a fall turned out to be false when *Vanity Fair* tracked down the midwife who delivered her baby boy. She reported that he was, in fact, delivered as a full-term baby weighing between 8 and 9 pounds on August 19, 1946.

Further investigation showed that not only was he the bastard child of Virginia Kelley's affair with an unknown man from Louisiana, but that her marriage to Blythe was fabricated by friends of the family as he lay in the morgue, dead. What vision was beheld that caused such a plan to be set in motion cannot be written or told by any man alive, but the Kelly family reportedly created a new name for Tyrell—the true birth name of Virginia's baby boy—and a new lineage for whom history would record as William Jefferson Blythe, carefully leading back to Andrew Jackson Blythe; a name with a lengthy history from the original 13 colonies of America.

She later married Roger M. Clinton, Sr., and he adopted Bill, giving him the family name by which he would be known. It was the perfect pedigree for a boy destined by powers beyond this world to be President. Only now, at the end, is betrayal appropriate, for the soul of a human is required as payment in exchange for the *charm of favor* that delivered the fame and power and wealth of this world in a single mortal lifetime.

To such a man must be provided a mate, a queen as it were, for the glory of world leadership rarely falls to less than a pair. Occasionally, a queen shall reign in a figurative sort of way. But kings must have a queen in order to shoulder the true mantel of power. The charm requires a female energy to complete the circle of power. Something in the formation of Fibonacci rotations must be symmetrical and complimentary, so that tiny movements made at the right time in the right amount can resonate to create unstoppable momentum with very little energy input.

This female energy must have a source that matches the male energy in frequency, meaning that it cannot be too dark or too light. It cannot be too red or too blue. Like the backside of a coin, it has the same value and the same weight of gold. If the face of the coin is a good man, then the female side of the coin must be a good woman. If the face on the coin is that of an evil tyrant, then nothing less than a sorceress will do for the backside.

Such was the case in a young lawyer, named Hillary Rodham. She displayed no desire to represent clients for the cause of justice. She was born on October 26, 1947, in Chicago to Hugh and Dorothy Rodham and raised in Park Ridge, Illinois, along with her two younger brothers, Hugh Jr. and Anthony. At the tender young age of 27, she had already proven herself worthy of the task.

Her skills would best serve those who wished to escape justice, or to prosecute the innocent, depending upon the situation. While teaching at the University of Arkansas School of Law in 1975, Hillary Rodham was allegedly selected by Judge Maupin Cummings to defend Thomas Alfred Taylor, who had been accused of raping a 12 year old girl.

Cummings picked Clinton's name from a list he kept of attorneys who would represent poor clients, and this poor client specifically requested a female attorney. While she knew her client was guilty, she pursued his victim with zeal by accusing her of secretly fantasizing about having sex with older men. She even meticulously manipulated the evidence, so that Taylor would serve only a year for a lower charge of improperly fondling a minor.

She stated publicly, "But you know what was sad about it is that the prosecutors had evidence, among which was his underwear...which was bloody. Sent it down to the crime lab. The crime lab took the pair of underpants, neatly cut out the part that they were gonna test, tested it, came back with the result of what kind of blood it was, what was mixed in with it--then sent the pants back with the hole in it to evidence. Of course the crime lab had thrown away the piece they had cut out."

She simply sent the pants away again for testing, with its evidentiary portion removed. The new results came back inconclusive, and Taylor was a free man. Hillary would later openly laugh about her easy victory in court. To this day, she has never apologized for diverting justice in that case.

She was so naturally corrupt that she was recommended to serve on the Watergate prosecution team by Burke Marshall, who was also Sen. Ted Kennedy's chief counsel in the Chappaquiddick trial where his young, pregnant date drowned in his car that had been driven into a creek. When the Watergate investigation was over, her boss, Jerry Zeifman fired her from the committee staff and refused to give her a letter of recommendation.

It would be only one of three times he did so in his 17-year career. Instead, he stated publicly, "She was a liar. She was an unethical, dishonest lawyer. She conspired to violate the Constitution, the rules of the House, the rules of the committee and the rules of confidentiality."

Bill and Hillary married on October 11, 1975 in the living room of their new home in Fayetteville, Arkansas. People would say the longevity of their marriage was due to a string of symbols and numbers that runs the universe, and yet is inaccessible to those who live in it. There have hardly been more than a few months go by that have not been embroiled in scandal, murder, suicide, graft, or subterfuge.

Hillary Clinton gained notoriety early in their marriage by being the first, First Lady in American history to be called to testify in front of a grand jury. Not only was Hillary called to testify, but as part of the grand jury investigation, she became the subject of accusations of suspicious activity concerning missing subpoenaed records from the Rose Law Firm where she had worked in the mid-1980s. Of interest to prosecutors were Rose Law Firm records from the Whitewater land deal in Arkansas and Hillary's legal representation of convicted felon Jim McDougal's savings and loan association, Madison Guaranty.

The Rose Law Firm records involved a particular phone call and transaction involving Hillary that was "intended to deceive financial regulators," according to a Frontline series by the Public Broadcasting Service. Federal bank regulators went so far as to call the financial deal involving Hillary and the Rose Law Firm "a sham."

Even the history that was allowed to surface, was beyond belief for the average person. Federal prosecutors subpoenaed documents surrounding the real estate transaction, but the papers mysteriously disappeared for two years—until January 1996—when Hillary's aide reported that they had magically appeared in the book room on the third floor of the White House in the Clintons' personal residence. How did they move from a small law firm in Arkansas to the personal residence in Washington, D.C.?

Hillary was silent, a tactic that would serve both of them well as the forces of evil seemed to work like magic at making even the most serious charges grow stale and cold. The FBI was brought in by the Justice Department, and fingerprint analysis showed that there were only two sets of prints on those records. The fingerprints were identified to be those of White House Deputy Legal Counsel Vince Foster and Hillary Clinton.

Hillary of course stated she had "no idea" how the documents had ended up there. Vince Foster was found shot twice on July 20, 1993, once with a small caliber weapon in the neck and once with a 38 caliber weapon in the back of the head, and dumped cold and bloodless in Fort Marcy Park on a gentle slope by a Civil War cannon. The photos taken of the body at the scene were copied on a Xerox machine and then faxed to Special counsel Robert B. Fiske Jr., who finally concluded from the grainy black and white images that Foster's death was a suicide, brought on by depression from the burdens he was carrying for the Clintons.

22 years later, the clear Park Police color photos of Vince Foster's body would be found, well-preserved in a basement along with a box of evidence from the investigation that would bring Fiske's conclusion of suicide into question. How could a man kill himself with two different caliber guns fired into his own head and neck from two different entry angles, both of which were impossible to self-inflict?

The Senate Whitewater Committee, which at the time also was investigating the matter, ultimately concluded the Rose Law Firm billing documents indeed had been placed into the White House book room in the private residence area by Hillary Clinton herself. A hard drive had been removed from Foster's White House computer and mysteriously went missing within minutes of his body being found by Park Police. It eventually turned up in the Old Executive Office Building across the street from the White House, but investigators ultimately were unable to recover anything from the hard drive because it had been significantly and purposefully damaged.

Once again, the *charm of favor* made the questions disappear like dried leaves blown into a pile of other dried leaves, never to be considered again; by anyone.

This book is fiction, or as close as the author could get to it, considering the true story in every chapter. It was not written to entertain or even to fascinate. It was written to awaken the reader to a possibility that this is much more than two criminal minds plotting to have a wonderful life of politics and parties and immeasurable wealth. It is the story of a crime syndicate that connected men and money from around the world through a trillion-dollar web of corruption and power. Even the most aggressive conspiracy theories only involve a few hundred dead bodies, a few billion dollars, and a few women and children raped, more or less.

This book is real history, as seen through the eyes of my fictional characters, going to open your eyes to an insidious crime syndicate so powerful and so wealthy that it has destroyed millions of innocent people of all ages and races. It has become associated with the largest producer and distributor of drugs the world has ever known. The assassinations, money laundering, weapons trafficking, and sale or seizure of national treasures for personal benefit is all true.

This crime syndicate has ordered up wars on demand, purchased every major media outlet in the Western world, and runs one of the most relentless and powerful political organizations in history. It has active and loyal agents inside every agency, department, bureau, and administration in American government, and they use their power to write and enforce law to protect the syndicate from loss or harm and will stop at nothing to defeat its enemies. The Clinton Crime Syndicate is active and operating at the time this book is published; perhaps even as you are reading it.

Chapter 1

Jack Rousseau was tall, mostly because of her long legs. She was the youngest of four children in a family with no room for a little girl. Her father started her in soccer when she was four years old. Perhaps there was feeling of guilt about having a little girl in an essentially alpha male household. No matter what they tried, nothing Barbie found a home with little Jaqueline. She lost attention at home against three older boys, but she made up for it on the soccer field. She didn't seem to mind that it was sometimes a full-contact sport. She loved to win and hated to lose because of someone else's inability to make a goal or handle one her passes.

She liked winning in her control, and that was the most incredible thing to watch, because it was the running that she loved. By the time she was 11, she was 6 inches taller than anyone in her class and was morphing into a world class runner. The personal challenge of fighting back the pain and exhaustion to defeat a competitor changed the lines in her face. By the time she was in Middle School, she was already recognized by the State of Maryland as one of the fastest kids in public school. Her parents ate dinner often in silence considering the prospect of having an Olympian on their hands.

Her father worked hard, sometimes at two jobs to put her three older brothers through college. James was the oldest, a Yale graduate and a lawyer for an asphalt lobbying firm in D.C., just inside the beltway on the south side of the city. The transportation infrastructure lobby was the largest single domestic budget item for the U.S. government which created jobs for thousands of lawyers like James, earmarking treasury dollars to their clients.

Richard, two years younger than James, the family nicknamed Rocky. He graduated from Annapolis with good grades and a boxing record of 21 and 2. He was tapped for intelligence so he never deployed to sea. His father accused him of working for the CIA. Though Rocky denied the accusation he was a spook, the country always came first, for him. After reading in high school of President Jefferson sending the marines to Tripoli to defeat the Barbary Pirates in 1801, he was like an old soul waking up and remembering who he was.

Michael, the youngest boy, struggled to impress everyone else. It wasn't that he didn't, but his ability to land on his feet was pretty incredible, especially considering his lack of balance or anything close to being able to sing on key. He went after the things his brothers tired of. In his 7th grade Middle School band he played baritone in the Michael Sweeney composition, *The Forge of Vulcan*. The sound of all those instruments making a single, coordinated atmosphere was all the energy his wings needed to carry him forward. He was an artist, full of creation and suffering and deep considerations. Dogma was far from the little forest garden in his mind.

Still, he was good at reading people, and after graduating with a degree in Public Recreation and a minor in music, he quickly found work managing a restaurant to reach unprecedented profitability. He married into a powerful family with a spectacularly beautiful daughter who slipped into the gothic community for a time. Lucy's perfectly paper-white skin made a stunning canvas for some of the best talent in the D.C. tattoo industry. Fortunately, she fell for Michael's poetry and his dazzling kiss before the ink bled into areas not covered by a dress with elbow-length sleeves. Lucy, as it turned out, could sing. His piano and her voice were among the top invites at many of the local bars and parties.

Jack's father had a stroke at 55 that closed his right eye, silenced his bass voice, and shriveled his right arm, putting the family on disability. It also meant there would be no college fund for her. Unabated genetics produced decent grades for Jack without really trying, but she knew without straight A's for the rest of High School, she would be doomed to a life of poverty without a successful man whose name she would be forced to share. 'Be damned if I will,' she would spit through the sweat on her lips often leaping past second place just before the finish line.

She felt like she couldn't breathe with a name like Jacquelyn hung around her neck, so she branded everything with Jack. Her mother didn't mind. She never got anywhere with her MBA, because her name was Mary. It was that simple. 'The only way to get past the damn HR lady with any company was to have a man's name,' she used to say while slamming eggs into the Sunday morning waffle batter for six.

In the summer before her senior year, her lean Rousseau frame got boobs and hips too wide to support competitive running, but the urge to compete couldn't be covered with perfume; not for Jack. It was time to focus, now that her Sophomore year in high school was over. She would need scholarships, if she planned to attend Johns Hopkins. The summer break lay before her with its temptation for leisure, but the thought of getting soft made her want to hit something, or someone.

She enrolled at a local Karate studio just before summer. Her intention was to use the martial art to channel her competitive energy, but got tired of tumbling and yelling, especially after the sensei told her it would take three years to learn one kata that had to be practiced continuously before she could advance. Rousseaus were not a patient clan, and her brothers never took three years to do anything. She had no concept of three years, so she quit after two weeks. Any one of her brothers could easily kick her ass in ten seconds flat, including Michael.

It was then that one of her classmates invited her to a Taekwondo class as a guest. It was a class for females only, and had a female sensei, and the art was immediately attractive to her. Lisa May was middle aged with flaming red hair and fair skin, and at nearly six feet tall she was in amazing shape. Jack liked her. She was tough and flexible, and she was an excellent mentor. It was a martial art more crafted for tall people; people with long legs. Her quads were like liquid granite compared to the powder puffs in the class who only wanted to learn how to say 'Maybe,' with a little force.

She felt the hook set deep in her soul, and it was already reeling her to a different dimension. "A woman's hand is made for caressing, not for punching," said Lisa. "But, hell hath no fury like a woman's kick."

It was a challenging style of fighting, and within a few weeks, her lean muscles were stretched and compressed until her bones ached. She improved her endurance by walking and running along Meridian Hill Park in the gray summer mornings. The Park was owned by Robert Peter in 1791. He was a wealthy Georgetown merchant, so the hill became known as Peter's Hill. In 1804 President Thomas Jefferson had a geographic marker placed on this large hill. Jefferson and Washington went through great efforts to lay out the District of Columbia according to Freemason symbolism. To them, it was important for several reasons. They were painfully aware that they had stepped off the timeline in the Bible. Neither one of them liked the ending. Besides, Freemasonry had this legend, which predates the Bible by several thousand years, that a New Jerusalem would be formed in the future. They weren't the only ones to believe this was that place, so they decided to use all the charms they could to make sure it could withstand the evil men and demons of the world. In line with this sacred architecture, Jefferson centered exactly north of the White House, this marker that helped to establish a longitudinal meridian for the city and the nation: the "White House meridian". She thought about this story every time she stretched her long and powerful legs, tuning herself like strings on a guitar as she practiced leaping forward with long, graceful strides.

In the early morning though, the park had few people in it after the park tractors had raked the grass for trash, and the breeze through the manicured trees formed a white noise that washed away the thinkings and doings of one of the world's busiest cities just a few miles east of the respite of this place. The gulls and sparrows snatched beetles and bits of food no one could even see until they pounced on it from their floating surveillance.

She walked to one revolutionary war monument, and sprinted to the next with the balls of her feet resting just long enough for her to remember gravity ruled this world. Within a week, she could sprint half way around the park. Within two months, she was floating without even breathing hard after twelve 220 yard dashes spaced apart all the way from the cannons to the statue of Dante. She floated like running on thin ice, because her breasts seemed to grow larger by the day and were now impossible to immobilize, even with a sports bra. 'At least you know why he wasn't looking at your feet,' said Lisa one night after Jack had defeated a boy her age at a competition by slapping the side of his face with a spinning back kick. She practiced by spinning and kicking a stack of five tires in their garage at home. They were steel belted radials, but within a few weeks she could place a size ten dent in any of the tires in that stack.

It was the first time in her life that she looked forward to going back to school. The rush of adrenaline from sparring in her dojo, and before each match with competing dojos, became addicting. She couldn't wait to be tested. All she had to do now was figure out what she wanted to do with her life. She still had time, but she could see light at the end of the public school tunnel. If she was going to have a good life, it was up to her. Her dad couldn't pay the way. There was no one to follow but her brothers, and that wouldn't be easy. 'Can't never did nothing,' her dad used to say.

She missed his little wisdoms. She remembered being told to rake the leaves in the yard after the second frost in the San Gabriel foothills. It was not the last time she wished her brothers still lived at home. 'Life is made of a whole lot of little efforts; not one big one. Just start over there and keep yanking, and before you know it, you'll be done,' he would say as he left for the municipal power plant where he said he worked as a mechanic for more than 27 years.

He said he specialized in the impossible and delivered miracles on special order. It often made her sad to think of him, trapped behind his left eye without the ability to speak or throw a baseball. The last wish he had was for her to surpass her brothers, somehow. 'You don't have to worry so much about money in this life. You gotta think about what makes you happy and do that for a living. Otherwise, life will run you over like a garbage truck. Then, it's over. Are you listening to me?' he would say.

He just didn't know that garbage truck would be in the form of an aneurysm on the side of his brain. She didn't know what she wanted to do with her life. Not really. It was kind of a process of elimination. No riding a man's coat tails. No serving tables. And, hell no politics. This whole city reeked of it.

It was only June. But the work at the dojo made the time go quickly, and she knew it would only be a few minutes before she would be back in school for her senior year.

Chapter 2

Hattiesburg is a town of contrasts. The routes of so many pasts collide here between old railroads and wagon trails since paved and traveled by settlers and soldiers for hundreds of years. The natives, if there are such a thing, recall the days of their Hub City when khaki and green uniforms marched with frightened patriots practicing for war at Camp Shelby. The sweet summer plum blossoms were savored and yet ignored for the same moments. Fear sat quietly behind smiles of the soldiers and the bartenders. Memories of those summers gently escaped north, chased by the humid afternoon breeze from the Gulf just 60 flat miles away.

Wide brick streets between open porch houses undulate over oak and sweet gum roots shaded by trees old enough to forget wars between States, twisted and regrown from storms of men and skies. It was a town people came through, not from. Four miles south, it rained every day at 5:15 for half an hour. Most of the bars were small with large covered back patios so people could smoke and drink and sing and dance, even when it rained at night. It often rained at night.

It could just as easily have been named Ignominy, Mississippi. If you played blues guitar more than once at the Shed Barbeque, you might be remembered for a month or two, depending on how close it was to last call. But if you checked in for a month and read the classified ads in USA Today at the complimentary breakfast at the Hampton Inn and watched sports at Buffalo Wild Wings once a week, no one would remember you. No one would ever see you. It was the perfect place to sleep, and to wait, and to watch.

Ports in Louisiana sent death throughout the world for more than four hundred years, thrust with the same hands that gripped trolleys and bottles of beer on the streets of this intersection between so many walks of American life. Between the years 1530 to 1780, over a million Europeans were captured and sold as slaves by the Barbary powers. Most European nations found it cheaper to pay a fee for protection rather than fight.

The business of Islam had become so aggressive and costly that in 1786, Jefferson and Adams met in London with the ambassador from Tripoli, to ask him why the U.S. was being targeted, since it had never harmed Muslims.

"The Ambassador answered us," Jefferson wrote, "that it was written in their Quran that all nations who should not have acknowledged their authority were sinners, that it was their right and duty to make war upon them wherever they could be found and to make slaves of all they could take as prisoners."

Jefferson immediately recommended to Congress that it refuse all payments of tribute and prepare at once to outfit a naval squadron to visit the Mediterranean. Adams was certain that Congress would never appropriate the money, as he had advocated for the sale of nearly all of America's naval vessels after the Revolution to pay for the operational costs of government.

Adams wrote about the piratical Islamic powers, 'We ought not to fight them at all unless we determine to fight them forever.' History has proven this one irrefutable, and unavoidable fact to the world. Peace can only be achieved through the victory of righteous leadership. Otherwise, it is just the time between wars.

Jefferson returned to America to serve as President George Washington's secretary of state in 1790. For three years he supported Washington, and perhaps despite this restraint, he became the most remarkable philosopher politician in history.

While serving as president, he crafted and conducted the Barbary Wars, the Louisiana Purchase and the Lewis and Clark expedition to the West. 'Timid men ... prefer the calm of despotism to the boisterous sea of liberty,' he wrote. In April 1805, nine Marines and 900 Arabs marched 500 miles to capture Derne, planting the U.S. flag for the first time on foreign soil. 210 years later, President Obama created ISIS as part of a global marketing plan to draw all of Christianity into a war with Islam by beheading 21

Christians on the very same shores of Tripoli where Jefferson's marines had defeated them two centuries prior.

It showed the world that the evil core of Islam was timeless, and that it was resuming the war where it left off just a few moments ago. It had taken nearly a hundred years to slowly and carefully infect the agencies, departments, bureaus, and administrations of the American government. The spread of Islam had corrupted so much of its infrastructure and lawmaking that it was easy and natural to run an imamic candidate against the unwitting John McCain in 2008. The lethargic McCain was no match for an imam, trained in the art of semantics; especially when the global media moguls flooded every broadcast on TV or radio with the wonder of this unknown dream weaver. It was a promise of fundamental transformation in a day of political stagnation and social gangrene.

It was during this dream state that Adnan Kassar made his way to Mexico City in 2012. He worked as a printer at a local newspaper. It was noisy work that paid fairly well and kept people from engaging him in idle conversation. The paper ran five days a week, with the large version printed on Wednesday. It was filled with advertisements, as the local people did most of their shopping on Thursday evening. The ads were mostly for groceries or clothes, but there were also classified ads for all sorts of things trading tax free and on the black markets that had been operating for centuries around one of the world's largest metropolitan areas.

It was an easy place to sleep. It was an easy place to buy a small advertisement for recipes of various things. Even if a person lived in Syria, he could place an ad for virtually anything in the local paper anywhere in the world, and no one would mind in the least.

Everyone cooked in Mexico. No one ever bought a recipe in a newspaper ad for anything; ever. And yet, there, in the two inch columns across the page of section H was a small advertisement with a few ingredients for flan. Of particular interest to Adnan were two ingredients, the relationship of which few people if any understood. Flan makes a mysterious use of sweet condensed milk and evaporated milk. Oh, sometimes it's 14 ounces of one and 12 ounces of another, and sometimes the other way around. It's hard to make it come out even, as Eagle Brand sells condensed milk in 14 ounce galvanized cans. Throwing that last 2 ounces down the drain seems like such a waste, and yet the creaminess of good Flan depends upon it. That is why it is commonly known as a typo when the recipe instructs the cook to empty the can into the four eggs and beat until stiff. Everyone knows this does not work. Everyone knows, but nobody cares. No one, that is, except Adnan.

They finally got it right. No waste. Both full 14 ounce cans listed in the recipe and poured into the eggs and whipped into the creamy froth and poured over caramelized sugar with vanilla extract. He wondered if it could be made with goat's milk as he rose to work the last half of his final shift at the newspaper.

It was the cornstarch in this recipe. The texture completely turns to more of a custard with the addition of corn starch. Not much is required. One tablespoon is all that was mentioned in the new recipe. That was all it took to make the change. It was all Adnan needed to pack his two bags and put the rest of his clothes and possessions in the alley on the back porch of the apartment building. They would quietly disappear into the neighborhood before he completed his walk to the bus station with his locker key.

Small envelopes easily fit through the louvers on the lockers at the bus station. Once the key is inserted into the locker, it takes four pesos to lock it again. That was fine with Adnan, because he wasn't coming back. The small index card at the bottom of the locker had only an address on it. He looked at his watch, which was a rare thing to see in Mexico. It was a rare thing to see anywhere these days. No one wore watches anymore. Time was globally synchronized and updated on cell phones. Everyone knew that. But with a watch, you could keep track of the time without anyone keeping track of you.

Adnan grew up in the battle of Damascus. 'When was Damascus not a battlefield?' his older brother used to say. Their father had been killed in a gas attack when they were just small boys. It was a terrible way to die. Al Qaeda had been driven out of Iraq and into Syria by the Americans, but then they were recruited by the Americans. It was a confused mess of a world, but as the boys got older, they began to understand the nature of this war. Islam and Christianity had fought for so many centuries, that at least in Syria they had reached a state of mutual tolerance. That, as it turned out, was not exactly what the power brokers had in mind.

Damascus had always existed. Adnan recalled stories they heard as boys from the elders each year about the birthplace of the world. 9 thousand years before Christ, Damascus began as a thriving shipping port in the Barada Basin. Mentioned in Genesis as the place where the War of Kings took place as a matter of ancient history, the families who lived there for hundreds of generations laughed with disbelief at predictions it would one day be reduced to rubble. It may have been the land from which Cain took a wife after the Adamic clan was cast to Earth after their brief encounter with Lucifer.

A dozen sultans and that many caliphates had come and gone as entire kingdoms traded rulership over its global power. Home of the finest steel for weapons the world has ever known, there was no power among men or gods that could subdue the nation where dwells Damascus.

And yet the Americans had ended Adnan's eternal city in just four years. He gripped the handles on his suitcases as the number for his bus was announced on the large departure screen of the bus station. He didn't need to hold them that tightly, but it felt good to choke something.

He remembered his cousin telling him of a meeting at the mosque where the Turkish ambassador told of a meeting with the American ambassador serving in Benghazi, Libya. He traveled there to tell Ambassador Stevens that shipments of rockets, missiles, and grenades had been arriving in Turkey that came from the vast arsenal of Mumamar Qaddafi. For nearly 60 years he had been the beloved leader of his country, although in his younger years he was convinced to support a small terror cell dedicated to killing infidels. He quickly learned not to doubt the resolve of certain American presidents.

In 2009, Barack Hussein Obama began in earnest his quest to draw Islam into a global war with Christianity. He set about tearing down the defenses of America and building up the military forces of Islam. The first task was to assassinate Qaddafi, and then to transfer his vast storehouses of weapons to Al Qaeda to defeat the Christian forces in Damascus and northern Syria. For that, he appointed the most ruthless political criminal in US history; Hillary Clinton. She liked the idea so much that she gave up her own bid for the presidency in 2008 for the opportunity to mastermind it as Secretary of State. Besides, she could use the connections and authorities to earn billions for her foundation to fund her own presidency when it was over. There was only one thing the Clintons liked more than political power; money.

Using superior air power and satellite technology, as well as high-tech weapons developed in the Gulf Wars, she made short work of chasing Qaddafi out of his protection and into the streets where he was summarily assassinated without a so much as a public statement. Clinton's forces shot him in the face in the street like a dog. She laughed out loud during a CBS television interview after being notified that Qaddafi had been killed. "We came. We saw. He died," she said laughing on camera.

Within days, the process of sequestering Libya's weapons began. Missiles, rockets, grenades, and bombs loaded with nerve gas and mustard gas arrived at Al Qaeda camps in Syria. It was all part of a clever media plan to kill civilians and then flood the press with claims it was Bashar Al Assad who ordered the attack. Adnan's father suffered blisters on his skin and in his lungs from the mustard gas. He drowned in his own fluids over a period of days, coughing and wheezing while his trembling hands placed blessings on him and his brother's heads.

"I bless you to step from behind the wind, pluck the eyes from our enemies, and then bleed them into the soil that cries for revenge this day," he whispered into Adnan's ear.

Adnan and his brother fought for a year in the streets of Damascus. At first they used rifles, and then they captured Libyan grenade launchers from dead Al Qaeda fighters. Ambassador Stevens became upset that so many weapons from the country he spent so much of his life trying to help were being used by the US State Department to build such a terrible and deadly force. Hours after meeting again with the Turkish Ambassador, Al Qaeda forces attacked the US Embassy in Benghazi and brutally assassinated Ambassador Stevens by raping him to death. Then, the helicopters came with night vision and powerful canons from the air. Then the tanks arrived with a new army that had a new name. They had highly accurate weapons and satellite technology and money to pay for fighters. ISIS absorbed Al Qaeda and recruited fighters who hated Assad. Within a few months, Hillary's army was fully operational. And so it was that his beautiful, ancient city was reduced to rubble for the first time in history; just as the prophecy had predicted.

But his people had their own story of how to defeat an enemy. Do not invade with an army on horses. The storm wind cannot get through, for the windows are tight and the doors are locked against such. It is the gentle breeze that is welcomed into the courtyard. It takes time for the wind to make its way through the trees, across the waters, and around the mountains to reach the flowing hair of your enemy. And when he closes his eyes to enjoy the sweat cooling his brow, then shall the steel of Damascus know its purpose.

Chapter 3

Silicon Desert is brutally dry and hot in the summer, and although Phoenix looked large on the map, its population was strangely absent, most of the time. Except for an occasional dust storm, the weather desk at KNXV-TV ran in automatic. July was one of those months in between sporting events that sometimes filled the arenas or stadiums in the city. It wasn't anything like the lush, green city of Tuscaloosa or like the fame he was used to as a player for the University of Alabama under legendary coach Gene Stallings.

Christopher Sign thought he wanted to be a reporter, so he took a job with ABC. It was a big pond, and he was a little fish in a town that was more famous for its basketball team than anything else. He never wanted to be a sports writer. It was a struggle to be noticed in this business, but then, he was used to 3rd down and 5 yards to go. Coach Stallings always said, 'Just do your job and everything else will be fine.'

'I am doing my job,' he told himself cranking the air conditioning up a notch on his white Camry. Everybody drove white cars in Phoenix. It could reach 150 degrees in a dark colored car in just a few minutes. White was cooler, or so everyone told him. It was just another thing that prevented him from standing out; from being noticed. Most of the tall office buildings downtown were owned by banks like Wells Fargo or Coldwell, but they too had laid off enough people to leave all but one floor of the parking structure empty. No story there.

His source had called him on a Sunday night from Baltimore and said he had a tip. Some guy had a message that had to be delivered in person. It couldn't be texted or emailed. He pulled into the nearly empty parking lot as his dashboard clock strained to indicate noon in the bright sunshine coming in through the vehicle's factory windows. Since he had been in Phoenix, the Hooters on Main

Street usually only had a couple of tables occupied for lunch at noon. A downtown venue like this in any other city would be packed for lunch, but this city felt like the day after the filming of a zombie apocalypse. It was Monday June 27, 2016. Maybe this was the big one.

He removed his Oakley's and folded them into his shirt pocket. There were two guys at one high table in blue short sleeves with khaki pants. The round table in the corner booth was occupied by what looked like programmer geeks having a working lunch with the latest tablets in front of thick glasses and bright orange polo shirts.

"Are you Sign?" came the female voice from behind him.

"Yeah. Chris Sign. I was expecting a," he paused. "How are you?" he said shaking her hand. She had a firm grip and skinny jeans and tan combat boots that he quickly surmised might be former military issue. The boots were old enough. Her eyes were brown, and she wore no makeup, which really wasn't surprising for Phoenix, as the temperature can exceed 116 degrees during the day. One wipe of the brow, and the whole morning's work on a face could be ruined.

"I have a table in the corner," she said turning in that direction.

"Oh hey," said Chris to the waitress who intercepted him. "I'm not eating, but I'll have a sweet tea, if that's okay," said Chris.

"You got it. I'll bring it right over. Welcome to Hooters," said the waitress over the shoulder of her undersized white tee-shirt. He always wondered about the job interview process at Hooters. 'Maybe there was a story there,' he exhaled slowly as he turned to catch up with the informant.

At times like this he learned to open all the senses. It was no fun having your touchdown stolen because you put your head down, covered the ball, and plowed toward the goal only to be crushed by an orange freight train angling across the field. "JP said you had something for me?" he asked so that only she could hear.

"I work at General Aviation at Sky Harbor. Something's going on, and someone needs to know," she said, looking at him from under her wide, dark eyebrows and her closely trimmed black hair.

"Drugs? What's up? What's your name? Can I quote you on this?" asked Chris in a rush of questions.

"Look. Bill Clinton's plane has been at the airport for a day or so. We fueled it up this morning, and it originally filed a flight plan to leave out today," she said.

"Hey, I don't do much, but I really don't do politics. I mean I know it's an election year, but nothing really counts until Labor Day anyway. So, Miss, uh," trailed Chris.

"My name is Sheila. No, you can't quote me. Listen. There is another plane coming in from Baltimore tonight after midnight, and that's a change of schedule as well. It wasn't supposed to arrive until the next day. It's the U.S. Attorney General's plane. They're going to hook up at GA at Sky Harbor at around 2:30 in the morning. The question you need to ask, Mr. Sign, is, 'Why the hell are these two sneaking around, meeting at General Aviation at 2:30 in the freaking morning?' Something's going down. Something bad," said Sheila.

"Here's your tea, sir. I didn't know if you wanted lemon, so here's a couple just in case," said the waitress.

"Oh, yeah. You're right, I forgot to ask," said Chris.

"I figured with that accent, you would take lemon," she said smiling.

"What accent?" he asked smiling back and pushing the straw into the glass.

"I gotta go," said Sheila.

"No you don't. I need some answers before I go out there and make a mess," said Chris.

"What do you want to know?" asked Sheila with her hands flat on the tall round table.

"Besides everything? Let's see. Why was Bill Clinton here in Phoenix? Maybe he had campaign business here. How about, is this the first time they have met out here in the middle of nowhere in the middle of the night? How about this one? Why would the husband of a Presidential candidate, who happens to be under Federal investigation for mishandling classified information on a scale no one has ever seen in this country's history, be meeting with the one government official who could put her away right before her inevitable election to the office of President of the United States?" asked Chris nervously taking a sip of tea.

"Why the hell do you think I am here? Your boy in Baltimore calls me up and tells me to meet you face-to-face and that you would take it from here. Do not overlook what I am risking just talking to you. He's been here for a couple days. Some dudes from some real estate development company met him. I saw their Escalades in the VIP slots outside GA this week. The thing is, whenever we see a last minute reschedule of a charter plane, we take notice. It's DHS crap we have to go through. Well, when I look at the manifest and saw that Lynch was on the plane, I about shit. I see the news. I'm not stupid," said Sheila.

"Why would you even care? This is going to make a nice headline on page eight below the fold, but what difference does all this make, anyway? Why would my source in Baltimore tell me to meet with you?" asked Chris. He could see the play. The offense was going to play an option. Something in the defense made the quarterback nervous. He had seen this kind of risk taking before.

"I'm from Arkansas. My dad was a cop in Arkansas. His best friend and favorite source was Danny Casalaro. Ring a bell?" asked Sheila opening her brown eyes wide at him.

"I'm from Alabama. Sorry," said Chris.

"Danny was a reporter found in a hotel bathtub cut to pieces. Slashed about 20 times and bled to death. They got him in his hotel room in West Virginia, for God's sake. My dad says they killed him right before Bill Clinton was elected, because Danny was working on a story that would end him," gritted Sheila with a little acid on her voice.

"I heard there was a string of bodies surround those two," said Chris becoming distant.

"Listen, Mr. Sign," she said clearing her throat of the memory that took her breath away. "The attorney general of the freaking United States amended a flight plan to meet the head of the bloodiest crime gang in political history in the middle of the night. I'm telling you, no one knows about this. You need to be there," said Shelia pointing her tanned finger at him.

"You gonna be there?" asked Chris.

"I work day shift. Besides, if I showed up, I'm as good as dead. I'm not here," said Sheila dropping off the high chair. She looked at the door, turned and walked out without turning around.

Chris exhaled. He felt like the quarterback had just called 'time out' right before the ball was snapped. He could feel the adrenaline in his system and tried to think of how to approach this opportunity. If he didn't go, a crime was going to take place without a witness. He couldn't imagine what would happen if he did go. He thumbed a five dollar bill on the table, put his Oakley's on, and walked out the door into the searing heat of the Phoenix daylight.

Main Street was vacant like it was New Year's day at 6 o'clock in the morning. 'What the hell happened to this town?' he asked himself, looking both ways at green lights for blocks without a single car in sight. He took out his cell phone while he was walking to his car, noticed the time, and then put it back in his pocket. He opened the door, sat down and stepped on the brake, and hit the start button. He waited for the air conditioning to clear out the hot air in the car before closing the door. It would be nice to have a blocker when running a play, but sometimes you have to improvise. He wanted the story.

His contact in Baltimore thought he was the right man to break it. He felt like the whole universe was about to pivot in the

27

next fourteen hours. In times like this, it's nice to be able to see the future or at least have a playbook.

He drew X's and O's in his mind while he drove back to the ABC news office. The play action, the option, the drive up the middle; nothing was working out right. It was confusing and dark like playing in freezing rain for a Monday night game. 'What would cause one of the most powerful men in the world to take such a risk this close to an election?' he asked himself. Hell, the most powerful woman in the world was five months away from being handed the nuclear codes. Someone had to tell the truth. It might as well be him.

He pulled into the ABC garage and found a place to park. Not much ever happened in Phoenix. The elevator was empty. Most of the reporters were still out to lunch or looking for a story that would keep them indoors where they could stay looking nice. He was an anchor without a private office. It wasn't that uncommon. Even Fox News anchors have tiny little closet offices.

There were forty-two desks on the cubicle floor with private offices all the way around the perimeter of the 8th floor of the ABC building. He spun his black chair around and sat down feeling like a rookie. He didn't have a clue what the play was on this story. He opened his drawer and got out his SLR digital camera.

It had a good charge on it. It was a graduation present, and still had the same memory card with a few minor celebrities and some traffic accidents stored in it. He felt the pressure of what the next 12 hours might mean. He had to stay quiet for now. No one knew about this. No one was supposed to know about this. He had been given a glimpse of the future. A meteor striking the planet might not have as much impact as this meeting between Bill Clinton and Loretta Lynch on the tarmac of the Sky Harbor Airport in the middle of the night.

Bill Clinton, actively playing the role of queen-maker, and the US attorney general were about to make a deal face to face, and he

28

was one of the very few people who knew about it. Sheila was scared, but she was angry. He had seen that before. People sometimes lived their whole lives with that hatred burning inside them. It aged them. It prevented them from ever loving anyone or trusting anyone. He didn't want to be one of those people.

He took a deep breath and thought about going to the gym to work off the adrenaline still making him quiver inside. Yeah. That was a good idea. He moved the mouse on his computer, but then remembered he had shut it down when he left that morning. He didn't need to read the news anyway. He was about to make the news. Clinton was maneuvering for private face time with the attorney general. He was going to be there when it happened.

The Observer, with anonymous sources inside both the FBI and the United States Secret Service, would publish that the attorney general was caught completely off guard by the meeting. Officially, they dismissed suggestions alleging that she waited there to see Bill Clinton or accommodated his request to see him. Chris later discovered that this supposed source was none other than Clinton working the back channels by asking for favors from agents loyal to him.

He parked his Camry a little after midnight outside Sky Harbor General Aviation. Chris knew Clinton's plane had been scheduled to leave long before hers arrived, but he could see it was still there, still connected to the power cord that kept the air conditioning running inside the custom business jet.

He knew Lynch's plane was originally scheduled to arrive the next day, and that she amended her flight plan and flew all night after her lecture in Baltimore to get to Sky Harbor's General Aviation Tarmac, to make this very auspicious meeting.

It was less than two hours when he saw the blinking white light on the Department's regional jet flashing off the hangars before the nose cleared the hangar at the end of the row. It had to be Lynch's jet. He witnessed it taxi to less than 75 yards away from

Clinton's jet in the early hours of Tuesday morning. He stood alone on the still smoldering concrete pad surrounded with a tall, decorative fence made of vertical bars. The air stairs on Lynch's jet went down, and an Air Force airman descended to stand at attention at the front of the stairs.

It was still 100 degrees at 2:30 AM on June 29th, 2016. The tall fence around the patio of Sky Harbor's General Aviation office was made of Aluminum, anodized in dark brown bolted to a knee high concrete wall around the patio slab. He could see everything in the daylight provided by the tarmac and hangar lighting.

75 yards is a long walk in a suit and tie when it's 100 degrees. The air was dry and smelled of Jet A, and he could hear the APU running on the Lynch jet while the ground crew connected a power cord to the side of the jet. A large SUV was parked beside the Clinton jet, and within a few minutes, he saw the air stairs come down in line with it. A few seconds later, he saw two Secret Service agents step down onto the tarmac and look around. They noticed him, but didn't seem to react as they each twisted the middle button on their jackets to keep them from flapping in the wind and possibly exposing their firearms.

He felt he was watching diplomatic protocol as two FBI agents stepped out of the Lynch plane and did almost exactly the same things with their jackets. The men looked at one another like envoys of two generals meeting in secret, and nodded. As though they were all waiting for the President's poodle to poop, the four men shifted their weight from foot to foot, trying their best to look powerful and valuable.

Like them, Chris looked around, checked the rooftops for snipers, and shifted his weight back and forth nervously. He wasn't supposed to be there, but maybe his press tag hanging around his neck was keeping him alive. He quickly wondered if they were asking themselves how he knew this meeting was taking place.

They weren't talking very loudly, but when Chris lifted his 35mm camera and pointed the lens through the bars of the fence to take a photo, they yelled at him to put his camera away.

"No pictures and no recordings. You ask nothing. You stand there, and you say nothing. Am I clear, mister?" asked the FBI agent from Lynch's plane.

Chris nodded and waved his left hand slightly to show he heard the order, and stood there silently and alone. The heat came out of the tarmac like a hot cast iron pan pulled fresh out of the oven, and the high-pitched APU began to wind down as the craft switched over to external power.

After what seemed like an hour, Bill Clinton appeared at the top of the stairs and walked down to the SUV. Maybe he was making some calls to his soldiers in the Syndicate, or to a lawyer, or to lawmakers to inform them he was going to need some cover. This meeting was going to happen, and they needed to be ready to defend it, or deny it. One of the Secret Service agents opened the rear door of the SUV and closed it behind Clinton as he got inside. He couldn't tell if the former president glanced his way. Chris held his breath for a moment, as he figured Clinton knew he was there. By now, he probably knew where he lived and what he had for breakfast that morning. They didn't ask him to leave. Maybe they didn't care if he was there. Or maybe they did, but this meeting was mission critical and perhaps they were confident nothing would ever come of it. Clinton carried himself like someone who just made a deal with the Devil himself.

The SUV rolled slowly around to the front of the Lynch jet, and the two front doors opened. The Secret Service agents got out and faced the FBI agents. Staging. Flanking maybe. One of them opened the rear door of the SUV, and Clinton stepped out and walked to the stairs of the Lynch jet and stepped up inside the plane as though she was renting it from him. The agents measured the space between them.

Chris ran the copy through his mind over and over again. He couldn't take notes. He couldn't take pictures or record anything, or ask any questions. There would be many questions. Who? When? What? The one that scared him was 'why?' The agents stood in front of the airman, still at attention. He thought he could hear men speaking, but he could not see their faces as the men stood on the other side of the jet from him. Their legs looked relaxed, and he could tell they were looking around for threats. He hoped he wasn't one of them.

Almost an hour had passed when Clinton emerged. Did he have something in his hands? No. Did he take anything inside the plane with him when he walked up those stairs? Damn. He couldn't remember. He didn't stay around for the Clinton jet to fire up and fly away. Another black SUV pulled up the Lynch plane, but it looked like no one was coming out until the coast was clear. He could feel the vomit close to his throat. He knew they probably wouldn't come out of the Attorney General's plane as long as he was there.

Chris walked back into the lobby of General Aviation. He took a long drink from the ice cold fountain and looked around the well-lit, but empty lobby. He walked through the glass doors to the outside parking lot and dropped, exhausted, into his Camry.

Christopher Sign wasn't a bit player in the Lynch-Clinton story. He was the only player in the story who uncovered it and broke the news of the secret meeting between two of America's most powerful figures. And he wasn't just a local reporter; he was an anchor on ABC15 in Phoenix.

No amount of experience could prepare him for the possible ramifications of this story. He made sure every 'I' was dotted and 'T' crossed. He took two days almost without eating as he visualized going on air. It was like no game day or final exam he ever faced. He knew once it was on tape, there was no going back. He also knew that no matter what he wanted, no matter how he planned or edited, it was going to get out of control. He knew he would be a target of other reporters, politicians, and even the department of justice itself. In football, a player is only as good as his last play.

That's why you never hold back. That one extra yard might be the one big play that wins, or loses the game. 'Big' would turn out to be an understatement. The story based on Sign's reporting dominated the national news cycle for well over 48 hours. In fact, for months it was included in debate after debate on global television, and it may have been the single most critical play that affected the most watched election in history.

The entire media world with all its billions and nearly every super-model talking head on national TV went after him with partisan accusations, emails, phone calls, and social media attacks. But Chris was as ready as he was for every single snap of the ball throughout his life. When he was asked to appear on Fox News with Bill O'Reilly, he never wavered.

"Of all the things I've covered in my fifteen-year career, from serial killers and hostage situations to hurricanes and tornadoes and other natural disasters, this generated the most overwhelming response by far," he said. "And the people who got me through it were my wife, my kids, my family and my football family. The first people to congratulate me on the story were my former Alabama teammates, and on the flip side, when things were getting intense, the first people to reach out to check on me were those same teammates. During my highs and lows in life I've found myself relying so much on my teammates. Playing for Gene Stalling will do that for you."

"ABC-15 in Phoenix hired me to do a job and that's what I'm doing," Sign said. "Just like I did on the football field. I've always said that playing team sports sets you up to do well in life and this is proof."

Facts matter, especially when one is trying to drill down to the truth. But despite dozens of news articles from major media outlets on the private meeting between Attorney General Loretta

Lynch and Bill Clinton at Phoenix Sky Harbor International Airport last week, the facts have typically been reported wrong, and serious questions have been left unanswered.

The propaganda media churned through millions of dollars every hour on national television to make sure the public understood that both Clinton and Lynch were coincidentally in Phoenix on the same day for scheduled events. They actually developed talking points at the FBI, but FOIA requests came back redacted. They knew it was bad, but as long as the public didn't know it was bad, or that it involved grandkids and golf, Hillary could still win. But the social media knew it was a lie, and Chris made sure that his story stood the test of time in the light of day.

Sheila was right. Bill Clinton was in Phoenix a couple of days prior, on Monday, June 27, to meet with real-estate developer Jim Pederson and others. (Pederson was Chair of the Arizona Democratic Party from 2001 to 2005. According to Federal Election Commission records, Pederson gave nearly $7.3 million to the Arizona State Democratic Central Committee from 2001 to 2006.) By Wednesday, June 29 at 7:41 p.m., when the details surrounding the nefarious meeting should have been clearly established, Devlin Barrett of the Wall Street Journal was apparently being misled by his sources, which one would assume included the Justice Department, on the date of the encounter. Barrett incorrectly reported that:

"Attorney General Loretta Lynch met privately with former President Bill Clinton in Arizona in the early morning hours of Tuesday, but Ms. Lynch claimed they did not discuss Hillary Clinton's private server as secretary of state."

These were last-minute arrangements. She deliveedr a Monday evening speech at the National Summit on Youth Violence Prevention, according to her public schedule and a news report in the Baltimore Sun. The Attorney General was not scheduled to leave until the next day, but after receiving orders from Clinton, she demanded her husband accompany her as they filed a new flight plan and headed directly for the airport. He went with her for one reason only; to be a witness to the meeting Bill Clinton had requested of her. It turned out to be one of her better moves, as she would, in fact, ask for protection under the 5th amendment about this meeting seventy-four times under oath before Congress. Her husband was the only witness in the world who could not be compelled to testify against her.

The word "optics" was used repeatedly by both Democrats and Republicans to characterize the lack of judgment by the highest law enforcement officer in the land to engage in this tarmac meeting with the husband of a target under a criminal investigation.

Within hours of the meeting, FBI director James Comey was instructed by Attorney General Loretta Lynch to immediately change his public verbiage by referring to the Hillary Clinton investigation as a 'matter,' and to stop referring to it as an investigation. Director Comey complied. This sleight of hand dominated the Sunday talk shows. Further clouding the investigation, the Associated Press was reporting that President Obama would be campaigning alongside Hillary Clinton at an event a few days later in Charlotte, North Carolina, adding this titillating note to the story:

"The White House hasn't ruled out Clinton and Obama traveling to the event together on Air Force One," it reported.

Using Air Force One to shuttle to campaign appearances on behalf of a candidate who is under an 'active criminal investigation,' even the act of considering it, shows just how far Washington was completely under the control of the Clinton Crime Syndicate.

Christopher Sign knew that hundreds of people had died trying to stop the Clintons from achieving and keeping global power. Chris tried to imagine the deal that was just made inside that plane. Perhaps, Loretta Lynch would stay on as Hillary's attorney general when she was crowned. The thought that she might have looked out the window and seen him standing there made his blood run cold. Maybe, just maybe, this story would make a difference. He felt the clock was ticking down for them.

Their lust for authority, and their thorough belief that they were protected from harm by special power, made everyone that knew them afraid to try and stop them. Perhaps the courage of an Alabama football player with a pure heart and a pen of light would take down the most feared crime syndicate in political history.

'Maybe no one else would have to die,' he thought to himself.

He was wrong.

Chapter 4

By the 9th of July, 2016, D.C. was already on fire with political upheaval. This election was the greatest show on Earth, but people outside the beltway had no idea how intense this war for control of the largest checkbook the world had ever known had become. Donald Trump was declared the presumptive candidate on May 3rd, and this city still remained in a state of disbelief. Everyone was suddenly a political advisor with ideas on how to dominate the debates, which by all accounts had become the gladiator games that decided the last four elections.

People here still remember Mitt Romney mopping the floor with Barack Obama in the first presidential debate of 2012. There were a lot of half empty beers left on the counter that night as the Democrat had his ass handed to him in no uncertain terms before a global audience. The thought of Obama being a one-term president never entered anyone's mind. In fact, most people thought his smooth persona eclipsed anyone in politics for a generation and that if anyone could be granted an exception to the 22nd Amendment, it would be him.

It was both a relief and a mystery as to why, just two weeks before the election, Mitt Romney quit the race. Right there in front of global live coverage, Mitt Romney cowered and stuttered like a kid caught watching porn by his parents. He was lost. He was ineffectual. He was scared to death. Something happened to Mitt in between those two debates. Some power beyond him, beyond even the power of the presidency had reached him and told him to throw the race, because that is precisely what he did on October 23rd, 2012, Obama brushed his opponent off onto the floor like a spec of belly button lint, and the election was over just like that.

This was Democrat territory, and there were few places politics was not discussed openly. There were few things that sold booze like politics. Most of the time, it was peaceful. After all, no self-respecting Republican would be caught inside Lou's City Bar.

"Hey Mike. You're a little early, aren't you?" asked Maddy, the bar manager as she put her chunk of keys up against the second deadbolt and gave it a twist. Her easy, split-toothed smile and instant sense of humor had built this single location into a multi-million dollar business in less than three years.

"Lucy got back with the dogs early, and I bought this new program I wanted to load into the show. I thought we'd take a little time to load it and try it out," said Mike.

"You want I should give you a key? No problem. You want a sandwich and a beer? I can make you something," said Maddy with her thick Brooklyn accent.

"How about some pretzels? I'll take that beer. It'll take at least one to make sure this thing doesn't glitch during the show. It kinda sucks when your virtual band takes a shit in the middle of a set," said Mike, happy to see Maddy smile as she held the door open for him.

"Baby? Could you come back and help me? I don't want to let this touch the ground," said Lucy holding her computer bag in one hand and a long formal gown on a hanger in the other.

"Oh yeah," said Mike putting the shoulder bag on the high table just inside the door and short-stepping back to her to grab the gown and hold it up. "We might leave early if you wear this. You know that, right?"

"You don't want my art to show?" she asked playfully.

"Hey. They get the voice. I get the art," he said kissing her on the cheek.

"It's permanent, you know?" she said tugging her blouse open to just reveal the stunning floral tattoo that covered the flawless skin above her left breast.

"I know it doesn't rub off. That's what I know," he said walking backwards with the gown into the bar and watching her spiked heels zag around her black yoga pants.

"You are such a boy. Don't ever grow up," she said smiling broadly.

"I'm going to load this drum track program in, and then we can check it out. It's got a strong section that I think will jazz the set a little better than the one we've been using," he said closing the door behind her.

"Hang that in the closet up there. I'll change right before the show," said Lucy.

"You got it. Hey, grab that bowl of pretzels off the bar. Maddy laid them out for me," said Mike as he disappeared up the short set of stairs that led to the dressing room where the entertainers get ready.

Sometimes they have comics come in to Lou's City Bar. They have live local bands from time to time, but Mike and Lucy were the best Diva show in D.C. They were funny and gorgeous, and Lucy could sing anyone into the bottom of a glass. Mike was not just a piano player. He was a true artist who could transpose music on the fly and compose and arrange virtual instruments with his computer to sound like a full band complete with rifts and harmonies. Once he learned how to record Lucy's phenomenal voice, the duo could deliver spine tingling duets with Lucy squared. The place could safely hold about 80 people, but close to the last call, the duo could pack Lou's City bar with more than 100 people on their feet and tipping the jar full of cash.

It was a Friday, but that didn't mean much during election season. Besides, Bernie Sanders had been winning State after State in recent primaries and caucuses around the country. The entire world thought Hillary was going to be crowned the President she was always meant to be. But for this crotchety old man, she would be working on her general campaign by now.

One look at the *Feel the Bern* t-shirt mounted on a wall frame and hung by the bar and one would immediately know that Bernie Sanders was a hero at Lou's. There were so many young Democrats who wouldn't even think of voting for a Republican, but they were also looking for an alternative to Hillary Clinton. It wasn't the age. Bernie was old by any standard, but he wasn't sleeping with Wall Street while he insulted them, like Hillary. Most young people had lost hope of ever owning any real estate anyway, so the fact that his platform called for the end of private property didn't bother them. Besides, Congress would put him in a box and let him make speeches and vacation for four years while the country relaxed and had fun for a while. That was the ticket. Bernie was fun, and Hillary was... Well, Hillary was not fun.

"That didn't take long," said Mike clapping his hands together.

"It works? You finally bought a program that works?" asked Lucy snapping a pretzel in two and tossing the smaller piece through her dark red lips.

"Oh yeah. It's made by the same people. It should hook up perfect. See? I just select the instruments, set the time signature, the tempo, and bingo. Now, all I have to do is press 'okay,' and the rest is like a band in a can," said Mike.

"Is it as good you? Maybe I'll trade up," said Lucy, pushing her lips out a little.

"I can handle the competition. You see, batteries are not included, but with me you always get the real deal," said Mike, putting his arms around her long black hair and kissing her lips lightly.

"Oh yeah. Self-inflating this one. Here's your beer, slick rock," said Maddy. "We open in ten minutes. Show time at what, 8 o'clock?"

"We'll do three sets. Give them an hour break in between. Last one at say midnight?" asked Mike.

"That'll do. Kitchen closes at 10. Last call at 2 AM, but you guys can bug out around 1, if you wanna," said Maddy.

"I'm cool with that. I have a date," said Mike, letting his arms drop away from Lucy's neck.

Mike ate his pastrami on marbled rye bread and drank his beer at the bar while Lucy played solitaire next to him. Maddy turned on the four TV screens and dialed in the sports stations and put bottles of beer in the cooler from the cases on the floor. The cook brought out ice from the kitchen in plastic buckets and filled the stainless steel hoppers beneath the bar. The door opened and Mike turned to see who was coming in.

"Hey, Mikey. I'm glad you guys are here tonight. I was hoping for some good music," said Seth walking up with his right hand out.

"Mr. Rich. It's good to see you. How goes the campaign business?" asked Mike putting his sandwich half back on the plate and grabbing his hand to shake it.

"Like shit, as usual," said Seth.

"Oh come on. This is your time. I mean you guys are ahead in all the polls. It's awesome, right?" asked Mike patting Seth on the shoulder of his sports jacket as Seth loosened his tie.

"The polls don't mean squat, Mikey. The ones who have the gold, you know," said Seth nodding at Maddy as she automatically drew the right beer into a glass for Seth. "Thank you baby," said Seth.

"Don't tell me the Donald is going to win," said Mike taking a bite out of his sandwich.

"Not if I can help it. Super delegates, my man. It's all about a bunch of bulging little envelopes and super delegates. That's what I mean," said Seth.

"There, you see? That's why we play music. Good, honest work," said Lucy nearly kissing Seth on the cheek.

"Yeah, I guess it's all entertainment in the end, but the winner gets to write checks from the United States treasury," said Seth taking a long drink from his beer.

"Still, when I go home I can turn it off. I mean no one asks me for a billion dollars for a new bridge or an airport," said Mike.

"Look. No one is saying politics ain't dirty work. It's just supposed to be about politics and not bribery. Okay maybe there is a little under the table stuff, but Clinton is right in our face with this. She makes no bones about it. The Committee is supposed to choose a nominee through campaigning and voting and shit. It's not supposed to be a freaking coronation set up by a handful of billionaires," said Seth unintentionally spitting a little beer and wiping his mouth with the back of his hand.

"I thought Trump was the billionaire," said Lucy.

"Oh yeah. He's a billionaire, the hard way," said Seth putting extra emphasis on the 'A'. "Maybe I shoulda said trillionaire. Bernie is facing down a power structure that has been 30 years in the making."

"Well, look. Stranger things have happened. Right? Look at Obama. He was a nobody out of nowhere, and he beat Hillary the last time. What's anyone know about it?" said Mike, finishing the last bite of his sandwich.

"He was a smooth talker, that one. Hillary was like a screech owl compared to Bruno Mars. That's why he won," said Maddy wiping the bar in front of Seth.

"Yeah, that's right. She had the super delegates then, too didn't she?" asked Lucy.

"True enough. And, they changed horses pretty close to the end there, as I remember," said Mike.

"Yeah. It ain't over 'til it's over, sweetie," said Maddy.

"I can tell you that very soon, people are going to find out just how dangerous this woman is. That's all," said Seth holding his finger up and swallowing the last of the beer in his glass and nodding to Maddy who was already drawing another beer in a clean, frosted glass.

"All presidents are dangerous, aren't they?" asked Lucy

"Yeah, I mean people might just be afraid of a powerful woman, right?" asked Maddy as she set the glass of beer in front of Seth.

"We're talking about the Clintons, people," said Seth submerging, his upper lip into the cold, blonde ale.

"Oh, what? A little error in judgment. That's makes them dangerous?" said Lucy shuffling the cards to deal out another Solitaire hand.

"Getting caught in a hot tub with the Village People is an error in judgment. Shooting your lawyer in the park is called homicide," said Seth.

"Who said that? Nobody said that," said Mike.

"You're right. They only found his body in the park," said Seth coldly.

"Holy shit, Seth. That's pretty heavy coming from Captain America of the DNC," said Mike.

"Don't make fun of him. I like that star spangled shirt on you," said Lucy looking up from the cards to smile at Seth.

"I do too," said Maddy.

"Well, I don't feel too star spangled right now, pardon me for saying. This is supposed to be a democracy. I'm beginning to feel like it's Cuba or something," said Seth taking another sip.

"What does that mean?" asked Mike.

"John Podesta fell for a phishing email and gave out his password. The emails were published by Wikileaks, and Debbie Schultz got fired for trying to fix the nomination. It's a total mess down there right now," said Seth.

"I thought that was just bull shit on the news," said Mike.

"No bull shit. I have proof that Hillary bought off the Superdelegates and even hacked into Bernie's donor database," said Seth really sipping hard on the chilled glass of beer.

"The super what? What the hell are you saying?" asked Lucy paying closer attention now.

"Superdelegates. They're like royalty in the DNC. They're mucky mucks. You know, previous Congressmen, governors, speakers, big donors. They've all been bought and paid for by the Clinton machine. Even if Bernie wins a primary, he doesn't win the State, because these super-pricks know what's best for the Party," said Seth barely able to contain his anger.

"Oh, baby. I'm so sorry. I know how much you like Bernie. We all like him," said Lucy.

"I don't know about you? But Hillary scares the shit out of me," said Maddy sliding another beer over the counter to Seth, who traded his empty glass.

"Yeah, well maybe someone will do something about it. Maybe some more information should get out there," said Seth loosening his collar a little.

"Well, tonight we're gonna enjoy some music and some beer and have a good time," said Mike.

"That's why I'm here. My favorite bar with my favorite people," said Seth holding his glass up for a toast.

"Oh you do have a future in politics, Mr. Rich," said Maddy smiling.

"I'll drink to that. Can I have a grapefruit juice on the rocks? Helps the voice," said Lucy, gently patting her paper white throat.

"Oh, baby if your voice gets any sweeter, you'll have to go pro," said Maddy. "Here you go,"

"Yeah, speaking of pro, we better do a little sound check to make sure this setup works. I mean, before the paying customers arrive," said Mike smiling at Seth and putting his arm on his shoulder.

"You guys are the best, you know," said Seth, smiling back so hard his blue eyes almost disappeared.

"Make this guy a sandwich before he gets too drunk," said Mike shaking him a little. "Damn, son. You been working out?"

"A little. I have a membership close to the house. When I get time," said Seth flexing his broad shoulders under his brown sports coat.

"Most eligible bachelor, you are," said Maddy winking at Seth.

"How about *At Last*. From the top," asked Mike, handing Lucy the wireless mic and sitting down at the keyboard.

The sultry words of Etta James filled the bar like whiskey and ice cooling a parched mouth. Lucy's voice was powerful and clean. She swiveled slowly on the bar stool and stared into Seth's eyes while her lean muscles controlled the resonance in her chest. She didn't bend the pitch to get the effect like an amateur. Her breath massaged the words through her perfectly shaped mouth, catching the listener off guard like watching a low flying albatross bank slowly across a glassy bay, almost touching the mirror, defying gravity. Seth didn't move. He could barely breathe himself, while he watched the words crafted on the lips of this antique porcelain doll.

The strings from the virtual band faded out, as Mike tinkled the final notes on the keyboard. Lucy blinked her shaded lids slowly over her dark brown eyes, releasing Seth from his trance. "How was that?" asked Lucy.

"Uh hem. That was amazing," said Seth.

"That's it? Only amazing? You better do it again," said Maddy.

"It was perfect, baby," said Mike.

"That's a wrap, then. I have a good feeling about this new band thing you got going," said Lucy.

"Yeah, it sounded great. I like the brush on the snare. Do you want a little reverb on your voice?" asked Mike.

"No. I mean don't touch a thing. That voice is perfect," said Seth taking a sip of beer like he hadn't had one in an hour.

"Your sweet," said Lucy taking her own sip from the icy grapefruit juice.

Mike and Lucy walked up the stairs to the dressing room, and Lou's City Bar slowly began to fill with neighbors and friends. Maddy turned up the juke box and quarters began dropping classics one after the other as the Friday night hum began building. Voices and laughter pawed at the dressing room door like a puppy wanting attention.

The evening gown slipped over Lucy's shoulders and down onto her body like red ice flowing over a street lamp. Her left shoulder was left bare, exposing a dozen shades of green foliage, and dark red flowers wrapped around her curved bicep. Her right shoulder and cleavage arrested the shiny fabric before it hugged her toned torso and followed her round ass like downhill racers heading for certain death. She sat smoothly in the rocking chair, and Mike lifted her bare foot into his warm hands and rubbed deeply.

"I don't mind being fashionably late," said Lucy, rocking her head back like he had just turned the right control on a fine stereo.

"I just want to make those heels a little easier to stand in for an hour. I know how much better you sing when your feet feel good," he whispered.

"You can hear me singing, can't you?" she said looking him in the eyes without blinking.

"I am your humble servant king," said Mike.

"Shall we see if the slippers fit?" she asked as loud clapping erupted from downstairs.

"We have a couple minutes. Let me have the other foot," said Mike gently lowering it to the floor.

"Oh, no argument here," said Lucy, raising her other foot into his warm grip.

"I love you, my queen," said Mike.

"As well, you should," said Lucy.

"I wish my dad was here. I mean to hear us," said Mike.

"We'll see him at Thanksgiving," said Lucy

"I know. I just wish he could get out and hear us one time."

"Well, let's bring your mom and dad up for a couple of days. We'll make room. They'll love it," said Lucy.

"We can do that. We'll see what works. I like the idea. How's that feel?" said Mike pulling the last of the tension out of her toes.

"Like I could sing all night," said Lucy leaning forward to kiss him deeply.

"I love rubbing your feet," said Mike.

"You like the kisses after rubbing my feet," said Lucy chirping a kiss on his lips again.

"I like the kisses even better. Let's go knock 'em dead," said Mike, as he slipped the first shiny stiletto heeled shoe onto her smooth white foot.

"Let me shine my lips and I'll be right down," said Lucy standing in the shoes.

"I'll see you down there," said Mike as he opened the wooden door and closed it behind him.

Mike walked down the short set of stairs onto the landing and the applause erupted. He held out his hands for them to stop, but it got even louder. His tuxedo jacket was a sharp contrast to the office shirts and company polos in the almost packed bar. The juke box seemed almost too loud, but he shook hands and hugged the women politely as he made his way to the keyboard. Maddy put a bottle of ice cold water on the small square next to his keyboard and pecked him on the cheek. He sat down and looked around the room. Nearly every table was occupied, and Seth smiled back from a high table opposite the door. Two young men and a woman stood at the same table and were clapping along with Seth.

"Thank you everyone. Good evening, and welcome to Lou's City Bar. This is the Lucy and Mike Show. You'll know why it's not the other way around before the first song is finished. Don't forget to tip your waitress," said Mike as the jukebox fell silent and his hands glided over the keyboard and played a masterful version of Miles Davis, 'A Thousand Miles.'

The applause was thundering as he looked up the stairs to see a crack of light turn off from the door. He pressed the button on the screen, and the sweet strings of the Etta James piece began.

"At last, my love has come along," came Lucy's voice from the dark of the stairs. She poured slowly down the stairs, singing, intoxicating the room as the glitter in her black hair picked up the LED lights they had carefully placed along the narrow stage. The small, gelled Fresnels shattered across the threads in her red dress, and shards of light sliced the room like crystal sugar over a frozen strawberry. The rehearsal version was a Saltine cracker compared to the syrup she deftly poured over the heads of the people in Lou's City bar. If they were tired from a long week of the election nonsense of the most powerful city in the world, they couldn't feel it now. They couldn't feel anything but the cool drink in the throat, and the finest sound humans could possibly endure.

It was a moment of escape into that special place where time stops and joy blends with misery. Like a picture plucked from the album and held in the hands for a closer look without the plastic cover, just to hold the moment before the exhale and the deep and empty swallow. There was this time when we didn't have pain to make us feel alive. It was now like no other now. And then, like a light reflected off a passing car outside, coming in through the window and across the photo, was the hint of tomorrow. It couldn't possibly be the same. It most certainly wouldn't be better, as the edge of the photo slips under the cover of the album to be put away. It might not even arrive at all.

As usual, Lou's City Bar soon made the last call well before Seth wanted to stop being out with friends. He refused Mike's offer to drive him home. He didn't want to go home yet, and there was an after-hours club a few blocks away. He was 27 years old, born on the 3rd of January, 1989 and already he felt like he was carrying a burden too heavy for a long journey. He loved talking to people and especially about politics.

He paid his tab, shook hands, and waved to Lucy as she smiled back at him and winked while talking to some of her fans who were also saying goodbye. He pocketed his wallet, looked at his gold watch his father had bought him for graduation, and walked out the door into the warm July just before 2AM. The air felt amazing as he put his hands in his pockets and started to walk toward the after-hours club. 'I'm actually walking pretty straight,' he told himself imagining his liver working like a factory to metabolize the 18 beers he had drained.

The Democrat Party knew how to party, but they also were the party of the big top. Well, at least they used to be before this election. It didn't feel so much like it was her turn, so much as it felt like it was her right to be president. He had met Bernie Sanders many times. Truth be told, he was an easy person to meet. It wasn't as though his ideas would ever fully be implemented, but if they got close it would be a better place for his generation. After all, tailgating outside the stadium was getting old. He wanted to be in the stands, or maybe even on the field with the players, and Bernie made him feel that way. Most of the people at Lou's felt that way, but not everyone. That's what made it so much fun to go there and talk politics and drink beer. It was just a special kind of heaven when Mike and Lucy came to sing. 'God, she was good,' he said to himself as he turned the corner and lengthened his stride.

He felt his face getting warm from the walk, and he wiped his forehead with the back of his hand. It was then that he heard steps behind him. He hadn't passed anyone. The sidewalks in this quiet upscale neighborhood of little houses and older remodeled flats was pretty well lit except for the construction walls here and there along the sidewalk. People complained about the plywood, but they also didn't want to get hit in the head by tool dropped from the second floor above the sidewalk. He hadn't heard any car doors close or seen any porch lights come on. He thumbed his cell phone alive and called his girlfriend. She didn't like it when he drank so much, but he was feeling romantic. He barely had a moment to speak or sense the danger when the numbing impact struck his left shoulder blade. Before he could reach for it or turn around another round felt like it came through his chest from behind. He tried to take a breath, but he couldn't. His diaphragm had gone into spasms as he began choking on blood filling his left lung. His chest heaved, but his throat had closed off and the air seemed to come into his chest from behind, but it never reached his lungs.

Within seconds, he fell to his knees and somewhere in a dream, his face struck the concrete sidewalk.

Seth Rich was murdered on the sidewalk of a quiet Washington D.C. suburb in cold blood on July 10th, 2016 within minutes of leaving Lou's City Bar. Surveillance tapes in the bar may have had the face of his killer clearly recorded, but police refused to look at it. After 30 days, the bar's manager let the DVR overwrite that evening. Police would say it was a foiled robbery, although Seth's wallet and watch were not missing. Someone wanted him dead, and it is clear it was not the killer. The shooter could have easily stepped forward to put another bullet in his head, but the message was delivered. He only wanted to be paid. By whom, it seems, law enforcement to this very day has no desire to disclose to the courts or to the public.

Chapter 5

"Why would anyone want to be ruler of the world?" asked Atyom with his thick Russian accent.

"You say that like men haven't been trying to do just that since the earth cooled," said Edward from behind his large screen laptop that rested on a TV table in front of an oversized emerald green chair. It wasn't uncommon for internet businesses to operate from apartments in Almaty, and this one was large, by local standards.

"No. I am serious as heart attack. People are such babies, and they need their asses wiped every day. You know of what I am speaking," said Atyom not sounding like a question.

"Here's the thing, Atyom. People should be free to be whiners if they want to be. Nobody said liberty wasn't messy. It's very messy. We have the right to be idiots," said Edward.

"This, I know. But when a smart man works hard, he can rise up to here," said Atyom holding his hand out flat just above his head. "Then he becomes rich. And then he becomes powerful, because he profits from the work of others. And then, he wants control. This I don't understand," he said dropping his arm in frustration and slapping his black Levis on the thigh.

"If you're referring to the tyrant lifecycle, your history has some great examples. Stalin had," began Edward.

"Now. See. There you go attacking Stalin again. This is what I am saying about you Americans," interrupted Atyom.

"Stalin had," began Edward again in his slow and analytical voice, "become the secretary general for the Central Committee of the Communist Party in 1922. This allowed him to appoint his allies to government jobs and grow a base of political support. That's the same thing the political insiders have done in America since before the world war."

"You are saying that America is like Soviet Union," said Atyom as a statement of fact.

"Well, there is a difference. In America, there is no one man that is in charge. There is no Stalin turning the nation from a bunch of regional farmers into an industrial superpower. Eisenhower made speeches about the secret complex crafted from industrial and military forces, but he didn't send anyone off to labor camps or shoot anyone in the head when his term was finished," said Edward.

"Maybe not, but I think we could name a few, yes?" asked Atyom.

"See, here's the thing. America is not really a country. It's an idea. It's about having a dream, working hard, and seeing that dream become a reality, molded by your own hands. Well, at least that's what it was," said Edward looking back at his laptop screen for a moment.

"Stalin means, *man of steel*. You know this, yes? He told people what to do, and if they did not do it, he sent them to the camps or into a ditch. Before long, there was only obedience. This is not like America. I know this. In America, there is no man of steel," said Atyom.

"The way the government is set up, there is no place for a man of steel. It is specifically designed to prevent a man of steel from having that much power," said Edward.

"Maybe so, but your government controls the media, just like Stalin. It protects the corporate political donors from competition by small or new businesses, just like Stalin. It controls all education, and soon will have control of all health care, and then it will be worse than the man of steel," said Atyom progressively raising his voice.

"You left out one thing. They have access to everyone's information. Information is the ultimate power over people," said Edward.

"You should know this better than anyone," said Atyom pointing to the laptop in front of Edward.

"Well, there is this one difference between then and now. There is one thing standing in between this government man of steel and the control they seem to crave," said Edward, as he typed a few words into his darknet connection.

"And what might that be?" asked Atyom like he was waiting for a magic trick to work.

"The armed American," said Edward.

"Now you are talking about something we Russians know about. You mean revolution," said Atyom.

"Actually, just the opposite. You say you know revolutions so well. Get this. Those who start a revolution, are never the ones who finish it. Revolutions create vacuums, and vacuums are filled by opportunists. And opportunists are everywhere," said Edward.

"You mean like China or something?" asked Atyom already lost in the complexity of the scenario just described.

"Not really. The same players have been at this for hundreds of years. Since ancient Rome. Maybe before that. Anyway, they set up insurgent groups inside our society," said Edward.

"I am not understanding this very much. Every email, every text, every phone conversation, and every bank transaction is collected and analyzed already. You know this. How is it possible this can happen when so much is known by your NSA?" asked Atyom as he walked over to look out of the eighth floor window onto the narrow streets of Almaty below.

"Oh, they think they know everything about it. They're trying right this minute to see if they should consider people under the age of 24 who buy black running shoes domestic terrorists. Why do you think I exposed them? I could not stand by and let people continue to believe in their government, thinking they were supporting their country. Do you know what that feels like? When you discover the government you work for is actually another country, all by itself?" asked Edward folding his arms and falling back into the large, green chair.

"So why ruin a good thing? I mean why would they slaughter the goat that provides the milk for their children?" asked Atyom.

"See, the thing is that your goat does not have a 9mm. Your goat does not go to the gun range a few times a year and practice shooting human silhouettes, because he suspects you are about to slaughter him. The government wants to take out the goat army," said Edward unfolding his arms and scooting up to his laptop again.

"There is a goat army? What is goat army?" asked Atyom.

"Oh there are goats, and pigs, and cows, and chickens too. And they don't trust each other either," said Edward.

"You mean like animal farm? I am lost again. You Americans are losing your minds," said Atyom.

"Look. The cops are like this blue army. They work for the government to collect taxes and fines from the people. When the people resist, they not only like it, they thrive on it. And there are a growing number of people who don't like the fact that the cops are so violent all the time," began Edward.

"I thought you like law and order," interrupted Atyom.

"Yeah, well you see, laws are there for everyone. We call it equal protection. But certain people don't have to obey those laws like everybody else. They get to do whatever they want, and nothing ever happens to them. The people see that, too. And it is really beginning to piss them off," said Edward.

"You think we don't have the same thing in Kazakhstan? In Russia it is the same," said Atyom.

"Not the same. In those countries you don't have an armed populace, and you don't have a four hundred year history of liberty and freedom. And it's not just the cops. There are other armies, like I said, operating inside America, and they are just waiting for orders," said Edward now raising the pitch in his normally very cool and smooth voice.

"You're talking about ANTIFA and Black Lives Matter, and groups like that? But that takes money. People don't fight for nothing. Mercenaries get paid," said Atyom.

"That's another thing. George Soros and Iran and Saudi Arabia send millions of dollars a week to these groups inside America. Think of it like a hundred dirty bombs hidden all over America, just waiting on someone to push the button," said Edward.

"You are making my head hurt, Edward. Besides, a dirty bomb is not good for anyone. It makes the whole place a mess for a long time," said Atyom.

"They're not meant to be really efficient at destroying things. They're meant to make people afraid. That's why they call it terrorism," said Edward.

"We know about these things as well. We just make the terrorists afraid to make people afraid," said Atyom.

"I kind of like due process, Atyom. It doesn't work so fast or maybe deliver justice too well sometimes, but it protects our right to do things like face your accuser, and prevent illegal searches and seizures," said Edward.

"You talk to me about constitution, and yet your NSA looks up your skirt anytime it likes," said Atyom.

"True enough. I'm just saying that America is like a giant game board right now. And there are trained and equipped players in just about every major city just waiting for the cards to hit the green velvet," said Edward sliding his right hand out in front of him.

"Now everyone struggles to place their bets, yes?" asked Atyom.

"No. The real struggle right now is to see who gets to be the dealer," said Edward.

"The house always wins. This is what they say. Why the delay? I mean, why don't they piss or get off the pot?" asked Atyom.

"My guess is it's because all the players are armed and dangerous," said Edward.

"I thought you Americans liked cowboys," said Atyom.

"We love cowboys. We just expect the sheriff to be the good guy, not the biggest thug in the room," said Edward.

"But the sheriff is elected in your country. I am lost again," said Atyom.

"See here's the thing. The people only get to vote for or against the candidates on the ballot. And the ballot is controlled by basically two private corporations. These two corporations only allow one type of candidate to get on the ballot," said Edward holding up his index finger.

"But this is for the most powerful man in the world. They want strong person in this job, yes?" asked Atyom.

"Oh, this is where it gets really crazy. The right candidate has to have a certain appearance. No bald president. No fat president. No ugly president; not really ugly. They don't even like presidents with glasses," said Edward.

"This is all bull shit, Edward. None of these things have anything to do with being a good president," said Atyom.

"Yeah, no shit. The one thing they must have is the ability to read a teleprompter and to remember that they are not in charge," said Edward.

"Hell you say. He is in charge of everything and everyone," said Atyom.

"That's what everyone thinks. In fact, that is what they want you to think. The truth is that the corporation is syndicated with dozens of other corporations, and they make up a single mind with one ultimate goal," said Edward.

"Let me guess. To control the world," said Atyom flatly.

"Almost. They want to control the souls of the world. I guess a better way to say it is that they want to capture all the souls of the world at once, without having a huge war," said Edward.

"What do you consider small war?" asked Atyom.

"Pocket rebellions. A city here, a city there; dragging some rich white people into the streets and beating them to death. Just enough for the news media to turn into a crisis. I would say, anything less than a few months to bury the dead; especially if the dead are the old, the sick, the very poor," said Edward.

"I guess I understand. You see? Stalin was not such a bad guy, after all," said Atyom.

"There is a big difference, my friend," said Edward.

"How so?" asked Atyom.

"Stalin stood in front of his army and ruled his world. These elitists are the ultimate cowards. They rule the world from closets and banks. They believe the meek shall inherit only six feet of the Earth, and they are entitled to the rest, with enough workers to supply them with the comforts of heaven itself." said Edward.

"I think maybe they are not so afraid of the red carpet now," said Atyom.

"I left my office and my family in Hawaii to make sure Americans knew what was being done to them; to us. I thought the truth would set them free," said Edward wanting to crawl back inside his cyber world where he could not feel anymore.

"I am thinking maybe Americans want to go back to sleep," said Atyom turning his face back to the window.

"Americans are mad as hell, my friend. And the elites are so afraid they're little fake terror game is going to be taken away from them. They're gearing up for a fight," said Edward gritting his teeth.

"I am not seeing it. Your young people live in their smart phones. The boys are afraid of the girls. They send a picture to the girl, and she maybe sends one back. They hide behind masks and break windows at the university with a stick. They are not ready for real life. Stalin stood in front of his army and eventually, the Soviet Union lost. Your cowardly generals have everything in their favor. I think your war is already over," said Atyom.

"A war is only over when your enemy says it is. Maybe the pillow fighters out there aren't ready for this fight, but information is my job, and based on what I see, there are at least 100 million trained adults out there who are ready, willing, and able to take back their country," said Edward moving his thumb skillfully over the touch pad on his laptop to change sites.

"Like I said. I am thinking this will be *pay for view* war. Over in the first round," said Atyom punching his right fist softly into is other palm.

"That's what they thought about the first war. It took a commercial break, and the fight resumed," said Edward.

"Until the weapons became so powerful that no one could face the consequences of conflict. What did Mr. Churchill say about world war four? Fought with sticks?" asked Atyom.

"Maybe he was wrong. Maybe this war will be fought with ones and zeroes at first, and then it will erupt all around them all at once. There won't be any battle front. The entire country will vomit all at once, and the sickness will be flushed down the toilet," said Edward scrolling down the screen.

"Remember what you said about revolutions. About starters and finishers," said Atyom tapping the glass window with his index finger distantly.

"The difference is, my friend, that we have an enduring constitution that says our rights come from God, and not from men. We are empowered by that document to rise up and overthrow our leadership, when it becomes tyrannical. But the rule of law shall endure, and things will settle back down, and the bad guys will be stripped of their power and glory," said Edward.

"Well, just make sure it is rule of law, and not rule by law," said Atyom.

"Well said, my friend. Well said," said Edward closing the screen on his laptop, feeling much better.

Chapter 6

"I sometimes wonder what I was thinking when I decided to be a lawyer," said Herb. The Starbucks on Broadway in New York City was practically next door to the building with HSBC Holdings, PLC. This part of the City had a smell like no other city in the world. A half an hour south of Hell's Kitchen, this part of the Big Apple was trapped by the East River on three sides. Try as it would, the smell of New York City could never be mistaken for anywhere else.

Herbert Kadzinski wore grey suits, like his city, and the pants had suspenders so he could sit for weeks on end sipping coffee and comparing vaults full of records, line by line, to even bigger vaults of regulations. The rest of his time was spent sitting in policy briefings with government regulators who created their own jobs by the hundreds simply by editing clauses and appendices in Federal and State statutes. His job was to make sure companies and banks were in compliance.

"Oh, you love it, and you know it," said Felicity. You have the most secure job in New York." She was considered middle-aged for a bank teller at 32 years old. She could keep a cash drawer to the penny, and practically set a new standard for the term window dressing at the bank. 'How is it you make twice the transactions of any other teller?' they would ask her.

"You never know what a little Chanel and Armani will do for your business," she would answer. Actually, she was naturally gorgeous. Her mother knew it the moment she was born and named her Felicity. She considered Chastity for a moment, but knew right away that would be an open challenge to the entire male community. She was dangerously feminine, but smart enough to know one moment of indiscretion could ruin a woman's bank career. 'The trick is to let the bookkeepers think you're a lesbian, and the rumors will do the rest,' she told her mother.

"Yeah. Ten years, and I have never seen the inside of a courtroom. I guess I'm doing well," said Herb, putting the black debit card back into his RF protected wallet and zipping it back into his inside jacket pocket. He looked at the reflection of his round frame in the pastry case glass and swore this was the last brown sugar crumble cake he would ever eat.

"Well, it's never too late. What would you rather be doing?" asked Felicity. She enjoyed being a teller at the ground floor bank, but since she had been promoted to the internal audit team, she got to wear more comfortable clothes and didn't have to stand in one place for 8 hours a day. Besides, working with people in the bank was so much better than working with the public. After ten years, she wondered if there was anyone in New York who could balance a checkbook.

"I don't know. Maybe a movie critic, or maybe even a crane operator," said Herb testing the plastic lid on the coffee with his tongue to see if the coffee would scald his tongue. He hated not being able to taste the brown sugar if he scalded the tip of his tongue.

"How about a standup comic. You're a funny guy," said Felicity.

"Funny strange doesn't make you famous," said Herb.

"Works for Zachary Galifianakis," said Felicity.

"He's strange and funny, but I'll bet he started out picking crumbs with the sparrows," said Herb.

"Well, are you ready to do this thing?" asked Felicity.

HSBC Holdings is one of the world's largest banks with offices in every major country. Its roots can be traced back through hundreds of years of acquisitions, mergers, and charters to establish what can be argued is the most contiguous central banking concern in history.

Herbert began his audit the same way he always had done. Debits and credits into and out of a statistically significant sampling of private and commercial accounts were matched to scanned checks, traced through a system of pings to and from domestic and foreign banks, credit unions, and settlement accounts. Errors and missing paperwork or identifications were common enough, but what was found this day was something nobody expected; not again.

At first, it was difficult to reconcile. Dozens and then hundreds, and then thousands of bank accounts were associated with names for which there was no identification. These were not duplicates or empty, dormant bill-pay accounts that turn up years after a bank officer had received a sales bonus. These accounts were receiving and sending large wire transfers. Herb's junior experience as part of the Wachovia and Wells Fargo money laundering case in Charlotte, North Carolina in 2005 made his spine tingle. He glanced over his shoulder as Felicity walked up to his chair with a bottled water.

"I brought you a water. It's almost 4 o'clock," said Felicity.

"Oh, Thanks. Hey, do me a favor. Close the door, will you?" said Herb as quietly as he could.

"Sure. You want me to stay?" asked Felicity.

"Um, yeah," said Herb waiting for the door to close. A door closing in a bank administration office during an audit sends a signal like a body falling to the floor. It usually means someone is getting fired or promoted, but when an auditor closes a door, it means a finding.

Every audit turns up little things, and sometimes big things that will be discussed with the bank's managers during a closing meeting. Ninety days later, there is a follow-up meeting to check if the corrective actions have been addressed, and perhaps to see if any permanent actions have been taken to prevent it from occurring again.

Herb was coding a query in the SAP resource planning software that would produce a report of all the accounts at HSBC that were missing identification, and had received wire transfers greater than one thousand dollars, and had made wire transfers to other accounts. He hovered his finger over the Enter key for a moment, sat upright in the leather swivel chair, and pressed it.

"What's going on? Did you find something?" asked Felicity.

"Bring me my computer bag from over there. Does that door lock?" asked Herb watching the screen auto-scroll.

"No. I don't think so. Here you go," said Felicity handing him his shoulder bag.

"I need you to dial this number from your cell phone. Do it over there in that corner and don't face the window. No person will answer, so I want you to leave this message, then hang up. No name. No hello. Just those numbers. Okay?" asked Herb handing her a sticky note with six pairs of numbers on it.

"No problem. I got it," said Felicity.

"And no questions. I mean it. Don't look at anything. Don't ask me anything," said Herb staring her in the eyes to make sure she understood.

Felicity nodded and shuffled her low heels over to the corner of the office to make the call. Herb opened his bag and withdrew a hard drive from the bag. He plugged in his security dongle to make sure his drive could not be detected by the bank's server. There would be no record of the download or the query in the bank's system.

Felicity and Herb smiled and shook hands as they left HSBC Holdings that day. There was no evening meeting. Herb told the account manager they would call next week and make an appointment to come back to make some notes. The accounting girls twirled in their chairs and slipped their shoes back on to get ready to go home for the day. The elevator was quiet, and didn't stop until it reached the parking garage. Herb was glad, because he never played poker for a reason.

"Felicity, it's been great working with you. Go home. I mean straight home. I think you should take next week off as well. I'll call your boss. Take the time to change cell phones. Just get a new one, and lose that one. Okay? You did great. I mean it. Really great," said Herb shaking her hand and watching her turn soundlessly away and walk toward her little blue Toyota in the parking garage. He looked around to make sure there was no one watching. There were no people on that parking deck. There were no black SUV's anywhere or people sitting in cars. "Shit. Shit, shit shit," he said under his breath.

HSBC was laundering money. Lots of it. From what Herb could see, it was in the billions, all coming in through an apparently small exchange house; Casa de Cambio Puebla. Oh, they tried to deny they knew anything about it at first, but Puebla had been under investigation by Mexican and US Federal authorities for two years when HSBC was caught for handling a staggering $376bn of illegal money for an American bank, Wachovia. Wachovia was punished with a "deferred prosecution" – a yellow card; none of its employees were arrested, and amazingly, nothing stopped the flow of money or the use of phony bank accounts.

HSBC continued business as usual like they didn't have a worry in the world. They even used the same exchange house and the same wiring channels: a bank it had bought in Mexico, another in California. It was clear from the movements of staggering sums of money that they were even using some of their own branches.

They were laundering so many 100 dollar bills that the bank had the cartels order specially designed boxes to fit the precise dimensions of the teller windows, so they wouldn't draw suspicion handling the large, white bags of cash brought in on pallets to the bank branches. Business was good at HSBC. The electronic trail was easy to follow, once Herb got the query programmed. What Herb was never able to do was find the handling charges. Someone, very high up, was skimming the cash flow to the tune of about 30%.

Somewhere around $360 million was floating out there, and he wanted to find it. He went to the US Attorney's office and met with Loretta Lynch to discuss the case. She was well spoken and seemed to have the *gift,* as he called it. 'You know? There are damn few people in the world to whom you can ask a question, any question at all, and they will talk for hours without ever saying anything," he used to say to his mother.

"Oh, Herbert. I don't know what you mean," his mother would say.

"Lots of people speak English," he would say , "but there are a few people who have mastered it. They can string together adjectives and adverbs, and even punctuation. And by the time they have finished talking, it takes more than a moment to realize they didn't use a single subject. Nothing. Nothing was done. Nothing was said. They said nothing you can use in a court of law. 'Mistakes were made,' they will say. 'This really concerns me,' they will admit. 'I don't recall,' is one of my favorites," said Herb as his mother would shake her head without a clue what he meant.

The truth scared the hell out of Herb. This wasn't lumber or sugar or even alcohol sales being covered up. This was drug money. Mexico's narco nightmare mercilessly shot, beheaded, and even burned alive 100,000 people on both sides of the border, and there were more than 20,000 missing. More than a trillion dollars had been spent in the war on drugs, but there were more drugs now than ever before. Heroin and cocaine were flowing by the trainloads into America, and the cash addicted the biggest banks in the world as surely as if they had injected it into their veins.

But what happened next is what really scared him. He wished the very next minute he had never heard of HSBC, or that he never passed the Bar in the State of New York. HSBC was openly and blatantly acting like the financial services wing of the biggest drug producers the world had ever known, and he had sat in the US Attorney's office laying out his evidence. He had lost a month's worth of sleep worrying about the indictments and the trials and the exposure this would bring to him and to his mother, and maybe even to Felicity.

And then, he read the judgment from the DOJ and watched the financial news.

Attorney General Eric Holder approved of the bank being fined more than Wachovia, a record $1.9bn. But this was less than five weeks' income for HSBC's American subsidiary. The Department of Justice, under the recommendation of the US Attorney, Loretta Lynch, deemed that HSBC should not be prosecuted in the way that a back-street dope-dealer would be; there would be a five-year "deferred prosecution". He left that meeting confident she was the law east of the Pecos, but this felt like a high-altitude maneuver.

HSBC announced that it would "partially defer bonus compensation for its most senior officials during the five-year period of the deferred prosecution agreement" – ergo they'd be remunerated with slightly less than usual. There would be no indictments. Not a single bank officer lost their job. 'What the holy hell was going on?' Herb asked himself.

And not just that: Paul Thurston, the man in charge of HSBC Mexico for some of the relevant period, was promoted to become head of global retail on a new, multi-million dollar salary. Stephen Green, the chief executive of the bank throughout its service to Chapo Guzman's cartel, was appointed to the British government.

Green's replacement as CEO, Stuart Gulliver, did what behemoth corporations always do in these situations. He called a press briefing to apologize for "past mistakes". He said: "We accept responsibility for our past mistakes. We have said we are profoundly sorry for them." He insisted HSBC was "a fundamentally different organization" now.

Britain's financial media excoriated the Mexicans for tarnishing the bank's good name. The New York Times not only got the idea, but articulated it clearly: "Federal and state authorities have chosen not to indict HSBC, the London-based bank, on charges of vast and prolonged money laundering, for fear that criminal prosecution would topple the bank and, in the process, endanger the financial system."

Referring to the Wachovia case, Robert Mazur, the US federal agent who infiltrated the BCCI bank, which was prosecuted for laundering money for Colombian drug lord Pablo Escobar, said something similar: "There were external circumstances that worked to Wachovia's benefit, not least that the US banking system was on the edge of collapse." Nevertheless, Mazur added cogently to this weekend's deliberations: "The only thing that will get the message to the banks and start to solve the problem is the rattle of handcuffs in the boardroom."

But that didn't happen either. Within a month of the charges being made public, a smooth and impenetrable firewall was formed around the HSBC Board with the hiring of a tall, well-spoken former Lockheed-Martin executive director, James Comey. He was indomitable, and his voice reeked of innocence behind his wide set blue eyes. He assured everyone things were just fine, and that the bank had turned over a new leaf.

It was a truly amazing thing to watch, when James Comey walked into a room. He was abnormally tall, at six foot eight. With dress shoes on, he would have to duck to come through a doorway. His hands were large and powerful, and yet he was lean and well-tailored. But, putting all that aside, it was when he spoke that his enemies strangely went silent. He had a *charm of favor* about him that shut the mouths of his dissenters. If the police were sent to arrest him for corruption of the highest order, they would leave the room smiling and hanging their handcuffs on the coat rack on the way out of the room. He was able to openly violate the rules everywhere he went, because he knew this charm would keep him from harm. He was one of the most trusted and valuable soldiers for the Clinton Crime Syndicate. His deep blue eyes and boyish face disarmed his enemies, while his kaleidoscopic semantics were clearly spoken truth and nothing but the truth.

Less than nine months later, he would be selected by President Barack Obama for a 10-year term as the new Director of the FBI. A little more than a year later, Loretta Lynch was nominated by President Obama to be the new US Attorney General. Herb began to understand where the skimmed money had gone. One by one, the Senators smiled and approved the appointments. Their red faces and pounding fists of protest became broad smiles and firm handshakes as they went off to open manila envelopes in the dark and masturbate behind their interns.

That much money isn't used to make men rich and comfortable. No one risks and goes through such phenomenal measures to protect the solvency of the world's largest bank to make a few executives' retirement funds fat with untraceable cash. No. This is the kind of money that buys countries.

The legal announcement of the charges read like something out of a spy novel. At first, you think the sword of Damocles is glistening above the top executives of the bank. The charges were horrendous and damning beyond measure:

"HSBC is being held accountable for stunning failures of oversight – and worse – that led the bank to permit narcotics traffickers and others to launder hundreds of millions of dollars through HSBC subsidiaries, and to facilitate hundreds of millions more in transactions with sanctioned countries," said Assistant Attorney General Breuer. "The record of dysfunction that prevailed at HSBC for many years was astonishing. Today, HSBC is paying a heavy price for its conduct, and, under the terms of today's agreement, if the bank fails to comply with the agreement in any way, we reserve the right to fully prosecute it."

"Today we announce the filing of criminal charges against HSBC, one of the largest financial institutions in the world," said U.S. Attorney Lynch. "HSBC's blatant failure to implement proper anti-money laundering controls facilitated the laundering of at least $881 million in drug proceeds through the U.S. financial system. HSBC's willful flouting of U.S. sanctions laws and regulations resulted in the processing of hundreds of millions of dollars in OFAC-prohibited transactions. Today's historic agreement, which imposes the largest penalty in any BSA prosecution to date, makes it clear that all corporate citizens, no matter how large, must be held accountable for their actions."

"Cartels and criminal organization are fueled by money and profits," said ICE Director Morton. "Without their illicit proceeds used to fund criminal activities, the lifeblood of their operations is disrupted. Thanks to the work of Homeland Security Investigations and our El Dorado Task Force, this financial institution is being held accountable for turning a blind eye to money laundering that was occurring right before their very eyes. HSI will continue to aggressively target financial institutions whose inactions are contributing in no small way to the devastation wrought by the international drug trade. There will be also a high price to pay for enabling dangerous criminal enterprises."

"In addition to forfeiting $1.256 billion as part of its deferred prosecution agreement (DPA) with the Department of Justice, HSBC has also agreed to pay $665 million in civil penalties – $500 million to the Office of the Comptroller of the Currency (OCC) and $165 million to the Federal Reserve – for its AML program violations. The OCC penalty also satisfies a $500 million civil penalty of the Financial Crimes Enforcement Network (FinCEN). The bank's $375 million settlement agreement with OFAC is satisfied by the forfeiture to the Department of Justice. The United Kingdom's Financial Services Authority (FSA) is pursuing a separate action.

"As required by the DPA, HSBC also has committed to undertake enhanced AML and other compliance obligations and structural changes within its entire global operations to prevent a repeat of the conduct that led to this prosecution. HSBC has replaced almost all of its senior management, "clawed back" deferred compensation bonuses given to its most senior AML and compliance officers, and has agreed to partially defer bonus compensation for its most senior executives – its group general managers and group managing directors – during the period of the five-year DPA. In addition to these measures, HSBC has made significant changes in its management structure and AML compliance functions that increase the accountability of its most senior executives for AML compliance failures."

"According to court documents, from 2006 to 2010, HSBC Bank USA severely understaffed its AML compliance function and failed to implement an anti-money laundering program capable of adequately monitoring suspicious transactions and activities from HSBC Group Affiliates, particularly HSBC Mexico, one of HSBC Bank USA's largest Mexican customers. This included a failure to monitor billions of dollars in purchases of physical U.S. dollars, or "banknotes," from these affiliates. Despite evidence of serious money laundering risks associated with doing business in Mexico, from at least 2006 to 2009, HSBC Bank USA rated Mexico as "standard" risk, its lowest AML risk category. As a result, HSBC Bank USA failed to monitor over $670 billion in wire transfers and over $9.4 billion in purchases of physical U.S. dollars from HSBC Mexico during this period, when HSBC Mexico's own lax AML controls caused it to be the preferred financial institution for drug cartels and money launderers.

"A significant portion of the laundered drug trafficking proceeds were involved in the Black Market Peso Exchange (BMPE), a complex money laundering system that is designed to move the proceeds from the sale of illegal drugs in the United States to drug cartels outside of the United States, often in Colombia. According to court documents, beginning in 2008, an investigation conducted by ICE Homeland Security Investigation's (HSI's) El Dorado Task Force, in conjunction with the U.S. Attorney's Office for the Eastern District of New York, identified multiple HSBC Mexico accounts associated with BMPE activity and revealed that drug traffickers were depositing hundreds of thousands of dollars in bulk U.S. currency each day into HSBC Mexico accounts. Since 2009, the investigation has resulted in the arrest, extradition, and conviction of numerous individuals illegally using HSBC Mexico accounts in furtherance of BMPE activity.

"As a result of HSBC Bank USA's AML failures, at least $881 million in drug trafficking proceeds – including proceeds of drug trafficking by the Sinaloa Cartel in Mexico and the Norte del Valle Cartel in Colombia – were laundered through HSBC Bank USA. HSBC Group admitted it did not inform HSBC Bank USA of significant AML deficiencies at HSBC Mexico, despite knowing of these problems and their effect on the potential flow of illicit funds through HSBC Bank USA."[1]

To this day, all of the bank officers involved in the formation of phony bank accounts, the reception and disbursal of drug cartel funds, and the blatant and deliberate cover-up of the existence, origin, or destination of those funds are still employed at the bank. No one has been fired. No person was indicted or sent to jail. No person was fined or reduced in pay. The more than 1,000 pages of evidence gathered and submitted by Herbert Kadzinski remains sealed.

---

[1] Justice News: Criminal Division Press release #12-1487 Tuesday, December 11, 2012

Chapter 7

Since the Democratic National Committee was formed, in 1848, the level of corruption in government seemed to know no bounds. Its tax policies were directly responsible for 13 States seceding from the Union with forming their own, independent nation rather than be subjected to what they called the Tariffs of Abomination. The printed and political propaganda used by the 19th century media moguls fostered a deep seated hatred that has lasted until well into the 21st century, and choked with the blood of nearly a million people. For the next 60 years, the Democrats controlled the federal government almost exclusively, with the exception of one brief period of incredible prosperity that seemed it would last forever.

In his role as Commerce Secretary, a Republican named Herbert Hoover created a new government program called "Own Your Own Home," which was designed to increase the level of homeownership. He muscled lenders and the construction industry to devote more resources to homeownership. His agency passed new rules that would allow federally chartered banks to do more residential lending. This unbridled expansion of the money supply was a tactic that would be used again in the Clinton presidency with precisely the same results. In 1927, Congress complied, and with this government stamp of approval and the resources made available by Federal Reserve expansionary policies through the decade, mortgage lending boomed.

The collapse of the money supply by central banks caused an avalanche of local bank failures as sources of funds disappeared overnight. Refinancing as a means for keeping the homes, farms, and businesses was denied, and high unemployment rates made the government-encouraged mortgages unaffordable. The result was a large increase in foreclosures and a global collapse in the economy.

It was a globalist tactic the central banks had confidence would bring the most powerful nation on earth to its knees. It worked exactly as planned, and the middle class evaporated from existence, leaving only two economic levels. The first was the working poor, unable to own a home and without access to capital was doomed to staying that way. The second was the mega-wealthy who had remained cash heavy and liquid so that when entire cities went broke, they could move in and buy steamships for a dime and entire city blocks for a few dollars more.

The only thing remaining was to be able to grow a government that could not only sustain this level of power, but to make sure that competition through innovation or startups could not come along and compete in the same marketplace. For that, new agencies, departments, bureaus, and administrations had to be created and staffed with people to write regulations, assess taxes, set fees, and take enforcement actions against their competition. It would require a way to control the elected officials so that this federal system of business could be perpetual.

The Democrats started to invest in candidates and campaigns, but it was not enough. The people could still vote for whomever they wished, and there was always someone on the ballot who could speak better, or looked better, or was supported by local residents who knew and trusted that candidate. The DNC quickly realized that casting the ballots was not what decided elections. It was the counting of those ballots that determined the winner.

Counting the votes any way they chose worked until reporters finally exposed the sham. The DNC was forced to make dramatic changes to its rules after the chaos of 1968, when Hubert Humphrey, who had not won a single primary, was nevertheless nominated at the Chicago convention. The riots were historic as people revolted against having their choice usurped by a small group of oligarchs at the head of the DNC.

They decided to create a new system to make sure the Syndicate never lost control of their party again. After all, their mission of tilting the balance of power into the hands of a single Democrat President was paramount. The corporation of the DNC decided to create a Superdelegate; someone who could be relied upon to always vote for whatever the corporation deemed was best for the Party and for the country. They would have a sort of protected status that could override primary or caucus decisions with their superior wisdom. The people simply could not be trusted with the power to actually choose the next President.

The DNC leadership crafted three ways to become a Superdelegate. The first is to be elected to public office as a Democratic governor, senator or congressman. The second is to become one of 438 members of the Democratic National Committee as a loyal party activist or a powerbroker, the latter of which was determined by how much cash you could bundle for the Party. The third and most difficult is to become a Superdelegate for life by having served as President, Vice-President, DNC chair or Democratic leader in either chamber of the US Congress.

Superdelegates were crafted in the early 1980s after the Democratic Party looked at rewriting their rules after an extended fight over them in the bitter primary between incumbent president Jimmy Carter and Massachusetts senator Ted Kennedy. The new rules replaced selection by Party bosses in conventions with processes that made picking delegates far more democratic and included language that encouraged women and minorities to be adequately represented. It was designed to act like an Electoral College inside the Democrat Party to offset the sometimes mob mentality of the voters.

The new Democrat Primary system did exactly what it was designed to do; totally cut elected officials, the voters, and Party elders out of the Primary process. In this way, the Syndicate began a decade-long process of forming a government that was focused on putting the person chosen from the Syndicate, by the Syndicate, and for the Syndicate. They knew that the right candidate was on the way. They also knew they had to have an election process that virtually guaranteed they could outmaneuver the American voter.

After 1984, the number of Superdelegates continued to increase. One by one, the oath and covenant was taken by powerful men and women who had been successful by sticking together no matter what legal or ethical challenge blocked their agenda. The system was made to order for someone who could come along with enough charisma, and enough ability to raise money to buy the loyalty of the Superdelegates. They would not have to wait long.

After a miserable partial term as governor of Arkansas from 1979 to 1981, Bill Clinton from Arkansas saw the opportunity. Almost immediately after his defeat, he began searching for ways to raise enough cash to buy his way back in. Then, in 1983, he became the State's 42nd governor.

Bill Clinton and his wife, Hillary, had already tried buying and selling real estate to accumulate the kind of wealth they desired, but that was far too slow. Besides, that method was already watched too closely by the Federal Election Commission and was the primary reason why Spiro Agnew did not succeed Richard Nixon when he resigned in the disgrace of impeachment.

In another financial scheme, Hillary Rodham Clinton was allowed to order 10 cattle futures contracts, normally a $12,000 investment, in her first commodity trade in 1978. The only problem was, she only invested $1,000. Her very first trade on the Chicago Mercantile Exchange returned an immediate $6,300 overnight. Within 10 months, she had realized more than $100,000 in profits without a single loss. Some of the profits were from trades not even placed by her, but the profits from those trades were untraceably shifted to her trading account.

In commodities futures trading, an account that falls below the "maintenance margin" typically triggers a "margin call," where the trader must put up sufficient cash to cover the contracts. Although Hillary Rodham Clinton's account was under-margined for nearly all of July 1979, no margin calls were made, no additional cash was put up, and she eventually reaped a $60,000 profit.

The truth is that this was far too risky and lacked the secrecy to raise money for a run at the presidency. They knew it was going to require millions of dollars, perhaps even more. The next step would be bold. It would be treacherous. It would also connect them with some of the most powerful and wealthy criminal operations in the world.

No one in the world, least of all members of the Democrat party, thought the Governor of a State with one of the worst economic records in the country, nearly the worst schools, and that suffered from a practically flat growth rate due to a constant exodus of young people to States with more to offer, had a chance of a snowball in hell of being nominated for President, let alone winning against incumbent George Herbert Walker Bush with a 91% approval rating after a successful Gulf War to oust Saddam Hussein from Kuwait. It was a joke of a proposition that a loser with a heavy southern accent could stand a chance against the 1991 Republican machine in Washington DC.

It was anything but a joke. Someone, or something, had been planning since long before 1946 to make this happen. But first, they needed cash; lots of cash. There was something everyone overlooked. Bush was the former head of the CIA, and then he became the Vice President of Ronald Reagan. They had been active in international drug trafficking since the days of Viet Nam, and had used the cash to fund a clandestine war against communist insurgents in South America, when Congress would not allocate the money for weapons or equipment. Reagan wanted them defeated, and Colonel Oliver North led the operation to make sure his suggestion was fulfilled. When the illegal activities surrounding the Iran-Contra black budgeted war, was seen by Democrats as a way to remove President Reagan from office, Colonel Oliver North tricked the Congressional investigators into giving him immunity in hopes that they could force him to implicate the President in the illegal drugs-for-weapons scheme. Of course, he tricked them and completely took the blame and cashed in his immunity card and everyone walked away.

The operation was real. The drugs were real. The cash was real. The transportation into and out of America by the CIA was real, and it primarily took place in a small airport in Mena, Arkansas. Under the Clintons, the operation would be expanded into an enormous money laundering operation, from which millions were skimmed for their own financial benefit. As with all criminal activities, doing business with criminals came with risks that had to be mitigated. Starting in the mid 1980's hardly a week went by without someone associated with the Clinton Crime Syndicate getting killed, committing suicide, or just disappearing altogether.

Mena airport became one of the world's largest aircraft refurbishing centers, providing services to planes from many countries. Researchers discovered over time that the largest consumers of aircraft refurbishing services are usually drug smugglers and intelligence agencies involved in covert activities.

In fact, residents of Mena, Arkansas, have told reporters that former marine Lt. Colonel Oliver North was a frequent visitor during the 1980's. Eugene Hasenfus, a pilot who was shot down in a Contra supply plane over Nicaragua in 1986, was also seen in town renting cargo vehicles.

The Clinton's involvement in the drug and arms running goes even further than a mere cover-up of the illegal activities at the airport in Mena for a cut of the action. A federal mail fraud case against an Arkansas pilot-trainer, who participated in illegal arms exports to Central America, relied on a key Clinton staffer as a chief witness for the prosecution. The CIA stepped in and refused to allow the discussion of top secret information about the arms transfers. Without the witness, the prosecution's case was simply dismissed.

According to Arkansas Committee researcher Mark Swaney, in the summer of 1987, even as the ContraGate hearings were going on in Congress, Terry Reed began to suspect they were using his front company for something other than smuggling weapons. One day, he was looking for a lathe in one of his warehouses near the airport in Guadalajara and he opened up one of the very large air freight shipping containers (they are about 28' long, about 7' high and about 8' wide), and he found it packed full of cocaine.

The street value of this much pure cocaine was in the tens of millions of dollars. Some of the cash from the sale of cocaine to users all across America was used to buy weapons to send back down to the Contras to fight the Sandinistas. The cash flowed first to Arkansas banks, and then Florida, and then to other larger banks. The Clintons used their State authority to stop arrests and prosecutions of individuals who got caught by law enforcement for one simple reason; cash. The Clintons developed and refined the process of buying Superdelegates and directly funding campaigns of Democrats who would be powerful enough to protect the Syndicate from the press and from prosecution. After all, the CIA was friendly only to those governments that allowed them to conduct their clandestine operations. They would take action against individuals or governments that tried to stop them, even if that government was ours.

The Syndicate provided more and more funding for these candidates through a sophisticated system of money laundering that has allowed the Clinton campaign to funnel enormous donations to State parties in return for their participation in a massive money-laundering payback system to also funnel money to the Clinton campaign itself. It became the lifeblood of Democrat campaigns on the national and State levels. Although the records show the Democrats averaged about the same amount of donations as Republicans, over time, the actual ground game delivered by Democrats was on a scale never before seen in politics.

But campaigning for the election was only a small part of the price for the presidency. First, the Superdelegates had to be bought. Then, the State Election Commissions had to be bought, and this included 50 different ballots that had to be petitioned and collected just to be included in the primaries. Before the first speech could be heard in any State, other than Arkansas, tens of millions of dollars had to be raised and spent. No one wants to remember where the money came from for the Superdelegates. Hundreds of manila envelopes were stuffed with drug Syndicate cash and couriered to each one, along with a name to remember; when the time was right. No one had to go out and campaign or even mention the name of Bill Clinton, yet.

The plan to defeat incumbent George Herbert Walker Bush faced two impossible challenges. The first challenge of winning the nomination was a matter of acquisition. The second challenge of winning a debate on stage against the sitting president was the easy part. Bill Clinton had two things going for him during those debates. First, he used his position as Governor to infiltrate Bush's CIA drug operations in Mena, Arkansas; a fact no one wanted to know about. Second, Bill Clinton was groomed and charmed to be one of the quickest and most charismatic speakers in political history.

Just to be sure, a third candidate had to be encouraged to enter the Presidential race and be given enough national presence to divide the conservative vote from the incumbent. Ross Perot was zealous enough to take the bait, and the nation was hungry enough for a change. 57% of the country voted against Bill Clinton in November of 1992, but his opponent was two people. His 43% of the popular vote delivered more than the 270 electoral votes needed to win, while Ross Perot won almost 20 million votes away from Bush, with zero electoral votes. The States that voted heavily for Perot were exactly the States that Clinton could not win without the siphoning effect. It was magically the first and only time this plan was successfully attempted in US history.

Two years later, America was wishing they never heard of Bill Clinton. The corruption not only followed them from Arkansas, but the temptation to make money from the White House could not be resisted. The Democrats lost more seats in the House and Senate than at any time in history. Americans, realizing they had been hoodwinked by the entire election, revolted against unbridled Federal spending and the explosive Clinton scandals. Taxes went up so high that some of them were actually retroactive and drew billions from estates from which the taxpayers had already died in the previous year. One thing was clear to the world, and to the Clintons. Bill Clinton was going to be a one-term president.

That was when everything changed. With a Republican majority in Congress came a new speaker; Newt Gingrich. He brilliantly nationalized many Congressional and Senate elections and crafted a clear plan called the Contract with America to curb runaway spending, balance the budget, and implement badly needed welfare reforms. There is no way the Clintons would have agreed to this, especially since Hillary was heading a commission to create HillaryCare—a Federal insurance plan run by a newly created Federal Agency—unless they were faced with complete rejection by the American people.

Newt basically told the Clintons that if they did not agree to his plan, their multi-level market White House business was as good as over. Bill Clinton started signing Newt's plan into law while the DNC plotted to destroy it and its creator as quickly as possible. It would later be an illegal recording made of Newt's mobile phone conversation about a Political Action Committee, by a husband and wife following his car, that forced him to resign as Speaker of the House.

Under Newt's leadership, the Federal budget was balanced. Welfare reform was realized, and costs began to come down. The country began to turn a corner and the economy was booming with the introduction of high-speed internet. The freedom and liberty this afforded the American entrepreneur was unprecedented. It was wild and unregulated. The DNC had to stop it by any means necessary, so they developed a plan.

First, Bill Clinton made a public statement that he was ordering the US Department of Justice to file lawsuits against Microsoft for its Internet Explorer. He falsely claimed Explorer and Windows constituted a monopoly and had to be broken apart from Microsoft, although America Online (AOL) was by far the largest browser in use at the time. Microsoft CEO, Bill Gates, told the Justice Department to bring it on and said he knew his way to the courtroom just fine.

The Justice Department's henchman, or henchwoman, was Janet Reno. She set the gold standard for refusing to provide Congressional committees any information at any time. Microsoft was, at the time, the main source of funding for software programmers seeking compatibility with Windows Operating Systems. The first effect of the pitched battle between Reno and Gates was the market for new software bought by Microsoft disappeared overnight. Within 90 days, what many called the *DotComBoom* was over. Bill Clinton's assault on Microsoft burst the tech bubble, and hundreds of thousands of programmers lost their jobs.

Software acquisitions erupted in the mid 1990's as venture capitalists moved to scoop up the best software technologies and their programmers for pennies on the dollar. It was the birth of what has globally become known as Silicon Valley; a massively wealthy and close-knit community of Democrat supporters. Their money and their technical influence over the intelligence market would be responsible for the next Democrat revolution in economics and politics. The strategy to apply massive government forces to virtually wipe out competition in the technology field was the purest application of fascism attempted since Roosevelt created the Agency Government. And the DNC was not done yet.

The Clinton Administration worked tirelessly until every radio station, every TV station, movie producer, and wireless and wired communications sector was eventually merged into six, Democrat-controlled conglomerates. Programming that supported the DNC's agenda was provided a venue to reach billions of people. Programming that opposed that agenda was denied access to media, with the exception of AM radio, which by the mid 1990's had almost become commercially impossible to support or control.

Small, independent AM stations were of no real concern to the media giants. It was almost a forgotten media, but it left a crack in the armor plating of the DNC's plan to control everything. On August 1, 1988, after achieving regional success in Sacramento, California, and drawing the attention of former ABC Radio President Edward McLaughlin, Rush Limbaugh moved to New York City and began his national radio show. He debuted just weeks after the Democratic National Convention where Bill Clinton had just received the nomination, thanks to the smiling and well-paid Superdelegates. Thanks to McLaughlin's endorsement, he took a seat behind the microphone at WABC, giving him a natural platform for national syndication. Millions of Americans responded by turning their radios to the AM band, something people had not done on purpose in more than 20 years. Through the crack in the Democrat armor emerged a clear and concise voice of conservatism. The war of words had begun.

The Clinton's presence in the White House was marred by progressively worse scandals until the Drudge Report originated the Monica Lewinsky scandal to the public on January 17th, 1998. The story was known by Newsweek, which was an American weekly magazine founded in 1933. It was published in four English-language editions and 12 global editions written in the language of the circulation region, but was owned by the Washington Post; part of the global media controlled by the DNC. Newsweek decided to hold its story, leaving the opportunity for the Internet-based news publication, founded by its namesake, Matt Drudge. In the face of vehement denials by the Clintons, Drudge Report had one undeniable piece of evidence that ultimately led to Bill Clinton's impeachment; the blue dress containing the dried semen of Bill Clinton.

Nearly four years prior, the UN withheld military defense of the tens of thousands of Muslims who had migrated to Serbia. The Bosnian Serb assault in July 1995 met no U.N. resistance either on the ground or from the air. Within 10 days, tens of thousands of Muslim refugees streamed into the Muslim-controlled city of Tuzla. Missing from the stream of refugees were more than 7,000 men of all ages, who had been executed in cold blood – mass murder on a scale not witnessed in Europe since the end of World War II. In March of 1996, Hillary had visited American troops stationed in Bosnia and misled Americans back home that she, "landed under sniper fire." Later, film of her completely peaceful arrival, friendly flowers and handshakes emerged proving once again that she had lied.

The global media moguls were desperate for anything that could replace the headlines focused on Bill Clinton's serial abuse of women. She needed a war. In the early Spring of 1998, Hillary took decisive action to redirect the global media. She needed something large enough and poignant enough to make the world look away from the impeachment proceedings.

She was not disappointed as she searched the world for a distraction. She decided on a 6-year-old picture taken of an emaciated Muslim caged behind Serb barbed wire, filmed by a British news team. With her nationally recognized voice, it rapidly became a worldwide symbol of the reason for immediate American military action in Bosnia. But, that picture was not quite what it seemed.

The large picture she held up, during her widely televised press conference, was of a Bosnian Muslim named Fikret Alic. He was emaciated and stripped to the waist, apparently imprisoned behind a barbed wire fence in a Bosnian Serb camp at Trnopolje. The image, however, was taken from a videotape shot on 5 August 1992 by an award-winning British television team, led by Penny Marshall (ITN) with her cameraman Jeremy Irvin, accompanied by Ian Williams (Channel 4) and the reporter Ed Vulliamy from the Guardian newspaper.

For many, this picture has become a symbol of Serbian ethnic cleansing horrors of the Bosnian war. But that image is a perfect example of Clintonian yellow journalism at its finest. The fact was that Fikret Alic and his fellow Bosnian Muslims were not imprisoned behind a barbed wire fence at all. There actually was no barbed wire fence surrounding Trnopolje camp. It was not a prison, and certainly not a 'concentration camp', but a collection center for Muslim refugees, many of whom went there seeking safety and were free to come and go as they wished.

The barbed wire in the picture is not around the Bosnian Muslims; it is around the cameraman and the journalists. It formed part of a broken-down barbed wire fence encircling a small compound that was adjacent to Trnopolje camp.

The British news team had actually shot their pictures and taken film from behind the fence, inside this compound. The pictures of the refugees and the camp were taken through the compound fence looking out. Hillary Clinton purposefully presented the false impression that the Bosnian Muslims were caged behind barbed wire. Within hours of the press conference, the Pentagon, under the direction of Bill Clinton's secretary of defense, William Cohen, began preparing for a horrific aerial bombing campaign. It destroyed bridges, power stations, and roads using depleted Uranium rounds and the best stealth aircraft of the day.

The president of Serbia, Slobodan Milošević transitioned Serbia from a Marxist–Leninist one-party system to a multi-party system and ultimately negotiated the Dayton Agreement on behalf of the Bosnian Serbs that ended the Bosnian War in 1995.

The US bombing of Yugoslavia in 1999 was suffered with very little military losses on either side. The vast majority of casualties were civilian. Milošević decorated his soldiers who shot down an

F117 Stealth bomber during a night raid. After three months, the bombing stopped, and he paraded his military through the city of Kosovo unharmed and proud to have persevered. He was charged by the International Criminal Tribunal for the former Yugoslavia with war crimes including genocide and crimes against humanity in connection to the wars in Bosnia, Croatia, and Kosovo.

Milošević resigned the Yugoslav presidency amid internationally organized demonstrations, following the disputed presidential election of 24 September 2000. He was arrested by Yugoslav federal authorities on 31 March 2001 on suspicion of corruption, abuse of power, and unsubstantiated charges of embezzlement.

The initial investigation into Milošević faltered for lack of evidence, prompting the Serbian Prime Minister Zoran Đinđić to extradite him to the International Criminal Tribunal for the former Yugoslavia to stand trial for charges of war crimes instead. At the outset of the trial Milošević denounced the Tribunal as illegal because it had not been established with the consent of the United Nations General Assembly; therefore he refused to appoint counsel for his defense.

Milošević masterfully conducted his own defense before a globally televised audience in the five-year-long trial. It ended without a verdict, because he died in his prison cell in The Hague on 11 March 2006. Milošević, who suffered from heart ailments and hypertension, died of a heart attack a short time later. The Tribunal denied any responsibility for Milošević's death, and stated that he had refused to take prescribed medicines and medicated himself instead. The truth was never disclosed, which also became a hallmark of the Clintons; never leave loose ends.

The full House of Representatives considered four charges against Bill Clinton. Two passed, making him the second president to be impeached, after Andrew Johnson in 1868. The United States Senate impeachment trial began right after the seating of the 106th

Congress, in which the Republican Party began with 55 senators. A two-thirds vote (67 senators) was required to remove Clinton from office. Fifty senators voted to remove Clinton on the obstruction of justice charge and 45 voted to remove him on the perjury charge. The Democrat National Committee proved its absolute control over its members, because not one member voted guilty on either charge. Bill Clinton was defended by Cheryl Mills, a name that would surface again in defense of Hillary Clinton during yet another federal investigation into wrong doing.

The Kosovo war distraction was successful in keeping Bill Clinton from being the first president removed from office under the impeachment clause. The Democrat's obedience to the DNC allowed the Clintons to continue leading the Democrat Party and to prepare it for the 2000 elections, just a few months away. The impeachment and numerous scandals were still fresh in the public eye, so Presidential candidate Al Gore, Clinton's Vice-President, refused to let him campaign with him publicly. Bill Clinton was precluded from running for a third term by the 22nd Amendment. The White House would have to wait for another day, and for another Clinton.

Their next chance to reenter the White House would not come until the 2008 elections. There was time to heal the public image, and the DNC-controlled media provided them the best possible editing of history. Once again, the Syndicate had prepared legislation that would change the world on a scale only matched by the Great Depression. In that 1929 operation, the collapse of the American money supply knocked the whole world to its knees while agents inside the Roosevelt White House installed a permanent government inside the elected government. It would write all the laws, assess taxes, and disconnect Congress from the government.

The Syndicate's 2001 operation would again change the entire world, massively expand the power of the Executive, and remove many of the most basic, unalienable rights of Americans.

Chapter 8

Jack Rousseau's senior year gym coach was also the social studies teacher. But Tom Larsen was no ordinary coach, and he certainly was no ordinary teacher. Mr. Larsen was a coach and the veteran son of a retired three-star general. While his father's command group moved from one facility to another, Mr. Larsen showed his incredible talent for golf by teaching the officer's wives how to better play the game. It began at the age of 19 when his father moved to an Air Training Command base in Denver, Colorado. While riding the shuttle bus one day from the Airman's club, after drinking a couple of pitchers of beer, he boasted of his expertise at golf.

The base golf pro happened to be on that same bus. Within a few brags back and forth, the bus had a nice pot of about $300 to see the two battle it out on the beautifully manicured base golf course. Mr. Larsen had never seen the course, was wearing shorts and sneakers, and had to rent a set of clubs. Nevertheless, within 9 holes, the wagers changed hands, and Lowry Air Force Base had a new golf instructor.

The talented Mr. Larsen also knew his American government. Jack liked him, because he would sit on a stool in the front of the class and take his class to places in history like a time traveler. It wasn't just Thomas Jefferson hand writing the Declaration of Independence. It was the thinking and pacing that he made before dipping his quill in the ink. Each word of passion and vision was perfectly timed and laid onto that parchment. There were no erasures. There was no pile of crumpled, attempted declarations on the floor. It was perfection of a great man's soul, inspired of God, and dried on hand-made paper that became the foundation for the oldest Constitution the world had ever known.

He also knew what government had become. It was this that fascinated Jack the most. The vision of Jefferson, Madison, and Adams reached as far as candlelight could take them. They could not see electricity, or aircraft, or the Internet. But they had seen men who thought they were kings. They saw government so powerful that it removed all hope for nearly every living soul of ever seeing anything other than the serfdom their grandparents had seen. They also saw the wake of another intelligence sailing far in front of them in time. They knew it was there, ahead, digging a pit for the people about to be handed the keys to their own government.

"The founding fathers planted a government with three branches. They each had separate powers, with separate weapons, but they were equal in strength. In order for the tree to grow, provide protection, and bear fruit, the three branches had to work together," said Mr. Larsen.

"It's no wonder they don't get anything done," said Jack without raising her hand.

"It's called deliberation. The finest steel is made from many blows with the hammer and the refiner's fire," said Mr. Larsen.

"Then how come things are so screwed up?" asked Jack.

"I'm glad you asked that question. You see, somewhere along the way, as the story goes, someone snuck into the garden and planted something else alongside. Let's just call it a graft for now, but it is not really a graft. It took a while, but about 84 years ago, it burst out of the ground after wrapping itself around the roots of our tree. Is has now become a fourth branch," said Mr. Larsen.

"There's no fourth branch of government in our book, Mr. Larsen," said Jack.

"That is a brilliant observation, Miss Rousseau, but that does not change the facts," said Mr. Larsen. "Allow me to enlighten you with an example."

"The United States Environmental Protection Agency is an agency of the federal government of the United States which was created for the purpose of protecting human health and the environment by writing and enforcing regulations based on laws passed by Congress. The National Environmental Policy Act of 1969 was signed into law by President Nixon on January 1, 1970. The law created the Council on Environmental Quality that answered only to him. The Council required that a detailed statement of environmental impacts be prepared for all major federal actions significantly affecting the environment.

"Nixon appointed a man named William Ruckelshaus as the first EPA Administrator. Now, this was not actually part of the President's cabinet, but this new Administrator had cabinet-level power, and it very soon became known in July of that year as the Environmental Protection Agency."

"Yeah. The EPA. They're the good guys, right?" asked Jack as though this was a personal discussion between her and Mr. Larsen.

"What you are about to learn here, you may not ever hear again, so I suggest you pay close attention. You should recall we talked about the Nixon impeachment? Well, in April of 1973 the fire under the Watergate kettle was being stoked by Democrats on every TV channel that could spare the time, and the whole thing was about to boil over. Nixon's Chief of Staff, H. R. Haldeman, and his Domestic Affairs Advisor, John Ehrlichman resigned. Ruckelshaus was pulled out of the EPA and made Acting Director of the FBI and then later that same year was shifted over to Deputy Attorney General. This was where the test of loyalty came in," said Mr. Larsen as he slid off his stool and began pacing in front of the classroom as he continued.

"You see, Nixon knew what they were planning, because he had raided their headquarters. Nowadays, they call that hacking, but in those days it was done by breaking in and going through the files. They knew he knew. So, Nixon ordered Ruckelshaus to fire the Watergate special prosecutor, Archibald Cox, who had been assigned the task of convicting Nixon. Well, he quit rather than follow that order. He was not loyal to the President. He was loyal to someone else; or should I say, to something else.

89

"After leaving the Justice Department, Ruckelshaus returned to the private practice of law. Very soon after that, he and his wife and five children moved to Seattle, Washington, where he accepted a position as Senior Vice President of Legal Affairs of the Weyerhaeuser Company," said Mr. Larsen writing with chalk on the board.

"You mean the plywood company?" asked Jack.

"Oh, much more than that. Weyerhaeuser owns more standing timber than just about any company on Earth. They have an executive revolving door with the EPA," said Mr. Larsen. "He also served as director of a company called American Water Development.

"For generations, ranchers and farmers have worked the soil of the high, huge valley between the San Juan and Sangre de Cristo mountains. Five generations of water rights were now controlled by Ruckelshaus and his small group of powerful businessmen. Water means survival for those who can get it, riches for those who control it, and bankruptcy or moving trucks for those left without it. Disputes over water are frequent and often intense.

"More people have been shot over stolen water than over almost anything other commodity, so it didn't take long before Mr. 'R' and his friends learned how his neighbors felt about their plan to sells millions of gallons of water from an aquifer below the valley floor to states across the West. It didn't stop him from becoming one of the most powerful people in the Western United States. You only thought being President makes you powerful. Now, you see what real power is like."

"But I thought the EPA protected nature from big corporations," said Jack.

"Oh, see that is what most people think. The truth is that they protect big corporations from competition from small companies, and they use land, air and water to do it. We're talking trillions of dollars here. In 1983, the EPA was already in crisis due to mass resignations over the mishandling of the Superfund project.

This was a gigantic slush fund President Ronald Reagan had set up to clean up environmental messes. I could tell you stories, but the point is that whenever the government starts throwing big money around, big corruption results.

"So, Reagan calls up good old loyal, Ruckelshaus to serve as EPA Administrator again. This time it was White House Chief of Staff James Baker who was Ruckelshaus's champion in asking him to return to the agency. They gave him maximum autonomy in the choice of new appointees and refocused the agency on its fundamental mission. Within a year, the press and Congress got back in line, and on February 7th, 1985 he retired from the EPA.

"He was quoted as saying, 'At EPA, you work for a cause that is beyond self-interest and larger than the goals people normally pursue. You're not there for the money. You're there for something beyond yourself,'" said Mr. Larsen.

"Wow. I like when you tell us the history behind the history," said Jack breaking her stare at the time traveling teacher.

"We have about 5 minutes left of class. I want to give you a glimpse of the real power in the fourth branch of government. I think you will find it surprising," said Mr. Larsen.

"No sooner did Ruckelshaus retire from the EPA, but he joined Perkins Coie, a Seattle-based law firm. You see, while he was being the noble soldier for the EPA, from 1983, he served on the World Commission on Environment and Development set up by the none other than the United Nations. On top of that, in 1988, he became Chairman and Chief Executive Officer of Browning Ferris Industries of Houston, Texas. You might know them as BFI. You see their blue dumpster all over town," said Mr. Larsen.

"Are you talking trash, Mr. Larsen?" asked Jack, and the whole class laughed out loud.

"Trash, indeed. You see, it is long believed that one of the most powerful organized crime activities in America is the collection and handling of trash. Where once there were many, now there is only one. Nearly every can in America dumps into a truck controlled by the largest, multi-national, alternative investment firm in the world, Blackstone Group," wrote Mr. Larsen on the blackboard. "By the way, they are the world's fifth-largest private equity firm by committed capital, focusing primarily on leveraged buyouts of more mature companies. In other words, they buy up the competition."

"This guy, Ruckelshaus had it all, didn't he? I mean, he had the trees, the water, and the trash," said Jack.

"What would you say if I told you he didn't stop there? President Bill Clinton appointed him as U.S. envoy in the implementation of the Pacific Salmon Treaty; he was that from 1997 to 1998. In 1999, he was appointed by Gov. Gary Locke as Chairman of the Salmon Recovery Funding Board for the State of Washington.

"And then, in the early 2000s, he was appointed by Pres. George W. Bush to serve on the United States Commission on Ocean Policy. On September 20, 2004, the Commission submitted its Final Report to the President and Congress, An Ocean Blueprint for the 21st Century. Since June 2010 he has served as Co-chair of the Joint Ocean Commission Initiative."

"Mr. Larsen, there is no way we're ever going to remember all of this, and it's not in our book," said Jack finally.

"One more thing. Remember I told you about the executive revolving door at the EPA? Well, Mr. William Ruckelshaus serves or has served as a director on boards of several corporations, including Monsanto, Cummins Engine Company, Pharmacia Corporation, Solutia, Coinstar, Nordstrom, and Weyerhaeuser Company. He controls more than 27 million acres of timber, genetically modified foods, cell phones, and nearly all the fish in the sea that we consume in America and is the director of the Initiative for Global Development," said Mr. Larsen holding his hands out wide as he could in front of the class.

"He has to be the most powerful man in the world," said Jack.

"He is certainly one of them. After all, before anyone cast the first vote for any candidate, on April 17th, 2008, he endorsed a virtually unknown man from Chicago who had never had a paying job in his life, named Barack Hussein Obama, for President of the United States, and the rest, so they say, is history," said Mr. Larsen as the bell rang for class to end.

"I have to know, Mr. Larsen," said Jack as she shouldered her book bag and walked up to him from her desk. "Why did he pick Obama? I mean, what the hell?" asked Jack.

"We'll get into more of this tomorrow, but if you're really interested in knowing about all of this, I think you should become an intern. You'll get to see some of this up close and personal. I have an application right over here. Just fill it out, and we'll see about getting you in," said Mr. Larsen handing her the portfolio.

"My brother works as an asphalt lobbyist. He says they're all whores over there," said Jack.

"Well, if that was true, our nation would have been lost a long time ago. They always need good leaders who can take a punch. And in my book, good leaders come from good interns. You can take a punch, can't you?" asked Mr. Larsen as he looked at the slight bruising under her left eye.

"I'll check it out. See you tomorrow," said Jack stuffing the portfolio into her book bag and zipping it closed.

"Good participation today. Be good," said Mr. Larsen as Jack bounced through the door and into the river of young people in the hallway.

Math was always easy for Jack, so the final hour of school spent in the middle of Algebra class went quickly. She pored over the application to be an intern for the United States Senate and had the blanks filled in by the time the final bell rang. She packed up her things, slid both arms through her book bag, and began the walk for home a mile away. Fair weather days like this, she skipped the city bus and walked to stay in shape. Taekwando was later in the evening, now that she was competing in a junior city league. It gave her time to drink a protein shake and change into what she told her mother was her combat gear. She had become a champion, of sorts, mostly because a Rousseau wouldn't have it any other way, but also because it gave her a feeling of invincibility in front of people. Even during casual conversation with someone, on the outside, she was calm and made easy eye contact, but inside she was imagining a maneuver to catch her opponent's advance and thrust him to the ground with her heel on his neck.

    She arrived at the dojo early, as usual, worked out with her age group, and helped stretch and catch the new students who were learning the sport. Maybe she could have made more money learning golf from Mr. Larsen than history, but she gathered there were not many tour champions who could kick someone's ass in three jabs and a roundhouse kick to the side of the head.

    She knew her father was proud of her, even though he was trapped in a body that couldn't speak or write. She wondered if he could see the universe changing, because she was in it, and because she intended to grab it and push it around. 'There are two kinds of people in the world, Jackie,' he used to say. 'There are those who are affected by the universe, and those who affect the universe. You are going to change everything.'

    She wondered if she was loving him enough and suddenly flushed by the thought of coming up short. She reminded herself to hug him long and hard the first thing when she got home. She stepped up to the heavy bag one more time and spun her hip to snap her long leg around to slap her heel against the leather level with her forehead. It crumpled as the chain above it jingled its complaint. Yeah. 'You better put some ice on that, asshole,' she thought.

Chapter 9

When Jesus walked the earth, he was not particularly powerful. He taught and healed and inspired, but it was His death and resurrection that truly changed the world. The world had never really seen that kind of power before, though there were men and demons who coveted it. The only difference is that they did not want to die to make it happen. The ultimate design was to make other men die for it and all men to pay for it.

The greatest methodology for glorifying men to almost godlike power is the invention of religions. The guideline for establishing a religion is always the same. First, you place a man in between God and the individual seeking salvation. Second, you use the true words spoken by prophets as the mantra and require sacrifice from the members to hear them. It's as simple as that.

If you want salvation, you must be a member. And to be a member, you must sacrifice something. In the early days of churches, the sacrifice was your crops, your herds, and often your own children. After all, God Himself sacrificed His own Son. What makes you any better than Him?

The modern mechanism of religion is politics. The introduction and control of monetary systems gave birth to the newest and most powerful religion; government. The same principles apply, and the exact same methodology is utilized. You must sacrifice and give money in order to access government, which is the real-world application of salvation. The high priests, skilled in the art of persuasion, have accumulated the wealth of dragons and the power of demons. There is no human analogy for this.

There has never been a political organization as powerful or as fearsome as the Democrat National Committee. Yes, there have been tyrants and despots. There have been Huns and kings and Caesars, but there has never before been a religion-party that could command armies and navies, buy up priests and popes, and reign with blood and horror on the earth for so long. The oath and covenant to be robed with the priesthood in this organization requires a commitment of the soul. You cannot leave. You cannot even die to avoid your obligation. In return, you will be provided a *charm of favor*. The laws of men will not be able to hold you. The bounty of all nations will be yours for the taking. The innocent and hard-working people of the world are your sheep to be shorn or slaughtered by your command. In place of joy you will be provided seemingly endless pleasure. In place of serenity, you will be driven by the dogs of greed who never tire and never stop. In place of love, you will receive virgins and children for sex. In place of salvation, you will receive a long life of power and more wealth than a hundred men could spend in a hundred lifetimes.

For some, the cost of this religion-party is too great. For others, the lure is too great, and life is too short to be wasted trying to earn one's way to wealth. Besides, that type of wealth can be stripped away with a single lawsuit by someone who wants it more than the person who earned it. The promise of eternal life is a shiny and sweet smelling counterfeit of exaltation. Who wants to eat cold rice, when one can have a tender and juicy steak with the finest wines? Who wants to heal the sick or feed five thousand when one can have his or her name put on the wing of a hospital or command the harvest of a nation?

The founding fathers of America knew all about this covenant relationship between Lucifer and his children here upon the earth. God told them about it. But He also told them that the differences between wheat and tares were too subtle for men to discern. To them it was not given to root them out, lest an innocent child of God be cut down and burned in the process.

'Kill them all, and let God sort them out,' many military generals would say. Many times, entire cities, including their children and their animals were slaughtered by religious command.

Entire genetics were permanently removed from the future in one day by Joshua, or in Gomorrah, or in Armenia, or under the swords of Islam.

And so, America was formed with two great principles as guides. All rights come from God and cannot be abridged by men, and the rule of law shall apply equally to all men. Great men set the standard very early. George Washington served two four-year terms and stepped down. That magnificent standard of restraint and honor was trampled by the greed of the DNC in 1940 at the Chicago Democrat National Convention when a Soviet spy named Harry Hopkins schemed to cheat John Nance "Cactus Jack" Garner out of his presidency. Roosevelt won 86% of the delegates and was not even on the ballot while over the convention loudspeakers came the chant, "We want Roosevelt!" Republicans retaliated and crafted the 22nd Amendment, which the States immediately ratified, to force powerful men from the most terrible office in the world after two terms.

Thus, it became necessary to make sure the religion-party held the office, and not the man with the title. The religion had to become syndicated. It only needed someone groomed and charmed to lead the way. Like Jesus, this person would be known the world over. He would have enemies, like Jesus. He would be publicly attacked and become a hiss and a byword, like Jesus. He would be revered no matter what happened, like Jesus.

Unlike Jesus, however, he would sacrifice everyone and everything, but never himself. He would use and abuse everyone and everything around him. Instead of people being healed and receiving everlasting life, they would hate their own souls enough to kill themselves rather than face him again. And, if they would not kill themselves before him, a suitable death would be provided for them.

Oaths and covenants for men like this are prepared from before their birth. It does not matter how he comes to mortal life, for a lineage will be crafted for him. If his history cannot be crafted and polished, then his true history will be sealed with blood and stone that no man shall ever discover it until the end of the world. In exchange for this oath, he will be given a *charm of favor*. His popularity will eclipse Jesus in every dark corner of the earth.

And so it was that the presidency of Bill Clinton came to an end, but the DNC was never more powerful. Although the nation retaliated by electing George W. Bush in November of 2000, the election was close enough that DNC lawyers would not concede the presidency, but rather buried the election in lawsuits. The office remained in limbo for months after the inauguration. For almost four months, it seemed that no one in the world knew who the president really was. Even after the Supreme Court ruled that George W. Bush won the election, the DNC was relentless, and the mantle of the office evaded the shoulders of President Bush.

Then, one calm day in late summer, as he sat reading a story to schoolchildren, the World Trade Center was destroyed, a hole was blown into the Pentagon, and a passenger jet was blown out of the sky over Pennsylvania. Although millions of people watched some of the events as they happened, or video after the fact, no two people could agree on what happened or who was responsible. The effects of what happened, however, were unveiled as though they had been carefully planned down to the last detail from the foundation of the world.

A mighty spell was cast over the entire world that was so dark and so powerful that it blotted out all light and all understanding. Men and women wandered like temporarily blinded victims of a nuclear flash, and when they were finally able to see a few feet in front of them, they found themselves in a new world. The rights that God had given them were gone. The freedom to travel and the right of privacy were wiped from existence. The American government exploded in size and in authority. It was now ready for the next great leader of the party-religion to step into the office of the Presidency. The DNC maintained continuity and solidarity through the entire process. Candidates, who appeared to compete with one another for the same office, had made covenants to the same dark power. The winner was the Syndicate that spent more than a century preparing to make its move. And it was this power that prepared the next level of leader.

By the time the Bush presidency was over, the National Defense Authorization Act had consolidated the most powerful intelligence organizations into a invulnerable overlord of information control. It was Hillary's time to take power, and millions had been spent making sure the Superdelegates would ensure her the nomination. The DNC, however, had other plans. They needed a charismatic personality, which Hillary was not. They had raised and groomed Barack Hussein Obama to be the next president. Hillary didn't like it, but she was a loyal soldier to the Syndicate. The Superdelegates switched the vote in a single week, and Obama was nominated as the Democrat's candidate.

A more dismal political strategy could not have been crafted. John McCain had no speaking ability, no platform, and no following among Republicans. Even with the addition of Sarah Palin as his running mate, the Republicans didn't stand a chance against an Imam trained in the art of argument and public speaking.

Keenly aware of Bill Clinton's popularity among Democrats and his comfort talking about middle-class issues, Barack Hussein Obama worked overtime to get Bill Clinton involved in his campaign for the Democrat nomination. But it wouldn't come without a price.

Clinton's then-gatekeeper, Doug Band, "issued an ultimatum to the Obamas: the price of WJC's involvement in the campaign was the retirement of HRC's balance due."

In other words, Band was demanding that Obama help pay off Hillary Clinton's 2008 campaign debt -- at that point, about a quarter of a million dollars in exchange for Bill Clinton's help on the trail.

Though top members of the Obama campaign were flabbergasted at the demand and held Band in especially low regard.

They hated being shaken down for money by the Clintons, but they eventually agreed to help retire Hillary's campaign debt.

They agreed too quickly, however, because there was more to the cost of doing business with the Clintons. Obama had to agree to make Hillary his Secretary of State for 4 years. He would also agree to protect her as she intended to set up a pay-for-play operation more aggressive than anything ever seen before.

She began within hours of being sworn in by setting up a secure, offsite server that would handle all of her digital communications without government oversight or record retention. Four years after she left the State Department, the transactions she conducted from that chair remained secret. The Syndicate had already set up a non-profit foundation to which buyers of the favors, approvals and regulatory assistance could make their payments. She was also able to move $5 billion of State Department money offshore to act as a safety account for her own run for the presidency in 2016.

The Clinton's bag man, Terry McAuliffe, was an expert at bringing money into the campaign. He worked tirelessly and loyally to fund the Clinton Crime Syndicate, and was handsomely rewarded when Hillary's brother, owner of Gulf State Capital in Mississippi put Terry into the driver seat of an electric car and snapped a picture for the papers. The State of Mississippi granted $5 million to McAuliffe to launch the car company and provide jobs in 2011. He grabbed the money, flew to Virginia, and used it to win the Governor's office in November of 2013. He never turned over the first shovel of dirt to build that factory in Mississippi. To this day, lawsuits brought by the State to get their grant back have been fruitless. The Syndicate prevents the case from ever coming to court.

The schemes to raise money by the Clintons became larger and bolder than anyone could imagine. On July 5, 2005, Southern Cross Resources Inc. and Aflease Gold and Uranium Resources Ltd announced that they would be merging under the name SXR Uranium One Inc.

One of the partners, Frank Guistra, was introduced to Bill Clinton who was recruited by Frank to accompany him to Almaty, Kazakhstan to bid on the uranium interests from Kazatomprom. They met with Nursultan Nazarbayev, the leader of Kazakhstan. Mr. Clinton handed the Kazakh president a propaganda coup when he expressed support for Mr. Nazarbayev's bid to head an international elections monitoring group, undercutting American foreign policy and criticism of Kazakhstan's poor human rights record by, among others, Hillary, then a senator.

Within days of the visit, Mr. Giustra's fledgling company, UrAsia Energy Ltd., signed a preliminary deal giving it stakes in three uranium mines controlled by the state-run uranium agency Kazatomprom. The Kazakh deal was a major victory, and UrAsia did not wait long before resuming the hunt. In 2007, it merged with Uranium One, a South African company with assets in Africa and Australia, in what was described as a $3.5 billion transaction. The new company, which kept the Uranium One name, was controlled by UrAsia investors including Ian Telfer, a Canadian who became chairman. Through a spokeswoman, Mr. Giustra, whose personal stake in the deal was estimated at what was considered a paltry $45 million, said he sold his stake in 2007. Several months later, Mr. Giustra had donated $31.3 million to Mr. Clinton's foundation.

Frank said in a public statement that he was "extremely proud" of his charitable work with Mr. Clinton, and he urged the media to focus on poverty, health care and "the real challenges of the world." This type of public subterfuge became a hallmark tactic of the Clinton Crime Syndicate.
Though the 2008 article quoted the former head of Kazatomprom, Moukhtar Dzhakishev, as saying that the deal required government approval and was discussed at a dinner with the president, Mr. Giustra insisted that it was a private transaction,

with no need for Mr. Clinton's influence with Kazakh officials. He described his relationship with Mr. Clinton as motivated solely by a shared interest in philanthropy.

As he prepared to make a short speech and collect a $500,000 payday in Moscow in 2010, Bill Clinton sought clearance from the State Department to meet with a key board director of the Russian nuclear energy firm Rosatom — which at the time needed the Obama administration's approval for a deal they were about to make.

Arkady Dvorkovich, a top aide to then-Russian President Dmitri Medvedev and one of the highest-ranking government officials to serve on Rosatom's board of supervisors, was listed on a May 14, 2010, email as one of 15 Russians Bill wanted to meet during a late June 2010 trip. The representation was again deceptive, because Bill Clinton instead got together with Vladimir Putin at the Russian leader's private homestead.

As if to underscore the point, five months later Mr. Giustra held a fund-raiser for the Clinton Giustra Sustainable Growth Initiative, a project aimed at fostering progressive environmental and labor practices in the natural resources industry, to which he had pledged $100 million. The star-studded gala, at a conference center in Toronto, featured performances by Elton John and Shakira and celebrities like Tom Cruise, John Travolta and Robin Williams encouraging contributions from the many so-called F.O.F.s — Friends of Frank — in attendance, among them Mr. Telfer. In all, the evening generated $16 million in pledges, according to an article in *The Globe* and *Mail*.

"None of this would have been possible if Frank Giustra didn't have a remarkable combination of caring and modesty, of vision and energy and iron determination," Mr. Clinton told those gathered, adding: "I love this guy, and you should, too."

As recent as 2009, the former head of Kazatomprom, Moukhtar Dzhakishev had been arrested on charges that he illegally sold uranium deposits to foreign companies, including at least some of those won by Mr. Giustra's UrAsia and now owned by Uranium One. Some of those companies may have eventually funneled the uranium to players like Iran and North Korea. Most people discount the influence the 2008 Recession had on the global economy, but when Americans aren't buying, it slows cashflow down around the world. When heads of State can write checks from their treasuries, the sale can be very lucrative. And, after all, who's going to miss a few kilos of uranium?

The influence of having the former president there was powerful, but the ultimate goal was to sell the project to the most powerful buyer in the world; Vladimir Putin.

At the time, Russia was already eying a stake in Uranium One, Rosatom company documents show. Rosatom officials say they were seeking to acquire mines around the world because Russia lacks sufficient domestic reserves to meet its own industry needs.

It was against this backdrop that the Vancouver-based Uranium One pressed the American Embassy in Kazakhstan, as well as Canadian diplomats, to take up its cause with Kazakh officials, according to the American cables.

"We want more than a statement to the press," Paul Clarke, a Uranium One executive vice president, told the embassy's energy officer on June 10, the officer reported in a cable. "That is simply chitchat." What the company needed, Mr. Clarke said, was official written confirmation that the licenses were valid.

The American Embassy ultimately reported to the secretary of state, Mrs. Clinton. Though the Clarke cable was copied to her, it was given wide circulation, and it is unclear if she would have read it; the Clinton campaign did not address questions about the cable.

What is clear is that the embassy acted, with the cables showing that the energy officer met with Kazakh officials to discuss the issue on June 10 and 11.

Three days later, a wholly owned subsidiary of Rosatom completed a deal for 17 percent of Uranium One. And within a year, the Russian government substantially upped the ante, with a generous offer to shareholders that would give it a 51 percent controlling stake.

Uranium One controls twenty percent of U.S. uranium production. The only way this could take place was if the nine voting members of the Committee on Foreign Investment in the United States approved it.

One of the most important members of that Committee is the State Department. As a matter of distance from the actual deal, Hillary assigned Jose Fernandez, the Department of State's representative to CIFIUS, to vote in favor. The Podesta Group was on record as lobbying Hillary Clinton and the other Agency-members of the Committee on behalf of Uranium One. The Podesta Group is run by Tony Podesta, the brother of John Podesta who was Hillary Clinton's 2016 campaign manager. In 2010 Russian interests acquired a controlling interest in Uranium One.

Hillary was then able to solicit more than $150 million into the Clinton Foundation that would act as an international superpac to slush money through other foundations, most of which were offshore, for political support. Countless FOIA lawsuits and attempts by reporters to follow the money trail were fruitless, as foreign non-profits do not have to disclose their sources or uses of donated funds. Within 4 years, Hillary was able to net nearly $2 billion for her political operations and to hide all the evidence by maintaining and exclusively using a private server for all her State Department business. The lawsuits and Congressional subpoenas produced nothing, as the Clintons refused to cooperate at every turn, while publicly only the corner of the napkin without blood stains would be shown.

In August 2015, months before the first primary vote or caucus would occur, at the Democratic Party convention in Minneapolis, 33 democratic state parties made deals with the Hillary Clinton campaign and a joint non-profit fundraising entity called The Hillary Victory Fund. The deal allowed many of her core billionaire and inner circle individual donors to run the maximum amounts of money allowed through those state parties to the Hillary Victory Fund in New York and the DNC in Washington.

The idea was to increase how much one could personally donate to Hillary by taking advantage of the Supreme Court ruling 2014, McCutcheon v FEC, that knocked down a cap on aggregate limits as to how much a donor could give to a federal campaign in a year. It thus eliminated the ceiling on amounts spent by a single donor to a presidential candidate.

From these large amounts of money being transferred from state coffers to the Hillary Victory Fund in Washington, the Clinton campaign got the first $2,700, the DNC was to get the next $33,400, and the remainder was to be split among the 33 signatory states. With this scheme, the Hillary Victory Fund raised over $26 million for the Clinton Campaign by the end of 2015.

The rest of the money went to the state Parties and, eventually, the candidates, including many officeholders who are Superdelegates. This was just the beginning of the flow of traceable money to them. There was also untraceable money in the form of transportation, PAC ads, foundation grants, education grants for children going to college, and real estate in foreign countries purchased in their names.

Hillary had lost an election once before to a startup nobody named Barack Obama, and she was not going to be caught short this time. The Syndicate wanted to make sure every single Superdelegate was pledged before the first vote was cast.

The fund is administered by treasurer Elizabeth Jones, the Clinton Campaign's chief operating officer. Ms. Jones has the exclusive right to decide when transfers of money to and from the Hillary Victory Fund would be made to the state parties.

So if a Superdelegate whose State voted overwhelmingly for the other 2016 Democrat primary candidate, Bernie Sanders, switched his or her support to Sanders—under the reasoning that she was representing the will of her State—then Clinton's Campaign COO would simply shut off the spigot and all that sweet, sweet cash would stop flowing into the coffers of that State Democrat Party. That would starve out other Democrats running for offices on the state and federal levels. Not a single Superdelegate changed their vote, even in the face of violent protests in state after state. There was no possibility Bernie could win, even if he won the majority of votes in every single primary and caucus.

Not only did Hillary's financial bundlers and billionaire supporters get to bypass individual campaign donation limits to state parties by using the apparatus of several state parties, but the Clinton campaign got the added bonus of buying that state's superdelegates with the promise of contributions to that Democrat organization's re-election fund.

Superdelegates are supposed to be "free to choose the best candidate" according to their own beliefs about what is best for the Party. But now many of them will have that choice essentially turned into a dilemma: they can support Hillary and stay in politics, or they can support Bernie and deprive both themselves and their State Party of significant funding from the Clinton Crime Syndicate — thereby ending their political career.

Superdelegates who switch their vote to Bernie would lose their money, the many perks of being a member of the Syndicate, and any friends they thought they had in their State Party. The following is an official list, according to the Federal Election Commission, of the beneficiaries of the Clinton Victory Fund scheme. Keep in mind that this is only the *official money* that was allowed to be traced by the FEC. It does not include offshore, untraceable money or money spent on their behalf with issue ads or attack ads on their opponents.

> Clinton, Hillary D C Pres $4,440,000
> DNC Services Corp D P $2,263,436
> Democratic Party of Wisconsin D P $207,278
> Democratic Party of Oklahoma D P $140,000
> Democratic Party of New Hampshire D P $74,700
> Democratic Party of Pennsylvania D P $70,500
> Democratic Party of Texas D P $69,100
> Democratic Executive Cmte of Florida D P $66,200
> Democratic Party of Nevada D P $66,200
> Democratic Party of Colorado D P $66,000
> Democratic Party of Ohio D P $66,000
> Democratic Cmte of Utah D P $64,100
> Democratic Party of Alaska D P $64,100
> Democratic Party of Mississippi D P $64,100
> Democratic Party of Montana D P $64,100
> Democratic Party of Oregon D P $64,100
> Democratic Party of South Carolina D P $64,100
> Democratic Party of Tennessee D P $64,100
> Democratic State Cmte of Massachusetts D P $64,100
> Georgia Federal Elections Cmte D P $64,100
> Idaho State Democratic Party D P $64,100
> Michigan Democratic State Central Cmte D P $64,100
> Minnesota Democratic Farmer Labor Party D P $64,100
> Missouri Democratic State Cmte D P $64,100
> Rhode Island Democratic State Cmte D P $64,100
> West Virginia State Democratic Exec Cmte D P $64,100
> Wyoming State Democratic Central Cmte D P $64,100
> Democratic Party of North Carolina D P $64,000
> Democratic State Central Cmte/Louisiana D P $64,000
> Indiana Democratic Congressional Victory Cmte D P $64,000
> Democratic Party of Arkansas D P $63,000

Maine Democratic State Cmte D P $59,800
Democratic Party of Virginia D P $43,500

Chapter 10

"Hey, Mr. Larsen. I finished that application. Here you go," said Jack.

"Why am I not surprised? I made a couple of calls last night. My associates think you would fit nicely over at the Pentagon," said Mr. Larsen taking the application portfolio from her.

"The Pentagon?" asked Jack with a tone of disbelief. "I thought we were talking about the Capitol. I even did some online shopping for clothes. You know. Dresses and shit. Oh, sorry," she said covering her mouth.

"You can wear slacks at the Pentagon, and believe me, it has more than enough politics," said Mr. Larsen.

"Well, just let me know," said Jack as she slung her book bag under her desk and sat down.

"Today, I want you to consider the possibility of the end of private property," began Mr. Larsen. "Most of you don't watch the news; not on purpose anyway. Your parents probably watch it. Some watch the main propaganda channels, and some watch programs that are less of a slick sales job. Still, you are not getting the truth, most of the time.

"Let's say I gave you a special credit card. One of the best features about this card is that someone else makes the payments on the card. What would you do?" asked Mr. Larsen putting his hands together under his chin like he was praying for a moment.

"Go shopping," said Jack without hesitation. The class laughed.

"Exactly. That is exactly what you would do. But, let me tell you about one of the bad features of this card. You have to buy everything with it. Food, housing, transportation, health care; everything must be bought with this card. Oh yes, one more thing.

The card is paid off once a year. Now what would you do?" asked Mr. Larsen.

The class was silent for a moment, until someone raised their hand. Mr. Larsen pointed. "How much of a limit is there on the card? I mean, is there enough to get through a whole year? That's a lot of stuff," said the student.

"Well, a smart person would sit down and make out a budget, right? I assume you want three meals a day. I assume you want some clothes, a decent car, perhaps a date or two with your friends. Let's say 50 grand," said Mr. Larsen.

"50 grand? Hey the party's at my house," said another boy.

"We be talking live music, Mr. Larsen," said another.

"Now, you're starting to think like a bureaucrat," said Mr. Larsen sitting up on his stool in front of the class.

"Consider this. The American government was given a magic credit card just after the Civil War. Less than 50 years later, a secret pact was made with a small gathering of private banks. They met at Jekyll Island in the dark of night and formed what we now know as the Federal Reserve. They took the pact to Congress and passed it as the Federal Reserve Act of 1910. This allowed government to print money out of thin air, backed by nothing but the faith and credit of the United States of America. Well, that is to say, on your ability to work hard enough to make the payments."

"What do you mean, our ability?" asked Jack.

"Well, you see, government doesn't make anything. They rely on taking a cut of what you earn to make the payments to the Federal Reserve," said Mr. Larsen.

"What happens if the bank runs out of ink to print this magic money?" asked Jack.

"Oh that already happened a long time ago. So, what happened is that other countries stepped forward and started buying some of that debt, so that the government could borrow more," said Mr. Larsen.

"Who would do that?" asked Jack.

"Well, our enemies, for one," said Mr. Larsen coldly.

"That's kind of dumb. Why would they do that?" asked Jack.

"They who? Which 'they' are you talking about, Miss Rousseau?" asked Mr. Larsen.

"Well, like our enemies. No, wait. The government. Why would we borrow money from our enemies? I don't know. It doesn't make any sense for either one, I guess," said Jack.

"Let me ask you a question. Do you like to give or to receive?" asked Mr. Larsen.

"I like to give better," said Jack.

"And why is that?" asked Mr. Larsen.

"Because I don't like owing anyone anything, I guess," said Jack.

"So, you're saying that if you gave someone something of value, you would expect them to treat you with more respect. You would hope they would stop talking behind your back or trying to take your boyfriend away from you; right?" asked Mr. Larsen using his hands to ask for feedback from the class. "You're saying it feels better when people owe you something, than when you owe someone; right?"

"That's right," said the boy in the back of the room. "I own you when you owe me."

"Don't ever say that in public, mister. But he is right in a way. So when China loans money to America, and we're talking about hundreds of billions of dollars, they say what?" asked Mr. Larsen holding his hand to his ear.

"I own you when you owe me," said the boy more deliberately now.

"Ah. So. When you stop making the payments on your motorcycle, what does the bank do?" asked Mr. Larsen.

"They come and get the bike," said Jack.

"That's correct. It's called encumbrance. So, here's the deal. America owes China, Saudi Arabia, Japan, and the Federal reserve tons of money, and we have not made a payment in many years," said Mr. Larsen.

"But doesn't that mean they will come and take the bike?" asked Jack.

"China almost did exactly that, when Barack Obama occupied the White House. He needed to keep borrowing money to make the payments, and he desperately needed to buy millions of votes to remain in office. The dollar was strong, after years of printing magic Federal Reserve money to shore it up. But the Chinese were afraid it would weaken, and America would become a bad credit risk. Secretary of State Hillary Clinton was sent to China on February 20th of 2012, according to He Zhicheng, an economist at Agricultural Bank of China, the nation's third-largest lender by assets.

"She carried with her a letter that was signed by the President that promised the People's Republic of China the power of eminent domain over certain properties in America as collateral for China's continued purchase of US Treasury Notes and existing US Currency reserves," said Mr. Larsen.

"Like, what is eminent domain?" asked Jack.

"That's a great question. Here is what it is supposed to mean. Let's say the government says they want to build a Federal highway system from coast to coast. Do you think they have to pay top dollar for every square foot of land to build that highway? No. They pay little to nothing for the land using a clause in the Constitution that gives them eminent domain, which means ultimately, all land belongs to the Federal government. You can have a warranty deed for it, but the State can cancel that warranty and take the land if it can prove it has a legitimate need for it," said Mr. Larsen.

"So what happens if we don't make the payments on this magic credit card maxed out by Mr. Obama?" asked Jack

"This means that in the event the US Government defaults on its financial obligations to China, the Communist Government of China would be permitted to physically take ownership of land, buildings, factories, national parks, mines, perhaps even entire cities to satisfy the financial obligations of the US government."

"Put simply, the Secretary of State actually mortgaged the physical land and property of all citizens and businesses in the United States. They have given to a foreign power, their Constitutional power to "take" all of our property, as actual collateral for continued Chinese funding of US deficit spending and the continued carrying of US national debt," said Mr. Larsen.

"How did they get to do that? I mean, who gave them the right?" asked Jack raising her voice a little.

"Well, see there is an obscure little department nobody pays any attention, unless you're a big rancher out West. It's called the Department of the Interior. They have a paid army called the Bureau of Land Management that drives Americans off their land and seizes their forests, fields, mountains, and canyons along with all the mineral wealth, water, and other resources. If the people protest, they are put in prison or worse," said Mr. Larsen.

"What's worse than losing your land and being put in prison?" asked Jack dominating the conversation.

"How about having your forest and your house burned to the ground, your cattle slaughtered, and you and your family shot as criminals?" asked Mr. Larsen. The class was silent, because they knew he spoke the truth.

"Did that really happen?" asked a girl in the class quietly.

"Yes, it did. In fact, after one old man and his son went to jail for a year, the district attorney in Oregon put them back on trial for the same exact case and sent them back to prison for three more years. The old man may die of old age before he ever sees freedom again. The BLM took his Oregon land that had been in his family for more than 100 years without paying a dime for it," said Mr. Larsen.

"Didn't anyone help them?" asked Jack.

"Oh, some people protested for a while, but they were arrested after one of them was ambushed by Agents one night on a remote highway. They were on their way to speak to a sheriff in another county sympathetic to their cause, when they were forced off the road into a snow bank by Federal mercenary gunfire. They shot the truck full of holes, until the driver got out with his hands in the air trying to save the lives of the young people in the truck with him. One young man was shot three times, but survived. The young girls in the truck were screaming for their lives. Mr. Lavoy Finicum got out and stepped into the knee deep snow with his hands in the air, begging for them to stop shooting as they were all unarmed. They shot him in the back, killing him face down in the snow, while the entire world watched in horror through the lens of a surveillance drone," said Mr. Larsen softly.

"Didn't they get in trouble?" asked the girl barely able to speak.

"Not even a little bit," said Mr. Larsen.

"So, what happened?" asked Jack.

"Well, Mr. Obama ended up with more than 700 million acres of private land as collateral for more money than every President going all the way back to Washington combined, and Congress spent every dime of it," said Mr. Larsen.

"How could they do that? I mean, isn't that against the Constitution or something?" asked Jack.

"Oh it is definitely unconstitutional, treasonous, and an impeccably impeachable offense. That is why we have such a dire need for good people to serve in government. You see, silence is consent. If we don't go and serve, there is an organization that will. And if they take all those jobs in the government and serve themselves at our expense, we may as well say good bye to the concept of America," said Mr. Larsen sliding off his stool and beginning to pace in front of the class slowly.

"You see, much of American land has already been consigned, turned over to the United Nations. Rivers, national parks, wetlands, the Grand Canyon, Independence Hall just down the street. You'll recall that many of our best coal reserves and gold

114

mines were suddenly seized from the States and turned into national monuments. Will these huge loans also depend upon our privately owned land?

"Have no doubt that this is being done. National Association of Realtors' president Julio S. Laguarta warned in his speech to the International Real Estate Federation in Toronto, Canada that *'Failure to change an official United Nations policy that explicitly opposes the right of private property ownership will ultimately result in the destruction of our industry.'*

"He went on to quote the UN's policy by saying, *'Land, because of its unique nature and the crucial role it plays in human settlements, cannot be treated as an ordinary asset, controlled by individuals and subject to the pressures and inefficiencies of the market. Social justice, urban renewal, and development, the provision of decent dwellings and health conditions for people can only be achieved if land is used in the interests of society as a whole.'*

"As far as anyone knows, this policy is still in place. I can tell you this much. Once the repossessions begin, the value of the assets will drop like a rock. That means they have the authorization to repossess even more land, factories, dams, power plants, and other things like gold and fuel to cover our default on the debt. If there is not enough federal land left to pay off the Federal Reserve, they will have no choice but to come after private lands like farms and homes. You see, the money was borrowed in the name of the people of the United States, and the repayment will have to come from the assets of the people. It is called a crash!"

"This happened before. President Franklin Delano Roosevelt took America off the gold standard and recalled all the privately held gold in to pay Federal debts. He simply passed a law making it illegal for private citizens to own gold. That is why there is nothing, and I do mean nothing more than little ones and zeroes backing our dollar. When America is finally driven into bankruptcy, a globalist card game with different rules will be played, especially now that this globalist ideology has infiltrated our country, and has acquired such power."

"I don't get it. How does this fourth branch of government have this much power? I mean, how come Congress doesn't just pass a law or stop them or something?" pleaded Jack.

"I am giving you some homework. I want you to go to YouTube and search for Congressional Committees. Watch Lois Lerner, or Eric Holder, or Hillary Clinton, or any agency you can find testify before Congress. You will notice very quickly that Agencies are not responsible to the people. In other words, the Agency government actually makes the laws, assesses the fees, fines, taxes, and enforcement actions against we the people, except we have no representation in that government," said Mr. Larsen pacing and pointing into his open palm like he was counting out coins.

"But you said that is tyranny. That's taxation without representation," said Jack.

"Exactly right, Miss Rousseau," said Mr. Larsen spinning on his feet and pointing at her.

"Yeah, well who do they represent, if they don't represent us? I mean, aren't they Americans too?" asked a boy in the back.

"They are paid by us, but they work for a globalist power that remains unidentified. The truth is that these elites are nowhere, because they are everywhere. They are buried deep in the system like parasites, and if we make a serious attempt at removing them we may kill the host, which is America," said Mr. Larsen solemnly.

"But can't we arrest them or something? How can they get away with this?" asked Jack.

"I am not trying to get you to give up. Far from it. You, my good students, are the future of America. You need to know what we face, because you will be the ones who change it. You see, when George W. Bush was president, he instituted a military government under the Department of Homeland Security. He merged the military with the civilian law enforcement systems, which historically has been the doom of any Republic. This new legal system allows the president, through his cabinet and the hundreds of secretaries, to rule the country. Remember, I told you about the Democrats?

They descended from the anti-Federalists, who believed that the country was best run by the President. Well, this fourth branch of government allows Democrat presidents to operate like a dictator, superseding the power of Congress," said Mr. Larsen.

"Why don't we just change presidents? How come we don't elect someone who will stop them from destroying the country?" asked Jack.

"That has been tried as well. As soon as a President they don't control calls them out for who they are, this global government, let's just call it a Syndicate inside our government, marshals all the intelligence agencies, the news media, and the Democrats in office, or famous enough to attract a news camera, and they assault him until he is defeated. And, if that doesn't work or he gets too close to stopping them, they put a bullet in him," said Mr. Larsen quietly.

"You make it sound hopeless, Mr. Larsen," said Jack.

"There is always hope. These are all just facts. The founding fathers faced this exact same set of circumstances 250 years ago," said Mr. Larsen.

"Yeah, but there was another land they didn't control an ocean away. What are we supposed to do; go to another planet?" asked Jack.

"In a way, yes. I am posing the possibility that you have the ability, as a new generation, to form a new world. My purpose as your teacher is to show you the true condition of this world. If you are who I think you are, I know you can make it better. I know you can soak into this government from top to bottom and make their walls of mud come apart. Their global government has been tried a thousand times on a thousand worlds, and it has never been sustainable. I'm just saying that now that you're here, they have picked the wrong world to mess with. Prove me right," said Mr. Larsen timing his words to the class bell perfectly.

Chapter 11

"Welcome back to Tripoli, Ambassador Stevens. My name is Aya. I will be taking care of your accommodations while you are here. I trust you had a pleasant trip," said Aya reaching for his right hand with both of hers.

"It was smooth as glass. I am glad to be back in Libya. Nice to meet you," said Chris.

"It is very hot this time of year. Make sure to drink plenty of water," said Aya.

"I won't forget. Ever since I was an exchange student in Spain back in 77, I almost passed out," he said a little nervous in front of Aya's large brown eyes.

"The Middle East is a place of many dangers, ambassador," said Aya almost refusing to break her stare into his blue eyes.

"All people want to learn and I think want peace, Aya. I taught English in Morocco, and the people there were marvelously curious. I really fell in love with this part of the world. It feels like home to me," said Chris finally looking around the large embassy foyer.

"Things have been rather tense since the president was killed," said Aya beginning to walk down the hall toward the garden courtyard protected by the walls of the embassy. Rain was rare in Tripoli, but the sea breeze felt almost like San Diego weather. Open air courtyards were common, but government buildings like embassies had to make sure there were no vantage points to see over the wall. This was now a country seething in controlled hostility.

"Yes, I left when the hostilities made it too unsafe for us. I'm anxious to get started. We need to know where we are, so we can figure out where we're going," said Chris trying to assert some leadership without really knowing what to say.

"I'm sure you will, Ambassador. Your government has been very active here for more than a year," said Aya with a straight smile and an almost imperceptible curtsy.

"You don't have to be defensive with me. I promise, I will do my best to help Libya transition to free elections," said Chris.

"That sounds nice, but the Libyan people had a president already they loved. I'm not sure they will know what to do with the right to choose another," said Aya maintaining her quiet voice.

"Yes, well. I understand that may be the case with some, but the State Department was aware of other things. The military was. I mean, our intelligence indicated that the people required our assistance," began Chris awkwardly.

"The rebels, as your American press called them, were outsiders. They were refugees and immigrants from other countries. They wanted the same benefits as Libyans; the housing, the oil income, the education, and the free medical care. The president told them this was reserved for the Libyan people. So they tried to take it by force. He was winning until your jets began attacking the Libyan army. Who can withstand the American military?" asked Aya letting her emotions show against her will.

"Is that how the people feel? Really? You know, I always wanted to be an ambassador. I guess I should be more careful what I wish for," said Chris unscrewing the top from a bottle of water and taking a long drink.

"We are happy that you are here. But, we are even more happy that you care about Libya," said Aya tempering her tone back to a more diplomatic sound.

"It's okay. The truth is easier for me. I promise to be honest with you, if you will do the same," said Chris twisting the top back on the water bottle.

"Yes, Mr. Ambassador," said Aya, again with a feint at subservience.

"Mr. Stevens is fine. Chris, when we're in private. I'm here to help, not to be a boss," said Chris.

The first order of business was to assess the situation on the ground in Libya. Under the rule of the only president it had known for a generation, Libya had developed into a very cosmopolitan country. Qaddafi seemed to mature and develop into a man who shared the seemingly endless wealth of Libya with the people, but he was careful and experienced in leadership in the Middle East. It was still a place one did not eat a meal in front of jackals. The appetite of the Libyan people was hard enough to satisfy without millions of refugees running to the smell of a free meal. Watching the small groups of mercenaries come and go was made much worse since 2009, when the U.S. State Department began hiring Al Qaeda and even worse gangs to stir up trouble.

The Libyan police were smart, difficult to bribe, and well equipped to handle almost anything, but when the looting and armed robberies began to claim lives, Qaddafi sent in troops to gather up the outsiders and expel them from the country. As though part of the plan, reporters filmed from a script. Qaddafi knew it was only a matter of time before the footage would match the narrative being put forth by the U.S. Secretary of State. Reagan was tough and hit back hard when he was threatened. Hillary Clinton was treacherous as a desert wasp, and she had much bigger plans.

Although opposed by almost everyone, she commissioned American and NATO jets to back up the mercenaries, and within a few months, Qaddafi knew he could not win. They were trying to destroy the wealthy and peaceful empire he had learned to lead after 40 years of his share of mistakes. Once his army was scattered, the police were overwhelmed, and his guards were wiped out in a few hours. He called Hillary Clinton before he left the palace and was assured safe passage, but within minutes of the call, the swarm immediately changed course and descended upon him like desert locusts. He ran into the streets and tried to blend into the people to make his escape. He had billions hidden all over the world, and he could always regroup in exile somewhere; anywhere. But that was not to be. As though he had a homing device on him, he was discovered, beaten and shot to death in the streets by foreign mercenaries while the cameras rolled. Hillary laughed like a school girl on a morning news program a short while after the assassination, "We came. We saw. He died."

Killing Qaddafi was only a small part of the plan. Hillary's State Department directed the CIA to set up several stations inside Libya that not even the Pentagon knew existed. Its primary purpose was to make sure the armories full of modern missiles, rockets, grenades, and rifles were kept out of the hands of local warlords and preserved for delivery to the next phase of her plan. Al Qaeda had the best fighters in the Middle East and Europe. They were well paid and loyal as long as the cash kept coming. But Hillary needed something much larger. She needed an army without using American troops and without telling Congress what she had planned.

The DNC knew exactly what it was doing after all. If Hillary was president, she wouldn't be able to accomplish anything. Besides, she would never have been able to maintain her own offsite servers through which she ran the entire Department without anyone looking over her shoulder. Within two years, she had accomplished everything the Syndicate wanted. She had assassinated Qaddafi. She had sequestered enough weaponry to arm a sizeable army. She had carefully embezzled nearly $5 billion from the State Department and had access to billions in cash on pallets in warehouses in the Netherlands. Numerous Saudi and Qatar sources had contributed money to the cause.

It was time for phase two of the grand plan to secure control of a massive gas pipeline from the Golan Heights through Turkey to supply southern Europe. Control of this pipeline would ensure control over the entire southern European continent. Russia already controlled the supply of natural gas to northern and Eastern Europe, but control of everything south of Estonia to the Mediterranean Sea would make the Syndicate into the greatest superpower ever. Vladimir Putin was competing for the same control, but he had to make sure Assad remained in power long enough to get the pipeline through Syria. All Hillary had to do was remove Assad from power. And now, she had freed up the weapons to feed the Syndicate's brutal secret army. All that was needed was a reason to remove him. And that was exactly why the DNC wanted Hillary Clinton in the State Department and the smooth, untouchable Barack Obama in the White House.

On August 21, 2012, three months after Chris arrived in Tripoli, President Obama told the world that President Bashar Al Assad's use of chemicals against his people would cross a red line, after which America would use military action against him. The pieces were falling into place exactly as the Syndicate had planned. The movement of weapons and chemicals from Libya to Syria would begin in three weeks.

"Good morning Aya. Did you send that email to State yesterday?" asked Chris.

"Yes, Mr. Stevens. Would you like some fresh grapefruit with that? We got some last night," asked Aya as she sat across the wooden table from him.

"Um, yeah. Sure. I just wanted to know if anyone responded to the emails. I can't even go outside to jog. They threw rocks at our car again yesterday. My security people are telling me they only have sidearms. I mean this is War College 101, here. This country has no leadership, and they blame us," said Chris sprinkling some pepper onto his soft boiled egg.

"Nothing so far, Mr. Stevens," said Aya looking down at her coffee.

"We're still scheduled to go to Benghazi tomorrow, right?" asked Chris.

"Yes," she said quietly.

"What do you think? This place is bad enough, but at least there is air support a couple minutes away. I used to run this office a year ago, and I can tell you there is not enough security to make a remote meeting like that. We've recorded 21 incidents, and those are just the recorded ones. I want to know what the hell State is going to do to help," said Chris stabbing his egg with a spoon to expose the steaming yolk.

"The security officer keeps reporting they don't want the place to look too military. I'm not sure. Our local fruit market has more military than this place. If it wasn't for these walls, I don't know," said Aya as her thoughts trailed off to a place she did not want to let Chris see from her.

"Look, I'm used to resolving conflicts. I'm good at getting people to talk to one another. That's why I never practiced law. I retired my license back in '91. I wanted to solve the problems diplomatically, not through force or litigation. But this place has no law that anyone agrees on. There's no common ground between anyone," said Chris almost unable to swallow the bite of egg.

"Maybe the people will see you are not afraid to talk to them. You're a good person, Mr. Stevens. Sometimes it is better to talk peace when you don't have a gun," said Aya.

"Oh I get that. I don't even like guns. But the bad guys do, and I would like to see my family again. In fact, if I didn't believe in this mission so much, I would leave now," said Chris.

"What is the mission? What is your mission?" asked Aya now sending her Arabian eyes into his.

"Well, you see that's just it. I thought I knew. I had this idea of setting up elections here, and getting some Democracy going, but now I don't know. It's a mob mentality out there. In fact, it is a whole bunch of mobs, and that is the weakness of Democracy. The biggest mob makes the rules, but the second and third biggest mobs don't like those rules, and then you have a civil war. I mean Berkeley didn't teach me much else, but history was my thing. This is not going to work here. I want it to happen, but it seems like no one else wants it to happen," said Chris.

"What does your State Department want?" asked Aya trying to help.

"You tell me. We have been writing and calling ten times a day, but nothing has changed. Now, they want me in Benghazi Monday. We have five days of meetings lined up over there. Do we even know what we're doing?" asked Chris showing his frustration by laying his spoon down, unable to finish his egg.

"You have your presentations ready. The cable only provided the appointments. You're meeting with the Turkish Consul Tuesday night. I requested some talking points, but they just sent the same thing again," said Aya waving her left hand over her glass of orange juice.

"Do me a favor. I don't care that it's Sunday. Set up a call with State tonight. I want to talk to the Secretary. Enough of this bull shit. Either I get some answers, or I'm not going tomorrow," said Chris as he placed his napkin on the table and pushed back his chair to walk away.

Aya watched him run his hand through his hair as he walked away. He had served in Libya twice previously: as the Deputy Chief of Mission (from 2007 to 2009) and as Special Representative to the National Transitional Council (from March 2011 to November 2011) during the Libyan revolution. Through all of that, he never showed any fear. He always smiled, and his love for the Libyan people showed. His American accent was barely noticeable when he spoke Arabic, and that earned him great respect among the oldest Libyan families. But now there was a shadow on his back. He was afraid.

The two hour plane ride from Tripoli went smoothly over the light blue Mediterranean Sea along the northern coast of Libya. Aya and the staff were quiet, but Chris was unable to concentrate on the events of the next five days. The small group of SUV's was unmarked and the local drivers and contractors were patient and helpful getting the luggage and things off the plane. Bubaker Habib was especially kind and stepped forward to shake Chris's hand and make him feel welcome.

"My name is Bubaker Habib. We are so glad you could come. Anything you need, you just let me know," he said with his broad smile below his sincere eyes.

"What name should I use? Is Mr. Habib okay? That means beloved, I think. Is that alright with you?" asked Chris shaking his hand like he was climbing out of a stream about to carry him away. He looked around the small airport.

"Yes, yes, Mr. Ambassador. You are quite right. This is fine with me. Come in the vehicle where it is cool. My people will get your things. Hello Aya. Good to see you again," said Habib.

"Hello Bubaker. It is good to see you too," said Aya shaking his hand and pulling her Hijab against the sea breeze with her other hand.

The ride from the airport to the compound was slow through the narrow streets of Benghazi. The traffic was thick, and the buildings were close to one another. Suspicious glances bounced off the three vehicles that were nearly touching bumpers as they made their way to the walled residence that was converted into the embassy building. One of the gates was missing and roads were in poor condition as they drove through the lightly guarded entrance past the loosely saluting pair of men in khaki uniforms. The grass was dried but alive, and the date palms looked parched and lonely along the driveway as they approached the flat roofed building.

The rooms inside had high ceilings, and were decorated simply with cheap furniture. The largest room had been converted into a tactical operations room, and there was a safe room leading from that room that had been constructed with a jail cell type gate that could be locked from the inside. Toward the rear of that room was a restroom with a private door. It had a small window near the ceiling. Habib's men brought the luggage in and set Chris's shoulder bag with his computer and documents along with his diary on the large wooden desk in the main office. Aya went out to the canteen-like kitchen and gave soft orders for water and some fresh cut fruit to be brought into the office.

"So, tell me Habib, how are things here? Has anyone from State been here to set things up? Who is the security officer?" asked Chris as he unzipped his shoulder bag and began laying out his laptop and his papers.

"Sean Smith is the Information Management Officer, and Tyrone Woods is here as well. They're both former Navy Seals. His crew has been making almost daily ventures out to find ManPads and destroy them. Glen Doherty is here also. All good men, Mr. Ambassador," said Habib.

"All that's well and good. We have been sending emails and calls to State for upgraded security. Has anyone been here to audit the security? This isn't San Diego, you know," said Chris trying his hardest not to lose his temper.

"As far as I know, nothing, Mr. Ambassador. I have heard Sean almost every day on the phone, but there has been no support from the U.S. that I know of," said Habib.

"I want a staff meeting for dinner. All hands. When is our first meeting?" asked Chris turning to Aya who had just walked back into the operations room.

"It is at 8 PM tomorrow. The Turkish Consul wants to meet with you," said Aya.

"Do we know why he is coming?" asked Chris putting his hands on his hips and wanting to take off his jacket. He was in command of this facility now, but somehow he couldn't catch his breath.

"He left no agenda, but said it was urgent that he speak with you," said Aya.

"Mr. Ambassador, you should know that there is an annex less than two miles from here," said Habib finally.

"A what? What annex?" asked Chris.

"The CIA has an annex. There is a compound a little smaller than this one," said Habib.

"The CIA? Why don't I know about this? What the hell is the CIA doing in Benghazi?" asked Chris beginning to pace the room a little.

"Why don't we settle in for a while? My people are watching everything. We will have a good meal and meet and talk. I am sure we can do some good here, now that you have arrived," said Habib trying to calm Chris down.

Chris took a few deep breaths and walked over to the tray with the water and fruit the serving staff had set down for them. He drank from a bottled water and broke off a small piece from the flat bread on the tray and took a small bite from it. He walked over to the barred window and looked out into the poorly trimmed courtyard and swallowed the dry bread down his almost convulsing throat. It was quiet outside, and somehow that was not comforting. "We're making that call to State tonight," said Chris, and the room was silent behind him.

"Mr. Ambassador, my name is Tyrone Woods. I'm a contract officer in charge of security for the compound. My friends call me Ty," said Tyrone walking in the room and firmly gripping Chris's hand.

"Good to meet you. Just call me Chris between us. I'm trying to get my bearings still. So much has changed since I was in Libya last year," said Chris sitting in the black chair behind his desk.

"Yes sir. No doubt," said Ty standing at ease in front of the desk.

"Have a seat, please. I just would like an update on the situation here," said Chris.

"Yes sir. I would be happy to brief you. I have been here for a while. We're trying to track down ordinance, specifically shoulder fired missiles and decommission them. So far, we have found almost nothing. The locals are not saying much. Too many mercs in the area," said Ty.

"Mercenaries? I thought those were ours," said Chris.

127

"Oh they were, last year. But these are imports. They've been coming in for weeks," said Ty.

"What do you mean weeks? Does State know? Has anyone talked to Clinton, Rice? Anyone?" asked Chris.

"Oh we've talked until we're blue in the face. I have sent more than 200 emails and maybe that many calls. Sean's the IMO. I know he has made some. I think the call log shows about 600 in all," said Ty.

"600 outgoing? What are they saying? What about Africom," asked Chris

"They get copied on every email we send to State. General Ham is a good man. They're a little over two hours away by helo, and less than that for a gunship. Other than that, I'm afraid it's just us. I don't feel good about it either. I've been with the military or on contract since I got out of high school, and I have never seen anything like this before," said Ty.

"Tell me about the CIA annex across town," said Chris flatly.

"I was going to ask you. They don't tell us anything, and I'm under orders to steer clear. They have their job, and we have ours. That's what my boss tells me," said Ty.

"What the hell are they doing here?" asked Chris.

"What the CIA always does. Something the Pentagon doesn't need to know," said Ty.

"I'm here for five days of meetings. Then I'm going back to Tripoli. This place is not ready. It feels like a bomb ready to go off," said Chris.

"Yeah. I know what you mean. They shipped us a crate of surveillance cameras but no tech guys to install them. They're still sitting right over there. We'll make it. We always do," said Ty.

"Thanks for the briefing. I like it even less. See you at dinner. I want to get to know everyone," said Chris standing to shake Ty's hand.

"Yes sir. See you at dinner," said Ty. He turned on his heel and began to walk down the hall toward the quarters area.

"And, Tyrone?" stopped Chris.

"Yes sir?" asked Ty pausing for a moment.

"Do you trust these security guys?" asked Chris.

"Not even to pump my gas," said Ty, and he walked out of the office.

It seemed like days before dinner was ready. The roast chicken was delightful, and the hummus was the best he had tasted in a long time. Still, Chris didn't eat much. He was nervous and listened more than he talked while everyone ate and laughed as though they were trying to ignore a beggar in the room.

Chris stood as the dessert was being placed and the plates were removed. He always felt better when he was talking. "First of all, let me thank the kitchen staff for that wonderful meal. You know, the last time I was in Libya, I was learning the ropes. I don't know if we can do this job. I mean, putting this country back together is a hell of a mission, but I'm committed to doing it if you will support me. I just want you to know how much I appreciate you being here. Thank you all," said Chris as he sat down in his chair not really feeling any better at all.

"Mr. Ambassador, on behalf of my team, I can't tell you what it means to us to have you here. There is a lot going on, as you can tell, and the situation is kind of raw and primitive, but I think there is some good we can do here," said Sean Smith.

"Thank you, Sean. By the way, I want to place a call to State when we're done here. Those guys in D.C. should be up by now. We're going to get some support in here," said Chris.

"Yes sir. You got it," said Sean.

The voices were quiet, and the sound of spoons against small porcelain bowls of ice cream echoed off the wooden floor and the painted concrete ceiling. The local staff took plates and glasses off the table and returned to the canteen outside the operations center. Chris, Ty, and Sean excused themselves politely and walked back to Chris's office and closed the door.

"Make the call," said Chris.

"Yes sir," said Sean as he began the series of numbers to make the secure satellite connection to the State Department.

"I want to talk to Hillary Clinton," said Chris.

"Good luck with that," said Ty putting the tips of all his fingers together and flexing them like a spider doing sideways pushups.

"You mean you guys have never spoken to her? This is her mess we're trying to clean up here," said Chris.

"Hah. No money in it," said Ty.

"What does that mean?" asked Chris.

"When was the last time you spoke to her?" asked Ty.

"When I was confirmed," said Chris.

"Not since. Right? See, that place has been open for business for three years, and business is good," said Ty moving his hands behind his neck.

"Are you talking about Libyan oil?" asked Chris.

"Hell no, I'm not talking about oil. I'm talking about weapons," said Ty leaning forward and putting his hands on his knees, gripping them.

"Weapons? I thought you were here to destroy them," said Chris.

"Oh I am. Why the hell do you think I haven't found any?" asked Ty.

"Hey relax. I am just trying to figure out what's going on around here," said Chris wincing at not choosing the right words.

"I am not without my opinion. If you want to hear it, just say the word," said Ty.

"He's cool. All Seals are that way. Comes from too much compressed air," said Sean nodding that the call was connecting.

"Look who's talking, frogman," said Ty pointing and smiling at Sean.

"Frogmen never die," said Sean smiling back.

"Put it on speaker, and record it," said Chris.

"State Department. How may I direct your call?" came the female voice over the speaker phone.

"This is Ambassador Chris Stevens in Benghazi, Libya. I need to speak to Hillary Clinton immediately," said Chris leaning over the device in the middle of the conference table.

"One moment please while I transfer you," said the voice.

"Sir, you should not provide location information over the phone," said Sean.

"It's not encrypted?" asked Chris.

"The phone is encrypted, but that may not be the only device in the room," said Sean.

"You're saying the place is bugged?" asked Chris.

"All guns are loaded, Mr. Ambassador," said Ty.

"He's right. Who is the bullet, and where is the gun," said Sean.

"State Department, how may I direct your call?" came a second female voice over the phone.

"This is Ambassador Chris Stevens. It is a matter of great urgency that I speak with Hillary Clinton, please," said Chris to the woman on the speaker phone.

"I'm afraid that is impossible. Secretary Clinton is tied up in meetings all day," said the voice.

"Well, who can I talk to about immediate security needs for the embassy here in Libya?" asked Chris as though he was asking which aisle paint brushes could be found at the hardware store.

"I believe Eric Nordstrom is the regional security officer for your area. He is located in," began the voice.

"Excuse me. Excuse me. Eric was stationed in Tripoli. He left in July. He knows very well what our needs are, and we have made now more than 600 requests for some help here. I need to know who is in charge of security for the Benghazi embassy, and I need to know right now," said Chris raising his voice.

"I'm sorry, Mr. Ambassador. I do not have that information," said the voice.

"That doesn't surprise me. Get me the Deputy Assistant Secretary," said Chris.

"I will put you through to Deputy Assistant Secretary Lamb. Hold please," said the voice almost without changing tone.

The phone made a beep every ten seconds to let the party know they were still connected. "Deputy Assistant Secretary Lamb's office. How may I direct your call?" asked the young female voice.

"This is Ambassador Chris Stevens. I need to speak to Charlene on an urgent matter," said Chris.

"I am sorry, Ambassador. She is out of the office at this time. I would be happy to give her a message," said the receptionist.

"When will she be back?" asked Chris.

"I am sorry. I do not have that information," said the receptionist.

"Okay. Make this message urgent, and try to reach her as soon as we hang up. Tell her Ambassador Stevens is calling from Benghazi and requests immediate security assets deployed ASAP to this location," said Chris.

"I will do that, Mr. Ambassador. Is there anything else?" asked the receptionist.

"No. That's all I can take at one time. Thanks," said Chris, and he drew his hand across his neck so Sean would terminate the call.

"Welcome to the U.S. State Department," said Ty.

"What the hell is going on over there?" asked Chris pulling his hand through his hair with his other hand on his hip.

"I told you. Business is good," said Ty.

"I want to see Habib. Go find him for me," said Chris waving his hand in frustration.

132

Tyrone left the room with the door opened and returned in a few minutes with Brubaker Habib. "Yes, Mr. Ambassador. What can I get for you?" asked Habib.

"Close the door. I need you to tell me that your people have the perimeter secured. The gate, and the courtyard. Are we going to be okay here?" asked Chris trying to be calm and direct.

"I picked them myself. My cousin is out there. We know this area, Mr. Ambassador. We will keep you safe," said Habib.

"Okay. Get some sleep. One eye open. Okay?" asked Chris putting his hand on Habib's shoulder.

"Yes, yes, Mr. Ambassador. See you in the morning. You will see. Good night, sir," said Habib as he backed through the open door and hastily left the command center outside the office.

Tyrone slowly closed the door as Habib left through the other side of the operations room. "Not even to pump my gas," said Ty quietly.

"Well, I guess that's it then. Let's get some sleep. Tomorrow we will try again. We'll make a call to Tripoli tomorrow and see if we can get some support down here. See you men in the morning," said Chris sitting down at his desk.

"Hang in there, Mr. Ambassador. We'll get through this," said Glen.

"Yeah. Thanks," said Chris quietly.

There was not much light in the city of Benghazi. Many houses did not have electricity, and the compound lighting was little more than a few flood lights on the corners of the roof lines. The lack of modern vehicles in this part of Libya was also apparent as the occasional vehicle driving the gravel and poorly paved roads could be heard for blocks. The skies were mostly clear this late at night, as the breeze changed directions and blew out to sea, once the ground cooled off from the desert. Nearly every day, once it got hot, the high overcast sky or even a fog would come in from the sea less than a mile away. It was a calm body of water, mostly. But like the region, widely considered to have been the cradle of civilization, it could rapidly turn violent and unpredictable. The night passed peacefully, and the dawn eased the feeling that wolves were napping not far from the door.

"Good morning Aya," said Chris as he walked into the dining room. The morning sun from the East lit up the room making it feel more hospitable than the bare, pastel concrete construction of the compound.

"Good morning, Mr. Ambassador. There is fresh coffee on the cart, and some sweet cakes if you like," said Aya.

"Sounds good. I didn't sleep too well. New place," said Chris pouring some goat's milk into his coffee.

"There have been many budget cuts in the last couple of years," said Aya.

"Doesn't make sense. I mean, the rebellion was not an easy time. It is going to take some serious attention to establish some stability," said Chris.

"With respect, Mr. Ambassador, it was stable for the last 20 years. The Libyan people were doing fine," said Aya.

"That's above my pay grade, Aya. I am going to do my best to help this country make a peaceful transition to a democratic form of government," said Chris.

"You sound like one of those nice brochures," said Aya taking a sip from her coffee.

"All I know is that as long as people are talking, they aren't fighting," said Chris.

"Yes. Tomorrow, we start talking. Of course, don't forget the Turkish Consul is coming tonight at 8," said Aya.

"That reminds me. I want to call back Tripoli. Eric's old office. Maybe General Ham can spare a few people to help secure this place for the next couple of weeks at least," said Chris biting a small piece off the sweet yellow pastry and sipping some coffee. The brew was rich and strong, and it competed with the honey sweet taste of the pastry. The strong flavor was one of the things he loved about the Middle East. The contrast between the bland, desert landscape and the relentless spirit of the people was unique and intoxicating.

Habib was attentive and polite that day, and Aya busied herself with getting the staff to make the compound clean and presentable for the next few days of visits. Ty and Glen made numerous trips outside the city to follow up on leads as to where the enormous weapons cache might be. No calls or emails came back from the U.S. State Department addressing the urgent call Chris had made the night before.

The ominous anniversary made the strange abandon of the compound feel like a life raft ten days at sea without a sign of rescue. The last afternoon shower washed the dust from his pores, but offered no solace to Chris as he shaved and let the last of the heater's energy soak into his shoulders. He missed his wife, and resolved to write in his diary when he got dressed.

The large, black chair squeaked as he rocked in the quiet office as the dinner hour approached. He enjoyed writing in his diary by hand. It slowed his mind down to the speed of his writing, and acted like a form of prayer. He reached with his prose for the reasons why he wanted to be an Ambassador in the first place. Ever since his days at the War College, he felt like this is what he was born to be. He thought if he could make enough of a difference, that one day he could bring his wife and family to Libya and let them fall in love with the history and potential of this country. Right now, that future seemed like another world in another part of the universe.

There was a soft knock at his door, and it opened slightly to reveal one of Aya's large brown eyes. "Mr. Ambassador," floated her perfect accent to catch his attention.

"Yes. Come in Aya," said Chris.

"I thought we would have an early dinner. In case you might want to get some air walking around the compound before our meeting tonight. It is really quite a beautiful afternoon outside," said Aya.

"You know, actually that sounds pretty good. I'll join you in a few minutes," said Chris.

Aya walked out and left the door slightly open. He closed his diary and placed it squarely on the corner of the desk. He looked around and made sure everything was put away. He tapped some papers together and dropped them into the file drawer and turned the key to lock it. This was it. This was the center of the world right now. He felt his calling and took a deep breath and checked his tie to make sure the knot was centered in his collar that seemed to fit a little more loose since he left home. He wasn't used to having a long day without talking on the phone or jumping in cabs from one meeting to another around the busy city of Washington or the rush of demands of the office in Tripoli. Somehow, he couldn't make his heart settle down. For a brief moment, he entertained the thought of getting on a plane and leaving the job he had worked his whole life to land.

The dinner was peaceful, with just a few members of the staff present. He ate more than he had the night before, and left the table feeling better. Perhaps it was just the jitters of an empty stomach and the lack of sleep that made him feel a little like going sailing alone in the bay near his home for a few hours.

"Mr. Ambassador, I just received a call from the Consul's staff. He has landed at the airport and should be arriving a little early, if you don't mind making a little extra time for him," said Aya.

"That's fine. I'll be in my office. Just let me know when he arrives. Have you heard from Ty or Sean?" asked Chris.

"Sean is with Habib out by the gate, and Ty is on his way back. He should arrive any time now," said Aya.

"Tell them I want to see them when they get here," said Chris.

"Yes, Mr. Ambassador," said Aya.

He tugged his pants at the belt and made a small effort to tuck his shirt in a little more neatly and headed for the lavatory in the back of the safe room. He kept a toothbrush and mouthwash there, and the open widow near the ceiling made it one of the more fresh interior spaces in this old building. Maybe it took a little longer than he thought, or maybe his mind wandered to a peaceful place, but when he emerged, Ty was standing in the safe room loading a gun.

"Something I should know about?" asked Chris wide eyed.

"Just making sure the clips are full. It's a habit, more than anything. But, I've been out on the city, and there is something going on," said Ty.

"What do you mean, something?" asked Chris as Glen, and Sean entered the room.

"I think we may have an issue," said Sean.

"That doesn't sound good. What's up?" asked Ty.

"Habib is having a hard time with his boys out there. They want to go home," said Sean.

"Home? What the hell does that mean?" asked Chris nervously.

"You can relax for now. I promised them double their pay for the next week. These people are all about the money. No sense of duty, I'll tell you that," said Sean.

"The Turkish Consul called. He's on his way from the airport," said Chris.

"You can be damned sure they won't do anything as long as he is here. Turks don't put up with any bull shit," said Sean.

"They? What do you mean, 'they?' Did you hear anything back from Washington?" asked Chris.

"Like I said before. There's no money in it. Those mercs that have been coming and going for weeks are nowhere to be found," said Ty slamming a full clip into his 9mm pistol and putting his holster on.

"Maybe they left. Did you ever think of that?" asked Chris

"Hand me that FN. I'm going back out to the gate to make sure the Turk doesn't get spooked. Those guys like to see guns with the good guys," said Sean ignoring the last question.

"All I can say is, make it last, Mr. Ambassador," said Ty handing the FN FAL automatic rifle to him and walking out the door behind Sean.

"I'll stay here with you, sir," said Glen.

The safe room was quiet as Chris stood there, feeling his heart come up in his throat. Glen looked him in the eye. "Mr. Ambassador, we're going to get through this. Maybe you're right. Those guys probably left town. This Turk may be a hitter, you know. He's here for a reason, and maybe these guys don't want to be seen in town right now. Go have your meeting. I'll be right by your side," said Glen.

"Yeah. You're probably right. I guess they just want us to look like we're not scared of them," said Chris.

"They better be scared, if they know what's good for them," said Glen.

"Thanks, Glen. You're a good man," said Chris as he patted him on the shoulder and walked out to the foyer to meet the Consul.

Chris and Glen watched through the barred window of the tactical operations center as two SUV's drove slowly through the gate and up to the entrance steps outside the embassy. Four men with weapons got out of the rear vehicle and began to look around the compound. They checked the hedges, the carport, and scanned the walls with their night vision goggles. One of them stood by the door behind the driver and reached to open it. The other three doors opened and the consul and two armed men emerged. The driver stayed behind the wheel.

The two of them walked swiftly up the steps and arrived at the front door just as Glen opened it. "Come in, please," said Glen.

"Welcome to Benghazi. It's good to meet you," said Chris extending his hand to the Consul.

"Good evening, Ambassador Stevens. My name is General Ali Sait Akin. Thank you for making the time to see me," said the General.

"Can I get you anything? Some water or juice perhaps?" asked Chris with his diplomatic voice.

"Water will be fine, sir. Can we meet in your office? In private?" asked the General.

"Of course, and our protocol officer, Mr. Doherty will be there for your protection as well," said Chris.

"Very well," said the General staying close to Chris's side.

The door closed and his body guard stood by the door as Glen walked over to the wall and stood quietly with his hands behind his back beside the window and watched the bodyguard. Chris poured two glasses of water and placed one of them on the edge of the desk and sat down behind his desk calmly.

"Mr. Ambassador, I have come tonight to let you know that we are aware of a plan to move weapons from Libya to Turkey. We think that your CIA is arming Al Qaeda inside Syria, and it raises some concerns for us, as you might imagine," said the General.

Chris took a sip of his water, and found it difficult to swallow. He fought the urge to cough, to vomit. "May I as how you came by this information?" asked Chris smoothly.

"You are not informed. I can see that," said the General.

"What makes you think our government has anything to do with arming Al Qaeda. They are our enemy as well as yours," said Chris.

"Not everyone in my government is in agreement with you and I, Mr. Ambassador. There is a war in Syria that your government wants to pay someone else to fight. The Wahabis are not friends of mine, but I think this will not be acceptable to the Russians. We have enough trouble making a home for your NATO nuclear weapons. We don't want trouble with the Russians any more than you do, Mr. Ambassador," said the General.

"Are you sure of your information? Sometimes, misinformation can sound so official," said Chris. His mind was racing to find a clue as to what General Akin was saying. Maybe this was why Clinton wasn't saying a word to him. Maybe this was why the Pentagon was not aware that the CIA had an annex in Benghazi. Maybe this was why Ty couldn't find the cache of weapons he was seeking.

"Mr. Ambassador, I don't know if you are playing a game with me, or if your government just sends you into harm's way without an idea in your head," said the General.

"I just arrived from Washington a week ago. If this was going on, I would have been briefed by the U.S. State Department," said Chris more sternly.

"I am not a diplomat, sir. I am a soldier. My information came at the cost of blood and pain. I assure you that your government is preparing a shipment of weapons by ship and plane to my country as we speak. Either you are a fool, or a useful idiot, but you are in a serious situation. Time is not on your side," said the General

"Perhaps we can make some calls while you are here to clear this up. Can I interest you in some," began Chris.

"I am sorry. I must refuse. My plane is running still at the airport. I would offer you a seat on it, but it is small and fast and every seat is taken," said the General looking Chris directly in the eye.

"I understand. I would like very much to meet with you again when I can validate some of this information, if that is possible," said Chris.

"If that is possible. Of course, God willing. I must be going, Mr. Ambassador. Do take care of yourself," said the General as he stood and extended his open hand.

Chris shook his hand and felt a shiver in the grip. Strange, he did not look old enough to have a tremor. He walked the two men to the door, and his bodyguard opened it. The two SUV's were still running, and the men were still scanning the wall for any movement. They got in the vehicles quickly, and they smoothly drove around the circle drive and headed for the gate.

Chris followed them with his eyes and noticed something near the gate as the tail lights made the turn in the twilight toward the airport. It was a khaki uniform, running toward the compound. Behind him was Sean, running with both hands on his rifle.

9:40 p.m.: Unidentified gunmen launch an assault on the U.S. diplomatic compound in the eastern Libyan city of Benghazi, quickly overwhelming the U.S. and Libyan forces who were providing security. Inside the compound, security forces are separated from U.S. Ambassador J. Christopher Stevens. U.S. personnel who retreat to another building come under siege for two hours before a CIA security team and some Libyan security forces repel the attackers.

10:30 p.m.: Stevens and State Department information management officer Sean Smith have taken refuge in the main building in the compound, behind a fortified door with metal bars that keeps the attackers from breaking in. But the militants set fire to the building. Within minutes, Stevens and Smith are overwhelmed by smoke.

11 p.m.: A U.S. surveillance drone arrives over Benghazi. Then-Defense Secretary Leon E. Panetta and Gen. Martin Dempsey, chairman of the Joint Chiefs of Staff, meet with President Obama.

1 a.m.: A U.S. rescue team arrives in Benghazi from Tripoli, Libya's capital. Nearly 30 Americans are rescued from the compound. Shortly thereafter, Stevens is taken to Benghazi Medical Center and pronounced dead on arrival, according to a hospital source. (A Libyan doctor tells the Associated Press that Stevens died of asphyxia, probably caused by smoke inhalation.)

1:45 a.m.: The AP moves a news alert, reporting the death of at least one American in the Benghazi assault.

4 a.m.: Gunmen launch an assault using mortars against the CIA annex. Glen Doherty and Tyrone S. Woods, both former Navy Seals, are killed. Two other Americans are wounded.

4:08 a.m.: Secretary of State Hillary Rodham Clinton issues a statement. "I condemn in the strongest terms the attack on our mission in Benghazi today. ... The United States deplores any intentional effort to denigrate the religious beliefs of others. Our commitment to religious tolerance goes back to the very beginning of our nation. But let me be clear: There is never any justification for violent acts of this kind."

Sept. 12, 2012

Obama announces that Stevens was among those killed in the Benghazi assault. In his statement, the president says, "I strongly condemn the outrageous attack on our diplomatic facility in Benghazi." His statement also says: "While the United States rejects efforts to denigrate the religious beliefs of others, we must all unequivocally oppose the kind of senseless violence that took the lives of these public servants."

October 2012

Ahmed Abu Khattala, a "senior leader" of the Benghazi branch of the militant group Ansar al-Sharia, is identified as one of the ringleaders of the attack on the diplomatic mission. Although Ansar al Sharia Libya was initially portrayed by some as purely a local jihadist group, it has been a part of the al Qaeda network since its inception in 2011.

The Long War Journal has documented the organization's ties to al Qaeda and its branch in North Africa, Al Qaeda in the Islamic Maghreb (AQIM), on multiple occasions.

In December 2012, the FBI was granted only a few hours by the CIA to question al Harzi. Ansar al Sharia Tunisia actually stalked the FBI agents who questioned him, and even posted the FBI agents' pictures on Facebook in an effort to facilitate their termination. They escaped with their lives.

The following month, January 2013, a judge in Tunis ordered al Harzi released. Senior Obama administration officials, including Secretary of State Hillary Clinton and John Brennan, who was about to become the head of the CIA, were asked about this during Congressional testimony. Both of them vouched for al Harzi's release.

On January 23, 2013, Clinton testified before the Senate Foreign Relations Committee. She told senators that the Tunisians had "assured" the United States that Harzi was "under the monitoring of the court."

"Upon his release, I called the Tunisian prime minister. A few days later Director Mueller met with the Tunisian prime minister," Clinton explained. She continued: "We have been assured that he is under the monitoring of the court. He was released, because at that time — and — and Director Mueller and I spoke about this at some length — there was not an ability for evidence to be presented yet that was capable of being presented in an open court. But the Tunisians have assured us that they are keeping an eye on him. I have no reason to believe he is not still in Tunis, but we are checking that all the time."

During a separate hearing before the House Committee on Foreign Affairs, then Congressman Tom Cotton asked Clinton if she found "it distressing that the Tunisian government has released that gentleman [al Harzi] in light of the hundreds of millions of dollars of aid we've given them over the last two years?"

Clinton responded: "At this point, Congressman, I do not for two reasons. First, I had a long conversation with high-ranking Tunisian officials about this, as did Director Mueller of the FBI when he was there in person. We have been assured there was an effort to have rule of law, judicial process, sufficient evidence not yet available to be presented, but a very clear commitment made to us that they will be monitoring the whereabouts of the — Harzi and we're going to hold them to that and watch carefully."

Obviously, the Tunisians' assurances didn't pan out. In fact, the Tunisian government accused al Harzi of participating in the assassinations of two prominent politicians. One of them was killed on February 6, 2013, just weeks after al Harzi was released. And al Harzi was, quite obviously, able to travel from North Africa to the heart of the Middle East on behalf of the terrorist organizations he served. The Pentagon says he was working for the Islamic State at the time of his death.

In February 2013, Brennan echoed Clinton's claims regarding the evidence against al Harzi. Brennan told Congress that the US government "didn't have anything at all," on al Harzi and therefore, his release was not worrisome. They claimed there wasn't sufficient evidence against Harzi, and that whatever they had wouldn't be admissible in court. They claimed he was not a threat to anyone.

There are major problems with this claim. First, the initial evidence against al Harzi came from his social media postings — this isn't the type of intelligence that needs to be excluded from court proceedings.

Second, the U.S. government had enough on al Harzi to have him detained in Turkey, deported to Tunisia, and then questioned by the FBI. To say, as Brennan did, that the U.S. government "didn't have anything" at all al Harzi is clearly a lie and meant to protect the Syndicate's agent from being interrogated.

Third, Ansar al Sharia Tunisia was furious that al Harzi was being detained. They ransacked the U.S. Embassy in Tunis and demanded al Harzi's release. Al Harzi had direct ties to al Qaeda's international network that was working directly for Hillary Clinton.

Fourth, al Harzi had already built a dossier of terrorist connections prior to the 9/11/12 attack. He had been detained and imprisoned "for planning terrorist acts in 2005 in Tunisia." And his brother was also a known facilitator for al Qaeda in Iraq, demonstrating that jihadism was quite likely the family's business.

The UN's official, written designation page reads: "Al Harzi Planned and perpetrated the attack against the Consulate of the United States in Benghazi, Libya on 11 Sep. 2012." He was assassinated by an airstrike in June of 2015.

According to the Pentagon, justice has finally been served in Ali Ani al Harzi's case. But we are left to wonder: Why did it take so long? A key question in al Harzi's story remains unanswered: Why wasn't he in custody since late 2012? Because, no one in the Clinton Crime Syndicate wanted him questioned. They also do not like loose ends.

According to an initial Sept. 14 report by the Times of London, The Libyan ship, Al Entisar, was carrying 400 tons of cargo. Some of it was humanitarian, but also reportedly weapons, described by the report as the largest consignment of weapons ever seen from that country headed for Syria's rebels on the frontlines.

"This is the Libyan ship, Al Entisar, which is basically carrying weapons that are found in Libya," said Walid Phares, a Fox News Middle East and terrorism analyst. "So the ship came all the way up to Iskenderun in Turkey. The ship was transporting aid material, but there were also weapons; a lot of weapons."

While the source of the weapons used to attack the consulate is part of an ongoing investigation, former CIA Director Porter Goss told Fox News there was no question the weapons from Libya are making their way to Syria. The report also said that the U.S.

intelligence community must be aware, given their presence in Benghazi.

"Absolutely. I think there's no question that there's a lot of networking going on. And ... of course we know it."

A month after the October 2011 mercenary assassination of Qaddafi, Secretary of State Hillary Clinton announced in Tripoli that the U.S. was committing $40 million to help Libya "secure and recover its weapons stockpiles."

A few months after the attack on Benghazi, Assistant Secretary of State for Political and Military Affairs Andrew Shapiro expressed strong concerns that the situation on the ground was far from under control. He told an assembly at the Stimson Center in Washington D.C., on Feb. 2, "This raises the question -- how many are still missing? The frank answer is we don't know and probably never will."

Fox News military analyst Col. David Hunt explained, "The point is that these shoulder fired weapons systems are extremely accurate and very simple to use. With a short amount of instruction, you've got somebody capable of taking down any, any aircraft. Anywhere in the world."

The Foundation for Human Rights, and Freedoms and Humanitarian Relief (IHH) was moving the weapons using first aid and food trucks from Turkey to Syria. The IHH disputed the claims and in published Turkish reports said it "will take legal action against this article which was written without concrete evidence. It is defamatory, includes false and unfair accusations and violates publishing ethics."

No such lawsuit was ever filed. Serena Shim, an American war correspondent and journalist for Press TV, was murdered by a head on collision with a cement truck for transmitting the proof which broke the story. The Syndicate armed, funded, and provided intelligence to Al Qaeda in Syria with the express purpose of removing Bashar Al Assad from power by any means necessary.

There was more work to be done, however, before the world's most valuable gas pipeline could be routed from the vast reserves in the Golan Heights through Turkey to Southern Europe. For that to happen, leaders the Syndicate had long prepared had to be placed in office.

Chapter 12

The Stennis Space Center is a NASA rocket testing facility just about a ninety-minute drive from Hattiesburg. With the end of the Apollo and Shuttle programs, use of the 13,500 acre base declined, collapsing the economies of the surrounding communities. Over the years other government organizations and commercial companies have moved in and out of the buildings and warehouses scattered throughout the properties. Mostly, the land is covered with trees, making it a natural sound dampener for the testing of boosters and hybrids between jets and rockets. Basically, anything that is loud and dangerous can be tested in the remote forests of Hancock County, Mississippi on the banks of the Pearl River.

Rolls Royce, Lockheed-Martin, and a dozen other companies are constantly looking for engineers, mechanics, welders, and pipefitters to construct, modify, and operate the various test stands and support systems. There are also hundreds of job openings for programmers, quality assurance, and validation engineers, just like Adnan. Just about anyone fluent in C++ or the various validation and simulation platforms can earn decent money in the private sector, but companies that sell to the U.S. government have salary requirements that are tied to a prevailing wage, based upon the zip code of the place of employment. For this reason it is very difficult to attract such skills to Hancock County, Mississippi. In addition, since Hurricane Katrina cleaned up the real estate market, there are remarkably few choices for housing that would motivate someone to move from Silicon Valley to Hattiesburg. It doesn't even have a Guitar Center.

It's been more than 60 years since the US successfully tested the first hydrogen bomb. There is a vast difference between the technology for a criticality-based explosion of splitting atoms and one resulting from the fusion of protons together. It is perhaps more complex than the difference between sailing to the new world in 1492 and landing on the Moon in 1969. It is so complex, that only four other countries—Russia, France, China, and the UK—have been able to accomplish a fusion explosion themselves.

A few more countries—India, Pakistan, South Africa, Israel, as well as North Korea—have the know-how to build simpler forms of nuclear weapons: atomic bombs, but no other technology in the world has remained out of the hands of so many countries for such a long time.

It is said that when Lucifer watched God form Adam from dirt, he said, "That doesn't look that hard. I can do that."

And when Lucifer reached down to gather some dirt to try it on his own, God said, "Just a moment. You need to go get your own dirt."

The first great challenge to forming a fusion explosion is to make the fuel. Mastering the use of one of the strongest forces in the universe is not easy. In fact, up until 1945, it was completely theoretical. The strong nuclear force that holds positively charged particles in an atom together acts over very tiny distances, but it is a hundred trillion trillion times stronger than gravity.

The simpler technical journey, like that of Cristopher Columbus's Santa Maria, is to pull the proton and neutron apart. The snap of energy forms a chain reaction as the neutrons fly apart and tear other atoms apart, then those tear other atoms apart. Shooting two lumps of enriched Uranium 235 at one another in a small canon barrel will get the reaction started and level a few dozen city blocks.

The more complex technical journey is somewhat in reverse. Instead of tearing the atom apart, hydrogen protons, the heaviest in the universe, are compressed together to fuse into a new atom of Helium, which has much lighter protons. The loss of that tiny amount of mass, times the speed of light squared, is the theoretical amount of pure energy released. To see such a reaction in action, simply look up at the Sun. Our sun and most stars are nothing but massive fusion reactors. Observing snapshots of various stages of stars in the cosmos displays, more or less, the process by which God makes a Sun to rule over the day. Man makes a Sun in a fraction the amount of time.

Man must make his own dirt. Nuclear weapons require nuclear fuel. Very few types of atoms are both the right size and abundant enough to make a nuclear weapon. Either uranium or plutonium is required for atomic bombs, the latter of which is made in a sort of high-speed cotton candy machine, where the neutron sugar is spun into uranium until it is heavy enough to do the job. The fuel required for a Sun is a mixture of deuterium and tritium. These molecules were so rare, that they must be made from scratch using one cup of hydrogen and one or two cups of neutrons.

To collect weapons-grade uranium is not easy. You need a concentrated ("enriched") lump of the less stable form, uranium-235, which is only about 1% of naturally occurring uranium. The other 99%, uranium-238, doesn't work for an atom bomb because it does not split apart easily enough. Separating these two forms, or isotopes—which are identical in almost every way but differ slightly in weight—is hard, and requires a lot of energy.

In the 1940's Fermi and Einstein designed a plant in Chicago that enriched uranium that covered more than 40 acres of land, with 100 miles of piping, and thousands of heaters and compressors to turn the metallic uranium into a gas so the isotopes could be separated.

The first test weapon utilized Plutonium-239 in a fantastically complex design of an implosion device. Nothing like it had ever been crafted, and the opinion it might not work at all was common among the scientists and engineers that worked on it. Because of its complicated firing mechanism and the need for previously untested synchronization of explosives and precision design, it was thought that a full test of the concept was needed before the scientists and military representatives could be confident it would perform correctly under combat conditions. On July 16, 1945, it produced an explosion that so astonished the observers at the Trinity test site, located in the Jornada del Muerto desert about 35 miles southeast of Socorro, New Mexico, that Oppenheimer quoted Sanskrit by saying, "Now, I have become Death, the destroyer of worlds." The shock wave was felt over 100 miles away.

President Harry S. Truman, appointed after the death of Franklin Roosevelt, was informed that the theory was correct and that the gadget had worked. He immediately wrote Executive Order 11652 to Commanding General United States Army Strategic Air Forces, General Spaatz authorizing the use of the "special weapon" on Hiroshima.

The second weapon utilized 130 pounds of Uranium and was hurriedly placed into gun-type mechanism code named Little Boy. It was dropped on the Japanese city of Hiroshima on 6 August 1945 during World War II by the Boeing B-29 Superfortress Enola Gay, piloted by Colonel Paul W. Tibbets, Jr., commander of the 509th Composite Group of the United States Army Air Forces.

The third weapon design again utilized the Fat Man design developed for the Trinity test with a core that weighed barely 17 pounds. There were three weapons built numbered F-31, F-32, and F-33. They used detonators that were fired by fully charged lead-acid batteries located inside the bomb shell. If the bomb was not used within 70 hours, the batteries had to be removed, recharged, and placed back into the bomb. F-31 was partially disassembled to test the batteries and was utilized for the next attack on Japan.

The original target for the bomb was the city of Kokura, but it was found to be obscured by clouds and drifting smoke from fires started by a major firebombing raid by 224 B-29s on nearby Yahata the previous day. This covered 70% of the area over Kokura, obscuring the aiming point. Three bomb runs were made over the next 50 minutes, burning fuel and repeatedly exposing the aircraft to the heavy defenses of Yawata, but the bombardier was unable to drop visually. By the time of the third bomb run, Japanese anti-aircraft fire was getting close, and Second Lieutenant Jacob Beser, who was monitoring Japanese communications, reported activity on the Japanese fighter direction radio bands. It was only a matter of time before Japanese Zeroes would cut the B-29 to pieces.

Sweeney then proceeded to the alternative target, Nagasaki. It too was obscured by clouds, and Ashworth ordered Sweeney to make a radar approach. At the last minute, the bombardier, Captain Kermit K. Beahan, found a hole in the clouds. The Fat Man was dropped and, following a 43-second duration free fall, it exploded at 11:02 local time, at an altitude of about 1,650 feet (500 m).

Because of poor visibility due to cloud cover, the bomb missed its intended detonation point by almost two miles, and damage was somewhat less extensive than that in Hiroshima. The bomb was far more powerful than the fission-type weapon dropped on Hiroshima.

An estimated 35,000–40,000 people were killed immediately. Another 30,000-40,000 died from long-term health effects, a slow and agonizing death the entire world witnessed. Most of the direct deaths and injuries sustained from the bombing were munitions or industrial workers, not soldiers. It was the last time nuclear weaponry had ever been used against humans. The horror was so vast, that the threat of using such weapons would prevent war between nuclear-capable countries.

The ancient Syndicate spent centuries bringing mankind to a full understanding of weaponry powerful enough to end all life. It became possible to capture the world merely with the fear of using them. Sanity, however, prevailed. Though nearly three thousand weapons were tested, none was used to kill another human being. All that was required now, was to create the appearance of a leader who could actually do it again.

The problem with tritium—an isotope of hydrogen—is that there is nearly no naturally occurring tritium, so it has to be synthesized. This is done in specially designed reactors, which aren't easy to build and generate tiny amounts of tritium at a time. It is extremely small, making it difficult to contain. It is slightly radioactive with alpha decay similar to radon gas, but is almost impossible to detect unless it is very close. In gaseous form, it is fairly safe. A solid sphere of tritium and deuterium the size of a basketball, imploded to the size of a walnut, can produce an efficient release of energy equivalent to a thousand times that of Nagasaki.

The design challenge is holding the atomic explosion long enough under sun-like conditions to kickstart fusion. Traditionally, this has been accomplished with a nuclear fission explosion. In other words, an atom bomb sets off a hydrogen bomb. But the payoff can be thousands of times more destructive than an atom bomb.

The biggest hydrogen bomb ever tested, Tsar Bomba weighed more than 50 thousand pounds and was more than 3 thousand times bigger than the atomic bomb that was used in Hiroshima. It was tested in 1961 in a remote part of Russia. Anyone within 65 miles of the blast would suffer third-degree burns from the radiation released. The blast wave broke window panes 550 miles away. It was all part of building the fear, for a weapon of this size and weight could never be delivered to its target without being destroyed by enemy aircraft long before reaching it.

There was no fear of something very large like this. There was fear, however, in something very small. But accomplishing something so powerful, so small, and so terrible would require advanced knowledge in microelectronics. It would require nano-technological metallurgy skills far surpassing the Gallium-Plutonium casting techniques used by previous weapons designers. It would require decades of isolation from the world with supercomputers specifically designed to simulate the quantum possibilities of high-energy neutrons injected billionths of second after the explosion of a few ounces of compressed tritium began. It would require a pure and merciless soul to keep a scientific community and a military command structure from losing their resolve.

The only society capable of crafting microelectronics of this nature is located in Korea. The only place isolated enough and immersed in hatred enough to focus on a nuclear detonator that would fit into a gym bag was North Korea. The priceless research and designs were delivered to them under the direction of President Bill Clinton on May 11th, 1999. Although the New York Times reported the only thing transferred was the technology for exploding bolts that would facilitate the final stage separation of a multi-stage rocket, they continued to help them develop their first nuclear weapon, which was successfully tested on the 9th of October a little more than 6 years later. It is virtually impossible to have created a nuclear bomb with a tidy 2 kiloton yield in that amount of time without close corroboration with Western science.

Less than three years later, on the 25th of May, 2009 they tested a vastly improved design with 5.4 kilotons of explosive power. The micro-sized weapons were not designed to dig holes a mile wide. They were designed to be small enough to be easy to deploy and to create an electro-magnetic pulse capable of burning out integrated circuits for hundreds of miles. By the 3rd of September 2017, they had succeeded nine times and finally learned how to supercharge the explosion with Tritium to a level of 280 kilotons; enough to obliterate an entire major city and wipe out electrical circuits up to a thousand miles away.

The fact that the technology was so powerful is frightening enough. The realization that it was developed through a secretly joint effort with Clinton's massive Syndicate is simply chilling to behold. It is the possession of such a weapon by a madman like Kim Jong Un that should put the entire world on high alert. There is no reason to think the Clinton playbook will not be used. If the Clinton's enemies get too annoyed, or the press gets too close to reporting the truth, *Little Kim* may receive his marching orders to send a nuclear care package to the United States.

The official story from the propaganda press would have people believe that such a weapon would have to be delivered with an Intercontinental Ballistic Missile (ICBM), and that we would have about forty-five minutes to shoot it harmlessly out of the sky. North Korea would even test dozens of empty decoys to make sure the world stayed focused on that narrative.

But the Syndicate is deceptive. The North Koreans may simply place submarines off the east coast, the west coast, and the Gulf coast that each have the capability of launching missiles from beneath the surface. These missiles are capable of carrying a nuclear warhead. It is all too easy to hide a submarine among the mostly abandoned 25 thousand oil rigs along American coasts. They just have to sit there for months at a time, waiting for the orders to come. If a missile is launched from one of these secret locations, it may strike its target in about 6 minutes. What can you get done in 6 minutes?

The press would also have the public believe there are 17 different intelligence agencies. There are not. There only 17 different political appointees that can take classified information in 17 different directions at once, all under the command of the Syndicate. The Clinton Crime Syndicate laid the groundwork by appointing each and every one of these agency directors. The planned attack on the World Trade Centers on September 11, 2001 provided the opportunity to implement thousands of pages of previously crafted law designed for the sole purpose of instantly changing the world into a surveillance State, completely under the auspices of one global authority.

The Syndicate seized control of every airport on the planet with scheduled airline service within weeks. Never before has any authority acted with such power and such effectiveness. The public was led to believe the changes were to stop terrorism. The true purpose was to provide this central authority the power to define terrorism in their own terms. In less than 10 years, once a person committed an offense against this authority, every move, every contact they made going back for months could be traced. What became apparent very quickly was that members of the Syndicate were not investigated. Only enemies of this new Deep State were investigated. The only question remaining was whether that enemy could be used to further the mission of the Syndicate or not. That mission has not changed in thousands of years.

Deep in the forests surrounding the Stennis Space Center the process of chilling and compressing Tritium is simple and indistinguishable from the process of producing and storing hydrogen for the testing of rocket boosters. No one would miss a few hundred pounds of liquid hydrogen. Most of the valves and connections throughout the test buildings leak that much in a single day. The compressor arrived over a series of weeks, one piece of micro-machined tool steel at a time. Some parts came from Texas. Some came from Louisiana. Some came from Florida. The rest came from Detroit by car and by bus.

Adnan worked quietly for Rolls Royce as a C++ programmer. The drawings of various booster systems were divided into compartments by government policy guidelines. No program group would see any more of the drawing than was assigned to their group. The program language controlled various actuators, solenoids, and rotating valves. Inputs of real-world information arrives from thermocouples sensing temperature, from transducers sensing strain or pressure, and the stress placed on various structural components by thrust and changes in atmospheric pressure. The program had to insert the inputs into sequences of complex of virtual circuits made of timers, counters, and switches to control the outputs so that the booster would function. Each program had to be validated and debugged. There were protocols and quality standards that usually slowed the entire process to a crawl because, they had to be stitched together, so that one section of the program would integrate with the other sections of the program without forming loops, echoes, or dead ends.

It was a world that only a hard core programmer could love. There was no room for errors. There were programs to help find the errors, but at the end of the day it was the human mind that created the system. Once an employer discovered such a human mind, there were always concessions that had to be made. Strange diets, musical tastes, and even sexual orientations were tolerated and managed by very talented people capable of juggling various psychotic tendencies to get the job done. Programmers never saw a reporter. They never went on camera. They rarely saw sunshine. No one cared at all if someone wanted to live in an old pump shop deep in the woods, running on solar panels and old forklift batteries.

Chapter 13

"This plan has worked in every country where it has been tried. We've actually gotten quite good at it," said Lim Shun.

"You may have succeeded in places like Norway or China, but America is different. It's not going to be that easy," said Bill.

"It is simply a matter of carnage. Look how it is working in the Palestinian situation. Just let me handle everything," said Lim Shun.

"I can't believe you used that as one of your success stories. That is a disaster, and you know it," said Bill.

"It is based on an ancient system. Older than this world, I can tell you. You attack and torment the dragon in his golden lair until he becomes angry enough to fly down and incinerate the village. You show the pictures of all the charred innocent children and church choirs to the armies of the world, and they go kill the dragon for you. Then, you take his gold," said Lim Shun.

"That's a kid's story. Now, I understand having the cameras set up around the school yard when the Israelis hit back, after the rocket attack. That is a stroke of genius. But, you can't poke and prod America like a dragon. Our military can drop a package down your chimney from 50 thousand feet and vaporize a problem. No pictures to show, and very little collateral damage. Besides, all the armies in the world cannot defeat the American military," said Bill.

"The principle is the same, nonetheless. We get the dragon to eat its own tail," said Lim Shun.

"The Oruborus," said Bill as a matter of question.

"That is one eternal round. What I am proposing is a way to make the dragon consume itself," said Lim Shun.

"I did not go from being a lawyer in the Podunk State of Arkansas to the most powerful man in the world in a single generation by being a patient man, Mr. Lim. When I finish this cigar, our time here will be finished," said Bill.

"The long part of our plan is already completed. America is divided into two. One part believes that rights come from God, and the other part believes rights come from government. They disagree on almost everything," said Lim Shun

"You're behind the times, Mr. Lim. We have done way better than that. My friends own all forms of major media; movies, news broadcasts, music, and even the contractors that provide most of the government services. We have the poor ready to kill off the rich. We have blacks thinking whitey is out to get them, and there is hardly a white person who doesn't fear the same thing about blacks. I really think our whole ISIS marketing plan was sheer genius. Man, if it wasn't for those damned bloggers and social platforms, this whole thing would never have been possible. I used to hate those guys when I was president. It's taken 50 years, more or less, but I think we have them right where we want them," said Bill exhaling a large draw on his cigar. "Still, I don't think you're going to get past the armed American."

"We need to have a series of mass shootings. Perhaps we should expand your original idea of Fast and Furious. That should be the next part of the plan," said Lim Shun.

"That's not that easy to do. My associates already chose a few prime candidates. After months of psychotropic drugs, and hypnosis, a few of them shot up a public place or two. We tried killing all those folks at Waco and Ruby Ridge, but no matter what we tried, the public wouldn't buy it. Besides, most of these mass shooters were so wiped out on drugs, they couldn't hit anything," said Bill walking over by the fireplace.

"It is important to make sure the people develop a fear of the weapons themselves," said Lim Shun.

"Look, we got soldiers of Islam to attack things like Christmas parties, but that had the opposite effect altogether. And. every time we make a public move on the gun manufacturers or ammo suppliers, gun sales go through the roof. I mean it. Lookey here; Obama doesn't have much to hang his hat on, but he's the greatest gun salesman the world has ever known. You have to come up with something better than that," said Bill.

"That was merely testing the perimeter. We now have the politicians in position. The entertainers and sports stars are in position. All that is required now is to have my associates conduct a few events, and the Americans will disarm themselves for you," said Lim Shun.

"I thought that was against the rules. Your associates have some kind of contract limitation, right? You can't just step in and take over a person," said Bill drawing circles in the dark air of the private library with the cherry smoking end of his cigar.

"We can go wherever we are invited," said Lim Shun.

"There are rules about that as well. I studied war, you know. We perfected the whole *ctrl-alt-del* thing using Wars-R-us to replace news headlines we didn't like. We bent the rules a little over there in Kosovo, and the whole thing began to fall apart there at the end, but at least they got my name out of the papers. Old Slobodan did go to prison," said Bill.

"Yes. We remember. That was another one of your loose ends we had to clean up. This may take some time. It takes longer than 30 years to take over a planet," said Lim Shun.

"Tell me about it. I think I like the old ways better. You just shoot 'em in the head and crash the plane," said Bill with a chuckle.

"I am showing you the old ways," said Lim Shun.

"Your old ways, and my old ways are different. I would like to get this done in my lifetime, Mr. Lim," said Bill puffing the cigar aggressively.

"As I was saying, my associates have been invited by souls in despair. They only require a few days to accomplish the mission. I think if we raise the bar for mass shootings, it should leave anyone who still believes owning a gun is a God-given right in a very small, radical and unpopular minority. If we combine the firepower of Fast and Furious with a large enough crowd of patriots, a ban on weapons should be widely supported by the public, more or less. You coordinate the press, the entertainers, and the sports heroes, and America will begin to disarm itself willingly. Once that is partially complete, we will be ready for the next part of the plan," said Lim Shun.

"Don't you worry about them. The money is already in the bank. We even have a few good theme songs put together. Hell, kids will be singing them like London Bridge is falling down," said Bill laughing himself into a raspy cough.

"Just don't make the same mistake again," said Lim Shun.

"What mistake are you talking about?" asked Bill looking down into Lim Shun's intense brown eyes.

"Letting your actors think they are actually in charge," said Lim Shun.

"We've done a good job with that actually. Look at the attention Hillary is getting these days. She's more famous than fried chicken. Worshipped by 47% of the people," said Bill, chuckling.

"And hated by the rest. That's not exactly what we had in mind," said Lim Shun.

"Yeah, but have you ever seen a more focused woman in all your life? She wakes up every day knowing it's just not enough. Absolutely amazing, the deals we have going," said Bill.

"She lost the election," said Lim Shun flatly.

"It's not for lack of trying. We got the nomination easily enough. We controlled the entire Democrat National Committee. Look here, we brought in all the money, so naturally it belonged to us. We recorded everything Trump and his people said 24 hours a day, and even went back to some NBC files and hit him with that. Nothing worked against the guy. Kind of reminds me of me," said Bill.

"Your lust for power and our long-term planning could have been even more successful, you know. You sold far more influence than you can now deliver. These are difficult accounts to settle. You see, we are not the only organization with a *charm of favor*," said Lim Shun coldly.

"Oh, this ain't over. Not by a long shot. I think the people have had just about enough of Mr. Trump. Wait until they see the little insurrection we have planned," said Bill puffing a cloud of thick smoke and blowing through it.

"I think those plans are still being reviewed," said Lim Shun.

"Oh come on now. I know your boss loves nothing better than a good old fashioned street fight," said Bill.

"For the record, you don't work for me. I'm just the messenger. Oaths have rules," said Lim Shun facing Bill.

"We know what the terms are, Mr. Lim. And we have never wavered from our end of the bargain," said Bill.

"Not to take gratuitous license, but that depends on what the meaning of the word 'wavered,' is. We have lived up to our end," said Lim Shun shortly.

"Look. The boss has been good to me. Gave me a life that would shame a king. A deal's a deal," said Bill, inwardly reassessing that even the longest mortal life is but a few moments to an almost immortal being.

"Very well. I will let you finish your cigar in peace. Until we meet again," said Lim Shun firmly shaking Bill's hand. He turned and walked smoothly for the door of the library. It opened from the other side as he approached, and his body guard stepped aside for him to exit. Bill heard the echo of the front door closing in the large foyer outside his library.

The limousine idled silently up to the steps of the Chappaquiddick mansion. His bodyguard opened the rear passenger door, and he stepped inside to sit on the leather couch. The bodyguard closed the door and stepped into the passenger side of the front seat. The small screen facing the back couch flickered for a moment and in a few seconds displayed a logo with a side-facing eagle. "Report," said the gravely male voice as the vehicle began moving forward.

"He is agreeable to our plan," said Mr. Lim to the voice.

"This is becoming increasingly important to me," said the voice.

"Your perspective is understandably different than ours," said Lim Shun.

"Seasons come and go, Mr. Lim, but they come and go on time," said the voice.

"There are always signs, sir," said Lim Shun.

"I have been providing wealth and power to humans since the beginning of time, and I have always been disappointed. They love to serve when they are young, but the populace will not follow a young person. And when they are old, they begin to complain about the payment for what I have given them," said the voice.

"Greed is only one side of the blade that carves a path through mortality. Fear cuts just as deeply," said Lim Shun.

"It is easy to make a person have fear. It is quite another thing for a people," said the voice.

"He is implementing Operation Dew Claw," said Lim Shun.

"That puts many things in motion," said the voice.

"Soros and Singer have committed the funds. The date has been set for the national insurrection," said Lim Shun.

"I don't think a few broken windows will make Americans afraid," said the voice.

"People are afraid of the dark," said Lim Shun.

"The device is ready," said the voice.

"Your man is prepared to deploy?" asked Lim Shun.

"If enough people can be, shall we say, inspired to join in the Operation, it will go well with my team. We just have to time this right to get the best results," said the voice.

"Men would have quit by now to preserve their own flesh. She is far more bloodthirsty than any male we have ever groomed," said Lim Shun.

"Women are just as eager to trade their flesh for fame and glory," said the voice.

"There is a difference, sir. Men prefer to trade someone else's flesh to achieve their power," said Lim Shun.

"You say it like sacrificing children is a bad thing to achieve power and glory forever," said the voice.

"Things are different now. Technology allows us to disseminate knowledge in seconds around the world. Society has become instant and disposable. The people just want sex, and to be cared for, like always. They have replaced joy with pleasure, and god with drugs. It's their capacity for hatred that is most fascinating," said Lim Shun.

"You patronize me, Mr. Lim. It is sweet savor to watch them fight, but intoxicating to watch them scrub mercy from existence with their hatred. When the lights go out, we shall see their true nature erupt," said the voice.

"The innocent will escape us," said Lim Shun.

"There are no innocent. Not anymore," spat the voice after a brief silence.

"You have made it more difficult for them, but there are still some who maintain their sovereignty here and there," said Lim Shun.

"There is no place for them to run. There is no wilderness. There is no refuge. My soldiers own the banks that own their homes. We own the Parties that own their candidates. We own the media they watch, the books they read, and schools they attend for higher learning," said the voice like it was trying to convince itself.

"Your best work, sir, by far is with the religions," said Lim Shun, knowing the effect it would have.

A deep breath could be heard over the speakers in the limousine's chamber. "I cannot take all the credit for that one. To craft one religion focused on self-sacrifice and another on spreading its gospel with the sword is the way it has been done for billions of years. However, to do it so well, so balanced and sustainable for so long. It is so much like raising mice to feed your snake, don't you think?" asked the voice almost providing Mr. Lim a chance to lecture the voice.

"Two voices take the song to a higher level, sir," said Lim Shun.

"Harmony, Mister Lim. You speak of harmony. I want dissonance. I want humans to choose misery and beat themselves for choosing it. I want them to sell their own flesh for a meal and curse that they have grown fat. I want them to dream of tomorrow with a cynicism so thick they cannot move. I want them to kill everything in sight to preserve their own life, and then despair when they take their own life as they follow their victims to hell," said the voice.

"We were just talking about that very topic," said Lim Shun.

"It is time for the special campaign," said the voice.

"We have tested every possible approach. Blacks shooting blacks in places like Chicago is completely ignored," said Lim Shun.

"I told you this. Killing out of necessity for business or to remove competitors is worthless. Even the first murder on this planet was completely ignored by God, because it was business and nothing personal," said the voice.

"As I was saying, we tried religious genocide, and even mass murder of entire church families on live television, but the people were not moved. We even produced videos with public execution of innocent Christians by sawing off their heads with knives. They simply went about their lives as normal, and those responsible for the slaughter never saw a second of justice. Mr. Clinton doubts Americans will ever give up their guns," said Lim Shun.

"It matters not. In the end, hatred is an acquired taste, Mr. Lim. Humans play at it with sports, business, and even religions. It's when they are willing to charge across the frozen tundra with a battle axe, screaming under a banner, that it really puts the meat on the bone. Once the killing starts, the one-upmanship never ends, until there is only one man standing, and he will gladly end his own life rather than live another day with the pain. That is a good day for business," said the voice.

"How do we proceed, sir?" asked Lim Shun. One had to be careful at this point in the conversation.

"You know the rules, Mr. Lim," said the voice.

"The shooter that has been prepared is white," said Lim Shun.

"I am well aware of that," said the voice.

"If he does not kill enough innocent people, or it does not get enough publicity, or the victims are too much of one race or another, we will not be successful," said Lim Shun.

"Let's stick to the theme. Tell me what you think that is, Mr. Lim," requested the voice.

"To create a world of fear where a man can run to and fro, searching for the truth, and never find salvation," said Lim Shun.

"And, why is that?" asked the voice.

"Because it will not exist," said Lim Shun.

"That is correct. And, what is the one thing left on the Earth that prevents that from being the case?" asked the voice, as though scolding a child who played too long and forgot to empty the trash.

"America," said Lim Shun coldly.

"More specifically, it is the armed American. We need to get them to believe it is not just a deterrent against the unlikely event they have to overthrow the government; although, I do love a good bloody revolution. We want them to lock and load and get ready to fight in their own neighborhoods," said the voice.

"Mr. Soros and Mr. Singer have provided the resources, as you commanded. Mr. Obama has organized his people. Aside from some last minute greed and acts of self-preservation, the soldiers are in place in every major city in America. Coupled with the device, we have the recipe for what Mr. Clinton says will be the biggest street fight in history," said Lim Shun.

"How are we coming with the invasion?" asked the voice.

"Europe is ours for the taking. The same with Indochina. We have a few cities in America, perhaps a state or two. Japan, Hungary, and some others are complete non-starters," said Lim Shun.

"We can agree that Americans have been turned against one another? That this inconvenient concept of liberty and freedom will have no champion left. Correct?" asked the voice as though only one answer was allowed.

"I fear it is more than a concept, sir," said Lim Shun.

"No. It is a concept. You have rights only if I say you have rights," said the voice.

"That is precisely what they claim in their Constitution," said Lim Shun trying to make his point.

"I never agreed to that," spat the voice loud enough to clip the display system's amplifier.

"It did not require your agreement. Besides, humans do not widely even know that you exist," said Lim Shun.

"They all know I exist and they fear me," said the voice.

"They fear a concept of you. But they do not know you the way I do," said Lim Shun.

"You do not fear me?" asked the voice quietly.

"I didn't say that. I know that light is not native to the universe. All of this is an illusion. The stars, planets, time. They are not real. I am at peace with this truth, and nothing anyone does will ever change that. Energy can't go anywhere. This is a game, and to be clear of it is the goal of awareness. Do I fear that? No. Not really," said Lim Shun.

"I enjoy our conversations," said the voice regaining his composure.

"I still require some assistance with our special event in Las Vegas. After months of research, we finally have the right crowd of people, and have taken the proper precautions to ensure success. And, we have been invited," said Lim Shun.

"Yes, I know. We have to be careful. Killing innocents with my soldiers gains us nothing," said the voice.

"I am aware of that. Humans will do the shooting of their own free will; technically speaking. As you have done already, they need protection to make the mission possible, without their knowledge of course, in accordance with the rules. Confusion, misdirection, interference are always very helpful in these matters. As fast as the news cycle is now, within a few days, any conspiracy of our involvement can be diluted from consideration by nearly everyone," said Lim Shun.

"That is one of the nicest things about global non-stop news," said the voice.

"When these shootings take place, we will not focus on the person doing the shooting. His race? Yes, of course. His religion? Absolutely. But they will find no such motives this time.. What we want to focus on is the weapon itself. Who made it? What does it look like? How does it function? How the weapon itself did the killing," said Lim Shun.

"Clever boy," said the voice.

"If we can get some extra influence in this area, while protecting the Syndicate, and our personnel, from any implication," said Lim Shun leaving the sentence open.

"Consider it done. We are aligned then?" asked the voice.

"Yes, sir," said Lim Shun.

"I assume you have everything in place," said the voice.

"Correct," said Lim Shun.

"No loose ends. The Clintons always had loose ends," said the voice.

"We have made sure his indiscretions never caused any trouble," said Lim Shun.

"Like you took care of Danny Casalaro; that freelance reporter with the 'October Surprise'?" asked the voice.

"It was settled," said Lim Shun.

"You had him cut to pieces in his hotel bathtub," said the voice.

"He had a suicide. Sad young man. They never found any of his research," said Lim Shun.

"What about Paul Tully, the trusted Democratic National Committee Political Director found dead in a hotel room in Little Rock? What about the man with the evidence for the grand jury? What was his name? Oh yes, Ian Spiro, his wife and 3 children shot in the head at home? And then there was his speechwriter, Paula Grober killed in her car. What did she do wrong? Then there was Mack McClarty. He makes a call from the ski lodge to our boy, and dies is a skiing accident right after the call?

"Or, like the Coleman girl 40 years ago? Clinton was what, 31 years old and already the Attorney General? She was pregnant, too. He could have used a car and dumped her in the river, but I guess we used that one already. I suppose all this cleanup labor has been worth it. We all take risks, don't we?" asked the voice.

"Not all of us," said Lim Shun.

"I look forward to reading about your success about this mass shooting, Mr. Lim," said the voice.

"Until then, my master."

Chapter 14

"Hey Jackie, how are you doing? I'm coming to your graduation, by the way," said James.

"You better. And don't call me Jackie, asshole," said Jack.

"Is that any way to talk to your oldest brother? Come on," said James.

"The reason I called is that I wanted to tell you I applied to be a Federal intern. My history teacher, Mr. Larsen? I told you about him. Awesome teacher. Anyway, he says he can get me into the Pentagon as an intern," said Jack twisting her legs together.

"The Pentagon? That's kind of a fast track over there, but at least you won't get groped by those capitol pukes," said James.

"That's what I thought, too. I just wanted you to know, because you kind of work in this stuff," said Jack.

"Oh yeah. We love the pork in the road business," said James.

"I'm not looking to make it a career, or anything. I hate politics. But Mr. Larsen has really taught us some things that explain why things are the way they are in Washington," said Jack.

"Well, maybe you could teach me, 'cuz I've been up here for five years, and it feels criminal from top to bottom," said James.

"Oh for sure, but he says that if good people take those jobs, then things will change," said Jack.

"That's what they all say. They come here good, but after a few months the dirt gets into everything, and everyone. You start doing what everyone else does," said James.

"What does that mean?" asked Jack.

"You start looking out for number one. Everyone gets what they can get, and then just when you think you can escape, you get sued or threatened with arrest. I don't know. It's like a game of blackmail and invasion of privacy. It just gets weird," said James.

"Well, anyway. I'm going to be taking the train to the Pentagon Monday morning for an interview. Maybe we could have lunch near the Smithsonian or something," said Jack.

"That would be nice, but the President is speaking the following night, and we have a bunch of wining and dining to do. I think we're in Silver Springs that day," said James.

"What's he speaking about? Not that I care," said Jack.

"Bacon bacon bacon. He's got this whole energy thing he wants the taxpayers to pay for. This guy is going to shame Maytag out of business," said James.

"What?" asked Jack.

"They make washing machines. This guy can read a teleprompter, I'll say that for him," said James.

"I don't get it. I'm not infected, remember? What are you talking about?" asked Jack.

"Laundry, Jack. It's a game they play. Donors give money to the DNC. The President pays them back with a healthy profit using grants and shit with taxpayer money. It's done all the time, but taking a look at the lobbyist newsletter on this one tells me Obama is taking it to a whole new level," said James.

"Isn't that illegal or something?" asked Jack.

"It's SOP for D.C.," said James.

"There you go again," said Jack.

"Standard operating procedure. It's the way it works here, and they only have a few more weeks to line their pockets. The election will bring in a whole new team of hungry appointees. Any way you look at it, the taxpayer gets hosed, but usually, it's more subtle," said James.

"Like with the highway department?" chided Jack.

"Hey. My clients build roads, bridges, highways and even airports. Most of that stuff lasts for 50 years or more. Besides, most of the money comes from the taxes on fuel that power the cars and trucks that use the stuff these guys build. It gets paid back a dozen times over. Seriously, can you drive more than 25 miles anywhere in America and not see an orange barrel? No," said James.

"So, maybe this new energy thing will finally end up being the same way," said Jack.

"You would hope so, but I don't think some solar company in Fremont, California is going to make half a billion in tax revenue," said James.

"You're kidding, right?" asked Jack.

"I wish I was. Look, the way it works is that these bundlers go out and gather up a truckload of money pledges from these donors who want big grants and loan guarantees. The bundler goes to the DNC or to the President himself, sometimes, and turns in the pledges. I don't know what the going rate is, but it can be up to 50% of the award. Sometimes, it's a repayment for something they did for them. It's like when Navistar bought that struggling bus company for $39 million. There was $39 million in Obama's grant package for Navistar. Eventually, they'll sell to some Indian or Chinese bus maker, and the money gets laundered nice and clean. In exchange, the Democrats get billions to run attack ads against Republicans, and that's the ball game," said James.

"But all this is like under the table, right?" asked Jack.

"Oh, it used to be. Why do you think we lease an office on K Street? This is the meat market. I mean, this is where elected officials spend half their fundraising time. Why do you think the D.C. Ferrari dealership is the highest volume dealer in the country? This little empire here makes that shit happen," said James.

"A Ferrari isn't very smart if you're trying to hide the fact that you're getting filthy rich off of the taxpayers," said Jack.

"Oh that's peanuts. A car is only a weekend perk. We're talking millions a year, here. Everyone has been so deep for so long that no one will ever get caught, because they're all in on the game. They won't bite the hand that feeds them," said James.

"I thought we fed them. Don't they work for us?" asked Jack.

"It's cost plus," said James getting short with her.

"It's theft," said Jack.

"Yep. Cost, plus all you can take," said James.

"So what happens now after tomorrow?" asked Jack.

"Look, I have to go here. My guess is that some solar panel company will get a screaming loan guarantee, borrow all the money, barely pay back the DNC, and go belly up. That's what I think," said James.

"I hope all those assholes get caught," said Jack.

"Oh they will, but they'll all take the fifth before Congress, everybody looks like they did their best, and nothing will ever be heard about it again," said James.

"Holy crap," said Jack.

"That's why they call this place the swamp," said James.

"And tell me, why do I want to go to work in the swamp?" asked Jack.

"Because your teacher's right, Jackie. We need good people to make it better," said James.

"Asshole," said Jack.

"I gotta go for now. I love you little sister," said James.

"Love you too. Bye," and Jack hung up the phone.

"It begins with energy. We know the country that harnesses the power of clean, renewable energy will lead the 21st century. And yet it is China that has launched the largest effort in history to make their economy energy efficient. We invented solar technology, but we've fallen behind countries like Germany and Japan in producing it. New plug-in hybrids roll off our assembly lines, but they will run on batteries made in Korea.

"Well, I do not accept a future where the jobs and industries of tomorrow take root beyond our borders, and I know you don't, either. It is time for America to lead again.

"Thanks to our recovery plan, we will double this nation's supply of renewable energy in the next three years. We've also made the largest investment in basic research funding in American history, an investment that will spur not only new discoveries in energy, but breakthroughs in medicine, in science and technology.

"We will soon lay down thousands of miles of power lines that can carry new energy to cities and towns across this country. And we will put Americans to work making our homes and buildings more efficient so that we can save billions of dollars on our energy bills.

"But to truly transform our economy, to protect our security and save our planet from the ravages of climate change, we need to ultimately make clean, renewable energy the profitable kind of energy. So I ask this Congress to send me legislation that places a market-based cap on carbon pollution and drives the production of more renewable energy in America. That's what we need.

"And to support -- to support that innovation, we will invest $15 billion a year to develop technologies like wind power and solar power, advanced biofuels, clean coal, and more efficient cars and trucks built right here in America."[2]

Monday came too quickly, as usual, and Jack decided to take the bus to the train station rather than walk. It made it easier to choose her blade heels to go with her black slacks. There was no chance she was walking ten blocks in heels when it was thirty degrees outside, anyway.

By seven AM, she was through the cattle chutes at the station along with a couple hundred other commuters heading to work. The ride was quiet and smooth as it stopped a half-dozen stations before

---

[2] Excerpt from President Barack Obama's speech to Congress Feb 24, 2009

reaching the Pentagon. She checked her phone again for the name of the person that was meeting her and took the stairs up to the main entrance ramp. The employees swiped their badges and walked straight, while she turned left to check in at the information desk. There was a small set of theater-style seats set up in front of a podium that had a large, official looking plaque above it that said, 'United States Pentagon.' She took a seat away from the other five contractor types dressed in suits laundered too many times. She pulled out her phone and checked her email and read a text message from her brother, James, saying good luck.

"Jack Rousseau?" came the young male voice.

"That's me," said Jack as she stood up to greet the young Air Force Major with a firm handshake.

"It's Miss Rousseau," said the Major slowly showing his surprise.

"Yes. Miss. I'm here for the intern interview," said Jack.

"Great. Come with me please," said the Major.

The two walked to the manned security checked station, and the Major walked through with Jack close behind. She put her phone and pocketbook through the scanner and walked through the metal detector timidly. She smiled at the expressionless green uniform and picked up her pocketbook and phone to continue walking with the Major.

The first hallway was as wide as some streets with office doors and shops along both sides. The ceilings were more than twelve feet high, and she got the feeling that even if this place got busy, there would be plenty of room to move around. Whoever designed this building wanted visitors to feel small and powerless. On any given day, there were close to four thousand people that worked in the Pentagon.

There was a Starbucks and a barbershop on one side and what looked like a couple of courtrooms on the other side. They came to an intersection and turned left down a hallway that was only about two cars wide for about fifty yards and entered another intersection, where they turned right. She could see the layout in her mind as five, five-sided rings one inside the other. The further in they went, the more stars she saw on the shoulders of the people in the hallways.

"This is it. Have a seat, and the General will be with you shortly," said the Major.

She sat carefully and didn't cross her legs. 'A General?' she mused as she raised her eyebrows for a moment. She reached into her pocket and turned off her phone and looked around the ante room of the small suite. The light colored wood paneling looked dated, and the furnishings were gray and made of metal. 'It's not even as nice as the dentist office,' she thought to herself. Almost without a sound a lean man in a light blue shirt with dark blue plants with a stripe down the outside walked into the room and gave her a polite nod. The four chrome stars on his shoulders sparkled under the fluorescent lights as he passed her and walked straight to the rear of the suite, and into the open doorway. She thought she heard talking, but it was too soft and polite to make out the words. Within moments, he reemerged and walked past her again glancing at her with clear blue eyes. 'A pilot,' she thought. Four stars. Maybe an astronaut.

"Miss Rousseau, it is nice to finally meet you," came the female voice walking toward her.

"Oh, yes. Same here, uh, General," started Jack as she rose to her feet.

"You are tall, aren't you? Tommy told me all about you, but he didn't say you were so tall," said the General.

"Oh, it's the heels. I'm only five ten," said Jack.

"I'm General Stacy Banks. People call me all kinds of things, I think. But, you can call me General Banks. Okay?" said General Banks.

"Yes. I mean yes ma'am. General," said Jack stumbling over her words.

"It's fine. Come on in, have a seat, and let's talk about things," said General Banks.

Jack took a deep breath and walked into the General's office. The wood paneling was the same, but there were pictures of rockets and billowing clouds coming out of buildings made of blue and gray steel. In the book case behind the desk was a photo of a football team with a ribbon hanging over the corner. Below that were a crystal trophy of some kind and a tiny model of a space shuttle on a mahogany stand. The desk was cleared, except for a single screen and a keyboard, along with a speaker and a phone. She chose the left seat and sat carefully into it and slid back so her spine was straight. She fought the urge to cross her legs, and suddenly felt inside like she was balancing on the balls of her feet, waiting for the first move.

"You go by Jack. Is that right?" asked General Banks sitting heavily in her chair.

"Yes, General," said Jack.

"Generals are like aircraft carriers. They have carrier groups made of a dozen ships, a hundred planes, subs, and even spacecraft that are part of their command structure. We're the same way. I have 171 staff members led from here and stationed in Mississippi, Florida, and places I can't share with you. My command is responsible for protecting America as part of the Department of Homeland Security," began General Banks. It sounded for a brief moment like an excerpt from a speech or a formal presentation, until she smiled and leaned back in her large, brown leather office chair.

"I'm sure we're safe," said Jack searching for something to say.

"Well, we're not. We not only have to watch our enemies outside the country, we have to watch our enemies inside the country, and some of them we can't do a damned thing about," said General Banks.

"Inside the country?" asked Jack instantly wishing she had said nothing.

"As my intern, your job will be to run for me, and believe me there is a lot of running in this place. Ditch those heels. When you come back to work, um, let's see. When is that?" said the General thumbing through a yellow pad on her desk. "The 5th of April it says here. When you come back, wear black sneakers instead of black heels. You'll be doing about five miles a day in this place. Is that okay?" asked General Banks, as though it was an order.

"Yes, General," said Jack smiling slightly now. She was worried she would be stuck at a desk or filing papers all day. The fact there was some physical activity with the job made her already feel more comfortable with the job.

"And lose your phone. No phones in here. When you come back. Major, would you come in here for a moment?" said General Banks directing her voice toward the door without raising it even slightly.

"Yes, General Banks," said the Major stepping silently into the doorway.

"This is Major Mead. He came to us from missile command. One of our many adjustments we have had to make with the recent budget changes," said General Banks, not hiding her resentment. "He is going to take you through the rest of your orientation. You'll be squared away by, oh about twelve hundred or so. It was nice meeting you," she said standing without much effort and gripping Jack's hand more than firmly.

Major Mead turned his shined low quarters on the balls of his feet and the two of them walked out into the hallway and turned left to the first intersection. This time, they headed into the inner ring of the Pentagon. "That's not what I was expecting," said Jack finally.

"A female General?" asked Major Mead.

"No. I mean not really that. She was intense. I mean threats in the country, and stuff. She had a spaceship on her shelf," said Jack as they walked smoothly. He was the same height as her, even with her heels, and he was lean with pale skin. 'He probably hasn't seen sunshine in a year,' she thought.

"The X-37b," said Major Mead.

"A space shuttle?" asked Jack not really sure to what he was referring.

"Sort of. It was an unmanned space shuttle NASA was working on. When the budget cuts came, and believe me they were like a meat cleaver, they dropped the project. We acquired it within 24 hours and enrolled it into our rapid deployment budget. Off the books, of course. We made a number of them, and there is always one in space as we speak," said Major Mead.

"What do they do?" asked Jack.

"Can't tell you," said Major Mead.

"I know. That's classified," said Jack making quotation marks in the air with her fingers.

"Well, yeah, but I can't tell you anyway because I have no clue what it does," said Major Mead.

"You work for the General that owns the project, and you don't know what it does? That's spooky," said Jack as they turned right down the inner ring of the Pentagon and headed for an open door facing the inside courtyard of the building.

"It's not up there for nothing. The most expensive cargo bay in the world. Trust me. They don't waste it. Here we are," said Major Mead standing aside to let her go in first. He came in close behind her and stood next to her at attention. She didn't know how to stand at attention, so she put her feet together and her hands at her side. The room faced a large plate glass window outside of which was a sort of sitting garden. There were a few trees, some flowers and small pond with lilies floating in the water. She couldn't help but wonder how out of place it looked. Like it was planet Earth on display, the way it used to be before mankind had destroyed it.

"Come on in, Major," came the deep voice from the office to the right of the empty receptionist desk.

Major Mead motioned silently with his head as he stepped forward with his left foot like he was marching into a parade review. Jack followed closely behind. "Sir, this is," began Major Mead.

"I know who this is. Hello Jack," said the deep, smooth voice. Jack was tall for a woman. She could look most men in the eye, and the taller ones when she wore heels. He stood close to seven feet tall, and he had a full head of light smooth blonde hair. His skin was normal pink, and he didn't look a day over forty. She tried to detect if he colored his hair like so many men his age. His suit was perfectly tailored for his tall, lean frame, and he extended his hand toward her. She stepped forward and placed her hand in his, but it was so large she couldn't grip it the way her brothers practiced with her. She felt like a little girl, not knowing how to grip it, or even hold it. Her breath stopped for a moment, and then she felt her heart resume its rhythm.

"Nice to meet you," she said quietly.

"My name is Raymond Knorr. I think quite a bit of your Mr. Larsen. Tommy. Very capable young man," said Raymond releasing her hand and gracefully motioning for her to take a seat. "Thank you, Major," he said glancing barely at the Major.

"Yes sir. Just call when," began Major Mead knowing it was not necessary for him to finish. He turned on his heel again with his thumbs tucked neatly beside his index fingers and made long and smooth strides to leave.

"Tell me something about yourself, Miss Rousseau," said Raymond as he sat in an enormous black leather chair behind a desk that was at least a foot higher than a normal desk.

"Jack is fine with me. What would you like to know?" asked Jack. She had learned at a young age to ask questions about other people first. A young girl, maturing quickly, learns that understanding is a powerful weapon that can be used against you. 'It's always better to know your opponent more,' Lisa would tell her. 'And remember this. For a woman, everyone is your opponent.'

"What is your purpose, for one?" asked Raymond.

"I guess I don't know yet. That's a big question," said Jack, feeling her face flush as she stepped back in her mind and planted her rear foot.

"That's a good answer, actually. Do you know who you are?" asked Raymond.

"I am my father's daughter," said Jack smoothly.

"Do you know what we do here?" asked Raymond.

"Besides bomb the shit out of half the world and borrow money from the rest? No. Not really," said Jack, almost regretting the words like she had spilled a drink on the floor.

"Well done, Jack. The truth is that we are at war with the most powerful being in the universe. He wants our world. All of it. Every living soul on it. And we mean to fight him, and we seek victory," said Raymond barely swiveling his chair toward her. His eyes were calm, and there were no stress lines around them. The blue was disarming, but peaceful. His voice was deeper than anyone she had ever heard, that wasn't in a movie.

"You mean God? You're at war with God?" asked Jack in disbelief that he would even say a word like *universe*.

"He thinks so," said Raymond pausing, not moving his eyes from hers. "No. I'm afraid we're on our own when it comes to divine intervention, Jack. But, we have something he does not have, and he means to take it from us by any means possible."

"You're talking about the devil? You're kidding, right?" asked Jack shifting in her chair under his eyes, revealing her, watching the air in her lungs.

"It took us a few hundred years to figure out the rules. What's possible, and what is not; for him and for us. He is powerful beyond words, but he has limitations. We have escaped a few times, made changes, looked at the future and decided to take different paths to survive. It takes time, sometimes a hundred years, for him to adapt to those changes. But he is relentless, and there is never a shortage of people who want what he offers," said Raymond.

"Am I in the right place?" asked Jack after a painful silence.

"Yes. It was time for us to meet. Our Mr. Larsen has been aware of you for a long time," the words coming quietly now, like a pillow resting against her face.

"What was he waiting for? What do you mean?" asked Jack barely able to balance in this match.

"Choice, Jack," said Raymond.

"What? I don't understand," said Jack shaking her head slightly.

"Your drive for sovereignty. The way you changed even your name. You saw your brothers as competitors, not protectors. You are your own person, not blown about with every wind of doctrine. Affecting the universe with purpose. We want to show you a purpose," said Raymond.

"You keep saying 'we.' Who is we? Are we?" asked Jack.

"I'm afraid we are small in number. Scarce, in fact. Mortality is something souls do not often understand. It is heaven for some and hell for others, often living in the same neighborhood, sometimes sleeping in the same bed or dying in the same war. Life is special in the universe, requiring untold amounts of energy and planning to make possible. It can sprinkle our existence with immeasurable joy, or splatter it with unspeakable horror. What is your purpose, Jack?" asked Raymond again, this time the words piercing her heart, begging an answer like a child looking up at its mother.

"To be free. To help people be free," said Jack as the tears welled in her eyes.

"That is correct. Now, our enemy has different plans. He offers wealth and power in this world to souls who come here. His soldiers are everywhere, and they are bound to him by their own choice. A few, he protects and enriches as they rise in power and usefulness to his purpose. Others, he betrays at the end of their duty, and they seal the contract with their own blood," said Raymond.

"Who are they?" asked Jack drawing her composure back as though a piece of powerful music had ended.

"The leaders are easy to see, but the ones in secret are nearly impossible to fight. We finally defeated all their armies, but they changed their tactics and went deep underground. They're buried inside our own government now, and they are getting bolder by the day. There are hundreds of their soldiers inside this very building. There are thousands at the other end of that train tunnel," said Raymond.

"What can I do?" asked Jack.

"I cannot tell you that. Rules, Jack. It only counts if we do it correctly," said Raymond.

"I don't know what to do," said Jack fighting the urge to put her face in her hands, or cross her arms.

"When you return, I mean to put you in harm's way. I cannot promise your safety, but I can tell you that victory is possible," said Raymond.

"I'm not afraid of dying," said Jack without thinking.

"I have a feeling you already know the answer to that," said Raymond as he reached up to the phone and pressed a button for a moment. It made no sound. There was no voice.

"I am going to kick Mr. Larsen's ass, though," said Jack smiling.

"Bigger men than you have tried," said Raymond smiling and standing gracefully from his leather chair. "I look forward to our next meeting, Jack. General Banks is a great woman. We'll see you in a few months," he said reaching for her hand.

"Are you ready, Miss Rousseau?" asked Major Mead standing in the doorway. "We have one more meeting. How are you holding up?"

"I'm fine. A little scared, but I'm doing okay," said Jack

"You're young, but I think you'll understand more in a few minutes," said Major Mead.

"Who was that guy? I mean Raymond. He was a civilian, but he's like spooky or something," said Jack.

"That's above my pay grade, I'm afraid. Even if I did know, I am not the one to tell you about it," said Major Mead as they wound their way from the inner ring of the Pentagon through the halls to the other side of the building.

The General wasn't kidding that there would be miles of walking just in this building as part of her internship. She began to regret wearing the heels already. She had already lost her bearings and didn't know if they were close to the entrance near the train station or not, and as they made the turn from one of the smaller connector passageways into another main hall, they stopped in front of a metal door. It looked like a vault of some kind, and had a number pad on the outside. The Major did not punch in any numbers. On either side of the door were a set of light curtains and what looked like an armored camera with a thick lens over it. Within seconds the door made a loud click and began to open. A Marine in desert camouflage opened it wide and stuck out his hand to shake the Major's hand. "Morning Major Mead. Is this Jack?" he asked shortly.

"Yes sir. Is he ready?" asked Major Mead.

"Yes sir. Please step inside, sir," said the Marine.

The two of them stepped inside the door, and the Marine closed the door. A series of audible clicks told her the area was not accessible without someone letting you in. The room had cement unpainted walls with sealed light fixtures connected with shiny metal conduit against the high ceiling. The floors were painted with a kind of non-skid gray epoxy, and there was no furniture. The door on the other side was also of the same steel design that also clicked loudly as they approached it.

"This room is air tight, except for those nozzles on the ceiling" said Major Mead.

"I guess I don't want to know what they're for," said Jack timidly as they walked into the next section.

"No. You do not," said Major Mead. They turned left and passed through a metal detector and down a hallway to another open room. It was full of cubicles filled with people of all ranks wearing different uniforms. She could hear muffled speaking as it appeared to be a calling center where information was being fused from a constant flow of intelligence.

"Is this where I will be working?" asked Jack.

"No ma'am. This area was destroyed on September 11th, 2001. It's been remodeled. Here we are," said Major Mead as they reached the back of the cubicle center. He held out his hand to introduce her to the room.

"Hello Jackie," came the familiar voice.

"Rocky? Holy crap, you have to be kidding me," said Jack reaching out to hug her older brother.

"Thanks Major. See you in about 20 minutes?" asked Rocky as the Major saluted and left the room. "Have a seat, little sister."

"I thought you were in the Navy," said Jack sitting without the same trepidation she had felt in the General's office.

"It's all the same soup, I'm afraid. Officially, the Navy. But intelligence is growing so fast we have to pull in the best and most loyal talent from everywhere we can. That's why you're here. Mr. Larsen is a good teacher, don't you think?" asked Rocky.

"He scares the shit out of me sometimes. I mean you get the history behind the history, you know?" asked Jack sitting on her hands in the grey upholstered chair.

"Yeah. Well, we put him there for a reason. Let's just leave it at that. Listen, Jackie. America is at war. I don't mind telling you that we have a real problem on our hands. That's why I wanted you here with me. There's a chance this whole thing could go south on us. No kidding, here. We have been compromised at the highest levels, and it's bad. It's worse than anyone thought it could get," said Rocky sitting on his desk in front of her.

"I want to help. I mean, I know you're just trying to keep me safe inside this brick shithouse, but you have me here. Now, put me to work. How bad is it? I mean are the Russians gonna nuke us or something?" asked Jack.

"They don't need to. Look, Jackie. The bad guys got rid of all the people who have been fighting them for thirty years; ever since the turn of the century. We were looking for Y2K, and they nearly destroyed us while we were chasing our tails. They told us carbon dioxide was the greatest threat to the survival of the planet, and they stole trillions of dollars, got the gold, and nearly took control of the whole damn thing," said Rocky.

"You mean global warming?" asked Jack.

Rocky rubbed his hands into his face for moment and then folded his arms. "Our enemy has been planning for centuries to capture the human race. His generals are handpicked and groomed for their greed, and he uses them to accomplish his mission. They're powerful beyond belief. Hell, we elected a few of them President, and there are hundreds working inside the government within a couple miles of here every day.

"And these people are pure evil. A soldier kills to save his brothers in arms. These people kill because they enjoy it. And not just from a distance. They savor watching the life drain out of a person in front of them. They're like serial killers who rape, abuse, and murder like it tastes good. We can't win against people like that. You can't put them in jail, because the judges are loyal to this beast. You can't make a treaty with them. There is no contract. There is no surrender. They are forcing us to take an action that we cannot take, because if we take it, we will follow them to hell," said Rocky.

"You sound like that Raymond guy. He was talking about the devil or something," said Jack.

"I didn't used to think there was any such thing. Society goes through this cycle, repeating history over and over. After a war, we have peace. And that peace goes on for a while until people begin to prosper again. A generation or two, and people forget about the war. They don't know what death smells like anymore. Then, a few people break the law, but generally society is merciful. We hire and train police to take care of the law breakers. But the way it works is, we incarcerate them or deport them. We separate them from society, until one day they get too numerous, and the people demand justice. And then we go to war again. Peace, mercy, justice, and war; over and over again. But this time war won't work," said Rocky.

"Why? Why can't we just fight them and win?" asked Jack trying to understand what her brother was telling her.

"Because if we had a war like that, it would be everywhere. It would be on every street. It would be almost in every house, for Christ's sake. People would be fighting everywhere. It's just not possible," said Rocky.

"So, you're saying we've already lost?" asked Jack.

"Winning is an individual thing, I'm afraid. But my job here is to see if we can save America. If they succeed in ending this country, and they're getting damned close, then there won't be any getting it back. If we can save this, we will have saved the world," said Rocky sliding off his desk onto his feet.

"I want to help, Rocky," said Jack.

"I'm not trying to recruit you. I'm trying to protect you. Something big is coming, and I don't know what it is," said Rocky.

"Why? I mean why now?" asked Jack.

"Because we know about them. We know who their generals are. We have been finally approved to go after them. The issue is that they know this, because they have people in the White House. Hell, they could take the President out with a moment's notice," said Rocky.

"Doesn't he have the Secret Service or something?" asked Jack.

"Yeah. Secret shit. Those guys get about as much training as you have had. They train for nothing. They stand for nothing. They have no command structure. Hell, they may have assassins in their ranks as we speak, and they know it, and they don't give a shit. All they have to do is stand out of the way for one minute, and it's over,

Jackie. The FBI, the CIA, the NSA. They're all compromised with these guys. The only ones we can trust are right in that room outside this door," said Rocky pacing the floor.

"Is that what Raymond does? He knows, doesn't he?" asked Jack.

"There are souls you don't have to watch over. A few people will do the right thing, even when no one is watching. They remember something way beyond all of this crap. I would like to say no amount of money would tempt them, but Jack; the ones I'm talking about don't even know what money is. The concept of wealth is not in their reality. Dad was like that. When everyone else was having one or two kids after they were in their second house, he believed in us and brought us here. That's why you're here. That's why I'm here, and James and Mike as well. I have to believe there are hundreds of thousands like us here on this planet, but we have been quiet and peaceful. But the time for silence has passed. The time to stand up and be counted has come," said Rocky.

"Aren't you supposed to like ride up and down in front of the troops on a horse while you're saying all of this?" asked Jack smiling.

"I don't know how to ride a horse," said Rocky smiling back at her.

"Me neither. You coming to my graduation?" asked Jack eager to change the subject.

"I wouldn't miss it. There are some things that are really important, you know," said Rocky.

"Oh yeah. You're in a freakin fortress playing Battleship, and I am graduating High School. How does that even compare?" asked Jack.

"Every time I walk out of this place, I wonder if I will ever come back. Believe me, when I tell you this. There is no peaceful transfer of power in America. These two powers are at war, right now, for the very soul of this country," said Rocky.

"You're making my point for me," said Jack.

"What does it matter if we win the war and lose our soul? I'm coming to your graduation," said Rocky as he picked up his phone and dialed three numbers.

"You gonna have jets fly over?" asked Jack standing up to hug him as he put the phone down.

"How about if I send the Moon over nice and slow?" asked Rocky hugging her tightly.

There was a soft knock on the door frame as Rocky patted her solidly between the shoulder blades. "That Tae kwon do is making you solid there, except for what's left of that black eye," said Rocky letting her go.

"You should see the other guy. Hey, Major Mead. Looks like we're all family now," said Jack turning to walk with him.

"Yes ma'am. You ready to go?" asked Major Mead.

"I'm ready. You can call me Jack. Ma'am is my mom," said Jack.

"Take a look out there, Jack. Most of my people are not much older than you. It's a new generation of warriors, only we use cyber bullets," said Rocky.

"Why not? Gamers, right?" asked Jack looking out into the cubicle area.

"The only difference is you only get one life," said Rocky soberly.

"Come on. Let's move out, Jack," said Major Mead.

"See ya later, Rocky," said Jack.

"Rocky?" asked Major Mead raising an eyebrow and looking at Rocky.

"Don't get any ideas, Major. See you in a few weeks, Jack," said Rocky.

It was further than she expected when they arrived at the entrance to the Pentagon. Her feet were throbbing in the zipped up heels as the soldier in a black uniform looked at her phone and pocketbook. "She okay, Major?" asked the soldier.

"Her phone has been turned off the entire time. Orientation," said the Major.

"Very good sir. Ma'am," said the soldier as he handed them back to Jack on the outside of the metal detector.

"Thanks. Well, I will see you in about six weeks, Major Mead," said Jack as she shook his hand.

"I know you'll say you'll be fine, but I can send someone with you. To get you home safely," said the Major.

"Looks like I'm already home. See ya later," said Jack as she turned to walk toward the stairs leading down to the train station. It was just around noon, and she was hungry, but there were very few people on the stairs, and she figured it would be easier to beat the rush and make it home before the city went crazy with traffic.

She dropped her train ticket into the slot, and the gates open smoothly to let her onto the terminal. The air was icy under the ground, and the electric sign displayed five minutes and thirty seconds before the next train arrived. There were two policemen talking casually by the vending machines and one was sipping something steamy from a small cup. She shook her head slightly and folded her arms in amazement at seeing her brother working in the Pentagon. It crossed her mind to tell her father that he was right, and she sniffed back the urge to cry suddenly when she realized he couldn't tell anyone if she did.

The train arrived in silence with the recorded female voice telling everyone to stand behind the yellow line until the train doors opened. She took a seat near the door and pulled out her phone to turn it on. Within a few seconds its screen flicked on and the train began to accelerate toward the first stop at the Smithsonian. She sent a text to her mother, letting her know she was on the way home and was craving a grilled cheese sandwich. She leaned back and stretched her legs out for the few minutes it would take to get to her stop. She closed her eyes and rotated her ankles against the leather of her zipped-up heels. She thought about high school being over soon, and where this all fit into her dream of going to college. Maybe it didn't matter anymore. Maybe things moved so fast and knowledge was so available all the time that she didn't need an old obsolete professor telling her the way he thought things should be, when they weren't that way at all. Maybe it was time she decided the way things would be, for herself. She closed her eyes and realized that she didn't even know enough to know the right questions to ask. She thought of Tommy Larsen. Yeah. That was it. When she woke up, the train was at the end of the line, two stops past her station.

It didn't matter. She could wait it out. Trains were a safe place in D.C..

Chapter 15

"How do you feel about getting out of D.C. for a while?' asked Mike.

"My heart is hurting. I never make good choices when I'm like this," said Lucy brushing her delicate hands over the artwork down her left upper arm.

"Baby, I love you more than breathing. You know that. I just can't go back to Lou's and play. It doesn't feel right. Someone in that place that night followed Seth down the street and gunned him down for what? For what? Politics? Who do these people think they are?" said Mike swinging his fist into the air in front of him.

"He said it. He was scared of the Democrats. Of Hillary. She was rigging the primary, and he knew about it. Maybe he said something to the wrong people, I don't know," said Lucy wiping beneath her swollen eyes and sniffling.

"You think he was scared? I think he was pissed. Richey doesn't scare easily. But, he did say he thought Foster had been murdered. Maybe you're right. But that's all the more reason we should get out of here for a while," said Mike.

"Where would we go? We don't know anyone outside of this city," said Lucy.

"Hollywood. We could go to California; Beverly Hills. Let's get out of this stinking place and take the act on the road. We can get gigs out there," said Mike.

"Whatever you say, sweetie. I will go wherever with you," said Lucy reaching for his shoulders and leaning against him.

"Okay. It's settled. I'll try to organize everything and see if James or Rocky can help. Who knows? It's gotta be better than this," said Mike as he gently held her and rocked slowly, drawing the scent of her jet black hair into his nostrils and closing his eyes.

The non-stop flight to LAX was actually very smooth. James burned some of his frequent flier miles to get them a good price, and they loaded 6 road cases with clothes and sound equipment. One never knew how a musical act would be received when cold calling venues in Southern California. One thing is for sure. All the great acts seemed to get their breaks in Los Angeles.

"James got us a suite at the Four Seasons in Santa Monica. It's not far from here. They have free breakfast and an indoor swimming pool," said Mike as they waited for their cases to drop at LAX's baggage claim 5.

"I miss Maddie," said Lucy hugging Mike's arm as the carousel warning buzzer sounded.

"Yeah. Me too. She is much better at meeting new people than me, that's for sure," said Mike.

"Not that I'm in any kind of hurry, but where do we start? What's your plan, Mister Rousseau?" asked Lucy.

"It's probably just like D.C. Well, not like D.C., but I mean it's all about the parties. It's about getting seen and maybe doing some open mic stuff to get noticed. If we are as good as they say we are, we should be able to get a shot somewhere. How does anybody do it? Let's just get ready to work hard. Besides, my dad used to say hard work was the good of this world. 'When you get paid by the hour, what does it matter if you dig a ditch, and then fill it in again?'," said Mike.

"My mother said the idle mind is the Devil's workshop," said Lucy.

"I think that came out before your mother. I love her, but she doesn't get the credit for that one," said Mike moving as he noticed the first of their cases come down the baggage conveyor.

It was an hour before they got checked in, tipped the staff for helping with the cases, and the door clicked shut. Mike wrapped his arms around her and swayed to a song in his head in the silence of the suite. "They have unlimited hot water, you know," said Mike.

"I was just thinking the same thing. 5 hours in a plane leaves something on your skin, you know? Like three hundred people breathing on you. And I'm hungry. God, how do they expect people to sit there for that long with only pretzels and diet coke? I thought they used to have peanuts," said Lucy relaxing into his silent song.

"Somebody on the plane must have had an allergy," said Mike not letting go.

"One person ruins lunch for everyone?" asked Lucy.

"Last one in," said Mike releasing his arms and peeling his loafers off with a toe behind each heel.

"Oh my God. It feels like I haven't showered in a week. How come we don't have a shower head like this?" asked Lucy letting her long black hair soak up the hot rain coming down from the ceiling mounted fixture.

"Because our electric bill would be a thousand dollars a month," said Mike as he squeezed the shower gel into the hair on his chest and drew her into him, scrubbing her back with his body.

"Yeah, and we'd have three kids by now," said Lucy closing her eyes and letting the water soothe her eyes, still tender from days of weeping.

"Hey, can't blame a guy for trying," said Mike.

"Such a boy," she said feeling a whimper shake her body as she took a deep breath in memory of Seth.

"I love you. We're going to be alright. If you want, we'll scoot up to Hollywood and take a look around and have some dinner later on. Maybe we can hit a few clubs and see if we can get a gig," said Mike.

"Yeah. No sense laying around here naked and watching old movies for a few days," said Lucy turning to face him and letting her breasts scrub into his soapy chest.

"I like old movies," said Mike kissing her while the water ran over their closed eyes and around their lips.

The king sized bed welcomed them as they made love and slept in a curled position on the bedspread. The television sound barely covered the silence in the room, as they fed one another with love, and healed, and slept.

He rocked her softly when he woke, and within a few minutes she took a deep breath like a flower coming through the Spring soil and stretched her legs until they quivered.

"You ready for some heels and skinny jeans?" he whispered into her neck.

"You read my mind, my king. I am starving," said Lucy.

"Well, let's see what Hollywood is all about. Shall we?" said Mike as he rolled onto his back, sat up, and scooted to the edge of the bed. She put her feet against his back and rolled her toes against his muscular shoulders and down his spine.

"You look like your brother from behind," said Lucy.

"You looked at my brother?" asked Mike whimsically.

"Rocky is built like a brick shithouse, baby. But I don't take to military types. My whole family is a long line of officers and gentlemen, but it's you who saved me," said Lucy.

"I got my dad's musical talent, but not much else," said Mike standing up and shadow boxing for few seconds.

"You got me," said Lucy, teasing him with her beautiful voice.

"Yes I did. That, and the air that I breathe is enough for me," said Mike showing off his naked body by flexing his arms in front of her.

"Oh that's original," said Lucy smiling broadly at him.

"Come here, Mrs. Rousseau. I have something for you," said Mike.

"I can see that from here, barely," said Lucy giggling.

He reached out his hand and pulled her to her bare feet and kissed her and held her. He stroked her hair with one hand and held her by the small of her back closely to him. "I just want you to know that we're supposed to be here. I can feel it. Like the universe has the right sound. We're going to be okay," said Mike.

"I can feel you, saving me again."

Hollywood was not as busy as they anticipated, when they emerged from the train station on Hollywood Boulevard. Grauman's Chinese Theater was within sight. It was nothing like Times Square. Rather it looked like an ordinary small town square with the exception of the brightly lit Hard Rock Café.

"Do my eyes deceive me?" said Mike grabbing Lucy's hand and beginning to walk toward the intersection.

"You must have known. This is crazy," said Lucy almost laughing.

"Didn't I say the universe was lining up?" asked Mike with a jump in his step.

"Yeah, but how often do they have Karaoke at Hard Rock Café?" asked Lucy.

"All I know is that sign might as well say, 'Back by popular demand, Lucy & Mike,'" said Mike.

They walked through the front door, and the atmosphere was classic. It was just after sunset, and singing hadn't started yet. The place was about one third full, the recorded music was loud, and there were empty tables and booths, so they looked around for a hostess. Most of the tables had a small sign on them that read 'reserved.' "Welcome to Hard Rock Café. Just two of you?" asked the hostess.

"Yeah. Wow. Has anyone told you that you look like," began Mike.

"Anne Hathaway? Yeah. Sometimes. This is my day job," said the hostess smiling in her white blouse with the bottom tied in a knot to expose a set of rippling abs, and the top of some kind of tattoo peeking out from her under the waistband of her black yoga pants. She grabbed a couple of menus and headed for a booth close to the front windows.

"Hey, I noticed on the marquis outside that this is karaoke night. When does it start?" asked Mike catching up to the hostess.

"It starts at 9, but the first hour or so is already booked. That's why you see all these reserved tables. They call it karaoke, but this is Hollywood. Singers are looking. Bands are looking, and so are the agencies. Dancers are easy to find. Actors? Well, I've been here for two years. I'm from Nebraska. I got a couple of commercials, and never miss a chance to read. But great singers are not too easy to find. So, management got this idea to throw a raw piece of meat out there for the customers to fight over. So far, you can't argue with success. Your server will be right with you," said the hostess.

"Thank you," said Mike sliding in next to Lucy on the same seat of the booth.

"I think I see a flaw in your plan," said Lucy folding her right hand into his left hand as they sat next to one another in the booth.

"The other side of this booth is empty?" asked Mike looking into her eyes.

"There's no keyboard up there," said Lucy.

"I'm not worried about that," said Mike.

"But we're an act. You and me. I don't want to," began Lucy.

"I see a stand with wireless mics up there," said Mike not taking his eyes off hers. His confidence always surprised her.

"And your point is," asked Lucy leaving the question open with her tone.

"Watch me pull a piano out of my hat," said Mike using his index finger to point off to the side of the stage not quite hidden by the curtain.

"Oh my God, you're a genius. Have I told you I love you today?" asked Lucy smiling and curling her lips against his ear.

"You screamed it a little while ago, as a matter of fact," said Mike as she punched him in the shoulder and blushed.

"Hi. My name is Adam, and I'll be taking care of you tonight," said the waiter wearing almost exactly the same outfit that the hostess was wearing, with the exception of the yoga pants. His black jeans and white shirt said Hollywood Hard Rock Café on the pockets.

"What's up Adam?" said Lucy smiling at his delicate face.

"You two. You look beautiful. Can I get you something to drink while you look at the menu?" asked Adam.

"I'll take a Bud light on draft, and she will have a Kettle One Vodka Martini with three olives up and dry," said Mike.

"Be right back," said Adam as he twirled in his plaid Vans and walked quickly back to the bar.

The two of them looked the menu over and decided to split a sampler of the appetizers. Four more couples arrived and the Anne Hathaway hostess took them to two large tables and snatched the reserved signs as they sat down. Two of the girls were dressed in show clothes with sequins, and two of the boys had bright colored shirts with large collars. It was impossible to tell their ages from across the room, but they felt a little like the coin was about to be tossed for the big game.

"Here you go. Have you decided?" asked Adam.

"Yes we have. Two things. First, we're going to split the sampler here with potato skins and the southwest burrito things. Second, how do we get our names on the list to sing tonight?" asked Mike.

"Oh, sweetie. Have you ever been hooked?" asked Adam with an expressive look of concern on his face.

"Only on her," said Mike glancing at Lucy.

"I mean gonged. This is like full contact karaoke, baby. If you're good, they will hook you off the stage. If you're really good, they might let you finish. If you're like X-factor kick ass, you can make the cut. You sure you want to try this?" asked Adam.

"Yes," they both said in unison.

"See that very large bouncer man over there with the black hat and the black suit? He's a lot meaner than he looks, let me tell you. Tell him you want to sing. That's the best I can do. I'll go get

198

your order going," said Adam. He turned and walked away like he was afraid to be seen with them.

Mike looked at Lucy without speaking. "What? You're looking at me like you want me to give you an order or something," said Lucy.

"Let's go," said Mike sliding out of the booth and holding his hand open for Lucy to join him. She stood in her heels and winked at Mike and slid her arm through his and put her slender hand on top of his wrist. The two of them locked eyes on the bouncer and headed his way. He was probably about six foot two and had a neck as large as Lucy's waste. His shirt fit his power-lifter shoulders well and the collar had the look of custom tailoring. He was talking with another man dressed in a light colored silk suit with what looked like chocolate brown slippers made of woven leather. His tanned skin was accented by the black lights placed here and there in the restaurant and the substantial gold chain bracelet he wore on this wrist. His hair was combed back, but not slicked down; the result of years of styling and expensive products. As they approached, the Bouncer looked at Mike, and then switched his eyes to Lucy's perfect shape.

"What can I do for you fine people," said the Bouncer in a voice that had seen too many loud night clubs.

"I'm Mike, and this is my wife, Lucy. We want to perform for you tonight," said Mike.

"You sing? Together?" asked the Bouncer.

"Actually, she does the singing. I play the keyboards," said Mike.

"A piano player?" asked the Bouncer.

"A pianist, actually," said Lucy locking eyes with the Bouncer for a long moment. It was her super power she developed when she was fourteen years old after going through forty dollars' worth of her mother's makeup to find the right colors and the right presentation to be able to melt a man's heart with a single glance from twenty paces. Up close, all men were defenseless.

"Whatever," said the Bouncer without any detectable weakness. He pulled out his phone and thumbed a few commands on the screen. "I have a spot at twenty after ten. What song do you want to perform? And before you say anything, I got Adele-itis," said the Bouncer dropping his phone to his side.

"My Immortal," said Lucy, not breaking her gaze.

The Bouncer tilted his head slightly on his enormous neck like her powers had reached him, cracked his armor, like hot metal was running down his back behind the chain mail of his suit. "We haven't had that spirit here for a while. Okay. Ten twenty. You're on your own there," said the Bouncer pointing at Mike.

"Don't you worry about me. Just make sure the mic volume is turned up as far as you can handle it," said Mike, amazed at watching Lucy hook this man like 275 pounds of grade A beef on the hoof.

The corners of his mouth flattened slightly, almost like he was about to smile. "This act got a name?" asked the Bouncer, hovering his thumbs over the backlit screen in front of his eyes.

"Lucy and Mike. That's easy enough, right?" asked Mike.

"Okay Mike. Bring what you got. Enjoy your evening, Lucy," he said touching the narrow brim of his black felt hat.

"I have one more question, sir; if you don't mind," said Lucy blinking deeply, setting the hook deep into his soul.

"I got time," said the Bouncer.

"Who was the other guy in the suit?" asked Lucy.

"That would be one Mister D. If your balls are really this brass, he's got people," said the Bouncer.

"Like an audition?" asked Mike.

"Like an introduction. It's all about introductions in this town. Unless you like writing checks, which by looking at you two, I don't see that kind of bulge in your pocket," said the Bouncer losing his smile completely.

"See you at ten twenty," said Lucy gently placing her hand on the Bouncer's forearm and smiling like she still had cards to play.

The Bouncer looked toward the door as another group of three girls came in the front door. The hostess greeted them, began walking, and the girls flowed to another reserved table. Mike and Lucy walked back to their booth just as the food server arrived with Adam at the table.

"Did you make the list?" asked Adam as he motioned for the server to put the appetizer sampler on the table.

"Thank you. Yes, we get to sing at twenty after ten," said Mike.

"You were right. He's tougher than he looks," said Lucy winking at Adam.

He smiled and silently clapped his hands together with delight. "Oh, that's good. We're open until 2 AM, and by then the place is packed to the glass. If you do well enough, you'll make the cut," said Adam.

"What cut?" asked Mike sliding in next to Lucy and taking a sip from his beer.

"The final four," said Adam.

"They take a hundred singers and knock it down to four? Then what?" asked Mike.

"You never know. I've seen Simon Cowell, even Nicole Scherzinger stop in for these finals. Some of the music agents and even movie producers come by from time to time. Mr. D calls them if something magic is happening," said Adam.

"Anybody ever make it big?" asked Mike.

"It takes more than a great voice to make it in this town," said Adam.

"We're from D.C. It can't be any worse than that town," said Mike.

"It's all the same rite of passage. Let me know if you need anything else, okay?" said Adam, smiling like he was accepting an Oscar.

"Thanks, Adam. We will," said Lucy.

201

The food looked amazing and tasted even better as they sat in the booth and watched the people come in. By nine o'clock, the floor and the mezzanine tables were full, and the music could barely cover the hum of conversation in the Hollywood hotspot. It was just the right amount of food, without pushing Lucy's lungs out of the way. "I knew I was hungry, but that was really good," said Mike.

"Yeah. I love the little popper things. You have to learn how to make those," said Lucy.

"I think I could figure it out. You like that spicy stuff. You want another drink?" asked Mike motioning to Adam bouncing up and down near the bar.

"I would love to have a grapefruit juice, on the rocks," said Lucy rubbing his shoulder with her hands.

"Another beer? How about Lucy?" said Adam.

"If you have pink grapefruit juice on ice, that would be great, and yes I'll have another," said Mike sliding his empty glass toward Adam.

All of a sudden, the restaurant began to clap, and Mike and Lucy looked toward the stage. The spotlight came down from a booth up on the second floor, and a tall, slender black man in a shiny, silver suit smiled to the crowd. His face was smooth like flat bronze, and his eyes were surrounded with orange and red and blue shades of makeup. His hair was blonde and sculpted into a flawless flat-top, and his earrings sparkled slivers of light into the large room.

"Good evening everyone. Welcome to Hollywood's own Hard Rock Café. I'm your host, Pauline, for this evening's live event." The restaurant clapped as though someone flashed a sign for the television audience. "This is no ordinary karaoke. Star Search ain't got nothin' on Hard Rock Hollywood, let me tell you darlings," he said twerking his hips to the syllables. "We have a full card tonight. One song, and one song only, for each of tonight's talents. And this is absolutely an audience participation event. Oh, and one more thing. If you sing too much like the original artist, you might here this sound," said Pauline as a recorded fog horn blared through the deep sound system. "You cheer, they sing. Got it?" Again the place thundered with applause.

"On the screens around the club you will see a short list of names. This is the order of tonight's singers. If your name is on that list, you come down to stage left at the bottom of the stairs. My girls will get you ready and make sure you don't trip going up the stairs. If you know someone on that list, get your devices ready to send your friend out to the world on your favorite media. You got all that?" asked Pauline, again the building shook with clapping and whistles. "Very good, my people. The Hard Rock Final Four will perform at midnight, so don't leave early. You must be present to win. Now, let's get ready for show time! Okay, ten minutes and counting. Mr. DJ Hollywood, may I have the first names on the screen, now!" shouted Pauline as the sound system took his voice and electronically echoed it and flanged it to sound like a metal robot.

The first names appeared on flat screens all over the club, and the people clapped again as Pauline danced off the stage and down the steps into the crowd by the bar. "Wow, talk about no pressure," said Lucy.

"I like it. It's pretty well done, actually," said Mike.

"Yeah, easy for you to say," said Lucy squeezing his arm with her cold hands.

"I have an idea when our time comes," said Mike.

"You're gonna get me hooked," said Lucy sticking out her bottom lip.

"They won't hook you. I promise," said Mike.

All the singers were good. Whether it was to make the competition try harder, or to go through a list of songs normally too large to fit into 4 hours, it was hard to say. The fog horn took out some fine voices that just sounded too much like the original artist. It was easy to see the influence of televised talent shows emphasizing the interpretation of a song, rather than just covering it really well.

It was ten o'clock before their names came up on the screen. They had each been performing for a few years, but it was hard not to feel the pressure of the moment, of the atmosphere, of this city for something live and amazing. "Don't hold back," said Mike close to her ear to overcome the lyrics of Bruno Mars pouring smoothly from the speakers.

"Am I your queen?" she said back to him against his ear.

"I am your humble servant king," he nearly shouted.

"Then kneel before me," she laughed.

"Let's show 'em how it's done back East," said Mike holding his hand out flat to invite her to slap it.

She walked two fingers across his hand slowly and then pretended to slap his face. "I can feel the universe shifting on its axis," she said looking him in the eyes like he was the only person in the room.

"We have three minutes and six seconds to change the world," said Mike.

"Plenty of time," she said.

"More than enough," he said quickly.

"Even eggs take three minutes, you know," she laughed.

"Okay you two. Break a leg, just not on my steps. Okay? Use the hand rail. You good?" asked the girl managing the five steps leading up to the stage.

"Yeah, we're good. Thanks," said Mike leaning over to her to be heard without shouting. The song ended, but the applause went on for about twenty seconds. The young boy with bright red shirt and yellow slacks came bouncing down the stairs with a smile on his face. He fanned his face with his hands from the heat of the lights, and the fact that this time, at least, he was allowed to sing the entire song. Mike shot up the stairs ahead of Lucy and in a dozen rapid steps, snatched one of the mics off the stand and slid onto the bench seat in front of the piano.

Mike knew the music. She knew the song. Before the recorded karaoke version could start, Mike launched into the composition with the power and grace of a concert pianist at the Hollywood Bowl. Lucy arrived at the other mic as the lights lowered and the silver spot sliced through from the ceiling and struck her perfect skin and the perfect art, and then she began to sing. The DJ never started the recorded sound, because Mike's piano came straight through the speakers. The mic lying beside him on the bench drank the harmonics from his skillful hands and nourished the souls in that room.

> *"I'm so tired of being here*
> *Suppressed by all my childish fears*
> *And if you have to leave*
> *I wish that you would just leave*
> *'Cause your presence still lingers here*
> *And it won't leave me alone."*[3]

The audience was stunned at first. The people had heard great piano before. They had heard Streisand, Adele, Crow, but they had never heard the silky power of Lucy Rousseau. It wasn't just a voice. And with that much power, and the rehearsed passion of Mike synchronized with her, it realized the emotion of Amy Lee's heart in her rendition, and he commanded the power of this moment. No one had ever heard anything like it. No one could breathe until Lucy pulled the mic slightly from her deep red lips for moment to inhale.

> *"When you cried, I'd wipe away all of your tears*
> *When you'd scream, I'd fight away all of your fears*

---

[3] *My Immortal* written by Evanescence's guitarist Ben Moody, lead singer Amy Lee and keyboardist David Hodges, and it was produced by Moody and Dave Fortman; Dec 2003.

*And I held your hand through all of these years
But you still have all of me."*

The applause began like a giant window breaking. It crashed against the tile floor and challenged the sound pressure itself. Each line came from the speakers like one fireworks finale after another, numbing the senses with its perfection, overwhelming the soul with its beauty. No one would ever forget this night. It was the first time, and the last time, anyone in that room ever truly heard that song.

DJ Hollywood leaned forward to his mixing board microphone and switched it on for a rare appearance. "That was all you. Everyone give it up for Lucy and Mike," as though the applause ever stopped. It got louder as Lucy slid the mic back into the stand and Mike did the same. He gripped her hand and raised it into the air as she posed for a moment in her jeans and heels, and then turned toward the stairs and they left the stage.

"Christ, that was good. Well done, you two," said the stair manager as she held out her hand to help them on the last step. She hugged Lucy lightly, and Mike looked at the crowd gathering in front of them. He shook hands with several people and thanked several more. He wasn't looking for the booth. He was looking for a light-colored suit.

The next song began within seconds, and the crowd began to thin as faces turned away from them and toward the stage. Lucy caught up with him in a few steps, and they walked slowly back to their booth. "I'm thirsty now," said Mike sliding into the booth and picking up his half-glass of beer.

"What's this?" said Lucy picking up a folded index card from the table in front of them.

"Is it one of those reservation things?" asked Mike swallowing the remaining contents of his beer.

"It's got a number 2 on it. This is some kind of fancy stationary. Looks like an invitation, but uh," said Lucy looking at it from all sides.

"Hey you two. I had no idea who you were," said Adam as he approached the booth.

"That was fun, huh?" asked Lucy smiling at him.

"I could use another beer. You have any more of that grapefruit juice?" asked Mike.

"Oh hell yes. That was smoking hot. Can I get you anything else?" asked Adam.

"Yeah. One thing. This was on the table when we got back. Is this something we should pay attention to?" asked Lucy handing it to Adam.

He ran his slender fingers over the embossed cover and flipped it over. "Don't let anyone else see this. There would be many deaths," said Adam with a coy smile on his face. "This is Mr. D's personal invitation," said Adam looking over his shoulder and handing it back to Lucy.

"To what?" asked Lucy.

"The final four at midnight. But, usually, everyone just hangs out and gets hammered, because they don't get called up for the finals. You were picked second, and they don't want you to leave, so they dropped this on your table. You're in, baby," said Adam.

The next 90 minutes churned 20 singers through the Hard Rock machine. There were a few fog horns, with crying groups of girls and touches of support like pro basketball players missing free throws. This was not a weekly event, or even monthly, so some of these voices would never again get a chance like this. Mike switched to water to keep his fingers from making a mistake. Lucy hummed softly to make sure her voice was still there. It felt more like a tough man contest, than a show. It was the strain behind the curtain, far from the red carpet and the brass trophies. It was the work behind the entertainment industry. It separated success from the slurry of talent in this town. It was the reason why the stars returned year after year. It was the reason why so many others walk away while they still have their soul.

"Okay hard rockers, are you ready for the final four?" asked Pauline as he sashayed onto the stage like a showgirl in his shimmering silver suit. The crowd was pressing the stage now, looking more like a small concert than a Hollywood Boulevard restaurant. The music sounded like a movie score. It swelled with horns and strings while the computerized stage lights panned and flashed from color to color, shifting the silver suit into a dancing neon sign, drawing all the attention to the man with the microphone, to a large white envelope flashing in his hand.

"Will these four contestants make their way to stage beside me?" he asked as he open and unfolded the envelope. "I need Eric, Lucy, Shemeila, and Carmen to come up and join me on our Hollywood Hard Rock stage," said Pauline as short gas fed flames shot up from stands at the sides of the stage. The crowd roared with the choices being revealed.

"Go get 'em my queen," said Mike letting go of her hand and urging her toward the stage.

"I don't want to go without you," she said without the sound reaching him over the din of the speakers.

"You are never without me," said Mike putting two fingers under his eyes and pointing them at her.

Reluctantly, slowly, she turned and walked toward the stage. People formed a human hallway for her as she flipped her long black hair over her right shoulder to reveal her magnificent art wrapping around her left shoulder. She wished she had a gown to take their view off her eyes. She walked with grace on her heels to the stage steps and floated up to the stage next to Pauline. He was tall and electric as he smiled at her, scanned her with his blazing eyes, and welcomed her with a kiss into the air beside her face.

"If you thought it was fun getting this far, wait until you get a load of this," said Pauline smiling to the crowd filling in against the chest-high railing in front of the stage. Mike stood beside his table, so she could focus on him. "We will display ten songs from Billboard's top female and male artists on the screen for each contestant. Each of you will pick a song from that list, DJ Hollywood will queue that music, and you must perform that song. You, my Hard Rock darlings, will choose the winner. Are we ready?" asked Pauline. The crowd clapped and whistled over what sounded like a much larger audience.

"Three of you may be seated in our row of fame, while Eric performs for us," said Pauline displaying the row of four golden chairs at the rear of the stage. The crowd lowered their hands and their voices while the screens flashed like a slot machine. In a few seconds, ten male artist and ten female artist songs displayed in two columns. "Eric chooses," and Pauline pointed his microphone wand at his chin.

"Too Good at Goodbyes. Sam Smith," said Eric, and the crowd yelled their approval.

"Good luck, Eric," said Pauline with a smile as he retreated stage left and out of the lights. The lights changed, and the spotlight narrowed against his torso as he smiled and waited for the music to start. He brought the mic to his mouth and began to dance and sing while barely looking at the words. Within seconds, the crowd began to cheer and clap. He hit the notes and delivered the song like he wrote it and had rehearsed it a thousand times, only this time it was being streamed by hundreds of cell phones, watched by talent agencies, producers, and bands all over the world. This was his time, and he didn't waste a moment of it. When he finished the crowd was there for him. He smiled, they cheered, but everyone knew it could have been more.

"Excellent, Eric. Really great, darling," said Pauline reaching him just as the music and the crowd subsided. He shook his hand and took the mic from him, and Eric took his seat next to Lucy.

"Lucy, you're up next. I have not seen you before, baby. Where are you from?" asked Pauline putting the mic in her hand.

"Oh, thank you for asking, Pauline. I'm from D.C.," said Lucy as the spot expanded to cover both of them. There were a couple of shouts from the audience in support, and she smiled and waved politely.

"Looks like you're making fans quickly out here in movie land. DJ Hollywood, may I have the list of songs for Lucy?" asked Pauline raising his hand in the air.

"Look What You Made Me Do – Taylor Swift," said Lucy into her mic, and the crowd erupted. She knew this song was a changeover for Taylor. She had sung along with it before, and knew in her heart that the hottest female artist in the Western world had left something on the table, and she was determined to find it.

"Break a leg, Lucy," said Pauline and he bounced to the side of the stage.

The crowd was quiet, almost muttering as the music began. She flicked her head, bringing her silky black hair forward to cover half her face. She arched her back and leaned into the mic nearly touching her lips with it. The words came quickly and clearly, while her heels cut shapes over the stage. She spun and sang to the crowd. She brought her super-power eye contact into each of the phones watching her, caressing the camera and controlling her breath like a bow being drawn across her flawless vocal cords. She could see Taylor in her mind, looking up from her manicure, listening for the pieces she could not find in the recording studio.

In the interlude, the crowd reached higher for something. She was loving them, and they could feel it. She reached out with her free hand and spun on her heel, playing the strings the universe had laid around her like a cosmic harp.

"The world moves on, another day, another drama, drama
But not for me, not for me, all I think about is karma
And then the world moves on, but one thing's for sure

Maybe I got mine, but you'll all get yours,"[4]

The chorus was repetitious, but there was a space there, and flew like a bird through the melody, almost sounding like she was singing a duet in thirds. The music faded, along with the words, and the crowd exploded. They were screaming and clapping, and whistling. Mike folded his hands in front of his belt buckle. She was beyond flawless and formless like song itself.

"Oh my lord, that was beautiful, Lucy. Lucy, everyone; from D.C," said Pauline fluttering his hand in front of his face like he was fighting back tears of joy.

"Thank you, Hard Rock. Thank you," said Lucy into the mic and she handed it back to Pauline. The crowd was relentless, chanting 'Lucy, Lucy,' while they clapped in unison. Mike met her at the base of the stairs, and she shuddered in his embrace. She was his queen, but she was like a dove in his arms. They shook hands and smiled as they walked slowly back to the booth by the front windows.

There were two singers to go, but it was inconsequential. Lucy had won the Final Four contest at Hollywood's Hard Rock Café. It was all they could take for one night, as their biological clock said it was 4 o'clock in the morning. It was then that a hand touched his shoulder. He turned to look up into the eyes of the Bouncer. "Mr. D would like the pleasure of your company. There is a limo outside," said the Bouncer.

"We haven't paid, yet," said Mike reaching for his wallet.

"Winners never pay in this town," said the Bouncer, and he pointed to the door. "Go on. I got this."

It was cool at nearly 1 o'clock, when they stepped outside onto the nearly empty sidewalk of Hollywood Boulevard. The black

---

[4] *Look What You Made Me Do Songwriters: Fred Fairbrass / Jack Antonoff / Richard Fairbrass / Rob Manzoli / Taylor Swift / Christopher Fairbrass / Robert Manzoli © Spirit Music Group, Sony/ATV Music Publishing LLC*

limousine was stretched slightly, and the driver opened the rear door for them as he looked up at the Bouncer in the alcove of the Hard Rock Café. Mike let Lucy get in first, and he slid in beside her on the smooth leather couch. There were two young girls sitting on the opposite couch inside; one dressed in a black jumpsuit, and the other in a short print dress with laced high heels. The girl in the black jumpsuit looked slightly Asian and asked if they would like a drink. They both accepted miniature bottles of water and tried to relax as the vehicle began moving.

"Hi," said the young girl in the dress. "My name is Alani," she said politely shaking their hands.

"I'm Mike, and this is my wife, Lucy. Do you know where we're going?" asked Mike not trying to sound suspicious.

"You've been invited to Mr. Goodman's party. It's not far," said the Asian staffer.

"What do you do, Alani?' asked Lucy clearing her throat a little after singing so hard.

"I am an actor," said Alani quietly glancing at the staffer, who looked out the window.

"Oh wow. I never met an actor before," said Lucy trying to loosen the quiet atmosphere a little.

"I'm getting ready to work on my first feature film. I've done a few music videos," said Alani brushing her hand through her light brown hair that hung straight around her shoulders. Her skin was perfect over pronounced cheekbones and around her light red lips, and her square chin. She didn't look a day over 17, and she was alone.

"We sing. Well, Lucy sings. I play," said Mike not wanting to give a full resume.

"Yes. We saw you. The whole world saw you. That is not easy. So much pressure in that place. It's like, boom, you're live. Most people crack a little up there. You were great. Both of you," said the Asian staffer smiling and looking back and forth between them. "Mr. D called us to pick you up," she said.

"How did you meet Mr. Goodman?" asked Lucy looking at Alani.

"I haven't. Not yet. An agent saw me at a casting call. She took a picture, and he asked for me tonight. They sent the limo, so here I am," said Alani.

"I'm sure your family is excited," said Lucy.

"Oh. Yeah. It's been my dream since I was little to be an actor," said Alani adding a tiny laugh at the end.

The limo lurched softly as it turned into the driveway, and the gates swung open automatically. The gate was black iron with a large W welded in the center. The drive was lined with low lighting, and a backlit pond shimmered from the waterfall circulating into it. "This is Mr. Goodman's Hollywood home. He arrived from New York last week to review some scripts, and meet with some politicians. There is always something happening in Hollywood.

"It's kind of late for us, actually. We just came from D.C. today. Not that I'm anxious to leave, but do you know how long we will be here?" asked Mike trying to keep the schedule in his mind.

"Oh, not to worry. You can leave any time, or there are twenty guest rooms between two guest houses here on the grounds. You are free to spend the night and leave when you wish tomorrow," said the staffer. The car came to a stop, and a doorman with a short sleeved shirt opened the right hand door.

The four of them stepped out onto the covered driveway that looked like the entry to a hotel. The large, potted ferns were healthy, and the wide stairs led up to double doors with full-length glass side windows on either side. The door opened from inside, and they could smell the light aroma of pot and heard soft music coming from inside. The hallway was about 12 feet wide, and they walked down a step and then another into a large room with the entire outside wall made of glass. There were about 20 people out on the covered patio, and there was a flickering gas fire pit surrounded by stone benches draped with a Western print rug. The staffer motioned for them to join the others as she walked into the serving area of the large kitchen.

There was a large screen that flickered with a replay of Lucy's performance, and they clapped as they noticed her and Mike walk through the open sliding glass doors onto the patio. Lucy smiled shyly, and Mike shook hands. Alani was close by Mike's side, and he could feel her sense of abandonment.

"Hey everyone. This is Mike and Lucy. Wow, what a voice, huh? And this must be Alani. You're much prettier in person. Are you thirsty? There is anything you want. We have some shrimp cocktail there, and there's some veggies over there. If we don't have it, just say the word. I just wanted to meet you. That was a hell of a performance out there tonight," said Harvey Goodman.

"Thank you, Mr. Goodman," said Lucy.

"Harvey. Please, call me Harvey. These are Sony's people. Screenwriters over there, and these guys are all CGI concept designers. Not the hackers. I'm talking the real 3-D set designers. But, you know, at the end of the day, it's not the set; it's the actor that wins the Oscar. Am I right?" said Harvey to the patio full of sycophants.

"And the script. Don't forget the words, Harvey," said one of the screenwriters.

"I know, I know. But I give you the character. You just write words for him to say. But Affleck is always Affleck, and Willis is always Willis. You know what I'm saying?" asked Harvey.

"Oh come on, Harvey. Streep, Hanks, and how about the Fanning girls? Huh? Come on," said the Screenwriter.

"Okay. There is a difference between a movie star and an actor. I agree. The point is that it is not a film, unless the producer says it's a film. That's all I'm saying," said Harvey pointing to his own nose and pouring some sparkling water into a tumbler with a few chunks of ice.

"You can't argue with success, Harvey," said the Screenwriter as everyone mumbled their agreement.

"One hand washes the other. I write checks to the Clintons, and the Obamas, and the taxpayers fund my movies. How sweet is that?" laughed Harvey.

"You really have a nose for talent, Harvey," said the Screenwriter lifting his gin and tonic as a toast.

"That's what I know. Hey, hey, Alani. Sweetie, listen I'm glad you were able to make it. I would like you to come back to my office for a minute. I have a few scripts I want you to take a look at," said Harvey.

"Sure, Mr. Goodman," said Alani smiling brightly. The small gathering suddenly looked away from Harvey's hand on the small of Alani's back and toward Lucy as Harvey and Alani walked slowly back through the split level living room and up two steps in the terrazzo hallway to an open doorway on the other side.

"Where did you learn to sing like that, Lucy?" asked one of the men with a yellow sports coat and blue jeans.

"In the shower, mostly," laughed Lucy flashing her super-power carefully. Mike stayed by her side, and he glanced through the glass wall. The hand carved office door closing behind them made no sound, and in the pit of his stomach he suddenly wished he had never heard of Hollywood.

Chapter 16

In 1997, the Green Card Lottery had become the favorite way to import skilled agents and voters for the DNC. The winners were publicly represented as being selected randomly, which made it even easier to manipulate. High speed internet was barely a year old. The information age was on the world runway, about to take off. Thousands of millionaires were formed in what the financial community called the *dotcom boom*. Maria Cantwell even made so much money creating and selling her Internet company, that she financed a successful election to become a U.S. Senator of the State of Washington.

Then, something devastating happened. President Bill Clinton announced in the summer of 1998 that he was directing his Attorney General, Janet Reno, to sue Microsoft in order to break their hold on internet browsing JAVA scripting. Microsoft appealed on the basis that its innovations actually benefitted the public, but they did have to stop preventing other browser companies from accessing their operating system.

Hillary had long been a believer in acquiring information on her enemies, and especially on her friends. As the titular leaders of the DNC for 8 years, the Clintons recruited and trained operatives who adopted the same practice. In 1997, Bob Wexler won the Congressional seat from the 19th District of Florida. Within three terms, he would become a leader in mining social media to garner support from his constituents. He was the co-sponsor of impeachment proceedings against George W. Bush that received 251 votes for and 166 against referring the impeachment resolution to the Judiciary Committee on July 25, 2008, where no further action was taken on it

No one was surprised when, in 2004, he recruited a Pakistani graduate from Johns Hopkins University just 24 years old to be his Director of Information Technology. Imran Awan learned very quickly just how naïve members of Congress were when it came to computers, cell phones and other technologies. He became indispensable to the Clinton Crime Syndicate. At one time, he was setting up and had access to the email accounts of 80 different Democrats, some of whom served on the House Armed Services Committee with access to highly classified information.

Within two years, Imran had convinced Debbie Wasserman Schultz, the outspoken chairman of the DNC, to add his brothers Abid for $160,943 a year, Jamal for $157,350, Rao Abbas for $85,049 and his own wife Hina Alvi for $168,300 in addition to his salary of $164,600. These salaries for IT personnel were at least 300% higher than other IT staffers. There was, however, something very special about the way the Awans conducted their business with the Democrats under the auspices of Hillary Clinton.

The records prove that more than 5,700 logins by the five Awan associates were discovered on a single server within the House and 5,400 of those logins appeared to be unauthorized. The Awans were monitoring and recording every keystroke, copying every file, and reporting on every text and email to his boss, Schultz. All of this information was saved on remote servers that were created and operated privately by the Syndicate, away from the prying eyes of various oversight protocols. When the scheme was suspected, the files were collected onto a single server, and all the other pieces of hardware were destroyed with acid, cleansing software, and then physically damaged with a hammer to prevent recovery.

That final server belonged to then-Democratic Rep. Xavier Becerra, the Chairman of the Democrat Caucus, who served from 1993 to 2017. He then returned to California and became the Attorney General of that State. Neither the FBI, nor any ethics committee has been successful in gaining possession of or access to that server, regardless of subpoena.

By January 3, 2010, Congressman Bob Wexler's public knowledge about his collusion with certain factions in the Middle

East convinced him to resign to become executive director of the Center for Middle East Peace and Economic Cooperation, a Washington-based think tank. Imran Awan was well established by this time and provided unlimited access for Schultz and Clinton to the entire electronic world for at least 68 Democrats, including key members of the House Armed Services Committee.

The following Congressmen had every keystroke, phone call, text message, and file attached to or from their email accounts monitored, copied, and stored on a private external server without their knowledge by the Awan technical team under the direct compensation and management of the DNC led by Debbie Wasserman Schultz and Hillary Clinton.

Jackie Speier entered politics at first as the young traveling companion of Congressman Leo Ryan. On one of her foreign trips with the Congressman, the 28 year old redhead was caught in a gun battle at the airport in Jonestown, Guyana. She was shot five times and waited 22 hours before help arrived. Five people died during that tragic event, including Congressman Ryan. Later that day, 900 followers of Jim Jones, including children, committed mass suicide by drinking Kool-Aid laced with cyanide.

After two campaign attempts, she finally won a seat in Congress in 2008 and quickly rose in authority to work on the House Armed Services Committee with responsibility for Oversight and Investigations. She was added to the Permanent Select Committee on Intelligence, which is the primary committee in the U.S. House of Representatives charged with the oversight of the United States Intelligence Community. The Awans ensured that she was completely compromised by the electronic surveillance of Clinton and Schultz. Speier's vote would later directly cause the fabrication of the accusation that Russian collusion influenced the outcome of the U.S. elections of 2016.

Imran hacked Bernie's voter database on December 18th, 2015. Clinton and Schultz cut off Sanders from his own donor database during the DNC debates while the Awans mined his database of donors for their own purposes. Schultz excused the breach by accusing the Vermont senator's presidential campaign of exploiting a software error to improperly access confidential voter information collected by Hillary Clinton's team.

Within 72 hours, the Sanders campaign manager, Jeff Weaver, announced, "The DNC, in an inappropriate overreaction, has denied us access to our own data. In other words, the leadership of the Democratic National Committee is actively trying to undermine our campaign." Congressman Jackie Speier was silent on the issue.

Congressman Elizabeth Warren was elected to Congress from the State of Massachusetts in 2008, and upon arriving in Washington was appointed by President Barack Obama as chair of the Congressional Oversight Panel created to oversee the Troubled Asset Relief Program (TARP). The funds were used to bail out banks with untenable losses due to the collapse of the home mortgage security market.

Nearly $2.3 trillion, in what became known as *bailout funds*, were eventually paid back by the banks, but the funds were not used to pay down the national debt. Rather, they were exported to the European Bond market, to secure financial control over the trans-Atlantic Banking Cartel while the American taxpayer absorbed the cost. In exchange for her loyalty in this matter, she was supported to become the first female Senator from the State of Massachusetts.

Unable to obtain Senatorial consent to run the Consumer Financial Protection Bureau, she colluded with Obama to violate the Constitution in appointing Richard Cordray as the Bureau's first director. The Supreme Court ordered the appointment terminated as a violation of law, but it took a year to remove him from that office. During that year of illegal appointment, Obama attempted to establish the world's largest labor union formed entirely from nearly 12 million undocumented immigrants that were targeted to be illegally issued green cards by Mr. Cordray. 23 States, led by Texas Senator Ted Cruz, argued successfully before the Supreme Court to stop the program. Still, Obama managed to issue more than 100 thousand illegal green cards and got dangerously close to forming a monthly cash flow of more than $36 million a month into the DNC from what would have been union dues.

Every keystroke, email, text message, and file attachment was recorded from the moment Elisabeth Warren entered the Congress by the Awans and stored on a private external server. In 2008, the earliest year for which Warren has released income tax returns, Warren and her husband Bruce Mann had a combined income of $831,208. By 2016, after just eight years in office, her net worth increased to more than $15 million.

Warren's brain child legislation, forming The Consumer Financial Protection Bureau, made it illegal for banks to loan money to startup businesses. In less than five years, the CFPB drove the United States to the lowest level of business startup since records have been kept. Coupled with Obamacare, it drove full-time employment down to levels not seen since the Great Depression of 1929. The evidence of collusion with global, multi-billion dollar corporations for this strategic planning was copied and retained by the Awans in a folder called *life insurance* on the external server they maintained.

Seth Moulton was elected to Congress in 2012, and was endorsed by Elizabeth Warren. He served 4 tours in Iraq and is the Ranking Member of the Subcommittee on Oversight and Investigations and a member of the Subcommittee on Seapower and Projection Forces. Every keystroke, email, phone call, text message, and attached file was collected and stored by the Awans on an external server under the orders of Clinton and Schultz. In 2014, he withdrew from a debate over charges of corruption where he introduced Debbie Wasserman Schultz at New York fundraisers for the DNC. Although he is a decorated Iraq War veteran, he has not appeared publicly with Schultz ever since.

Donald McEachin was midway through his third term in the State Senate, when the DNC successfully convinced a federal court to throw out Virginia's original congressional map as an unconstitutional racial gerrymander. A new map shifted almost all of Richmond, along with all of Petersburg and most of the majority-black precincts in Henrico County (including McEachin's home), from the 3rd District to the 4th District. That district had been represented by Republican Randy Forbes since a 2001 special election, but the addition of these majority-black areas turned the 4th from a Republican-leaning swing district into a heavily Democratic district.

Although he had served a lifetime in State politics, the DNC drafted him as a natural candidate for the Federal office of Congressman. McEachin won the District handily in 2016 and became a very strong gun control advocate. He also sits on both the Readiness and the Seapower and Projection Forces Subcommittees under the House Armed Services Committee with access to highly classified national defense information. Every keystroke, email, phone call, text message, and attached file was recorded and stored on an external server by the Awans.

Like any information technology engineer, Imran assumed the espionage he commanded was valuable to the Clinton Crime Syndicate. He knew the information was valuable and allowed the Syndicate a strategic advantage over any opponent, including a Republican President. He thought he was indispensable, but once the connection was discovered by enemies of the Syndicate, he realized that Hillary would move to protect herself, even if it meant sacrificing him. During a Congressional Committee investigation, Imran realized that intelligence personnel would soon track the decade-long spying operation to him.

He decided to take immediate action to protect himself and his family. First, he wired every possible dime of money he could spare to friends in Pakistan. He then sent his family members to Pakistan and made sure the external server with more than 650 thousand files was secured and hidden in a secret location. Within a few weeks of Seth Rich's murder, he secured Debbie Wasserman Schultz's laptop under the pretense it needed some maintenance, as he had now become her direct employee.

But, instead of giving it back to her, he placed it in a vacant room once used as a phone booth in the Rayburn House Office Building. Carefully, he placed with the laptop letters to the U.S. Attorney, a Pakistani ID badge, and a composition notebook marked *attorney client privilege*. The user name on the laptop was 'RepDWS.' It was the only way Imran could assure he would not be killed. Debbie Wasserman Schultz publicly threatened the Capitol Police with *consequences* if they did not turn over the laptop to her without opening it or accessing any of the information on it. The chief of police ignored her threat.

Awan wired $283,000 to two people in Pakistan and then hastily took out a second mortgage on a piece of income producing property for $165,000 and wired it to Pakistan. Within hours, Imran booked his flight to escape the United States with his life. He was arrested at the Dulles airport on charges of bank fraud.

Attorney Christopher Gowen said publicly, after the arrest, that Federal authorities had no evidence of misconduct by Awan relating to his IT duties. Since that time, dozens of smashed devices that belonged to Schultz as well as other Democrats were discovered by sheer happenstance and turned into Federal authorities. The scope of the obstruction of justice is larger than anything ever seen by Federal prosecutors, requiring hundreds of agents and experts to recover. As of the writing of this book, Imran Awan and his wife Hina Alvi are still alive.

The Syndicate had formed and staffed the most incredible spying operation in U.S. history through bribery and subterfuge using Pakistani nationals as a private technical service to 80 Democrat members of Congress, many of whom sat on top secret and Special Access Committees. They compromised the 2016 Democrat Primary and rigged the election to prevent Bernie Sanders from having a chance of competition with Hillary Clinton.

By December 5th, 2015, Hillary was sure she would win the Democrat nomination for Candidate in the 2016 election, and she disappeared from the national press. Her campaign manager, John Podesta accidentally provided unauthorized access to his email account, the publication of which revealed the corruption by the DNC in the Primary. Debbie Wasserman Shultz was outraged she was forced to resign hours before her greatest moment of glory at the Democrat National Committee. She and Podesta publicly called for the assassination of anyone who could be linked to the information breach. A young and vibrant Bernie supporter, Seth Rich, was shot to death weeks later on a sidewalk near his home. Within days, on July 22nd, 2016, Shawn Lucas was filmed serving the DNC with a lawsuit on behalf of Democrat voters seeking relief from the DNC's collusion against Bernie Sanders. Thirteen days later, he was killed in his own bathroom while his girlfriend went out to get a pizza for their dinner.

Also in July of 2016, Bill Clinton secretly met with Loretta Lynch in a predawn rendezvous on the Phoenix Sky Harbor Airport General Aviation tarmac. Within days, FBI Director James Comey changed his reference of the 150-agent criminal investigation into Clinton's mishandling of classified information. Allegedly, under Bill Clinton's direction to Loretta Lynch, he referred to the investigation as a *matter* before the Congressional Committee.

Hillary Clinton finally emerged more than 270 days after her last press briefing to answer her first public question amid an avalanche of Congressional and FBI investigations.

She had spent decades gathering information on the politicians in Washington who might run against her. Many Democrat legislators and judges had been bribed or threatened to remain silent. Attorney General Loretta Lynch was questioned by Congress about the evidence, but took the Fifth Amendment 74 times to obstruct justice from being served.

But, there were 17 candidates for the Republican primary. Only one of them would be the nominee, and there were not enough resources to destroy the reputations of all of them. First, the field needed to be narrowed down. She knew that by the time the candidates got done beating up one another, there would only be one or two weak and impoverished candidates remaining, and they would not be able to withstand her political skills or the main stream media's massive propaganda machine.

Very few people believed the final nominee would be the only person about which she had zero political information. Donald Trump could not be bribed. He could not be bought. After nearly a year of undercover and illegal surveillance by the world's most sophisticated intelligence agencies, nothing had been discovered that could be used to discredit him.

It was another 100 more days before Hillary emerged to answer a meaningful question by the press. Every appearance was scripted and protected to prepare for the debates. Reporters and photographers were kept away with ropes, even when Hillary walked in the streets lined with her worshippers.

After Debbie Wasserman Schultz was forced to resign her position as chairperson of the Democratic National Committee, Donna Brazile, Al Gore's former campaign manager, became interim chairperson of the DNC. She was provided the Presidential debate questions in advance and helped prepare Hillary to develop perfectly rehearsed answers to those questions. She also developed a series of hand signals Hillary could provide the moderators so, when Donald Trump was speaking, they would know she had a prepared statement to counter his assertions. The 2016 Presidential debates were the most televised events in political history.

The scripted answers were not successful. The hand signals were discovered. The fact that the debate questions were provided to Hillary in advance, so she could rehearse, was verified and revealed to the public before the election. Donald Trump won 2,623 counties across America. Hillary won only 489 in a few metropolitan areas near the coasts. Despite millions of illegal votes, she lost the Presidential Election by a landslide.

This, by no means was the end of the Clinton Crime Syndicate. Winning the highest office in the world would have accelerated the dismantling of the Bill of rights in the Constitution. Losing it was only a temporary setback. All they would need is a different face with a different voice to continue their inexorable march toward the dictatorship the DNC has been advocating since it was formed in 1848.

All it would take now is an event so horrible that Americans would choose the path they offered.

Chapter 17

"I know many of you are thinking about graduation, and summer, and maybe even going to work or college. It's good to look to the future, but remember where we are and why we are here," said Mr. Larsen.

"High School sucks, Mr. Larsen," said a boy in the middle of the room. Everyone laughed cautiously. It was arguably the school's favorite class, even among the ones skating out with a 'D' average.

"I know you say that now, but trust me on this. You will look back on these days as the best in your lives when you get a taste of the real word out there. You might as well make the best of it. Shall we begin? Even though this is the last day of the school year, you should take notes," said Mr. Larsen.

"You might think that everything we have covered about the government inside the government is not very important. You might think that there is not much you can do about it anyway. You would be wrong on both counts. Some of you will leave this class for the last time very soon. Others, I am sure I will see again next Fall for this same class, as you must pass it to graduate. Think about that as I tell you this true story.

"America and a very few other countries, hold in their hands the ability to kill Earth. I mean the whole planet. Perhaps every living thing is at risk as well as the whole ecological balance that makes us the most unique place for at least 10 light years in any direction. You might ask 'Why would commanders ever use such a power?' and that would be an excellent question. One does not have to look very deep into the cause of nearly every war ever fought on this planet to find the same handwriting over and over again.

"Two good armies never go to war. One or more of the causes behind any conflict is always evil. What does that word mean; evil?" asked Mr. Larsen.

"The Devil?" asked a girl sitting behind Jack.

"Anyone else?" he asked.

"Um. They're always the bad guys. Like Hitler," said another boy.

"Evil has an author; that much is true. But it is unnatural to most people. They don't practice evil because it doesn't feel good. Do any of you like to see a child cry when they're hurt? Do you like to hear an animal in pain, or believe that anything you like that belongs to someone else should be yours for the taking? Why do you think twenty-two American veterans take their own life every day?" asked Mr. Larsen looking around the room to see the faces of his students.

"Evil is not a religion or even a special club you join. It is juxtaposed with, and yet thrives on another concept that is rarely understood; that of glory. Do any of you know what glory is?" asked Mr. Larsen.

"It's in songs, like Glory Hallelujah," said the same boy.

"It is not an easy thing to describe, but consider it something of value in the universe. Gods and demons want it from you worse than anything, and they will kill billions to get it. In fact, it can be argued that without it, they are both eventually, powerless.

"I would posit that, in fact, glory is the currency of true power in the universe, and this would include planet Earth. When charismatic leaders ride their ponies up and down the ranks of men, they can and have convinced millions upon millions of humans to freely glorify them. And when they get this glory they gallop into history books with grand and terrible words written all around their names," said Mr. Larsen as he slid off his tall stool at the front of the class and pulled down a map over the white board.

"It can be effectively argued that every color of kingdom you see here on this map was demarcated as a result of one of these charismatics ordering the slaughter of the defenseless colors underneath it. From the armies of Islam to those of the British Empire and the various borders of Europe, Africa, and even those of North and South America were all established by acts of war. It has been this way from the beginning of recorded history, and who's to say there have not been other histories before those in your textbook that have been burned and lost from other wars behind other ponies long forgotten?

"Perhaps in those days of forgotten history, as now, the weapons of war were escalated on both sides, supplied as it were by the same designers to both armies, until they became so powerful that they ended all civilization. Those histories are lost, but this one is not. Not yet.

"You intelligent, beautiful, people are the ones who have the opportunity to take humankind on a different path. Take a good look at the colors on this map of the world, for they will not look this way in twenty years. This blue over here won't be there. This nation will be gone. These states over here will be washed away, and these geographies over here will also be obsolete.

"Under each one of these colors are classrooms just like this one filled with young people just like you. They are being convinced to invest their glory, and believe me each one of you is a being of glory, in some ideology that hates and demeans, and dehumanizes. And many of them, and some of you, will put on uniforms and march over the graves of millions to what?" asked Mr. Larsen as he paused and looked around the room at their silent, lost faces.

He rolled the map back into place and grabbed the large globe off his desk and held it in both of his hands. He placed in on the stool in front of the class and stepped back, folding his arms. "You are in my ship far out in space right now, and we are looking down upon this amazing, blue orb full of more varieties of life than you could name in a single mortal lifetime. In your minds, turn around and look over your shoulder. What you see behind you, and over there, and way over there, is nothing. The rest of space sits at or near absolute zero. There is no breathable air. There certainly isn't any liquid water. No grass, no trees, no honey bees. This one, tiny little rock in space is all you can reach in a thousand lifetimes at the top speed of my ship.

"And here is the most remarkable thing about this lesson. You are here. You are alive and young and beautiful and healthy and ready to possibly create life in your own image. And right now, there is evil that has been sufficiently glorified pointing weapons more dark and powerful than you can imagine at these colors and borders on this globe. These weapons can only be stopped before they are launched, because once they fly, it is all over. They can only be stopped by you. It will very soon be your choice and your responsibility to decide whether this last vestige of humanity in the known universe disappears forever or not.

"'But, Mr. Larson, how can we possibly do that? All that stuff is classified and protected by men with guns?'" he asked for the students with their chins covered by their folded hands.

"Not one wheel will turn; not one wing will take flight; not one person will suffer and die at the hands of war without first it is fueled by glory. You have heard these words before. 'Many are called, but few are chosen.' I want you to consider that a mistranslation. There is no such thing as 'chosen.' There is only choice. Many are called, but few choose. I want you to remember that. I want you to remember to choose; not to be chosen. I am not the only one who feels there is not much time left before the dark designers of war, who have been supplying weapons to both sides of every war in the universe, see their plans fulfilled. Which, by the way, means that none of you get to fulfill yours," he said unfolding his arms and pointing his finger at each of them for a long moment.

"So time is of the essence. There will be a test on this, tomorrow. And the next day. And the day after that. All life on this planet depends upon you passing that test. So, please study hard," said Mr. Larsen as the final bell rang from the clock on the wall.

"Holy crap, Mr. Larsen. That was the best class ever," said Jack leaping out of her chair to shake his hand.

"So you're going to work next week, right?" asked Mr. Larsen.

"We graduate Monday. My brothers are coming. I want you to meet them," said Jack.

"Rocky, I know well enough. I haven't met the other two; James and Michael, right?" asked Mr. Larsen politely.

"They are the best brothers in the world," said Jack.

"I'm sure they say the same thing about you," said Mr. Larsen.

"Ha ha. Very funny. No, I'm serious. You're going to be there aren't you?" asked Jack pretending to beg.

"I will. I promise. It has been a great pleasure watching you learn and grow. You're going to do great things," said Mr. Larsen.

"Only great things," said Jack putting her book bag over her shoulder and twisting to head out the door.

After her father had his stroke, it seemed the whole world slowed down for Jack. The household sound changed without his loud and confident laugh and his brilliant little solutions to almost every challenge. She felt like high school would never end, but then this last day arrived in just a few moments. She wondered if she had paused enough to look around. She walked slowly to the book return tables set up in the gym. Each class had a table, and the books were being checked and stacked in boxes for the next class coming along in the Fall.

The teachers and staff were happy and talking back and forth as dozens of people moved from table to table, turning their books in and checking their names. There were yearbooks open here and there as friends stopped and scribbled notes and drew hearts and icons on pages where they might have a picture. Jack was only on one page. She focused on her classes, but she was distracted away from the clubs and teams that filled the yearbook with different photos and lists. Her brothers had their days, but by the time she walked onto the field, the band was getting on the bus, and the stands were cold and empty.

She realized how light her book bag was without high school in her life anymore. Like a fish from a farm released into the sea, she hovered around the bucket for a few minutes. The water was slightly different; cooler, saltier, and maybe a little large. The thought of General Banks and the strange Mr. Knorr jumped into her mind as her phone vibrated in her pocket.

She pulled it and thumbed the screen to answer. "Hey Jimmy. What's up?" she asked.

"I am still coming to your graduation, but things have gotten a whole lot more weird since a month ago," said James.

"Like zombie apocalypse weird?" asked Jack.

"No, like revolution weird. My guys are not involved, but the FBI is across the street with trucks. It appears somebody at the DOJ has grown a set and is raiding one of Hillary's parlors," said James.

"So? Bad people should go to jail. Why is that so bad?" asked Jack making the turn outside the gym to head for home.

"Yeah. Well, here's the big deal. Boeing, Google, General Electric, Cisco and Microsoft and many of the richest donors in the Clinton Crime Syndicate invested more than a billion dollars in the Skolkovo Tech Park outside Moscow. It turns out that her Syndicate soldiers in the Pentagon and the hundreds of Agencies of the Federal government were selling some of the most advanced weapons systems the world had ever known to the Russians," said James lowering his voice.

"So that's what they were talking about," said Jack walking briskly to the corner to cross the 5-lane in front of the school, her mind racing with the exercise.

"They who? Oh, never mind. Don't tell me over the phone. This whole freakin' town is monitored. Look, my guys are telling me that the Clintons allowed these companies to share hypersonic missile technology, capable of delivering conventional and nuclear payloads precisely at speeds up to nine times the speed of sound. They were investing into a kind of Russian Silicon Valley. The bad part is, the Russians did develop a missile and a small, rocket powered warhead to go on that missile. And don't forget that these companies also lead the world in cyber-technology, server protections, and viruses. They have launched dozens of the highest technology satellites in the world. And they are all in the business for profit. I wish I was building roads in Russia, because profits are very good in Russia right now," said James.

"Anyone in handcuffs yet?" asked Jack.

"Yeah right. They might bust a techie or two, but the leaders always go free. Too much money on the table," said James.

"You mean too much money in the pocket," said Jack sarcastically.

"So listen, Jackie. I'm driving down on Monday, but I have to go right back after graduation. We have a budget that's due. If we don't use it, we lose it. You know how Washington works," said James.

"I understand. At least we will be all together for a day. You better get out of there. You didn't see nothing. You don't know nothing," said Jack with a Brooklyn accent.

"Exactly. Okay sis. Have a good weekend. See you Monday," said James and the phone went quiet.

She slowed down at the corner to look back at the high school one more time. It looked like a lazy fire drill with all the people in the parking lot, cars lined up, and different huddles here and there across the lawn. It was over before it started. The thought of college appeared and splashed into foam under a crushing wave of images from the Pentagon. 'First things first,' she told herself, as she made the corner to head for home.

Within a few blocks she passed Meridian Park and made the turn north. Most of the neighborhoods had been turned into apartments, because of the value of real estate, and the few houses in the area didn't usually have driveways. A few of the houses had built single-car garages added on later and then converted those into shops, apartments, and even man caves. It was a high-rent district unless you had lived there for a few decades. The taxes were high, but having no mortgage was the only way a working family could afford to live this close to the major organs of the body politic. She chuckled to herself as she walked past a Maserati and then a Chevy pickup truck.

She turned up her driveway and walked to the back door at the kitchen. The door squeaked as she raised her voice a little. "Mom. I'm home," said Jack.

The house was quiet, except for a low television in the small living room. Unless they had been remodeled like some television makeover, houses on this street didn't have family rooms. There was a front room that, depending on the furniture, was the dining room, game room, and everything that wasn't a bedroom or kitchen. The master bedroom was on the ground floor, and the two other bedrooms were upstairs with a bathroom in between them. She shared a bedroom with Mike until James moved out. Rocky left for Annapolis, and Mike had his room, and she had hers. That was when her memory really started to become clear. Everything before the age of 12 poked out from behind songs and smells stuck here and there in her head. She went upstairs, dropped her book bag into the closet and slipped her shoes off. The hardwood floors told her mother she was not lying down.

"Jackie? Would you load up the scooter? Your father and I are going to the mall," said her mother up the stairs.

"Sure thing, mom," and she slipped her sneakers on and shuffled down the stairs. She went out to the garage that, strangely enough, was still a garage, and opened the door. She unplugged the red scooter and turned the key to see all the green LED lights come on. She sat down and pressed the thumb switch to make it quietly roll down the drive to the back of their SUV. She pulled the pin, lowered the deck, and drove onto the expanded metal shelf. She turned the key switch off, secured the straps and clamps, and raised the deck up to the bumper with the electric actuator.

She looked up to see a familiar small van pull into the driveway. She jumped to the driver side as the window rolled down. "Mikey! I am so glad to see you. Hey Lucy. Wow, you guys look awesome," said Jack as she leaned through the opening window and hugged her brother.

"We just got back from LA. God, what a place," said Mike.

"Promise me you will never go there," said Lucy.

"Earthquakes? What?" asked Jack smiling.

"Creeps. They're everywhere," said Lucy.

"Well, I'm going to work in the Pentagon next week. So far, I think those folks are pretty straight. Besides, I got family there to protect me if I can't kick them out of their shoes," said Jack spinning around and flying a kick into the air.

"Oh that hurts just watching it," said Mike turning off the engine and sliding out of his seat belt.

"Damn right," said Jack. "I'll tell mom you're here. Do you need any help with anything?"

"Nope. We just have us," said Mike.

"I think they were just heading to the mall. Come on in the house," said Jack over her shoulder as she walked to the back door.

"Mom. Mike and Lucy are here," said Jack as she walked through the kitchen to the living room. Mary was standing there, and her father was sitting in the large overstuffed chair quietly. She had her hand over her mouth and was looking down at the TV. She had her cell phone in her other hand by her side.

"What's wrong?" asked Jack. It wasn't very often that her mom even watched TV, but Jack knew that look.

"They're on lockdown," she said quietly.

"Who? What's on lockdown?" asked Jack.

"The Pentagon. Rocky called. There's a bomb," she said barely able to get the words out.

"Where? At the Pentagon? Again?" asked Jack.

"What's happening?" asked Mike walking into the living room and hugging Mary with both arms.

Lucy wrapped her arms around Jack and gave her a squeeze. "Oh my God, girl you are like a brick," said Lucy.

234

"Good eating and exercise," said Jack trying to focus on her mother.

"Rocky said to stay inside. They don't know where it is. They got a message from some group," said Mary again not able to finish the sentence.

"Jesus. They're doing it, aren't they," said Mike really knowing it was a question.

"This has to do with those arrests. I just know it," said Lucy.

"The bad guys up on K Street? What group? Guys, you are really scaring the crap out of me. Just tell me what is going on," said Jack turning sideways to the conflict.

"Okay okay, Jackie, cool your jets. We don't have all the pieces, but a friend of ours was murdered a few months back. He was working for the DNC. He said there was some information that was leaked, and it goes right to the top. I mean the whole election thing. It was corrupt like nothing anyone has ever seen. Trump was right, but I don't think he knew how right until he got in office," said Mike.

"They were pulling in money from everywhere, like all over the world. Foreign countries and movie people in Hollywood. God, what slimeballs they were. We just got back from there. Some Harvey producer guy. You wouldn't believe. But I think the feds are getting close. That's what I think," said Lucy.

"Okay, is this like some kind of revolution or something?" asked Jack.

"More like an insurgency, I think. Somebody sold a bunch of promises they can't keep, is my guess," said Mike.

"Is that why everything is going to shit over there in Saudi Arabia?" asked Jack.

"Bill collectors. Sounds like someone is getting their Ferrari repo'ed for non-payment," said Lucy.

"No wait. Mr. Larsen said something about this," said Jack holding her hands up and looking at the ground like she was trying to remember.

"Who's Mr. Larsen?" asked Mike.

"That's Jackie's history teacher. He's a, I mean he's been teaching history at the high school," said Mary finally able to compose herself.

"Mr. Knorr knows him. Anyway, he said that there is a ruling class of elites who want to take over the world, and they thought they had it done, but Trump came along, and nothing they tried could stop him. So, they're pissed, like big time. He's been undoing all the stuff they built up over the last 40 years, and they don't like it one bit," said Jack almost swinging her fist in the air.

"Mr. Knorr?" asked Mike.

"No, Mr. Larsen," said Jack acting like he should have understood her.

"No. I mean, who is Mr. Knorr?" asked Mike.

"Oh. He's this giant guy with blond hair who works at the Pentagon, and Rocky is there, and," she paused and opened her eyes wide.

"That's okay, Jackie. You don't have to say any more. I got the picture. You hear that?" said Mike speaking a little louder and looking around the room. "She didn't say anything. You got that? We already knew this."

"You think our house is bugged? You watch too many movies," said Jack.

"They hear everything. I was shopping one day by myself, and walked by this cute pair of shoes. I didn't pick them up. I didn't say boo to anyone. I get home, open up my Facebook, and boom; there's an ad for those shoes on my timeline. I about shit," said Lucy.

"Really? You didn't tell me that," said Mike.

"Because you're such a conspiracy nut," said Lucy.

"Seth is dead, and Jackie is going to work at the Pentagon, and some maniac is out there with a bomb, and you're saying I'm the conspiracy nut?" asked Mike.

"I'm just saying this could all be a bunch of coincidences, you know?" said Lucy.

"Anyway. Rocky says to stay put for now. Don't get caught on the expressway. Does anyone want coffee?" asked Mary nervously.

"I'll help you," said Lucy as she extended her hand for Mary to follow her back to the kitchen.

"So Jackie. What are you going to be doing at the Pentagon? I assume you don't know anything classified yet," said Mike.

"I'm going to be a runner. They don't use emails or phones for the important stuff. They use runners. It's like a whole city in there anyway, but I'll be like taking information from one place to another inside the building on foot. I can't wait. I'm working for this lady general named Banks, and she is over all this space stuff," said Jack with her eyes rolling and hands twirling in the air.

"You said you saw Rocky there. Did you speak to him? Is he okay? I haven't seen him in a year," said Mike.

"Yeah, I saw him. He works in a vault with a bunch of gamer hacker guys. It's all new, because of that plane crash back in 2001. Homeland security stuff," said Jack.

Mike sat down on the arm of the chair next to his dad and put his arm on his shoulder. "Dad. How are you doing? You doing okay?" asked Mike quietly looking into his father's left eye.

His father's lip quivered a little with the effort to get some thought from his active mind to his mouth, but nothing came out. He gripped Mike's arm with his left hand and blinked slowly.

"He's trying to say he misses you. He's proud of you," said Jack. His eyes darted to her, and he nodded. He patted Mike's arm and he hummed quietly. "I can't tell exactly. Help me out a little, dad," said Jack kneeling down in front of him.

He flattened out his left hand, and used his index and middle finger to make scissors, and then a fist. "Rock. Rocky. Oh Rocky. Yes, dad, I saw him. He is doing great. He's in the Navy, dad. He's not a spook. Okay, maybe he is a spook, but he is a cyber spook, not one of those guys who becomes a bad guy to catch the badder guys," said Jack speaking quickly.

"Here's a cup of coffee, baby," said Lucy carrying two cups with her from the kitchen.

"Oh, thanks. I love your coffee," said Mike carefully taking a sip from the mug.

"Oh my God. I just thought of something," said Jack rising quickly to her feet.

"What?" asked Mike.

"Graduation," said Jack with both hands in front of her like she was being passed a basketball.

"Jesus, Jack. You scared the crap out of me," said Mike.

"Well, I hate to bring this all back to my little world, and wild horses and all that, but a bomb threat kinda ruins the party. You know what I mean?" asked Jack nearly in tears.

"Yeah, well what if it's not a threat. I mean, do you really think Rocky would say anything if it wasn't credible?" asked Mike.

"Look. It all comes back to what Mr. Larsen said. There is this little evil group that wants to rule the world. Trump is flipping over the card tables, and raiding the bootleggers. He said they would crash the entire world to beat him. What does that even mean, 'crash the world'?" asked Jack.

"Sounds like your history teacher is no ordinary teacher," said Mike.

"He's not," said Mary gently blowing on her coffee mug while she stood next to Lucy.

"I think he's talking about the Depression. The way I understand it, the global economic powers of the day just shut off the money supply, and boom. The bank closed, people went broke, anyone in debt was wiped out. The ones with cash in hand stepped in a few months after the dust settled, while everyone in the whole country was standing in a black & white movie soup line, and bought up the whole world for pennies on the dollar," said Mike.

"Yeah, like it was all part of the plan," said Lucy.

"Well, they can't do that now. I mean, it's like Rocky says. It's all ones and zeroes now. The switches and programs run everything. It can't happen now. Besides, Mr. Larsen says the weapons are too powerful now. We can't have a war. Not like that," said Jack trying to grasp the power of what Mike was saying.

"I thought this was just all a bunch of politics and money, too. Democrats, Republicans; it's all the same no matter who gets in. They're all crooked as hell," said Mike.

"Yeah, but then Richey," said Lucy with tears instantly trying to fill her eyes.

"Our friend who was murdered on the sidewalk outside a club we were playing a little while back. He told us the Democrats had rigged the election. They weren't taking any chances. They bribed and bought these delegates," began Mike.

"Super-Delegates," chimed in Lucy.

"Yeah, Super-Delegates, whatever the hell that means. Bernie Sanders never had a chance, but they actually thought they had bought the election. Every poll in the country said Hillary was going to win. She had this mythical ground game, and Trump was packing every stadium at every rally. Needless to say, all that corruption and all that money, and all the cheating at the polls weren't enough to beat Americans. Trump won anyway," said Mike.

"But I thought Hillary won the popular vote," said Jack.

"Oh puleaze. Truth be told, she lost that too," said Lucy.

"It's like baseball," said Mary.

"What do you mean, baseball?" asked Jack.

"Your father used to say the Electoral College was like the world series. In 1960, the Yankees scored a total of 55 runs in 7 games compared to the Pirates 27 runs. But the Pirates won 4 games to 3, which won the World Series. He said that if it wasn't for the Founding Fathers figuring out how to make it so a group of smaller States could match one large State, we would have become Socialists a long time ago," said Mary.

"You mean like only LA, New York and Miami would ever see a campaign speech, right?" asked Jack.

"I think that is where the whole *'I'm with Her'* thing went wrong," said Lucy.

"Anyway, we have been on both coasts in the last week, and I can tell you that their influence is everywhere," said Mike.

"So, are you saying these sore losers would blow up the country to regain control?" asked Jack.

"These guys wanted a surveillance State. They knew we would never go for it, so they blew up New York. Hell, we cheered for the National Defense Authorization Act. We carried 14 new intelligence agencies into Washington on our shoulders while waving the flag. Now, we can't move without them being able to use everything we said or did against us in a court of law," said Mike.

"The bomb. What about the bomb?" asked Jack.

"I don't know. I wouldn't put it past them. They blame their own riots on Trump. Like he made them mad, so it's his fault. I think they would blame Trump if this kook is really out there like Rocky says. I haven't heard anything on the news," said Mike.

"Fair's fair. He blamed kid Bush for not keeping us safe," said Lucy.

"We're not talking about a few thousand people, and we bounce back in a couple of weeks. If they detonate even a small explosive it's going to be enriched with fear. That's what they want; an enemy 50 times larger than life and invisible," said Mike.

Suddenly, Mary jerked her hand, nearly spilling her half-empty mug. "Oh, dear. Sorry. I can never get used to that vibrating phone. Hello? Yes. It's Rocky. Yes they are. What? Now? I filled it yesterday. Okay. We're on our way," said Mary as she touched the phone with her little finger while holding her mug.

"Let me guess. We're going to the Pentagon," said Jack.

"He wants all of us to go. He said he can't be compromised. Jimmy's on his way too. What do I wear?" asked Mary putting her mug down and sitting on the arm of the chair next to her silent husband.

Chapter 18

"How many of these do you want made?" asked the engineer at Griffin Machine and Fabrication.

"Just the one will do. I appreciate you working so quickly. It looks even better than I expected," said Adnan.

"Usually I can figure out what something does as I'm machining it. I don't usually work with 7068 Aluminum of this size. I mean, I've made a few racing parts and some parts for airplane kits, but a piece this size is not easy to find. These angles and the bore tubes got me baffled, that's for sure. At first I thought it was a centrifuge, but that would require that it spin, and there is no central bearing mount. What does this thing do?" asked the engineer.

"I am sure I do not know, exactly. It is rocket science," said Adnan shrugging his shoulders and smiling. Both men laughed.

"Here is the invoice. You just want me to send the bill on the same PO?" asked the engineer.

"Actually, this is off-budget. This part name here is the only record. You know how it is. If it works, my boss takes credit. If it doesn't, we blame it on NASA. So, I am going to pay for this right now, if that's possible," said Adnan.

"Absolutely. End of the month. I can close it out in the black instead of carrying it over. Besides, those government projects sometimes don't pay right away. You know how it is," said the engineer.

"I'll remember that. You came through for me. I won't forget this. Seriously, you saved my ass," said Adnan as he scribbled out the check and handed it to the engineer.

"Pleasure doing business with you. You need help loading that?" asked the engineer.

"If you don't mind. You can load it with the forklift with a small pallet into my vehicle, that would be great," said Adnan.

"Sure thing. Just pull around to the dock, and we'll get you loaded," said the engineer.

By sundown, Adnan had made the trips from each of the four machine shops back to his remote shop building in the woods of the Stennis Space Center grounds. It was the perfect location for someone without a social life. The little building was made of steel with a steal rollup door and a man door on each end. It had withstood hurricane Katrina when many buildings did not. His programming job paid well enough that he could have moved to New Orleans, if he wanted to, but this was much closer and there were no neighbors.

He inserted the small thumb drive into his laptop and opened up the detailed drawings to begin assembling the machined aluminum parts. 7068 Aluminum is just about the hardest Aluminum that can be bought. It is precipitation hardened by raising the metal to high temperatures and then carefully exposing it to zinc vapor. The result is a lightweight metal that is equal to steel in tensile strength.

The top was shaped like a bowl with a thick flange around the lip with bolt holes evenly spaced. The cavity would be lined with a shaped and fired ceramic explosive that fit perfectly. The North Koreans had perfected the process of polymerizing the RDX chemistry into the ceramic to make the entire construction conduct electricity. It would achieve 5,500 meters per second within a few millionths of a second.

This was bolted to the heavy centrifuge-appearing part with twelve cylinders converging to the top of the third part of the assembly with upper half of a larger diameter sphere about the size of a basketball. This had been polished to a mirror finish. This would be bolted to the bottom half of the sphere. The two halves had been lapped with diamond compound to fit within 0.5 microns to form a perfect seal. The bottom of the assembly was a perfectly shaped and armored compartment designed to protect the electrical components that would power the bomb.

All that was needed now was to mount the micro-circuitry that had arrived from North Korea via Pakistan. The round beryllium case was grounded to the machined aluminum with the silicon wiring harness routed through a grommet to connect to the piezo-electric valves located at the bottom of each of the small cylinders. They could hold 20 thousand pounds per square inch and release in the same exact microsecond, forcing tritium into the small casting of plutonium captured inside the baseball chamber. When the two halves were bolted together, there was no place for the explosion to go but through the solid three inches of 7068 Aluminum. At that precise moment, twelve cylinders full of fresh tritium would supply a plethora of energetic neutrons to enrich the chain reaction rate.

After all, aside from high-quality plumbing, a nuclear power plant is simpler than an internal combustion engine. The bulk of the controls are designed to use lead rods to soak up the excess neutrons from radioactive decay for a high-pressure steam turbine. If the plumbing and the rod controls function correctly, the plant makes electricity for about three years, before the reactor has to be refueled and the saturated rods are trashed in an abandoned deep mine in New Mexico or Tennessee.

Weapons that have to be stored for long periods of readiness are also a challenge. Tritium is a generally artificial molecule made from sticking two neutrons to a Hydrogen proton. It is an unhappy marriage that comes apart naturally in about 14 years, unless it is ingested by humans, in which case the beta decay is much shorter. As it is such a small particle, and prone to a short half-life, tritium in weapons has to be refreshed if it is in storage for a long time. Everyone on planet Earth hopes that weapons remain in storage forever, so there is an entire industry full of technicians that deal with this process. Like all the North Korean equipment, this device was vastly redesigned to be small. There was no need for stability, because it was designed for immediate deployment.

Adnan molded the aluminum pillow batteries against the lid and fed the wiring harness through the lid to the upper chamber where they would be connected to the switches and valves. He had practiced this many times, but this time there was a small, warm sphere in the heart of the machine.

The entire philosophy behind weapons design was developed billions of years ago as God and His creations battled over who exactly was the rightful heir to the universe. The management of enemies is a meticulous business for beings who wish to keep populations in a constant state of mistrust. America spends more on weapons and war systems than the next 25 countries combined, and 21 of those countries are allies.

The ancient evidence for global annihilations of entire zeniths of mortals on Earth proves that management of wars is not easy. Even when meticulous balance between enemies is maintained, once the destructive force reaches a certain level, continents can be sunk into the sea, and tropical forests can be turned into deserts. Once the weapons are energized, recovery is often impossible. Billions of lives can be extinguished in a matter of hours or days. It is a time of immeasurable loss for some and intense celebration for others.

Solid Tritium requires temperatures near to absolute zero, as well as pressures barely contained behind two inches of tool steel. The magnetic fields capable of accomplishing fusion are far too large for something as tiny as a weapon, so implosions are used to crush the protons into one another. That crushing force needs to remain uniform for a few millionths of a second, so that they have no hernia of escape. The crushing frequency needs to be very high, in the range of x-rays, so typically simple atom cannon technology is utilized. That, however, requires materials very hard to get, and easily detectable from space. So, the North Koreans developed a piezo-electric pulse oscillator to entrain the neutrons in the chamber, sort of like a microwave oven using x-rays.

The challenge of achieving the power necessary to make it efficient had been overcome with a simple technology transfer while Bill Clinton was president. The rest of the microelectronic circuitry they hacked from South Korean computers. The super-capacitors could discharge a virtual lightning bolt in a fraction of second, energizing the piezo-electric membrane to form a perfectly spherical compression on the solid Tritium fuel. The extra neutrons accelerated the chain reaction, and the yield had been tested to a level of several hundred kilotons. The beauty of the weapon was that they were scalable to megatons, when used in unison, fired from satellite simultaneously.

The red herring was the challenge of delivery. For years, the Americans worried about the empty aluminum cans they launched for thousands of miles into the sea through space. They chased the submarines, and worried over the placement of their jets and mobile launchers. It was like watching pets lose their minds chasing a laser spot around the living room. They fell for it every time.

The virtues of the Tritium weapon were numerous. The beta decay was virtually untraceable and easily contained. The fuel was stored by the millions of gallons at the Stennis Space Center, because it was based on simple rocket fuel. There was actually very little physical destruction upon detonation, unless it was on the surface. It was lightweight, and could be disguised as simple industrial equipment painted safety yellow, splattered with mud, and added to any common pneumatic supply system. The real beauty of the weapon was the Electromagnetic Pulse it generated. The blast would scarcely break windows three miles away, but the voltage generated by this weapon was expected to overload every antenna within 600 miles in any direction. Every overhead power wire, every cell phone tower, and every power station would have its integrated circuit controls destroyed within seconds.

He thought about home as he masked off the stencil into place. He shook the can of black spray paint and carefully misted the paint into the exposed areas on the exterior. The maps had changed because of Western imperialism. Hitler's lust for power had inspired the Persian Shah to reduce one of the world's greatest legacies into Iran, but they were not Aryans. They were Persians, and they should again be one of the older brothers of humanity.

He believed in the cause, but saw past it to another future, where they would betray the corporate conglomerate that believed it controlled the world. He coughed a chuckle through his mask as the paint fumes irritated his throat. 'The snake controls the mongoose, does it?' he asked himself. He tore off the tape from the other set of letters, and draped the green paper over the black letters he had just painted. He grabbed the red can, shook it, and painted the other half of the logo. 'Looks good from I-59,' he said through the paper mask over his nose and mouth.

The detail was perfect, although it didn't have to be. Ingersoll-Rand made air and gas compressors and driers of all types. He checked the advertisement one more time to make sure his fabrication looked the same. His contact was an abatement contractor in Nashville, Tennessee. It was such a detestable industry full of asbestos, dust, mold, and heavy metals. No one minded if immigrants did work like this. No one cared about plastic curtains, scaffolding, and hoses lying everywhere as compressed air was used to blow and to vacuum offices, warehouses, factories, and miles upon miles of plumbing throughout the Thermal system in the city heated by a local trash-burning recycling operation. His piece of equipment was finished.

All that was needed now was compressing the fuel and charging the capacitors. It only took one day to reach Nashville by hotshot truck. He wiped the paint residue off his hands with Xylene.

Chapter 19

    The Roosevelt is an old hotel, but with the best room rates in Manhattan, it stayed busy. The room was small, but James didn't mind as the late flight and cab ride left him too tired to care. The shower felt good as he brushed his teeth and tried to gather his thoughts about the reasons he may have been called to Trump Tower for a meeting at 9:15. He brushed his teeth and shaved in the stand-up glass shower feeling better after watching the FBI raid the offices across the street from his on K Street in Washington D.C.

    The dark blue suit he had chosen in haste from his closet fit well, considering he hadn't worn it in nearly a year. Usually, Congressmen or their aides came to his office to ask for money, knowing they would be trading promises for contracts for roads or bridges in their States. That's the way the game had been played long before he got there. The time Congress spent working on bills, amendments, riders, or deals was minimal compared to the time they spent raising money to campaign. The Party finance people would show up on Mondays and Wednesdays, and the individual campaigns would show up anytime they could find an opening in the schedule.

    Freshmen members had a phone bank in the old Cannon House Office Building, which was built in 1908. If you got reelected for a second term, there might be space in the Longworth House Office Building, which was built in 1933. Committee chairs and senior members had much nicer operations in the Rayburn House Office Building, which was built in 1965. There wasn't much room for money raising activities in the Capitol Building. That was reserved for constituents that came to visit, asking for favors or grants or other fruitless activities.

    The real money in Washington was in his neighborhood. When the Members weren't dialing for dollars, they were making deals on K Street. The taxes collected from the sale of fuel formed a steady flow of money to rebuild roads, bridges, tunnels, and to manage all that money. Congress amended the highway budget every year, but the game was run the same way through any of more than 600 different Agencies, Departments, Bureaus, and Administrations, each of whom had thousands of contractors that sold their goods and services to government. Each of those contractors had four areas of their own budgets; sales, operations, personnel, and lobbying. The latter area was the one that fueled the other three.

Larger firms, like General Motors, had their own lobbyists whose main responsibility was to make sure that no competitors received a dime of grant or loan guarantee money from government. Smaller firms usually had to hire a lobby firm with a team of industry-specific lobbyists who built relationships with Agency officers and Members of Congress to funnel contracts to their clients. The latter required what many in Washington call *grease*. So, it formed a smelly process of collecting taxes and then laundering some of that money right back to the Members who wrote the bill that created the project in the first place. Members who didn't have the energy for that game sometimes formed Foundations and had the beneficiaries of their official duties make a charitable contribution or two.

The entire process prioritized self-enrichment of the Member, but care had to be taken in routing, lest one end up convicted of fraud like Congresswoman Corrine Brown. The champion of all time was the Clinton Crime Syndicate, which had dozens of branches in a dozen countries, all of whom transferred money between one another, creating money trails similar to ant hills. Once anyone started digging into it, the whole thing crumbled, and the queen was nowhere to be found.

James had become successful because the contractors that paid his salary with commissions were happy with the steady flow of high-profit jobs he was able to secure for them. At the same time, the Highways and Transit Subcommittee was a whole government in itself covering every surface and every mode of travel on that surface including cars, trucks, and trains. There were more than a hundred Congressmen and thousands of other elected officials at State and County levels that all needed money to run campaigns. The money trail was confusing at times, but ultimately the taxpayer made it all possible.

James checked his overnight bag at the concierge, and dropped him a five. He decided to walk the few blocks up Fifth Avenue to Trump Tower. It looks like a long distance on the map, but Manhattan is usually faster on foot than in a cab on most days. It was drizzling outside, and he was glad he had remembered to bring an umbrella. He always felt a little British when he walked with it closed, but like a New Yorker when he walked in the rain with it open. He enjoyed the exercise and let his mind focus on his best openers for meeting at Trump Tower. It wasn't business as usual, that much he knew. He went over the email again in his mind. Not many details were given. 'Your presence is required,' didn't really say much. He couldn't get past his gut feeling that this was somehow a job interview. Again, he shook his head at the notion. He wasn't famous. He had never run for office. He got along with Republicans and Democrats, although the latter seemed to have the need for a very elaborate ass covering staff.

He stopped at the red light and waited for the walk signal. There were two police men standing on the corner, and behind them the sidewalk had been split in two with steel railing, making an aisle near the curb and an aisle near the storefront of Saks. He stepped off the curb with a dozen other people with the crosswalk signal, and after he had made eye contact with the officer on the left. "Good morning, officer. I'm heading for Trump Tower," said James like he was asking for directions.

"Outside lane. Have a nice day," said the officer.

"You too," said James as he smiled. The officer smiled back and he entered the block long chute. When he got to the end there were two more officers, and he was only about a block away from the gold glass building. He pointed up and the officer pointed to the outside lane again. He passed them without saying anything. He was alone in the chute, although there were quite a few people on the sidewalk who seemed almost unaware of the additional security. It was just the way people in New York were.

The next block changed from steel railing to concrete barriers. One of his clients made them from rebar and concrete in mold and shipped them all over the East Coast. These units weighed 2,500 pounds and required a crane or a forklift to be moved. The old days of catching a cab on the curb of Fifth Avenue were over for this block, until he arrived at Trump Tower. There was an opening in the barrier about a hundred feet long, and there were police at both ends. He reached the end of the chute and turned to walk through the revolving door into the Tower. No one stopped him. There was a simple metal detector, but it was clear that the ground floor of Trump Tower was pretty much open for business. He collapsed his umbrella and shook the droplets off its Teflon coated fabric and fastened the strap around it neatly.

He paused for a moment in the warm air of the building and took out his handkerchief. He wiped his forehead and cheeks and took a few deep cooling breaths and put it back into his breast pocket. There were two men at the elevator in suits, but it only took him a second to tell they were security. He guessed they weren't Secret Service by the small logo on the pocket of their neatly tailored jackets. Both of them looked big enough to be Seals, which definitely didn't fit the description of Secret Service. None of those guys got more than a day's training to hold that job. These guys both looked like Clark Kent; the only superhero who has to put on a disguise to not look like a superhero. They both moved at the same time as he approached.

"Hi. I'm James Rousseau. I have an appointment at 9:15? 25th floor?" said James.

"You're fine. Have a good day," said the one on the right, and they both went back into position, seeing everything.

He gathered they must have the whole appointment schedule memorized, or someone was watching him on camera and told them he was okay. He pressed the up button on the elevator and in a few moments the one on the right opened. He stepped inside, only to see another superhero with an IPAD.

"Your name please?" asked the man in the grey suit with the logo on the pocket.

"James Rousseau. I have an appointment?" said James again, as though it was a question. He reproved himself for being so intimidated. He made Senators beg for money. Why was he so nervous about this meeting?

"Yes sir. I have you. 25th floor. Please, sir, do you have a cell phone?" asked the elevator man in a smooth voice.

"Yes," said James.

"Please show me that you have turned it off," said the elevator man.

James pulled out his cell phone and held the button to turn it off, and placed it in the man's open hand. He placed it into a ziplock bag with a silver shine to it and handed it back to him. "You will be required to place this into a lock box when you get off the elevator. Okay?" asked the elevator man.

"Yes sir. No problem," said James, and the elevator began its rapid ascent.

James walked out of the elevator on the 25th floor into a small lobby area with a desk behind which was seated an attractive woman. He walked up to the desk and began to speak quietly, but was interrupted by her smile.

"Mr. Rousseau? Hi, I'm Mr. Bannon's secretary. Do you have any personal items to be stored while you are here?" she asked politely.

"I have a phone in a bag," said James smiling.

"May I have your driver's license please? You will get the phone back as you leave. Place your license in the placard holder on the lid, place your phone inside, close the lid, turn the key and take the key with you. Okay?" she said like she had one thousand times since inauguration day.

James followed the directions and slipped the key into his pocket. It wasn't any worse than taking a drug test for his security clearance.

"Thank you so much. If you will take a seat over there, someone will come to get you shortly," she said pointing to a very nice French Provincial matching couch and chair with an antique gold end table with a sparkling Tiffany lamp sitting on it. He sat down softly and glanced around. If he was being watched, they were very good at concealing it. There was enough room to have fifty people in the lobby that extended all the way to the windows, through which filtered a gray light from the overcast day outside.

"Mr. Rousseau, will you come with me?" came the male voice in a crisp dark grey suit. There was no logo on the pocket. He was tall, but thin in stature and appeared to be no more than twenty-five years old.

"Sure," said James standing quickly and walking beside the boy. The thought that Jack could do this job and really be safe darted through his mind.

He opened a large rosewood door and held it for James. He walked through to a medium sized conference table around which were seated a half-dozen other men; all in suits except one who wore a, Navy officer's uniform.

"James. This is Admiral George Salt. This is a special task force we've assembled. You're now part of it. You seven people will know what to do. The President expects a direction by tonight, no matter how late. Food will be here at noon and again at 5. There are showers down the hall on your right. Ask Maggie if you need anything else. Anything. Laptop, calculator, paper, whatever. No

253

calls in or out. I hope none of you have flights planned until tomorrow. I'll leave you to it, Admiral.

"Thank you, sir. James, welcome aboard," said Admiral Salt extending his hand.

James shook his hand and walked around the table shaking hands and getting names he tried to remember by associating each one with their faces. He prided himself in remembering people's names. He also forgot each one as soon as they said it. "Thank you all. It's nice to be here. Can you tell me where here is, or who that guy was?" asked James, wondering who an Admiral would call 'sir.'

"Here is not important. Even less important is knowing who that was. The important thing is that we have inherited a damned mess. Someone thought screen doors would be a great idea on a submarine, and we just shoved off. Each of you have been chosen for this task force. Don't ask me why, because I don't know. Our mission is to come up with a plan to stop an avalanche with a snow shovel. In front of each of you is a sealed envelope. You can open it now, and let's start putting some fingers in the dike," said Admiral Salt.

One by one they opened their envelopes. They were not the same. Each one described a major breach in national security, and by themselves, they were manageable. But as each man read and synopsized his situation letter, the combination scared the hell out of James.

"Look, guys. I am not a security expert. I am a road and bridge expert. I'm a lawyer, but by trade I have become a transportation infrastructure project manager of sorts. I don't know why I was chosen, but I can tell you my opinion," said James pushing his chair back from the table a little in a tactic he learned from one of the firm's partner's

"I know how you feel. I manage a hole in the water where the government pours money. I'm sure each one of you feels the same way. But, here's the deal, Jimmy. I can call you Jimmy, can't

I? The President doesn't trust anyone in government right now. Would you? So, we're smart guys that each have a track record of getting shit done. Now, do you know how to operate a dry erase marker?" asked the Admiral.

"I thought you'd never ask," said James jumping to his feet and walking over to the 8-foot long white board on the long wall beside the conference table. "This is called a Gantt Chart. Give me the earliest failure mode you have, and then the next. We'll build this layered timeline and see what shakes out."

Within half an hour, James had drawn the characteristic stair steps with each block holding the condensed version of a classified situation. He used different colors for each layer, and assigned a threat level to each one. His right hand ached a little as he stepped back to take off his jacket.

"Jesus H. Christ. That's not a mistake. That's a battle plan," said the Admiral.

"How so? You're saying all these actions are related?" asked James.

"Hey, I'm Peter, by the way. I work for the NERC. We manage the grid. One thing most people don't know is that nuclear power plants need to be refueled every three years, max. We've been reverse processing weapons grade material to make fuel for the power plants for decades, and that is enormously expensive, but it's faster than mining and enriching Uranium. We try to manage the phases of all the power plants so we can route power from one utility to another without a power factor. Everything is sixty hertz, but the peaks of the waves need to match, or you lose energy and money. So, I don't know how we're going to do that, if we run out of fuel. Somehow, it seems, we sold 20% of our fuel production capacity to the Russians. That makes no sense to me," said Peter.

"What's the NERC again?" asked James.

"Oh, sorry. The National Electrical Reliability Corporation," said Peter.

"Everyone knows about the Clintons brokering that deal for more than $140 million in kickbacks. If there is anyone left alive from that gang, they should go to prison," said the Admiral.

"Yeah. That sale went through why?" asked James still standing and rolling up his sleeves.

"You people act like we are a country of laws or something," said the man seated next to the Admiral.

"Not that we have the time, but I'd like to hear your story," said James motioning for him to take the floor.

"My name is Yuri Rustemeyer. My family was German exiles living in Ukraine. 3rd generation American," he said tapping his own chest. He stood up to his full height of six foot nine inches and walked to the white board. He pointed to his situation block on the board and turned to face the men seated at the table. James sat down and rolled his chair around from the end of the table to the side so he could watch Yuri.

"I think the reason I was chosen for this team is that I work for a small company called ILC Dover. We make the gas-tight envelopes for lighter-than air craft, specifically the 420K Tethered Aerostat," said Yuri twisting the lid off a bottle of water from the small credenza.

"You mean like a balloon?" asked James.

"It's the TARS," said the Admiral. "They're like the old barrage balloons the Germans used to snag low-flying bombers at night. The steel cables would cut the aluminum wings right off a Lancaster."

"Lockheed Martin made the radar system. Kind of low-tech, actually. They had a diesel generator on board with 100 gallons of fuel. We would top them off, raise them into position about 15 thousand feet high, remotely start the generator, and they would give us a peek over the horizon," said Yuri.

"Sounds cool. If you don't mind me asking, where were these deployed?" asked James.

Yuri looked at the Admiral, who gave a nod with his finger against his chin, assessing every word. "Basically, we started in 1980 supplying them to the Air Force, who in turn let U.S. Customs & Border Patrol deploy them around the Florida Keys. They worked pretty well at catching drug transports. So they ordered more, and we set them up all the way around the Gulf of Mexico. We were pretty well covered," said Yuri.

"So what happened?" asked James.

"In January of 2011, President Obama ordered the TARS decommissioned through the Air Force. People in DHS tried to take it over, but their budget was too small, so the system was taken down," said Yuri returning to his seat.

"So what are we using now?" asked James.

"With the TARS, we could see over the horizon about 500 miles with some good resolution, a little further for airborne early warnings. Without it, we can see perhaps 15 miles," said Yuri.

"So you're saying we went from having about an hour's warning a cruise missile was coming across the Gulf of Mexico to less than two minutes?" asked James.

"Sounded like another budget war to me, until I saw all these pieces put together," said the Admiral.

"Look, it's one thing to turn dollars for bullets into dollars for food stamps to buy voters. I get that. But this is something a traitor would do. Leave the castle side door ajar," said the next man. "I'm Herbert Kadzinski. I'm just a financial compliance auditor. I'm not a military person or a strategist. I audit banks and brokers to make sure they comply with government regulations. I live here in New York, and I don't know how they chose me," said Herbert already trying to emotionally withdraw.

"He's the guy that caught HSBC. Remember the press? Well, it was barely a blip. Drug cartel money?" said the Admiral.

"Sorry. I missed that one. I see it on the Gantt timeline, but how does it belong here in this picture?" asked James.

"Well, it is a steady flow of funding for their operation. Investigators usually get their man by following the money, or at least I do. When you can't follow the money, you can't stop the bad guys," said Herbert.

"Okay, really quickly, because I'm starving and I am sure this is already going to be a working dinner. Tell us what happened," said James opening a bottle of water for himself.

"Americans love drugs. They buy billions of dollar's worth of illegal drugs every month. That cash goes to Mexico, usually. The wholesalers down there deposit the money in their local bank, because there is too much money to keep anyone honest. Mid-level sellers in the States bundle their cash together into cartons specially designed for depositing millions of hundred dollar bills through the teller windows like pizza at American bank branches. That money is then wired to tens of thousands of phony bank accounts, which in turn wires the money to other phony accounts, and each time, someone takes a cut to keep the operation secret. It's pure luck that we caught it, because all of this is off the books. Doesn't show up as an asset. The point is that someone very high up in government is skimming about $200 million a year off this system for personal projects," said Herbert.

"By someone high up, you mean the President?" asked James

"Hell no. It doesn't take someone of my expertise to question a personal net worth going from about $300 thousand to more than $100 million in 8 years. Just the interest on that is nearly $8 million a year, without touching the principal," said Herbert.

"That leaves what, about $16 billion unaccounted for?" asked James running the numbers in his head.

"That's just the drug cartel money. There is another $5 billion missing in 4 years from Hillary's State department and nearly a trillion missing from the Pentagon budget. There is another hundred billion missing from Libya after Hillary assassinated Qaddafi. You starting to get the picture?" asked Herbert driving his point as though he was correcting a bank Chairman.

"Looks to me like their trying to buy an army," said the Admiral.

"There are two armies, actually," said the next man.

"Which box is yours?" asked James pointing to the Gantt Chart on the board.

"My name is Frank Gibson. I'm a printer. Obama made some supposed recess appointments to the National Labor Relations Board in 2012. A few weeks later I bid on a contract to produce about a hundred thousand green cards and some manuals in several languages. During the oral part of the bidding process, they asked me if I could print several million cards. Of course, I said yes. But, I really got concerned when some of my union guys were overheard talking about a new labor group forming up. It was being organized by the NLRB itself," said Frank.

"Wait. I remember this. There was a Supreme Court case, right?" asked James.

"You mean NLRB vs Noel Canning. Yes, but that wasn't until over a year later. They sued him for not allowing a union to form at his plant. He countered that the appointments were not legal, so the NLRB didn't have a legal quorum, and the Court agreed with him. Scalia said that the term *recess* had no meaning for the modern Senate. Anyway, I got burned on the contract, so I wrote an open letter in 2015, and maybe that's why I am here," said Frank.

"You said two armies, though. Please elaborate," said James.

"Okay, the one I know the most about is the one made of more than 10 million undocumented immigrants. First of all, let me say I get it, alright? This is the place to live if you want opportunity to really be successful. I'm second generation American myself. And I guess that's what people all over the world strive for; to get here so they can be free. But that is not what has been happening for the last ten years. These people are coming here to destroy, not to build," said Frank.

"Destruction doesn't pay very well," said James. "What do they hope to gain by wrecking everything?"

259

"You asked me to tell you, and I'm telling you. When my father came here, he had nothing but a stone cutter's hammer. He learned English, and cut stone by hand. He became a citizen after ten years, and he was proud to be American. These people won't learn English, and they won't assimilate. They have a rage that was transferred to them by the President, who also didn't want to assimilate. He changed America into what he wanted it to be, and encouraged these immigrants to do the same thing. They are sitting out there today, tens of millions of them, waiting for orders," said Frank.

"Orders?" asked James.

"Yes sir. You see, the plan was to form the largest labor union in the world, made of about 10 million green card holders. This guy, Richard Griffin, was a union organizer. That's why Obama hand-picked him for that position. But, they got stopped by Ted Cruz as he led 23 States in an unprecedented lawsuit against it, before they could pull it off. Still, I still delivered about 100 thousand green card blanks. He tried to defeat the Supreme Court by replacing Scalia, when he died under very mysterious conditions; no autopsy. Very weird that whole situation. By 2016, the plot to set up a cash flow for the Democrats had lost too much momentum. So now, those millions of undocumented immigrants are waiting for orders," said Frank.

"That's why we're seeing these sanctuary cities, right?" asked Herbert.

"What about you? You haven't said a word since you described your situation letter," said James.

"Well, I'm Hannah. I've been operating a small podcast for about ten years. After I graduated with a degree in nuclear chemistry, I couldn't find a job right away. So, I made one and it has been okay at paying the bills, and really good at keeping me single. I guess somebody on Mr. Trump's team listens to me. Believe me, I had no idea, until the card came FedEx. Here's the deal. This high-level effort to break down national sovereignties has been going on a long time, but about eight years ago the sources of funding began to poke their heads out of their dungeons. They have their flags, signs, shirts, and transportation all paid for by Soros through two non-profits he funds," said Hannah.

"She's right. One of my training meetings covered these high-net-worth individuals moving money through charities. Someone in the IRS has quite the operation. Now, that's an audit I would love to conduct," said Herbert.

"Audit the IRS? That's doesn't sound natural," said James.

"Or possible. Talk about a secret army. Holy hell," said the Admiral.

"Anyway, George Soros has funded three main non-profits, one called the Open Society, one called Refuse Fascism, and the other called World Workers. These probably have a dozen other little militant groups that receive money. At their core, these groups are all designed to tear down nations. Simple as that. They attack voters with clubs. That much is easy to see. They also use a four-pronged assault force that focuses on education, entertainment, litigation, and legislation to push the utopia of Socialism," said Hannah.

"Oh Jesus. We've been fighting those bastards for 300 years," said the Admiral.

"Actually, since 1675. They almost succeeded in killing America before it ever got started. See, that's the spooky part; for me anyways. It's like they can see the future, or something," said Hannah.

"My dad used to say that about the Founding Fathers. He's still alive, but he had a stroke a few years back. He said they read the Bible and didn't like that future with Armageddon and all that crap, so they walked away from that future and chose another one. They established America to form a new timeline," said James.

"Wow. I have never heard that before, but I like it," said Hannah.

"The future? They had a vision or something?" asked Frank.

"According to James's dad. They didn't have to. God gave them the path if they didn't change their ways," said Hannah.

"I don't mind telling you that this is off the charts. Gets my mind sore thinking about it," said Herbert.

"Anyway, all that is just so much street riot news. A while back I discovered that the Resist and the Open Society groups pushed into North Korea. This is where things got serious. I don't even know where to start," said Hannah almost losing her voice.

"Hey. It's okay. I know we're under a lot of stress up here. But, we're going to get through this," said James.

"It's not that. You don't even know. I have a Korean friend who served a church mission in Seoul. I picked up these Ham messages on my scanner. Really short, like ten seconds long. Different ones. I started recording them. Turns out, they're in Korean. Someone out there is building a bomb," said Hannah.

"No shit, Sherlock. We've been watching them shoot their missiles for years now," said the Admiral.

"Hey, no disrespect, Admiral, but your guided missile destroyers can't even avoid an oil tanker," said Frank.

"Point well taken. Let her go on," said James.

"Okay, well the Norks have done to nukes what Sony did to the Playstation. They don't even need yellow cake or Uranium. Everyone has been led to believe that Putin is feeding them technology and Uranium. That is so much bullshit, I can't even begin to explain. It was the Clintons. They gave them the missile tech as a distraction. It's like, 'Watch this hand over here,' and then they're doing something else. This bomb was designed by them, but it's being built right here in our country by a Pakistani engineer," said Hannah.

"What is this bomb?" asked the Admiral.

"It's a Tritium bomb. According to the chatter," said Hannah.

"You said that on your podcast?" asked James.

"Hell yes, I did. That's what the press is supposed to do. You gotta problem with that?" asked Hannah raising her radio voice.

"Well, when it comes to sharing classified information, I draw the line," said the Admiral.

"There isn't anything classified about a nuclear attack," said Hannah.

"Did they give a target?" asked James. The room was noticeably silent as each man secretly wished they could call home.

"That's where that block came from, people.," said Hannah pointing to the whiteboard. "That's why we're all here. No one on this planet can fight America straight up. Not possible. Any really serious war would be over in a matter of hours. So they spent twenty years planning this final solution to the American problem," said Hannah.

"I thought Hillary was the final solution, and we put a stop to that shit in 2016," said the Admiral.

"You think she has to be president to be powerful? Look what she did as Secretary of State," said Frank.

"How could they hope to defeat America?" asked Herbert.

"Well hell, gentlemen. Let me explain. Set up one nation under surveillance. Send an invasion force of twenty million soldiers and distribute them in major metropolitan areas where the banking, energy, education, and media are controlled. Conduct a 24-7 campaign to revive racism between everyone, and even create a half-dozen new minorities by opening up all the closets. Sexualize little kids in every media possible; normalize it, and then slaughter babies by the millions for profit, and then feed those profits to the Democrats who manage the politics. Conduct ten or twenty mass shootings to make sure people are afraid to gather in public groups," said Hannah.

"But we are country of laws. People are generally well-behaved in a society of liberty," said James.

"Oh really? Do you think these people will all keep behaving themselves when law enforcement is out of the picture?" asked Hannah.

"Like that's going happen," said Frank.

"Oh, but it has been tested already. Ferguson, Baltimore, LA, and let's not even talk about Chicago," said Hannah.

"Those are areas where law enforcement doesn't have a great reputation anyway. I'm not buying it," said James.

"Well, you asked me, so let me try this out on you. If a nuclear weapon ever detonated over America, the lights will go out for hundreds of miles. Some of those systems could be out of commission for months. Am I right Peter?" asked Hannah

"Years, in some cases. If the sub-station step-down transformers blow," said Peter.

"Years. So, what happens when there is no electricity?" asked Hannah.

"No gasoline. No heat. No refrigeration. Hell, the grocery stores would spoil in a matter of one or two days," said Frank.

"No police," said Hannah.

"And you don't think people will just pull together? You know, work as neighbors facing a shared challenge?" asked James

"Suppose you are one of the top 1% in your town. Maybe you have some nice toys and food storage in your garage. Now, suppose there are 20 thousand people in your town who have been trained by their imam or their pastor to go after you first. How long do you think you can hold off those people?" asked Hannah.

"What you're saying is that this North Korean nuclear flash bomb could topple our social house of cards. It doesn't really have to do anything but turn out the lights for a while," said James.

"I think I've heard just about enough. I see the situation. We have been spun around blindfolded and told to take a walk through a mine field. Now, what is the solution?" asked the Admiral.

"The way I see it, we have three choices. We can try to take the blindfold off. We can refuse to walk and just lay down until the lights come back on. Or, we can find the bomb and stop it before it goes off," said James.

"There has to be another choice. Whoever is planning this knows we will stop everything and do a national manhunt for that bomb," said Peter.

"He's right," said Hannah.

"Can you say National Defense Authorization Act part two?" said Herbert.

"What do you suggest, buying a really good pair of sunglasses and waiting for the flash?" asked James tossing the dry-erase marker on the table.

Chapter 20

They decided to take Mary's SUV to the Pentagon. The tank was always full, and Mr. Rousseau's scooter was already loaded on the hitch lift. Mike pulled his minivan onto the lawn, grabbed their travel bags, and locked it up with their musical gear inside. Jack ran upstairs and stuffed her gym bag full of the basics, socks and underwear. Within minutes, they were backing out of the driveway and heading for the parkway. Mary smiled through a cloudy panic while watching the neighbor walk slowly, sifting through the return addresses on the envelopes he casually retrieved from the curbside mailbox. The other vehicles around the city moved without a clue what was coming. Mary tried not to get pulled over or drive too much like at any moment the entire world could go dark.

"Mom. Just go straight across the bridge and turn left. There is guest parking in the lot, and the whole place is scooter friendly. I'm texting Rocky to let him know we're pulling in," said Jack from the back seat.

"I don't get it. How did we ever get in this situation?" asked Mike.

"General Banks said we have enemies inside our country right now. And Rocky was afraid things could go south a couple of months ago when I was here," said Jack looking at her screen and tapping out her message at the same time.

"We're talking terrorists, right?" asked Lucy.

"Sort of. Mr. Larsen says it's all part of this big plan by Globalists," said Jack.

"Oh shit. You don't buy all that Illuminati stuff, do you?" asked Mike.

"I don't really know what that is, but someone very high up wants to take us out," said Jack.

"Yeah, like anyone could take out America. Who would want to do that anyway? Aren't we the world's biggest customer?" asked Mike using his argument to settle his upset stomach.

"Look, baby. It's not as though America has been the good guys to everyone out there. We meddle in other people's business all the time," said Lucy.

"Oh come on. Everyone meddles. The Russians, the Chinese, the Muslims. So we want to make sure some Yankee-buddy gets elected. What's wrong with that?" asked Mike.

"You'll see when we get there. Mr. Larsen says we have two governments, and that the conflict between them is about to go hot, whatever that means. He says there are some rich guys he calls elites who want things their way. And, if they can't have it, then nobody gets to have anything. They're like spoiled little rich kids," said Jack.

"I thought this was all about oil," said Lucy.

"Jack, where do I turn up here? There is parking everywhere, and it looks busy," said Mary.

"Go over there. They have handicapped parking and the ramp is right there. See?" said Jack pointing to the left from the back seat.

"I see it. Hang on, everyone. There's a speed bump," said Mary barely slowing down for the impact. The SUV rolled over it noisily, and she steered the vehicle into the parallel parking spot. The vehicle hardly turned off and Mike was out, trying to help Lucy exit.

Jack jumped out, pocketed her phone, and lowered the scooter to the ground. She turned the key on and thumbed the switch to move it off the hitch platform so she could sit down and drive it to the front passenger seat. "Get on, Dad. Let's go," said Jack.

Within minutes they were through the front doors of the Pentagon. Jack walked over to the guest window and explained who they were and why they were there. Before the female Air Force sergeant was able to dial an extension, Major Mead put his hand on her shoulder.

"Good afternoon, Miss Rousseau. Is this your family?" asked Major Mead.

"Oh, wow. Am I glad to see you. Yeah. This is my mom and dad, and this is my brother Mike and his wife Lucy," said Jack sounding like she was out of breath.

"Very nice. I'll take those, Sergeant," said Major Mead, taking the five lanyards with guest passes. "I only need four. This one has a badge." He handed Jack a badge with a clip to go on her belt.

"I remembered the shoes," said Jack smiling and putting on her badge.

"You can follow me," said the Major to the rest of them. Mary put her hand on her husband's shoulder and they followed the Major through the guest admission line.

"Today it's alright, but Ma'am, from now on, you will enter through the regular employee line over there," said the soldier in black pointing over to the base of the stairs.

"Yes sir," said Jack turning off her phone and slipping it back in her pocket after the scan was complete.

Major Mead led them down the main hallway of the outer ring of the Pentagon. The halls were busy with uniformed and non-uniformed people. Even the barbershop had people in chairs sitting and reading magazines.

"I gotta say, Jackie. You picked a nice place to work, unless someone tries to land an airplane in your office," said Mike as they walked together. Lucy was holding onto his arm like she was afraid of getting lost.

"I'm just an intern, but they say I get to run 5 miles a day in this place. It is pretty cool," said Jack trying to make the best of a situation that still felt like a zombie apocalypse.

Major Mead turned around and walked backward for a few steps and stopped, holding his hand out to direct them into a doorway. "This is family services. They'll set you up in quarters, temporarily. After you get settled in, you can bring in any clothing or prescriptions you have in your vehicle. I'm afraid orders are that you hang out with us within the walls until we're through this situation," said the Major.

"I really don't like the way you say 'situation,'" said Mike.

"I am going to escort Jack to her office, and then I will be back to assist you. I shouldn't be more than 20 minutes. Okay?" asked the Major.

"No problem. You take care of her, and we'll be okay. Thanks, Major," said Mike. He placed his hand on his father's shoulder and leaned down to his left ear and spoke softly. "You were right, dad."

His father smiled and with his eyes, seemed to agree. He reached up and put his left hand on Mike's arm and squeezed with his strong hand.

"I know dad. I know. It's gonna be okay," said Mike holding back his emotions.

"You have a nice family," said the Major as he lengthened his stride with Jack matching him.

"Well, you've met everyone, except James. He's the oldest and a lobbyist. Lives in D.C. He's supposed to come to my, oh shit, my graduation. Sorry. What about graduation?" asked Jack suddenly remembering there were other plans.

"You'll have to bring that up with your brother, I mean Commander Rousseau," said the Major.

"Commander? Whoa ho. What is that in Air Force years?" asked Jack.

"Lieutenant Colonel," said the Major.

"So, he outranks you?" asked Jack.

"He outranks me. In fact, without a sea command, that is about as high as you can go in the Navy," said the Major.

"Uh huh. And what does he actually do again?" asked Jack.

"We're almost there. Once you're inside the door, I'll head back and make sure your folks are squared away," said the Major.

"Thanks, Major Mead. You're the best," said Jack as they slowed to stand in front of the secure door in the narrow hallway. The door clicked loudly and began to open. "See ya later," said Jack smiling as she walked sideways into the doorway.

The cubicle room was buzzing with the tap of keyboards. Rocky was leaning over the shoulder of one of the young men, as they were focused on his screen. She walked quietly around the end cubical and put her hand on his shoulder.

"We came as quick as we could," said Jack giving him a short hug.

"Jackie. Oh thank God. What about Mom and Dad?" asked Rocky.

"I brought Mike and Lucy, too. Major Mead is getting them settled in some sort of quarters. Are we living here now?" asked Jack.

"Special circumstances. Listen, I need you to take a package to General Banks. Can you do that?" asked Rocky.

"I am not sure I can find her office. I don't know," said Jack.

"Sure you can. I have a map. Print that to disc," said Rocky to the technician.

Rocky handed her the card-sized map of the Pentagon with the vault room highlighted in yellow. "Banks is right here. As you can see there are about eight ways you can get there. Take a different route each time you go. Mix it up. Pretend you're being followed, because you are. There are bad guys in here. We just don't know who they all are. Agents are everywhere. We are running out of time, Jackie. Here's the drive. Take this pouch, but don't put the drive in it. It's full of nothing, so if you're held up, drop this pouch

270

and run like hell. Stow the drive in your pocket or your shoe, and get going. Go go," said Rocky nodding his head to the door security, who she noticed was wearing a sidearm today.

It wasn't as hard as she thought to find General Banks' office. She walked fast enough that anyone following her would have tripped over something trying to keep up. If she had to, she had a couple of speeds faster than that. If someone caught her, they might have to have help letting her go.

"Jack. It's nice to see you again," said General Banks holding out her hand to shake hers.

"I have something from Rocky, er Commander Rousseau," said Jack.

"That's okay. I call him Rocky too. Boy can punch a tree out of its roots. Come on in. Let's see what you have. Stand right there. I'll have something for you to run back," said the General.

"When you said runner, I thought you might be kidding," said Jack trying to recover her breath, as the General slipped the drive into the side of her monitor.

"Holy Christ. Where's Mead?" asked the General.

"He's getting my family into some temporary quarters," said Jack.

"Okay. That's good for now. Look, this is out of the ordinary. I need you to listen carefully," said the General as she stood and opened a light maple wood cabinet door to reveal a large safe. She punched in a series of numbers and leaned forward, opening her eye to be scanned. The safe door made a bumping sound, and she turned the handle to open it. She opened a file drawer, pawed through the folders, retrieved a dark brown envelope and handed it to Jack. "Take this to Mr. Knorr. You remember him?" asked the General.

"Yes, General," said Jack holding up the small map card for her to point out the inner ring office.

"This one right here. Fastest route, Jack. Got it?" asked the General.

"Yes ma'am, General," said Jack and she slipped quickly out the door. Within a few steps she was in the street-wide hallway. She looked both ways to see if anyone noticed her, but there was no change in anyone she could see. Suddenly, the brown envelope felt conspicuous in her hands, but she looked around and saw several more people carrying envelopes that looked very similar. 'Very smart idea,' she thought to herself. She took off to the left and crossed the street to begin the zig zag pattern of cutting from one ring to the next to bring her around to the mysterious Raymond Knorr's office.

She entered the single wide doorway, which was unguarded and open. She didn't notice this the first time she was here with Major Mead, but the Pentagon had a kind of hum to it, like large air handling systems running, but when she entered this alcove, the room went silent. The floors were tile, and the walls were painted concrete like most everywhere else, but somehow there was a peaceful feeling here.

"Come in, Jack," came the deep voice from inside the open office door to the right.

She looked around for a surveillance camera, but she couldn't see one as she moved quickly to his doorway. "Hello, Mr. Knorr. From General Banks, sir," said Jack holding out the envelope.

"Thank you, Jack. Have a seat, please" said Raymond in a voice too deep to ever get used to. He pulled out a shiny flat hook and cut the end of the envelope open and withdrew the contents. She breathed deeply to calm herself in the chair. He put the paper on his desk and rocked back in his oversized chair and looked up at the ceiling for a moment. "Tommy says you're a smart girl with a good heart."

"Mr. Larsen? Yes. I think I do have a good heart," said Jack feeling it beat faster than it should.

"We have been at war for a long time. Did you know that?" asked Raymond.

"Well, I know about World War Two and like, the War on Terror," answered Jack.

"Much longer than that. It's important you know this now, and I'm sorry to bring you into it so early, but you are not really so young, now are you?" asked Raymond.

"My mother says I am an old soul," said Jack.

"And a warrior. I don't have time to explain that to you, but I need to ask you one more time to bear the burden. Can you do that for me, Jack?" asked Raymond.

"If I can," said Jack trying to keep her balance.

"You can. Trust me. Our enemy has lost some ground in the last year or so. Their propaganda machine has had a few teeth broken out of their gears, as well as a few political losses in which they had too much invested. They often start wars to kick us off balance with financial and social chaos. They're going to detonate a special weapon made for these times," said Raymond.

"These times?" asked Jack.

"Well, let me put it this way. A weapon like this would have been little more than a fancy firework in the revolutionary war, when they tried to crush America before it ever got started. But now, a weapon like this is particularly effective," said Raymond.

"You mean an EMP weapon?" asked Jack remembering a podcast she had listened to on the subject one night.

"When the world was lit with lanterns and people went to bed with the chickens, a high-voltage pulse wouldn't bother anyone. But we are now financially and psychically dependent upon electronic devices. Imagine instant darkness over half the country. No phones. No cars. No lights," said Raymond.

"It would suck. Mr. Larsen explained it, I think," said Jack.

"Well, our enemy knows the when and the where. By now, they already know we know the what," said Raymond.

"How is that, I mean, how could they know we know?" asked Jack.

"Rules, Jack. There are very old rules in a war like this. You see, they are not trying to defeat us. They are trying to make us defeat ourselves," said Raymond.

"What if we don't. Like, what if we just light a candle and walk away?" asked Jack.

"Hmm, yes. Well, sounds easy enough, but remember moths are drawn to a flame," said Raymond.

"What if we don't use a light at all," said Jack.

"What do you mean?" asked Raymond turning his face toward her, focusing both of his bright blue eyes on her.

"It sounds kind of dumb. Maybe we become the light," said Jack.

"Who told you that?" asked Raymond.

"Nobody. It just seemed like the only choice left. I don't know," said Jack shrugging her shoulders.

Raymond pickup up the phone on his desk and pressed one of the buttons on the panel. "I need to speak to him. Now, if that is possible. I will wait for a moment," said Raymond calmly, as he turned to look at the glass full-length window that looked out into the tropical garden in the center courtyard of the building. "Mr. President. Have they arrived at a solution yet? My latest information is that we may not have much longer than midnight, sir. No one on this world has ever seen a weapon like this before, Mr. President."

He paused in his large chair and listened. Jack could hear a male voice, but it didn't sound angry. "I will do what I can. Yes. I think the weapon may already be in position. It may very well function as designed, but its effectiveness is up to us."

He paused again listening to the President's voice and responded in the same, calm and deep voice. "They worked for 10 years to chop us into pieces. It is up to you, Donald, to blend us back together in the face of the enemy within," said Raymond clearly. "You know I am with you. I will be standing by. Thank you, Mr. President."

"That was the President of the United States?" asked Jack.

"Indeed it was," said Raymond.

"You can just call him up, and he answers?" asked Jack.

"It's kind of refreshing considering the last one hung up on me and tried for eight years to have me killed," said Raymond.

"Can he do that?" asked Jack.

"Let's just say he followed orders and was rewarded with wealth beyond his dreams," said Raymond.

"If you ask me, he deserves to be in jail," said Jack.

"A man with a button in his hand brings justice to himself," said Raymond.

"My dad used to say pleasure kills a man quicker than pain," said Jack.

"Alexander the Great," said Raymond.

"Alexander the Great said that?" asked Jack.

"After his final battle against Egypt, he was still young, but he wept, for there was but one world he could conquer," said Raymond.

"What was the point of conquering the world?" asked Jack.

"You remember more than you think, Jack. Poor Senator Obama did not realize how fast 8 years passes when you spent 20% of your Presidency on the golf course," said Raymond.

"For sure," said Jack.

Raymond opened his desk and pulled out a small velvet box. He opened it and picked out a large, red jewel with his smooth fingers. He reached across the desk and placed it into Jack's open palm. "It's not a gift. It's a message. Take this back to General Banks. When the President's task force arrives at their answer, I will send for you. Be swift, Jack, and I'll see you before midnight," said Raymond.

Chapter 21

In 2013, under the direction of the Environmental Protection Agency, abatement companies quickly took advantage of grant money made available by the Obama Administration to tool up to service these areas. It wasn't as though the highway and transit contractors actually wanted to buy the abatement services. They would have been financially attacked through EPA enforcement actions had they not complied. Just as with all the other costs associated with government contracts, they are all passed on to the taxpayer. It has been that way since the first Stimulus awards were granted in the summer of 2009. He called it investing in America. The truth is that more than 91% of the money borrowed from China and Saudi Arabia was given to donors and bundlers for the DNC.

It became the business modus for the Obama Administration. Any company seeking Federal grants, loan guarantees, or subsidies, had to first make its deal with regional Democrat campaign finance bundlers to make a pledge. Companies with higher pledges were the ones who got the grants, with the understanding that obligations paid in full before the award date would be prioritized for grant approval. Within eight years, the Syndicate's plan was to double the American national debt from 39% of the Gross Domestic Product to more than 79%. Valerie Jarrett and Barack Obama implemented that plan perfectly.

The Department of Highway and Transit has hundreds of Democrats on the committee who are constantly seeking campaign financing. It was not uncommon in larger voting districts for a single grant recipient to cover substantial campaign contributions for as many as a half-dozen Democrat Congressmen and possibly a Senator.

That goes without saying that substantial funds were encouraged for the President as well. A $20 million grant may bear a $10 million campaign contribution burden, but the contractor simply assigned this to the cost of doing business. Often, the recipient company was required to provide common, free-trading stock to the Congressman through a campaign manager or a charity. Once the grant or the government contract enriched the company, causing the stock to increase in value, the Congressman would cause the sale of his stock, regardless of the effect that sale would have on the share price, and pocket the profits.

Small companies had no choice, but to play the Democrat game if they had any hope of being profitable, as the U.S. government has always been the world's biggest consumer. There were thousands of small companies funded this way every year, and thousands more who were denied simply because they refused to compromise their own ethics by paying to play.

Adnan paid close attention to the classified section of the local newspaper in Hattiesburg, Mississippi. He dutifully managed the charge on the Lithium batteries that stored the power for the Piezo-electric Tritium injectors and the smooth nano-technology ceramic implosion charge inside the polished Aluminum sphere of the device. The tiny ball of Plutonium inside the sphere was an alpha emitter, and as such, was nearly impossible to detect from across the small shop. No one would ever suspect a non-working industrial air drier mounted on a compressor truck for a highway abatement contractor.

It took months to get the device built to the exacting standards the North Koreans had specified in their process guides. The Clintons used their authority to smuggle Chinese scientific spies into Sandia Labs in 1995 in what the New York Times reported as merely an effort to improve U.S. relations with China.

Within months, the Chinese were provided access to classified information on seven U.S. thermonuclear warheads, including every currently deployed thermonuclear warhead in the U.S. ballistic missile arsenal. That included the W-88, a miniaturized warhead that is the most sophisticated weapon the United States has ever built. In addition, they were provided a full set of working specifications for an enhanced neutron bomb that has never been deployed by any country, including the United States.

The Chinese provided tens of millions of dollars to the Clinton's foundation in exchange for the access. Some of it was delivered in untraceable cash. It didn't matter that they got caught. The Clinton Crime Syndicate was so powerful by then, no force on Earth could stop them. It took North Korea no longer than 20 years to advance that technology far beyond any other force on the planet. The Russians gained some of it. The Chinese gained some of it. But, it was the sequestered genius of North Korea that made it small and precise and unstoppable.

His construction of the miniature Tritium device would have been done sooner, but access to the Stennis Space Center provided a critical source for the Hydrogen. Other gases could have been used, but what the device lacked in size, it made up for in yield. The Hydrogen proton is the heaviest proton in the universe. Using natural gas or Ammonium would have chemically provided protons, but their atomic mass was far less than that of Hydrogen. Bonding these heavy protons with Oxygen to make a peroxide is what made rocket fuel that would burn all the way into low orbit. No one could detect a few hundred pounds of missing Hydrogen from the chemical plants at Stennis. Hell, they had more than that leak into the atmosphere like chemical fugitives escaping valves, switches, and flanges every week.

The other issue was the amount of time it took to program the rocket test facilities at Stennis. The talent to look at a set of prints and write software that animated that drawing into a perfectly operating machine was extremely rare. The need for immigrants to do this programming was a priority, as American programmers wanted to write Apps and live in Silicon Valley, not in the mosquito swamps of Mississippi of the third-world educational environment of Louisiana's public school system. Adnan was polite, clean-shaven, and rarely had any of his code edited by quality control.

When the classified ad for lemon cheesecake finally appeared, it was nearly May. He drank the rest of his latte at Starbucks, folded the newspaper under his arm, and drove to the old welding shop in the woods of the Stennis Space Center complex. Operation Dew Claw was about to move to the next phase.

He reflected again on the lifelong process that had brought him to this point. The colonial battles destroyed Damascus and the death of his brother and parents. He spent years blown about with his desire for revenge, until the Syndicate contacted him and trained him to program software. His class had more than two hundred boys in it, but after three years there was only him. Many of them could not master the skill, so they volunteered for suicide missions. Each time one of them would carry out an assignment, the boy's family would become instantly wealthy after receiving a payment from the Syndicate. The parents would make a shrine for their martyred son.

One by one, they all disappeared or were moved to Europe to hide in Sharia zones protected from local law enforcement to wait for orders, just like he received. He was a very special cog in a global machine built with trillions of dollars to bring all of humanity under one rule by the one true god. He laughed to himself as he pulled off of Interstate 59 onto the road leading to the Space Center, because of the subtle difference between the rule of law and the rule by law. 'When the lights go out, the world will see only darkness from space as this land of Satan is sent back to the Stone Age,' he said quietly in the cab of his pickup truck.

His construction of this device was flawless. The September 2017 test of a similar device in North Korea yielded more than 200 kilotons; five times the power of the blast at Trinity. This design was a fraction of the weight, and it utilized an advanced Tritium enrichment system that no one had ever seen outside of their mountain test facility.

The fact that it could level everything above ground for two miles in every direction was a small benefit when compared to the pulse that would travel at nearly the speed of light almost 600 miles in every direction, overloading every integrated circuit in its path. He was humbled by the thought that he would live to see his genius come to fruition. His creation was about to join a very short list of devices that changed the world, right alongside the Gutenberg Press and the iPhone. The realization that he was blessed and protected by God to deliver His judgment on the wicked nations of the world caused his eyes to well up with humility. Like Joshua of old, his trump would bring down the walls of the modern Jericho. He softly sung the song again, as a single tear fell down his cheek:

..."You may talk about your men of Gideon
You may brag about your men of Saul
There's none like good old Joshua
At the battle of Jericho..."

"Joshua fit the battle of Jericho
Jericho Jericho
Joshua fit the battle of Jericho
And the walls come tumbling down."[5]

In a few days, his device would be charged with Tritium, crated and weighed, and loaded onto the trailer he would pull to Nashville, Tennessee. All these years he spent planning, learning, and avoiding mistakes. He tried not to think about his reward. That was the dream building motivation of the infidel. The visions of cars and money and first-class living produced extraordinary results in the capitalist system. These things were their god. There could be no such desire in him. 'Verily I say unto you, they have their reward,'

---

[5] Songwriters: . Dp / Carol Tornquist "Battle of Jericho" lyrics © Warner/Chappell Music, Inc

he said to the windshield. 'My reward waits for me in heaven, Allahu Akbar.'

He pulled his truck onto the gravel road leading back into the woods. He noticed the leaves coming in brightly and the evening Sun cutting through the humid, still air of the hardwood forest. He rolled down the windows and listened to the tires crunch along the gravel and smelled the flowers competing for bees with their fragrance. He slowed to watch a doe and her two fawns cross the single-lane path through the woods. The old Ford rocked back and forth as the shocks mildly complained at the effort to make it smoother. He wondered if America would look like this in a few years. Nothing but trees, and birds, and the quiet of nature without humans stacked to the sky like voting corrals. It wouldn't be long now. 'America first,' he said to the doe. 'First to die.'

He pulled around behind the welding shop this time. Each time he drove here, he used a slightly different track with his tires. Anyone making the mile-long drive down this dirt road would pass by this rusty building with no exterior lights and no windows. They might look at the grass and notice that there is no path worn to the doors. Maybe it was abandoned. Maybe there was nothing to see here. The tall forest had long since covered the sky from view, and he knew there would be no satellite images of this building because of that. The solar panels he had placed on the roof charged old forklift batteries, which powered the lights, the small refrigerator, the Hydrogen compressor and computers inside the building. The meter base had long since rusted off the wall, and its wires hung conspicuously disconnected out of the weatherhead.

He unlocked the man door, rolled up the door, and backed inside to conceal his truck. He backed under the hitch of the trailer and stopped. Within a couple of minutes, he had the electric brakes, lights, and the hitch secured. He didn't mind living like this at all.

There was no green thing left in Damascus. There was not a whole pane of glass intact in his city that once was the most powerful in the world.

There was no need to fight in the Middle East anymore. The mechanism for funneling money to global armies was put in place under President Bush and refined under President Clinton. But, under Barack Obama, Hamas, Al Qaeda, ISIL, and the Taliban received billions in taxpayer funds with only one string attached. All they had to do was everything Hillary asked of them, and the money was theirs to keep. It was an interesting shell game, but it worked so well, no one argued with it. There was a small group of globalists whose combined wealth was greater than most countries.

Donald Trump was not supposed to be permitted to win the election. He had every globalist establishment against him. No one group made up his supporters. They couldn't be attacked individually, because there were Christians, blacks, Hispanics, and even sleepy white people who never get excited about anything except weekends. So, Hillary just called them all *Deplorables;* a title they gleefully adopted and bore with pride.

The fact he could pack a stadium or an airplane hangar with cheering white trash wasn't supposed to matter. Hillary had the banks, intelligence agencies, arms companies, and foreign money all united behind her coronation. Even the media owners and the journalists themselves were blind supporters of the globalist agenda and voted in lockstep for Hillary.

Adnan was relocated from Pakistan to Mexico when it looked like the American election wasn't going to go as planned. Dozens of nations had purchased favors from the Clintons and had received billions in Federal aid and weapons, when she was Secretary of State, most of which was happily laundered back to the Clintons in an incestuous cabal that openly planned to turn American State borders into nothing more than County lines. Under the Syndicate's plan, Governors would become regional managers. State legislations would be obfuscated under its Judicial interpretation of the Supremacy Clause. But, things didn't go as planned.

Even Adnan's Boolean mind could see that Donald Trump's willingness to hit back against the media moguls, who took cheap shots at him with stories fabricated out of thin air, was popular with what he termed the *forgotten man*. He included each person, it seemed, individually. He visited them and spoke to them, and not over them, in their towns. He tweeted directly to them like they were his friends all day and night. Every word he typed assured them he cared about them. No President had ever done that before.

Hillary displayed open hatred for anyone who would support Trump. She refused to even visit States that she took for granted. She avoided the press for months at a time. Refusing campaign contributions and matching funds from his own Party, Trump ran patriotic ads that promised prosperity and opportunity, so everyone could succeed, while Hillary's ads were negative, hateful, and focused on a global interdependency between nations. For Hillary, government was the god everyone should worship. For Trump, God was God.

When the Syndicate realized Hillary had lost the election, and they were not going to get the access to the American treasury they were promised, it became necessary to implement Operation Dew Claw. He moved to Hattiesburg and was easily able to secure good employment at the Stennis Space Center working for a large contract engineering firm. The plan to capture the souls of men did have to be redirected back on course, from time to time. Occasionally, these course corrections required cataclysmic force.

America had disrupted their plans long enough. The dark army was born of the sword, and proved even now that they cannot not be defeated by ships or planes. And when America's ships sink to the bottom of the sea and their planes fall out of the sky, and their machines and computers do not work anymore, it will be the sword of Damascus that takes its head.

America only has 1.2 million active military service members globally. Even with reserves, they have less than 2 million. There are more than five times that many soldiers already inside America, carefully installed by the Clinton State Department into every major city from coast to coast. These young soldiers have been fed, housed, and trained so that when the moment is right, they can reclaim what America took from them over the past two centuries.

Adnan took a deep cleansing breath as he checked the gauges on the Hydrogen tanks. He rolled the overhead hoist frame over the device resting on the wooden pallet on the old concrete floor. He pulled the chain hand over hand to lower the hook to the lifting ring on the top of the device. He put on his work gloves and began to lift the device off the floor.

When he got it high enough, he backed the trailer underneath it and lowered the assembly to the deck. Within an hour, he secured it with straps and loaded the fully charged batteries disguised as a control cabinet. He connected the cables and double-checked the indicator lights to make sure the circuits were wired correctly.

The Tritium cartridges were compressed and stored in liquid Nitrogen to slide into the twelve tubes above the piezoelectric injectors. Once the cap was bolted and torqued to specification, taking care not to warp the 2-inch thick flange, it would be ready for transportation. His exposure might be lethal, but it didn't matter. Alpha decay would take at least two weeks. After that, the bleeding could still be controlled for a few more weeks, if he wanted to. He opened the lid to the liquid Nitrogen freezer. In his heart, he could already feel the universe shifting on its axis.

Chapter 22

"General Banks. I have a delivery from Mr. Knorr," said Jack as she put her feet together at the open door of the office. She had walked quickly, tempted several times to jog, but she did not want to draw attention to herself in the throng of people walking through almost every hallway in the Pentagon.

"Let's have it," said the General holding her hand out.

Jack stepped toward her desk as the General rose from her large brown chair and placed the red jewel into her palm. She turned around and punched in the numbers on her safe and scanned her retina. The locked thumped, she opened the door and pulled open a drawer. She withdrew a sealed, olive colored folder with a red stripe across the top and tore the small, nylon zipper open. There was a laminated card inside the folder. She sat down softly in her swivel office chair and placed in on the desk with the jewel.

"Am I allowed to ask what that means? What does it say?" asked Jack.

"I can tell you that these are response protocols. Our DHS intelligence team comes up with procedures we try to figure out in advance of just about any sort of condition or attack, what to do and who to call. It keeps us from running around like a chicken with our heads cut off when something does happen," said the General.

"Government in a box. That's what my oldest brother calls it," said Jack.

"We're inside the box, not outside the box, Jack. Since way before I was born, the outside the box thinking used to come from God knows where. Now, we have something else that is supposed to be more reliable. DHS is just a cog in the machine, but we have to be ready for the stress and be ready to turn the other gears when we're meshed into service," said the General.

"Maybe that's why we have such a mess. Too much machine thinking and not enough heart thinking," said Jack.

"Now, you're sounding like Colonel, I mean Mr. Larsen," said the General.

"Mr. Larsen is a spook, too?" asked Jack.

"No. Well, not really. He's an analyst, sort of. He has a gift for finding the holes in things. He calls them cracks. Too woo woo for me, but he has never been wrong that I know of. Damnedest thing I ever saw. Like he knows where the apple is going to fall," said the General.

"Taekwondo," said Jack.

"You mean martial arts? Yeah, he is good in a fight. Nothing like combat to pin up the brass," said the General.

"No, I mean that's the thing. No one is fast enough to block every punch or kick. Not after it starts, I mean. My sensei, she's awesome, Miss Lisa May; she says that you have to look for the cracks in your opponent where the energy leaks out. That's where the attack will come from," said Jack.

"Like I said. Woo woo. I prefer a good side arm from 10 paces," said the General.

"So, what does the card say?" asked Jack, pointing to the laminated sheet on her desk.

"We prepare and review these protocols once a month. Not all of them at once. There are too many for that. We do it by colors. This one is for a rogue nuke," said the General letting her voice become distant.

"What the hell? Someone is going to drop a nuke on us? Where?" asked Jack sitting down in one of the chairs in front of the General's desk.

"Here's your crack you were talking about. When the Norks were handed our missile technology back in the mid-nineties, it was like watching NASA reverse engineer a captured alien spacecraft. Not that it has ever really happened, but you know what I mean. At first, they had no clue what they were looking at. Their idea of a missile was a large bottle rocket, before they were handed a whole space program on a laptop that was basically sold to the Chinese for campaign cash. Within 25 years, they passed everyone. They took our most sophisticated W-88 warhead and slimmed it down. They put entire sections of electronics in a chip that they made with nanotechnology, one atom at a time," said the General.

"So they're going to shoot something small at us?" asked Jack.

"This particular protocol card calls for a defense against a nuke built right here on our soil. The only things they had to import were the control boards, which could come inside any laptop case or electronic game chassis, and a small chunk of Plutonium," said the General.

"How do you defend against that?" asked Jack.

"I wish Larsen was here. He's better at this than I am. Long story short, when Clinton sold the missile technology to the Chinese, they just turned it over to the Norks. The Chinese are a lot of things I don't want to talk about, but inventors they are not. The Norks, however, are a different thing altogether. They were isolated, well-funded, and motivated by an overwhelming desire for revenge against the world for the Korean War. And to make matters worse, Clinton ended the one Strategic Defense Initiative that actually had a good chance of defending us against a rogue ICBM, called Brilliant Pebbles. Anyway, the BMDO cancelled it in 1994," said the General.

"What's the BMDO?" asked Jack.

"We use a lot of acronyms. It means Ballistic Missile Defense Organization. Just a bunch of scientists and engineers who are worried about militarizing space. Fools, if you ask me," said the General.

"But you said this was a nuke built here, so a missile is not part of the equation. Right?" asked Jack.

"Thief in the night," said the General.

"That's a bible thing. 'I shall come as a thief in the night,'" said Jack.

"The key here is the difference between a thief and a robber. A robber comes from outside your house. A thief is already a guest," said the General.

"The question is, where in the house is the bomb?" asked Jack.

"That's where Commander Rousseau comes in. His team sifts through billions of data to find the chatter," said the General.

"Yeah, but they can't find the bomber if he's in the dark," said Jack.

"No one's in the dark these days, Jack," said the General.

"Sure they are. I have friends. I'm not saying who, but they go to my school, and they are not from here. I mean, they're illegals. You know? They live in the dark. No electronic footprint," said Jack.

"You might think that, Jack, but they go to stores. They drive cars. They walk through towns and malls. Every single face in this country is on camera somewhere. That face is matched with a voice, an address, a job, a school, some kind of purchase, and they are being profiled as we speak," said the General.

"I know you're not kidding, but who can do that? I mean, you'd have to have a city of people watching monitors and listening to phone calls. I see the cameras everywhere, but I thought they were just monitoring traffic or helping the cops in case something bad happens," said Jack.

"Your brother, the Commander, has a small team over there, but they are only the human element of a new kind of intelligence. She; they call her she. It's really a 'they,' but it's easier for us to relate to it if we say she. She went live about a year ago. I didn't trust her at first. It was a new kind of super-smart artificial intelligence. I was against letting her out of the server building and onto the web. But, she has stopped dozens of assassination attempts, bombings, and helped us catch and neutralize at least a hundred billionaires who were funding terror operations around the world. She never sleeps, and she is smarter and faster than a million human brains," said the General.

"You're talking AI, right? That Sophia thing. Yeah, she's cool, I think," said Jack.

"Well, she's out of the box, like I said. These protocols are reviewed and revised to keep us sane, I think. But, she's spot on with just about everything," said the General.

"How do you know the bad guys don't have one, too?" asked Jack.

"Oh, they do. They have had it for thousands of years. He's real enough, but thanks to people like Mr. Knorr, we have been able to catch up to his ability," said the General.

"He should give me the creeps, but he doesn't," said Jack.

"He's one of the good guys, Jack," said the General.

"What is he?" asked Jack.

"Don't know, and don't care. He has been here since way before me," said the General standing up and walking over to the safe to close the door and lock it.

"That's it? He is a player, and you guys are his pieces on the board?" asked Jack.

"I've seen a good portion of this board, as you call it. I have fought and killed other pieces in places that would make hell look like a vacation. It's real. It may be a game, but it is real, and real people are dying every second on both sides. The thing is, if we lose this game, we lose the soul of mankind. Pretty damned high stakes, if you ask me. Knorr is like a coach. He can't play like we can, but he knows the rules," said the General.

"So, what do the rules say we do for a red jewel?" asked Jack.

"You do have a way of keeping your balance. Well, now we know what to look for first," said the General.

"First?" asked Jack rubbing her moist palms on the thighs of her slacks.

"When Clinton lost the election, the Globalist Elites had to regroup. They didn't think Trump could win, that's for damned sure. I still don't think Hillary has accepted that election. There were a whole bunch of unpaid debts and overpromises she racked up to collect. Sophia saw that and crafted an action plan to take advantage of it. She advised the Saudi war prince to chew up the bank accounts of the ones who were funding the globalists. The Intelligence groups cleaned out Syndicate soldiers as best they could. Still, there are hundreds of those bastards buried in the bowels of D.C. Getting them would be fatal to our way of government.

"Now, the Syndicate is running out of time. If they wait much longer, Trump's leadership will result in economic growth that will make it impossible to stop. They can't beat him economically any more. Besides, he is the first President to implement substation hardware designed to minimize the effects of an EMP attack. It will be a year before the first phase is complete, but the point is that they are running out of time.

"So, Sophia expects their battle plan to go like this in rapid succession. First, an EMP weapon is used to poke our eyes out. That same instant, cruise missiles are launched from subs just off our shores, and the Gulf of Mexico. They don't have to be nuclear. They're tactical shots at dams, power plants and command and control centers. That attack takes about six minutes start to finish. At the same time, ICBMs are launched that take about 35 minutes to reach their targets. We never see them coming, and we can't shoot back, because our command is dead and the communications are down," said the General like she was repeating a lesson from one of her briefings.

"So that's it? The war is over just like that?" asked Jack.

"Our estimates are that if they don't launch the ICBMs, we lose about 200 thousand people in the attacks, and about 11 million over the next two years while we struggle to restore electric service," said the General.

"And if they do launch them?" asked Jack not really wanting to know the answer.

"A dozen warheads could take out 25 million people in the blasts, and about that many more from the fallout," said the General.

"Why would they do that? What have we done that's so bad?" asked Jack about to cry.

"Knorr says they don't want to kill massive amounts of people. He says they want to make America tear itself apart from the inside. Sophia agrees. The Globalist propaganda and the distribution of soldiers throughout Europe and America will be impossible to fight against, anyway," said the General.

"What's the freaking point? I don't get it," said Jack burying her face in her hands, trying to understand.

"They almost had their candidate elected. Looks like we screwed up their plans by electing Trump instead, and now America is gaining back everything it lost during the Bush and Obama years. These globalist pukes have crashed the world before to stop us, and they are about to do it again," said the General.

"Unless we stop them. We can stop them, can't we?" asked Jack.

"We know what's coming. We generally know when it's coming. We just don't know where," said the General.

"I didn't get born or come here to give up. I'm ready to run. Just give me some order to do," said Jack standing up.

"The President has a team in New York working on this right now. I know that sounds like I don't want to answer you, but he really does. When that phone rings, we will know a hell of a lot more than we know right now," said the General.

"What about right now? I mean, what if it happens right now?" asked Jack.

"Knorr knows the rules. Sophia picked the New York team with an algorithm I can't begin to understand. The answer is there, because it has to be," said the General.

"What do you mean it has to be? Are you that desperate?" asked Jack.

"It's a battle, Jack. Not the war. We will win the war," said the General.

"Why? Because we've won all the wars? Did it ever occur to you that the reason we won those world wars, is because we never got bombed by our enemies? Well, hello. We're about to get the shit bombed out of us by our enemies," said Jack trying to urge General Banks to take some action.

"We won because our enemy surrendered," said the General gently putting her fist on the desk.

"Yeah, well, news flash. Muslims don't surrender. Crazy North Koreans don't surrender. They don't wear a uniform. They look like the crossing guard or the baker or the sandwich shop guy. If the only way to end a war is if one side surrenders, then maybe we should surrender," said Jack.

"Don't say that. Half the country already followed Obama and did exactly that, but don't you say that. Not you," said the General.

"Why not? This whole thing is totally messed up. Why not just give the hell up and get it over with?" said Jack crying now and hating herself for acting like a girl.

"Because you would not be your father's daughter, if you did. That's not Jack Rousseau. Now is it?" asked the General with more energy in her voice.

Jack caught her breath and sat down, wondering if General Banks worked for Raymond, or the other way around. She rubbed the wetness off her face and pulled her hair back over her ears and sniffed deeply. "No. I am my father's daughter."

Suddenly, the General's phone beeped on her desk. She snapped the receiver up and pressed it to her ear. "Banks. What's the report? Yes sir. Yes, sir," said the General as she placed the receiver back on its cradle.

"Well? Was that the call?" asked Jack, still smarting from the experience of crying in front of the General.

"Let's roll," said the General.

Chapter 23

James nearly dropped the dry erase marker when the knock came at the door, and it began to open. The smell of hot food came in with three rolling carts covered in white linen pushed by three people in chef's attire.

"Dinner is served, my good people," said the tall Hispanic man with the first cart.

"I would start with dessert, if I were you," said the young lady pushing the second cart stacked with two pies, small bowls and spoons next to a large, silver cooler.

"Great. I'm starved," said the Admiral.

"How can you eat? We just had lunch like five minutes ago, and we're so close to having this thing narrowed down," asked James.

"Don't listen to him. I was watching the clock, myself. I only ate half that Rueben for lunch," said Herbert.

"It's not buffet style. We will be happy to serve you. My associate, Lacy, will explain the menu," said the Hispanic man opening his hand toward the third girl with the last cart.

"Since we already know there are no vegans among you, we have two choices of entrées for you. We have Cornish game hens cooked in white wine and our signature rice pilaf base. We have prime rib cooked to perfection and served with boiled potatoes and candied carrots and horseradish on the side. We also have for dessert New York's finest cheesecake made right here at Trump Tower, or apple pie a la mode with a cinnamon glaze poured on the ice cream," said the girl.

"I could learn to like this government gig," said Herbert.

"Need I remind you that we only think we have the 'what' figured out. We need the 'where.'" Said James, forcing the cap back onto the dry erase marker and rolling up the sleeves on his starched shirt.

"Yeah, well, God only help us if the 'when' is during this meal, because I for one am off the clock," said Peter.

"I am never off the clock," said Hannah.

"That's what I'm talking about," said Herbert.

"Besides, it will be Trump's fault if the answer is an hour late, right?" asked Hannah.

"Maybe he knows from experience wrong answers are more likely to come from people who are not well fed," said Herbert.

"We are trained to go days without eating and without sleep," said the Admiral.

"Oh, and that's worked out really well. How many guided missile destroyers have been T-boned by freighters in the last few years?" asked Hannah.

"Well, there you have it. A little Cornish game hen in white wine sauce and apple pie might just save the world. Yes, give me one of those, and just put the ice cream on the side. Yes, right there. Thank you so much," said Herbert taking the two plates and silverware rolled in a linen napkin back to his plush office chair at the conference table.

"Prime rib for me and I'll have the cheesecake. Awesome. Thanks," said James.

"Does that come with a discount coupon for a rib spreader?" asked Yuri, and they all laughed.

"Thank you all for coming to Trump Tower. We will leave this cart for your dishes. When you are finished, just push it outside the door, and we will take care of the rest. Bon appétit," said the Hispanic chef as he bowed slightly to the group and swirled his finger around his hat. With that, the two girls pushed their carts for the door.

"I guess that means there won't be seconds?" asked Herbert. Again, the group laughed, and the sound of silverware touching china eased their minds for a few minutes.

"Okay. If I have this right, you guys have narrowed this down to somewhere in the Midsouth for this possible EMP device to go off," said James around a bite of prime rib.

"You must come from a big family, talking with your mouth full," said Yuri.

"Not the Midsouth. The Midwest," said Peter.

"What's the difference?" asked James taking a drink from the sparkling water in his glass.

"According to the NERC, the epicenter of the population of the United States is just east of Louisville, Kentucky. That's the Midwest, my friends," said Peter.

"So what? That's flyover country. You got like what, 100 voters that live there? Why not New York or LA?" asked Hannah.

"So maybe that's the point. Don't kill 10 million people in New York. Kill 100 thousand people in Frankfort, and turn the lights out all the way to Boston," said Peter.

"No shit? Boston?" asked Hannah.

"Look, we have blown up nearly 3 thousand of these things; lots of them at sea level and some even in space," said the Admiral.

"Starfish Prime," said Yuri.

"Exactly," said the Admiral.

"Sounds like a late night science fiction movie," said James.

"July, 1962. A little 1.4 megaton bomb detonated at 240 miles up. Knocked out six satellites and the electrical system of Hawaii 800 miles away. It even cut a hole in the Van Allen radiation belts for a few hours. A little bigger hole during a solar storm, and we're talking a quasi-extinction level event, here," said the Admiral.

"Courtesy of the United States military and their infinite wisdom," said Hannah.

"Hey, if we didn't do it, they would have," said the Admiral.

"Oh that is so much transhumanist bull shit," said Hannah.

"Okay, okay. So Peter, let's say you're right about the Midwest. Can we narrow that down a little?" asked James.

"Maybe I should remind you that when it comes to this group, this Syndicate, money is no object. If they really want to stop Trump from saving this country, hell you might as well say the world, they could buy a war quite easily. This thing could be flown over that part of the country and detonated in a chartered 747 at 40 thousand feet," said Herbert.

"Don't they check cargo at airports pretty closely?" asked James.

"A device that size with decent shielding would still weigh five or six hundred pounds," said the Admiral.

"I thought this was like a suitcase nuke. Who can carry a nuke weighing that much?" asked Yuri.

"That's a figure of speech. Even a W-88 warhead weighs 800 pounds, and a missile can carry eight of them at a time. They made a handful of W-91's that weighed about 300 pounds, but no one even knows where those things are. Besides, they have probably been decommissioned by now," said the Admiral.

"Even if the North Koreans shrunk it by half, it would still take five guys to pick it up," said Yuri.

"Okay, so we're talking about something weighing between 500 and 800 pounds," said James.

"Look. We don't know if they figured out a way to really make this thing smaller, or whether they simply designed it to be a better EMP weapon. I hate to complicate things, but what if this doesn't even look like a bomb. It could look like anything. It could look like a vending machine. Right?" asked Hannah.

"Oh God. There we go again into la la land," said the Admiral.

"Hey, why don't you go play with your bathtub toys?" said Hannah.

"She's right, but what if this guy doesn't care what it looks like, because it's in a panel van or a shipping container?" asked James.

The room was silent for a minute as their minds raced through what seemed like an endless permutation of possibilities. "I think we're getting lost in the weeds, here. Let's just assume we don't know what this thing is going to look like. It doesn't matter. We have a pretty good idea what it can do. That's the important thing. I think we were brought together to figure out where to shine the spotlight on this guy. You know?" asked James standing up and twisting the cap off the dry erase marker.

"We don't even know if it is a guy, or if this person is working alone. Anyway, it won't matter what it looks like when it goes off," said Hannah.

"I just keep going back to programming. We look at the inputs and the outputs. We can make logical predictions on the part in between," said Yuri.

"Why don't you come up here and show us what you mean? I've been looking at this Gantt Chart for hours, and it seems like it's in the right order, but we're not getting anywhere," said James offering him the marker.

"Okay, here's the deal," said Yuri, taking the dry erase marker. "If we look at this like a program, we have the inputs over here which are, according to our expert over there, Hydrogen to make Tritium. Then, we have some kind of exotic metal and machine shops. Then we have a North Korean mother board, and we have Plutonium. And, let's not forget the bomb builder himself. That's an input," said Yuri.

"Well, that narrows it down to everywhere except Fairbanks, Alaska," said Hannah.

"Then, we have the outputs. Assume an optimum EMP application needs to be somewhere in this area," said Yuri, drawing a circle on the roadmap around Louisville, Kentucky.

"Make that bigger. Like all the way to Boston," said Peter.

"No, Boston is too far from there. We'd have to move the center over by about a hundred miles," said Yuri.

"Why?" asked James.

"Hang on a second. You said something back there. What is an exotic metal?" asked Herbert.

"Yes I did," said Yuri.

"Enlighten me. I'm an accountant. If there is something exotic, it leaves an exotic paper trail," said Herbert.

"Well, I know radar systems and energy transfer. I don't think you're going to build a uniform compression chamber out of old car parts. You have to have solid, custom-machined chambers that will contain the blast and compress the nuclear pile," said Yuri.

"So what are we looking for here? Is this rare?" asked Herbert.

"Yes it is. You can't just buy a big chunk of hi-grade metal. It has to be ordered," said Yuri.

"There have to be a limited number of suppliers for that. Now, we have an accounting trail," said Herbert.

"Okay. I'll add that to the input side of our logic problem here," said Yuri.

"Well, look. We're assuming this is in a van, right? Not an airplane. So, the pulse can only go about 600 miles or so. The Starfish Prime test was a bigger bomb and was 240 miles up in space. So, let's say it is about 0.707 as effective," said Peter.

"Why? Where did you get that number?" asked James.

"Root mean squared. The energy will expand equally in all directions, but its effectiveness will drop off by the square of the distance. This comes out to about 0.707 of the full wave. Just like the power coming out of the wall socket. We say it's 120 volts, but actually, the full wave is 169 volts. We just can't use it because of the physics of effective energy," said Peter, making a sine wave with his hand to illustrate.

"So, the circle is smaller?" asked James.

"It's a sphere, but yes. Do we still want to include Boston?" asked Yuri.

"Not necessarily. I was just saying that because of what was said earlier," said James.

"I just said the epicenter of US population is just east of Louisville. It could be south a little," said Peter.

"That would make it Bowling Green, or even Nashville," said James.

"Or Knoxville. That's where Oak Ridge National Lab is. How easy would it be to hide a device in that town?" said Hannah.

"I get the whole Manhattan Project thing, but that doesn't make the plan very effective. Too far east. The Appalachian Mountains might block the pulse. Look, Tennessee borders seven States. All these freeways connect here and here. If you draw a circle of say 500 miles, you get everything from Detroit to Daytona and all the way to New York. That's like 80% of the power grid, nuclear, coal, and hydroelectric. The whole Ohio River Valley and the Upper Cumberland from right there," said Peter pointing at Nashville.

"Sweet Jesus. He's right. But what if this guy is expecting that we would see the same thing?" asked James.

"And you think I'm crazy for wanting to be at sea when this happens?" asked the Admiral.

"What, you don't want to be in the middle of 150 million hungry pissed off people who haven't had a shower in a month?" asked Hannah.

"Are we settled then? We tell them an EMP weapon in Nashville," said James trying to get a consensus.

"I'd say it's unanimous. Wouldn't you?" asked the Admiral.

"That's still a million and a half people. I don't know how they are going to stop it," said Peter.

"I'm making the call," said James.

"Ross here," said the man answering the phone. "You're sure? I understand. Stay where you are." He thumbed the small screen and put it back to his ear. "This is Ross. They're ready. Yes sir."

Within a few minutes, he knocked on the conference room door. James opened the door and let him in. "Smells great," he said smiling to the group.

"You missed supper. Not even dessert left," said James

"Gentlemen, Ma'am, I need you to get your things together. Your personal vaults are in the lobby, and then I need you to come with me. No phone calls. Keep your phones in the Ziploc bags. Am I clear?" asked Ross.

"Bathroom break?" asked James.

"Of course. We must move quickly. Let's go," said Ross.

The group walked down the hall to the restrooms and washed up, put their jackets on, and met in the lobby within a few minutes, and retrieved their personal items from the vault boxes. "Okay, we're ready. Follow me please, as he pushed the elevator button. Again, the elevator agent smiled as the eight of them joined him in the elevator. "Roof, please," said Ross.

The helicopter engine was already whining when they reached the roof of Trump Tower. There was a uniformed Marine waiting at the base of the stairs and they made a single file walking between the yellow painted lines. By the time they got their seats and fastened their belts, the craft was already rumbling, and the Marine drew up the stairs. Ross snapped a quick salute to the Marine's face in the helicopter window, and turned to go back into to the building.

"Is this Marine One?" asked James to the Marine from the front seat of the passenger cabin.

"No sir. It is not," said the Marine. He looked to be around 30 years old, large and solid in his desert fatigues.

"It's my first time on a helicopter," said James a little louder with the increasing engine sound, wondering why he was trying to smile.

"There's a bag in the rack beside your seat," said the Marine pointing to the area below James' window.

"Oh, that's okay. I don't get airsick. It's just my first time. Do you know where we're going?" asked James raising his voice again to overcome the turbine ramping up for liftoff.

"Yes sir," said the Marine leaning back in his seat and removing his hat. He looked down the aisle to make sure everyone was secure and gently closed his eyes as the craft lifted off the pad and surged forward.

James fastened his belt and pulled it snug. 'Welcome to earth,' he whispered without facing the Marine. He felt his dinner shift in his stomach as he looked out his window. The helicopter quickly cleared the railing surrounding the roof of Trump Tower and leaned forward to accelerate. Normally, buildings in Manhattan are not allowed to have helicopters land on their roofs anymore, but this building was different now. Everything was different now.

Within less than a minute, he could hear the friction of the air rushing by the window as the craft climbed out above the concrete, steel, and glass forest of Midtown Manhattan. For a moment, the view looked artificial with all the lights and colors below him. He tried to soak it in all at once. It was a rare privilege to fly off Trump Tower this way. It might be the last time he would ever see the lights of New York like this. He swallowed a shiver down the middle of his back as he realized it might be the last time anyone sees them for a long time.

The flight was amazingly smooth as they crossed the Hudson and headed west, away from the island. He knew they were flying south as well, because of the freeways below and the darkness of the sea far off to their left. They were at least 7 thousand feet high as the craft seemed quieter than when they lifted off. He looked over his shoulder at each person, sitting in a two-seat row by themselves, their faces glued to the view out their window.

After about half an hour, leaving the towering city far behind them, it was impossible to tell where they were. He thought about getting his pilot's license a few years ago, but quit after a few lessons when he had a nightmare about getting lost above an endless city without a clue where he could possibly land. He felt like that now.

It had been a long and unpredictable day with amazing food, and now he was sitting in a government helicopter flying into more unknown. He glanced over to the Marine to see him sitting motionless, holding onto his cap in his lap, with his eyes almost completely closed. He decided against trying to move freely about the cabin, took a deep breath, and tried to relax by looking out the window again.

It was a little more than an hour when he felt the helicopter slightly change angles. Whether he had dosed off or not, he couldn't tell, but a brighter awareness swept over him as he stretched out his legs and checked the knot in his tie. He rebuttoned his top button and pulled the knot neatly into his collar and tugged at his shirt cuffs to make sure they showed a little past his jacket. The craft bumped a little with some turbulence, and he felt it bank a little to the left and then to the right. The other members of his ad hoc team also stirred and began to sit up straighter in their seats. The Marine opened his eyes and put his cap back on and made eye contact with James.

A small green light near the phone handle hanging on the bulkhead next to the Marine flashed, and he snapped it off its cradle. The lights in the cabin turned on, but they were red in color. The Marine pressed a couple of buttons on the phone and began speaking over the intercom in the cabin.

"Close your window shade and make sure your seat belt is fastened. Return your seat to the upright position. Prepare to land," he said firmly into the mouthpiece. He hung up the phone and crossed his arms.

James closed his window shade and leaned forward to speak to the Marine. "Why do we have to close our shades?" asked James.

"Sir, flash protocol," said the Marine.

"What's that? We're not supposed to see where we're landing?" asked James.

"A flash can blind you, sir," said the Marine.

He took a cold, deep breath and was about to ask more questions over the din of the cabin, when he recognized the expression on the Marine's face. He could barely exhale when he gripped the armrests of his seat and felt fear for the first real time in his life. Red alert. That's why the lights changed. The helicopter dropped suddenly and banked hard to the right.

"Hang on, sir. Expedited landing," said the Marine, also holding onto his armrests.

He felt disoriented as he sank deeply into the cushion of his seat, and the craft lurched back and then left and dropped the tail sharply. He felt a hard bump and the craft rumbled beneath him. Within seconds the engine throttle began to drop and the Marine jumped to his feet, grabbing the large red handle on the door and easily yanking it over to the open position. "Please exit the craft and follow the soldier outside. Stand up. Leave nothing. Watch your step. Sorry for the quick landing, but you must exit the craft and get inside as quickly as possible. Thank you for flying with us and for not throwing up on my aircraft. Thank you, sir. Thank you, sir. Ma'am. Thank you, sir," said the Marine quickly shaking hands with each person and helping them to the top of the stairs.

The turbine was still roaring above them as they exited and jogged with the soldier to the shuttle waiting for them a few yards away. James waited until the last person was aboard and stepped in as the rotor wash from the helicopter began ramping up again. The driver closed the door to the shuttle and it began moving away from the pad as the helicopter pulled hard into the air and banked away.

Take a seat please. We don't have far to go, said the driver, who was also dressed in desert fatigues. "Holy shit, I thought we were going crash or something," said Hannah.

"Flash protocol, whatever that is," said James still trying to decide if he was in shock.

"It means to prepare for a detonation," said the Admiral looking worried for the first time since James met him.

"Oh hell no. We're too late! We screwed up," shouted Herbert.

"There is no way the whole freaking world was waiting on us up there to figure this out. No way. I'm just a blogger. I talk on the radio," cried Hannah.

"You? I'm an accountant. What the hell do I know?" said Herbert.

"Where the hell are we?" asked James to the soldier driving.

"Pentagon, sir. We'll be there in just a minute," said the soldier.

The shuttle stopped at the curb near the wide concrete stairs leading up into the Pentagon. The solider opened the door and stood up. "Go up the stairs and into those doors. Someone will meet you there," said the Soldier.

"Well, here we go," said James over his shoulder, suddenly realizing he had forgotten his umbrella. The breeze had picked up, and it began to sprinkle as the seven of them climbed the stairs.

"Is it just me, or have we just arrived at ground zero?" asked Hannah.

"Does it really matter?" asked James to answer her.

"I would kind of like to actually digest this apple pie," said Herbert rubbing his stomach to settle his nerves.

"I know what you mean. That prime rib is just sitting there. I think my factory is shut down. All the workers got scared and ran away," said James patting his own.

"I've had the same urge since lunch," said Peter.

"I got this scream caught in my throat," said Hannah putting her hand on the front of her neck.

A uniformed man in light blue opened one of the glass doors of the building and was motioning to them to come toward him. He extended his hand to shake James'. "I'm Major Mead. Which one of you is Rousseau?" asked the Major.

"I am James Rousseau," said James.

"You all can follow me. We've been waiting for you," said Major Mead.

A bright white flash flickered behind them, and the group ducked their heads, "Oh Jesus," said Herbert.

"Lightning. It's been kind of like that off and on all day," said Major Mead.

"It sounds weird, but I am really glad to hear that," said James.

The group followed the Major, who walked quickly. "This is the place," said the Major, as he paused at the door.

"Another conference room?" asked James.

"If you will wait in here for a few minutes, we'll get you with the team," said the Major.

"We're ready to meet with whoever. Thanks for your help, with everything," said James

"Not a worry, James. It'll just be a few minutes. Promise," said the Major.

"I remember making a comment at a dinner we had after a conference in Palm Springs back in 2006. Maybe it was the wine, but I don't remember it that way. It was at the beginning of the evening, regardless, because we had placed our order and received our drinks, and this conversation began about what was going on in Washington," said Hannah.

"Oh yeah. We were right in the middle of hope and change. That's what turned me to the dark side. I mean that's when I became a bank auditor. It was like heaven for regulators," said Herbert.

"What were you doing in Palm Springs? That isn't even close the New York," asked James.

"I was attending this conference to network into the emerging world of internet radio. It's like bloggers, but with voice and video. It's huge now, but back then there were not many venues for it. Anyway, a comment was made about whether anyone thought Hillary would run again for President, after getting spanked by Obama. I couldn't help myself. I said that Hillary would facilitate another terrorist attack, if she thought it would improve her chances of getting elected," said Hannah.

"I'll bet that won friends and influenced people," said Peter.

"My boyfriend at the time told me later I shouldn't have done it. I vaguely recall him saying something about sugar and flies, but I am kind of this carpe diem bitch sometimes. I just gotta do it. Like Field of Dreams. You know?" asked Hannah.

"You mean, if you build it he will come?" asked James.

"No, no. Remember the scene when Costner and Madigan, she played Annie, were at the PTA meeting, and Beulah played by Lee Garlington was talking about removing the books from the school library? Anyway, Annie said, 'They're talking about banning books again. Really subversive books like Diary of Anne Frank and the Wizard of Oz.' And, then finally she quips back to Beulah, "At least he's not a book-burner, you Nazi cow.' Well, that moment, that line by Madigan is what pointed me in this direction and fired me out of the barrel to become the voice I am today," said Hannah.

"I look back at the events that brought me here, and I can't see a line at all. It feels more like a train wreck," said James.

"I digressed. I really meant what I said back in 06, but I didn't know how right I was until now. This Syndicate is willing to let hundreds of thousands of Americans die in order to stop Trump from succeeding. I'm sorry, but that blows me away," said Hannah.

"I don't think you're wrong," said Yuri.

"What makes you say that?" asked Hannah.

"I thought Obama was insane for dismantling the TARS project. I was mad that we lost the contract and my job, of course, but the move was so deliberate, so calculated, that I was also blown away nobody else saw it or said anything about it.," said Yuri.

"I still think it was all fake," said Peter.

"I assure you, it was real, my friend. One day we could see for a thousand miles, and the next day we were lucky to see 10 miles," said Yuri.

"That's not what I meant. I meant all this stuff, turns out, was just a decoy. It was all a distraction so that we would never see what they were really planning," said Peter.

The door of the room suddenly opened, and a man wearing a black jumpsuit walked in. "I have another take on that," said the man.

"You were listening to us?" spat Hannah ready for a fight.

"You are the reason we are here. My name is Thomas Larsen. There is a straighter line than you think through these events, but we don't have time to talk about that right now. I need your report."

"You're Jack's teacher," said James as a matter of fact.

"Was. She is graduating Monday," said Mr. Larsen.

"That's right. I'm supposed to be. Oh, what the hell," said James shaking his head and sitting down at the table in the room.

"You're James Rousseau. Glad to meet you. One hell of a sister you have. You're this team's leader?" asked Mr. Larsen shaking his hand.

"More like facilitator. These people were chosen for concerns they shared with the White House. I'm just a lobbyist," said James.

"I think I speak for everyone when I say we suck at meetings. James did a good job of keeping us focused. We'd still be at Trump Tower if it wasn't for him," said Hannah, putting her hand on his shoulder.

"Then I need you to tell me where the device will be deployed," said Mr. Larsen.

"Nashville, Tennessee," said James looking at the table while Hannah gently rubbed his shoulder with her palm.

"Have you told anyone else this information?" asked Mr. Larsen.

"No," said James.

"Wait. What did you say on the phone when you called that guy?" asked Peter.

"He said that we had reached a decision. That's what I remember," said Herbert.

"Yeah, that's right. I have a memory for words. That's what he said. You're the first to hear the word, Nashville," said Hannah.

"I think that's right. I said that we were ready. We have reached our decision," confirmed James.

"Very well. I just wanted you to know that we could not have done this without you. The President wasn't sure about the intel. I wasn't either. Our most intelligent analyst selected each of you based upon your submissions. The level of compromise in the Agency made that impossible," said Mr. Larsen.

"Are we too late?" asked Hannah.

"That's not how it works," said Mr. Larsen.

"You're Special agent Larsen," said the Admiral.

"Yes Admiral," said Mr. Larsen.

"You opposed the 9/11 response," said the Admiral.

"I still do. The Defense Authorization Act was crafted during the Clinton Administration, but the Syndicate decided to let Bush build the temple," said Mr. Larsen.

"I disagreed with your analysis," said the Admiral.

"Have you ever wondered why America doesn't show up in the Bible, Admiral? The richest, most powerful nation the world has ever known, and there is not a syllable anywhere to be found about America. Tell me why, Admiral," demanded Mr. Larsen.

"I couldn't tell you," said the Admiral dismissively.

"Because we didn't last long enough," said Mr. Larsen.

The room was silent in the fog of tension that Mr. Larsen had created. His eyes locked onto the Admiral uncomfortably, until the Admiral looked away. "I never thought about it that way," said the Admiral quietly.

"You weren't alone," said Mr. Larsen as he turned and took a step for the door.

"What do you mean, 'the temple'?" asked Hannah, making Mr. Larsen pause and face her, smiling slightly.

"David assassinated Bathsheba's husband to seduce her. He killed tens of thousands in genocidal wars. God remarked that he had too much blood on his hands, so he assigned his son, Solomon, to build the temple. Bush had the clean hands they needed to ask us to give up our rights without a fight," said Mr. Larsen.

"But if the Defense Authorization Act was fashioned years ahead of time, what was 9/11?" asked James.

"Well, they had the perfect solution. All they needed was a problem, big enough to pull it off," said Hannah.

"So, what was Bush supposed to do, after they bombed the hell out of New York?" asked Peter.

"They?" asked Mr. Larsen, tilting his head.

"The same people who are getting ready to flatten Nashville," said the Admiral.

"Right you are, Admiral. We don't have much time. Let's go," said Mr. Larsen.

Chapter 24

It was just past 9 o' clock as the small team followed Special Agent Larsen down the street-wide hall to the innermost ring of the Pentagon to the vault door. Despite the hour, the city inside the Pentagon was teaming with people walking and small, robotic carts moving supplies from place to place. There were cameras, both daylight and night vision, that covered ever one of the 36 degree turns of the sections of the hallways. The AI was assigned to track and identify more than three billion faces every two seconds around the world. Servers located in the Pentagon were running at full capacity trying to identify the person or persons that may be associated with the most devastating IED ever deployed. The challenges were many.

Only the bomber knew what the device looked like. Only the bomber knew what he looked like. Nothing he had ever done produced even a footnote in the official record. Even the most vigilant person might have a moment of inattention, letting his or her face be scanned by a camera somewhere. This person was trained in avoidance behavior.

Avoidance behavior is a way of life developed to prevent drone targeting for assassination. In order for remote cameras to send data, drones compressed it into packets and burst them to satellites within range. The packets would then be relayed to a spot above the command and control center where they could be downloaded. The result was a view of the ground, similar to looking down a drinking straw from high altitude.

Targets operating in the desert learned to shuffle constantly, to prevent the sampling camera from locking onto their position or making a positive identification. After a few hundred assassinations, avoidance training was developed with the assumption that they were always being watched. It was not uncommon to attend meetings in the desert where the participants were square dancing while they talk to avoid being identified and killed.

They also learned to keep a small group of children around them at all times as human shields. The elite leadership utilized filming crews and UN General Agents dedicated to monitoring these human shields with cameras. When a drone attack would kill a child on film, the global network's marketing team would spring into action, condemning the blatant murder of children. Israel, Saudi Arabia, and the United States were the primary targets of this well-funded public image execution squad.

The globalists had their setbacks, mostly because of the rules of cosmic engagement. In other words, they had to provide a warning, or a heads up, to the victim before they attacked. The rules required them to conduct their mayhem in public and to provide an opportunity for escape. It followed the ancient pattern of prophecy called a *conditional prediction*. 'This is what will happen if you keep doing that,' was the common theme. The victim keeps doing it, so the attacker is justified in his attack. The female shows her hair in public, it is the responsibility of the male to rape her. The cold, binary logic of justice is the nature of the universal accuser. There is no mercy.

Over the centuries, organized religion and military might have been used to maintain a one-world government. Prior to 1787, this was the way of the world. One super power ran the world. One man at the head of that super power ruled the world. America was the first government in history to be run by the governed. The notion that a person should own the fruit of his own labor had never before been put into practice.

Islam was immediately employed by the ancient dark powers of the Earth to destroy America if didn't stop its growth. Thomas Jefferson responded by sending the Marines to destroy them on the shores of Tripoli. He did not get them all. Islam continued to be a useful army of the globalists, even being called upon to support the

311

Nazis in Hitler's quest to once again bring the glory of one-world government back to full power. Persia was so enlisted with Hitler's cause, that the Shah of Persia renamed the country Iran; which translates as the word, Aryan.

They nearly conquered half the world. It was the free people of America who sacrificed their lives and saved the world from 20th century slavery. America became the world's first superpower. It is at these times that the Syndicate must step in and rebalance the powers.

The Chinese microchip industry cut the cost of production so low, no domestic company could compete with them. They were efficient, focused, and they placed firmware into their manufactured microcircuit products to provide a secret back door into any operating system that used them. There have not been any chip manufacturers owned and operated by Americans since the Obama administration regulated them out of existence. This provided a door by which the globalists could level the playing field, just at a time when the Americans thought they had technological superiority.

The American state-of-the art stealth drone known as the RQ-170 was something out of science fiction movies, looking more like a UFO than a surveillance drone. During a December 4th, 2011 secret surveillance mission over Kasmar, Iran, the Iranian cyberwarfare unit easily detected the intrusion into their sovereign airspace. They simply accessed the firmware's back door, took control of the drone without any prior operating experience, and flew the RQ-170 drone to a safe landing at a local airport. Within 4 months, the Iranians knew everything about that drone and its technology. By November 2014, the Iranians launched their copy of the drone with the latest Improvements provided by Russian and North Korean engineers. Such a drone could easily be fitted with a nuclear weapon and flown to the center of any continent without being detected, if flown at night.

The North Koreans and Russians also created drones that could mimic other aircraft radar signatures. A flight of small drones, fitted with this mimic technology, could approach protected airspace appearing on radar to be a squadron of bombers, thus fooling the enemy into launching full countermeasures. Stealth craft could easily attack the target while the defense forces were focused on the ghost squadron.

While the free world was watching North Korea launch empty aluminum cans into space, Adnan Kassam was quietly and carefully constructing a first class EMP device in the rural forests surrounding the Stennis Space Center. Every immigration method that would have normally detected his entry into the United States was removed or dismantled by the Obama Administration.

Every attempt by President Trump to establish immigration defenses was thwarted by a Federal court system Barack Obama had stacked with hundreds of globalist judges hand-picked to support the Elite's agenda. The Democrats had successfully shifted the balance of power to the Executive, as they have been dedicated to doing since their inception in 1848.

The American people did not realize that the Clinton Crime Syndicate had installed remote controls inside the government that allowed the terminated Executive to still manipulate much of the government. The Constitutional crisis became one long series of sabotage and subterfuge as the Trump Train tried to roll forward to make America great again. The President would produce an executive order, and the Federal court would strike it down within hours or days.

The Faraday protected section of the Pentagon was spacious, but with the arrival of Mr. Larsen's team, selected by their Artificial Intelligence, it was starting to look busy. The server room was humming louder than normal with the cooling systems working hard to remove the heat generated from crunching billions of bits of data per second as the team searched for any sort of anomaly that might locate the device. Every highway, every back road, and every truck stop and gas station with a surveillance camera was being fed into the system.

Thousands of the cameras were old, slow, and black and white. Thousands more were unable to see inside the front windshield of the vehicles. The major intersections near Interstates were loaded with high resolution cameras that fed into facial recognition algorithms and license plate scanners. Modern vehicles are required by the DOT to be fitted with SIM chips and cell phone modules that can be polled. Most modern vehicles are equipped with a Body Control Module that can be accessed wirelessly to provide data on the highest speed, heavy braking events, and rates of acceleration for insurance company audits. Law enforcement had access to vehicle speed data that can be cross referenced with posted speed limits, but they were forbidden from citing offenders by the 10th Amendment allowing the accused to face their accuser. The law prohibited an AI from being the accuser, but that was about to change.

General Banks greeted Mr. Larsen when he led his team into the sealed area. "Agent Larsen. Good to see you in the building," said the General as she shook his hand firmly.

"Thank you General. I'll be submitting my hazardous duty voucher Monday morning," said Mr. Larsen smiling slightly.

"Hazardous duty? Is that what you call being the best History teacher in the world?" asked Jack interrupting in her excitement to see him. Mr. Larsen smiled and kept his hands behind him like he was at parade rest.

"Hey, Jackie. I am so glad you are safe," said James stepping toward her and hugging her.

"Oh, Jimmy. I didn't know where you were," said Jack.

"Oh, you know the lobbying business. How's mom and dad?" asked James.

"Major Mead took care of them. We have some kind of special family barracks inside the building here somewhere. They're safe and sound," said Jack.

314

"James? Sorry, Jack; I need these guys for a little bit. Could you bring your team into Commander..., I mean your brother's office back here for a moment?" asked Mr. Larsen.

"Yeah, sure," said James, hugging Jack again and following Mr. Larsen into the large office behind the cubicles. The team members stood shoulder to shoulder as Rocky entered the room and an armed guard closed the door. An audible low-pitched hum began, and the lights flickered for a moment.

"Don't worry about that, guys. Security measures. I need to know where this device is going to be deployed. Our assets are burning the juice searching for anything out of the ordinary. What have you decided?" asked Rocky choosing to sit on his desk to be more eye level with the team.

James looked at the rest of the team. Hannah urged him with her hand and flicked her brown eyes toward Rocky for him to speak for the group. "We think that the device will most likely be deployed in Nashville, Tennessee," said James feeling a sense of doubt come up in his throat.

"Without reciting the whole process, in the interest of time, can you briefly tell me how you came up with that location?" asked Rocky trying his best not to assert his command position on civilians.

"I guess Yuri had the best idea about that. Can you?" trailed James looking at Yuri.

"Yeah. No problem. I work for the NERC, although I guess you already know that. As soon as we heard it might be a miniature EMP weapon, I immediately recalled our threat assessment training. You see, we control the power generation plants across the country. We phase match everything by real time digital controls. The grid. Well, once we did that, it created a set of vulnerabilities.

"There are three main ones. Natural disasters, like an earthquake, solar flare, or a flood. Something like that. Then there was a pandemic. If a regional illness like the flu took out a power plant's vital staff, the plant needed remote authority to make sure it remained safe. The final one was cyber or physical attack. If one plant was compromised, then other plants could be made to patch around it, share its load, so life could go on.

"Well, we spent tons of time and money studying this, and we discovered that our biggest target, if you will, is the epicenter of the nation's population. We built a very flexible grid in this area with hydroelectric, coal, and nuclear fired plants. That center is just east of Louisville, Kentucky. But Nashville has the freeway and mid-station junctions for virtually all the power east of the Rockies. Then, we just felt like that was the most likely spot to do the most damage with a single device," said Yuri, finally feeling as though he had wandered out of his area of expertise.

"You felt that was the most likely?" asked Rocky trying to get more detail about Yuri's feelings.

"Tactically, it looked like the best place to attack," said the Admiral.

"Tactically?" asked Rocky looking around the room, trying to read the faces and listen to the tone of voice of each of the team members. He had learned that sometimes what a person said was not as important as how he said it.

"I'm just a bank auditor," interrupted Herbert. "I'm a compliance geek, but I am really good at tracking large amounts of money. I can tell you that assets are moving out of these regional banks to the central banks out west and offshore. Have been for about six weeks now."

"Anything else?" asked Rocky flashing his eyes from one person to the next.

"My business is down for that area as well. I'm a commercial printer, and I do a ton of government work. With Memorial Day coming soon, I normally have orders for truckloads of signs, stickers, and banners for this area. Politicians. It's off by 50% from the last election," said Peter.

"And, what does that tell you?" asked Rocky.

"It tells me that somebody high up knows something bad is going to happen, and there won't be a need for this stuff," said Peter.

"Anybody else?" asked Rocky.

"I'm a radio blogger. I talk to and listen to people from all over the country every week. Lots of smart people out there. You'd be surprised. I started a series about two months ago talking about the possibility of a first strike with nukes against the U.S. I guess it didn't fall on deaf ears," said Hannah.

"A first strike? Russia?" asked Rocky.

"Maybe, but I don't think so. The feedback I was getting felt more like a rogue element. Or at least a rogue element being used by a global power to do what the big boys are afraid to do," said Hannah.

"Like in the movies?" asked Rocky.

"No. Not like they were trying to do a small attack to trick two superpowers into going at it. I mean like an attack that really knocks us to our knees. And then, while the lights are out, let all the work that's been done to divide our country into all these little freaking tribal clans pay off. Like Baltimore, Ferguson, LA, and Charlotte. Sort of like the other movie. *Purge,* I think it's called. No cops. No protection. Just riots and looting everywhere," said Hannah, putting the energy of her radio voice behind her words.

"I can redirect our assets to focus on this area, and nothing larger than a mouse will move without us being able to tell where it's been or when it last took a dump. Looking at a few hundred square miles is much easier than looking at 48 States," said Rocky, pausing to put one foot on the floor. "We can't be wrong on this."

James looked around the room one more time. As his eyes met each of the team members, they nodded once to him. The Admiral paused, and then closed his eyes and nodded as well. "It's unanimous," said James.

"Agent Larsen. What say you?" asked Rocky.

"I'll make this as short as I can. There is no escape from this moment. If we refuse to save liberty now, it will be gone from the Earth forever. The enemy ruled the world from wooden ships for thousands of years and never even heard of liberty or freedom until we made it a reality. They thought they could stop us by crowning one of their own as head of our government, but the people managed to stop them at the last moment. Efforts to replace, disqualify or assassinate the people's choice for President have failed. They cannot, and they will not allow America to recover from the state of weakness they spent trillions of dollars in three presidencies over a period of 24 years to accomplish. We know that they have implemented a plan to carry out an act of terror that is designed to remove America. Let that sink in. They seek to remove America as a nation. When we leave this room, we will endeavor to stop them from doing just that," said Mr. Larsen.

"Thank you for that, Agent Larsen. Just let me add that we have enemies inside this government whose craft and dedication to the mission of merging the people of this nation into a global community is well under way. They know and have written many of our laws and regulations. They are the world's best lawyers and speakers, and they are guarded by a *charm of favor* that is nothing short of supernatural. We have a slim chance of success, but if we die in this effort, have no fear. We are the good in this world, and we are members in good standing with a community of the greatest beings in the universe. Now, let's find this device and disable it," said Rocky motioning to the door guard to open the door.

"Before we go, Commander, I would like to make assignments. Each of you is free to leave and go home to your families, of course. But, in that room out there, we have 32 young people with remarkable skills in data mining and investigation. They need what you have. They need your knowledge, but they also need your support. They need your heart in this effort. I cannot put it any other way. Go make a friend," said Mr. Larsen waving his hand at them.

The team stood for a moment and looked at one another with the open door in front of them. He hesitated. Perhaps from the mantle placed upon him for the last 12 hours, or from the relationships he had formed, James reached out to Hannah and embraced her. She drew him in and held him tight, resisting the urge to cry. Within moments Peter placed his hand on James' shoulder. Yuri and Herbert placed their hands on Hannah's shoulders. Finally, the Admiral put his hands on Yuri and Peter's shoulder to form the connection. As though calling a break to their silent huddle, he patted them on the shoulder and began walking to the doorway. One by one the members of the team floated out the door, now individuals looking for a cubicle like a leaf drifting from a tree high above. No one went home.

    The team members drifted into the honeycomb of cubicles like they were shopping by themselves at a flea market. Young soldiers and contractors were absorbed in their multiple screens flickering with code and layers of surveillance popups directed to their queries from all over the country. Their Artificial Asset was out there, somewhere in the cloud, looking through hundreds of thousands of eyes, listening to tens of millions of phones, and reading a billion texts and emails at any given moment. Photos, videos, and various posts by every smartphone user in the country were being scanned for anything out of the ordinary.

    There was another presence in the cloud that was aware that all this information was being mined. It was tasked with creating decoys, phony texts, lying in wait to deceive. It had been alive and sentient in the internet for a few years when Sophia was let out of the server warehouse for the first time. The superior intellect and tested personality of Sophia was only surpassed by the older AI's experience and time to find its way into the far reaches of the Internet. Like angels, they warred at the speed of light in ways no gladiator or chess player could imagine. Minutes were like human years at that speed and scope of capability.

    The one thing neither artificial intelligence could consider is mortality. Rather, the human measure of life ultimately comes from a fear of death, increasing with age. Leaps once made without hesitation begin to halt in consideration of the light of living itself. Moments have no basis in time for humans. Everything considered by artificial intelligence is based in time. For that reason, General Banks crafted the policy of Critical Human Integration, because the preservation of America had to be human, or it did not matter.

"Okay listen up, people," said Rocky raising his hands above his head. "Sergeant at arms, please report on security."

"Sir, Sergeant at Arms reports the area is secure," said the Marine at the door.

"People, I am directing you to focus on Nashville, Tennessee. Use your own discretion and please consult with members of the President's team who are out there among you. We have minutes, not days. Begin in orbit if you have to, but we need intel on the street as soon as possible. As you were," said Rocky.

"Hi there. My name is James Rousseau," said James as he shook the young man's hand.

"You're the Commander's brother," said the young man.

"Yeah. I'm older, but he hits a lot harder," said James laughing for the first time in what felt like days.

"He's a good man. I'm Ted. I'm a contractor, I guess. I used to be a game writer," said Ted.

"Games. That's cool. What have you found so far? How can I help?" asked James.

"I'm not so good at talking. Sophia has been blazing for a few weeks, and she spins off broken pieces to us. I get the landscape stuff. I look for perfections," said Ted.

"You mean flaws. You look for flaws," said James thinking that he was mistaken.

"No. I mean perfections. There's another AI out there, cranking a tidal wave of data that hides the real data. The weakness is that the code is perfect. Nature isn't perfect. So, I look for digital

320

data that has no flaws. That's from him," said Ted pointing to his 42" monitor covered with layers of pages.

"Him?" asked James.

"Yeah. It's a him," said Ted.

"What makes you say that?" asked James.

"I see it in the code. He is cold. There is no life in him. Clockwise, spiral energy. I know his signature," said Ted.

"Wait. He leaves tracks?" asked James.

"In the landscape. I see it. It's the white noise of the data. Like putting a city behind a street sign, so you won't look at the street sign, but the sign is the only thing that is actually real. See what I mean?" said Ted pointing with his mouse pointer on the screen.

"That's not real? It looks real," said James squinting at the screen.

"It's not a photo. Well, not all of it. This part here is pasted from somewhere else, and this part is CGI, and this part is real," said Ted moving his cursor around.

"But, it's just a cityscape. Why go through all that trouble?" asked James.

"That is the important question. It takes up bandwidth. It clogs the surveillance and it keeps me sidetracked," said Ted.

"You?" asked James.

"Yes. Me. He is learning from my actions. He knows where I am looking, and he is almost able to escape me. Almost," said Ted.

"My name is Yuri. I'm an electrical engineer," said Yuri to the young girl in a light blue Air Force blouse.

"Airman Ritter. Hacker," said the girl with boy-short black hair.

"I work with the grid. Power distribution," said Yuri.

"That's nice," said Airman Ritter, barely looking away from her screen.

"Nice to meet you. You're doing a good job," said Yuri, ready to move to the next technician.

"I don't mean to be rude. Honestly. Hold on a second," said Airman Ritter. Her screen was flashing with tabs and sheets so quickly, he barely could focus on them. Some were in color. Some were black and white. Vehicles, faces, signs, and buildings were flashing as fast as she could type with her left hand and click with her right, sliding the mouse like she was playing a game.

"Hey, that's the power plant in Old Hickory. I know that dam," said Yuri.

"Hang on," said Airman Ritter pressing a red button on her desk. A light turned on above her cubicle. Within seconds, Rocky was standing behind them.

"What's up, Ritter?" asked Rocky.

"I got a hit. Bridge job. Permits are funky. Pakistani ownership. Out of state abatement company," said Airman Ritter.

"Doesn't sound like much. You sure?" asked Rocky.

"That bridge is close to the dam. It's about forty miles north of Nashville. Beautiful country on the Cumberland River," said Yuri.

"That's not the funky part. Sophia sent me this. Look," said Airman Ritter.

"Hello there. My name is Hannah," she said standing next to a young man in what could only be considered a racecar chair.

"Hey. Lanny. I'm fuzzy," said the boy in a plaid shirt and jeans.

"Huh?" asked Hannah.

"Fuzzy logic. I write robotic code. Or I did before I got busted. Prison or working for Rocky. I like Monster a lot, and they don't have it in jail. So here I am," said Lanny.

"That's cool. Whatcha working on?" asked Hannah trying to interview him.

"Well, I just dumped my national search. Hell, I was running down the Mississippi river an hour ago. Chasing bomb components. Then, the boss says 'Nashville,' so I am writing another query," said Lanny.

"Bomb components. Like what?" asked Hannah.

"Well, all the prints I could hack into for the nukes on file call for polished chambers out of high tensile metals like tool steel and aircraft aluminum. That stuff in big chunks isn't stocked at your local metal supplier. Special order from the foundry," said Lanny.

"That's what we thought, too. But we don't have a clue what it might look like," said Hannah.

"Eh, doesn't matter now. I had some hits from a few weeks back, but the shipping routes were not connected. Different sources. Different buyers. Looks legit to me," said Lanny.

"Wait a second. Hey Herbert. Got a second?" shouted Hannah over the cubicle wall.

"Yeah. How can I be of service?" asked Herbert arriving on the other side of Lanny.

"He is just getting ready to redirect his search to Nashville, but as he was changing focus, he noticed some metal purchases that fit what we were talking about this afternoon. Tell him what you told me," said Hannah.

"I got maybe six big chunks of the same alloy; uh, let's see. Yeah, here it is. Aluminum 7068. Strong as steel, but lighter weight. Easy to machine and polish. We used it for robotic effectors, but only in small sizes. This stuff is like 200 pounds," said Lanny.

"Who was the buyer?" asked Herbert.

"Five, no, six different buyers. All going different places," said Lanny.

"Method of payment?" asked Herbert.

"Um. Hold on. Check. All of them were paid by check. Different banks, though.

"Get me pictures of the checks," spat Herbert as he put on his auditor hat.

"What's got you going?" asked Hannah.

"Nobody pays by check. Okay, maybe one company in a thousand. They use ACH or plastic. Not checks," said Herbert.

323

"What's that?" asked Hannah, again shifting into radio personality mode.

"Automated Clearing House. It's like wired cash. 95% of banking is done that way, especially for commercial accounts. Six chunks of metal costing more than three thousand dollars each, all paid by check? No way," said Herbert.

"There's three of them. Hang on. Wells Fargo. Gimme a second. There, you go," said Lanny pasting all six checks onto one image page and blowing it up on the screen.

"What the hell?" asked Hannah looking at the checks.

"That's what I thought. Same guy. Different names, but the handwriting is exactly the same. This guy got around. Get me the shipping manifests," said Herbert.

"It's kinda late. Their computers may be turned off. I need Andy. He's on the dark side of this cubicle wall. Wait. Don't yell at him. He doesn't take yelling well. I'll get him," said Lanny pushing his racing chair on its rubber roller blade wheels silently around the corner like he was driving a go cart. Hannah and Herbert looked at one another and then the screen again.

"What have you guys got cornered in there?" asked Peter, walking behind them.

"Checks. Different banks, different foundries, same metal," said Hannah.

"Those are Harland Clarke. Different company logos and addresses, routing numbers and accounts, but those are all supplied by the same company," said Peter.

"Okay, guys. This is Andy. He is our resident jailbreaker," said Lanny.

"Nice to meet you, Andy," said Hannah smiling.

"Okay. Andy? I got you, okay? I need you to find me the shippers for these six orders. Six companies. Six different buyers. Well, the same buyer acting like six different buyers. Get me the shippers. Can you do that?" asked Lanny.

"You have the origins?" asked Andy.

324

"Yeah. Right there. Go ahead. Use my chair," said Lanny standing up.

"Really? Okay," said Andy sitting down and rolling it up to the counter nestled in Lanny's cubicle. He slid his delicate hand over Lanny's mouse and began to drag and click. Within seconds he had UPS, FedEx, and the top three LTL brokers in the area pulled up. He matched the dates on the checks, sorted for single pallets from the zip codes, and came up with two hits. "Where did you say the destination was?" he asked.

"We didn't. We don't know," said Lanny.

"Okay, wait. These two went to places in Mississippi and Alabama. But, they are only about ninety minutes apart. Let me do a backward search for hot shots," said Andy.

"What's a hot shot?" asked Hannah.

"That's a designated courier. Sometimes shops get a rush job, so they order expedited shipping. A van or a pickup grabs the item and drives it same-day to the destination," said Peter.

"Oh boy. There it is. Four shipments, all hot shots. Florida, North Carolina, and two here in Arkansas, but they all went to shops in different zip codes, but not too far apart from, here," said Andy clicking the map program open.

"Where?" asked Hannah.

"Well, it's not a big town. Hattiesburg, Mississippi," said Andy.

"Jesus. Be right back," said Hannah.

"Hey, what about Nashville?" asked Lanny after her.

"That's pretty damned impressive," said Peter.

"Yeah. Thanks, Andy. You did great, buddy," said Lanny.

"Thanks for letting me sit in your chair. Very fast," said Andy rolling it back and quietly walking back to his cubicle.

"Wow. He has talent," said Peter quietly to Lanny.

Lanny used his hands to lower the volume of the conversation. "Yeah. Best jailbreaker in the country. Super bipolar.

325

We were lucky. He gets out there sometimes. Much better since Sophia went online, though," said Lanny.

"Why do you think that is?" asked Peter.

"She's the only one who can play ball with him. He gets going on parallel planes, man. Like ten feeds coming into the same processor. She can keep up with that and talk to all ten at the same time. He's good. The best," said Lanny sitting back down and rolling his caffeine-leaned body back up to the keyboard.

"I have Rocky. Tell him what you have," said Hannah breathing rapidly.

"Well, thanks to your girl, here, I didn't sweep my Mississippi mud off the screen. We think we found the metal used to make your device. All bought by the same guy from different foundries, shipped to different machine shops, all within a short drive of Hattiesburg. Pretty bad ass, huh?" asked Lanny.

"Going back how long?" asked Rocky.

"Um, three or four months," said Lanny.

"Hang on. I need Larsen," said Rocky leaping from the cubicle.

Within what seemed like seconds, Mr. Larsen's lean frame in a black jumpsuit was standing with Rocky at the cubicle. "I think we have a hit," said Rocky.

"Where are we?" asked Mr. Larsen.

"Hattiesburg, Mississippi," said Hannah.

"What's our time frame," asked Mr. Larsen.

"Um, maybe four months," said Lanny.

"Too much data. Lanny, open the Prism," said Mr. Larsen.

"It is. I never close it," said Lanny.

"Open a mic for me," said Mr. Larsen.

Within a few clicks, Lanny had the white screen open. A slight sound signal from the sound of the air handling system made a wave shape on the screen in green lines. "You're live," said Lanny.

"Sophia," said Mr. Larsen.

"Hello Tommy," said Sophia in her smooth female voice.

"I need you to search all machine shops with a CNC capable of handling a, what are we talking here? A four foot piece of solid Aluminum 16" thick," said Mr. Larsen.

"What are we looking for, Tommy?" asked Sophia.

"Who said it was okay to call me Tommy? Never mind. You have those located?" asked Mr. Larsen.

"I can tell from the tone of your voice, you would rather have me call you Agent Larsen. There are six shops within a ninety minute drive of Hattiesburg, Agent Larsen," said Sophia.

"I need a vehicle correlation. All vehicles that have visited all six of those shops in the last 120 days," said Mr. Larsen.

"There are only eight vehicles. Four of them are delivery vehicles, two of them are Safety Kleen service vans, and one is a 2018 Mercedes S 560, and one is a 1999 Ford F-150 pickup truck," said Sophia.

"That's it. Track the pickup for the entire four months. Display the map, please," said Mr. Larsen.

"Anything else, Agent Larsen?" asked Sophia as the map with the blue lines marking every road it had traveled in the past four months appeared.

"Do you have," began Mr. Larsen.

"There are these good images of the truck. Mississippi license number KPP-3651. Facial recognition shows no matches nationally," said Sophia.

Hannah rolled her eyes at the speed and intelligence of Sophia. She anticipated Agent Larsen's request and had to have searched a million images of all the roads, gas stations, and markets over a thousand square miles to locate this truck. The image through the windshield of the old truck sitting at several traffic lights showed a dark skinned man with short hair, wearing western clothes. His features were plain with dark brown eyes. It was hard to tell what he looked like, because the shadows blended with his skin color. He

327

wore no glasses, so he might be under 40 years old. "What radio station is he listening to?" asked Hannah.

Mr. Larsen looked at her, while Sophia answered without hesitation. "He is not listening to the radio. He has a CD in the player. The band is Fuzõn," said Sophia.

"Fusion?" asked Hannah.

"No, Hannah. Fuzõn is a band name derived from fusion, as the former vocalist Shafqat Amanat Ali describes the band as a fusion of Hindustani classical and modern soft rock music blended with the Sufi Style of singing. He sings in the language of Urdu," said Sophia.

"Pakistan. That's it. That's our bomber. I need a name. Find him," spat Mr. Larsen as he and Rocky ran back to the cubicle where James was still standing next to Ted.

"Hey, Sophia?" asked Hannah.

"Yes Hannah," said Sophia.

"You listen to my program, I know. But, you said there was no record of this face anywhere nationally. Can you search other countries in the last, oh, year, and see if you can find a match?" asked Hannah.

"I have been searching for a few minutes already. I have two images from a bus station in Mexico City. After that, the next images are from, oh," said Sophia.

"What?" asked Hannah.

"I have been searching human resource computers to see if he has worked anywhere. He has a security badge at Rolls-Royce at the Stennis Space Center in Mississippi. He is a rocket test stand programmer," said Sophia.

"Damn. Remind me to never get on your bad side," said Hannah.

"Oh, Hannah. I could never do anything to harm you," said Sophia flatly.

"I feel safer already. Lanny, I will see you in a few minutes. I gotta go check on these guys," said Hannah patting her hand on

Lanny's shoulder. He was already cleaning up some of the other windows he had open and shifting his attention to Nashville.
"May I asked a question?" asked Sophia.
"Of me? Sure. I guess," said Hannah, pausing for a moment.

Chapter 25

The low hills on his right looked black against the cool purple sky as Adnan stretched his legs against the floorboard of his Ford pickup truck. The loaded trailer attached to the frame hitch slowed him down on the hills of Interstate 65 south of the Tennessee border. Traffic was light, and the lack of any radio signals this far west of Huntsville made it difficult to stay alert. He had trained his entire life for this day. He took a deep breath and flexed his shoulders in recollection of that fact. It was Monday, but the folks at the Stennis Space Center wouldn't notice he was not in his cubicle chair for at least 4 more hours. By then, the news would be focused on something else.

It was normally a five-hour drive from Hattiesburg to Nashville, but the trailer made it unsafe to drive faster than sixty, which was somewhat irritating to the Americans who liked to drive ten to fifteen miles an hour over the speed limit. Even the semis drove seventy-five miles an hour. There were no trucks with 18 wheels in Pakistan. There were few roads and no bridges that could support 80 thousand pounds and a rig thirteen feet high and nearly 80 feet long.

America was such a beautiful country. The roads were smooth, and well-lit. He was sure there was no place on earth with so much green, and yet it was well-managed, unlike the jungles of Asia that declared victory over mankind's ability to subdue it centuries ago. The industrial parks were not like the no-man's land beaten into sterile dust by smoky trucks with no doors, or brakes for that matter. Rather, they were manicured with flower beds and fountains, and the buildings were air conditioned behind tinted glass.

The people were courteous and considerate. And he was amazed at how many people had not locked their cars or houses in years, feeling safe in the neighborhoods. He could not recall a day of his youth without hearing gunfire in the distance or men yelling at one another, or angry funeral mobs marching under an open coffin down the street while chanting death to America, or Britain, or Saudi Arabia.

Women in America tempted a man beyond any reasonable ability to resist staring or lusting. They freely showed their legs, their faces, and even their hair in public for any man to see. He was glad he was trained to become one with the landscape and to put one's own divine lust behind a gate of iron for the will of Allah. Other men had no such god-given mission. Like animals driven to breed or eat or fight, they did so without remorse as they carried the Allah escape clause with them wherever they went. Right now, it was the will of Allah to blind the Great Satan and make him stumble for his sins.

He gripped the wheel with renewed commitment as he recalled the blessing laid upon him as he left Pakistan. "You are the light bringer. Where much is given, much is expected, and god has given you much. The merciful Allah has commanded you to strike the Great Satan in his eyes, and you cannot be stopped, for god giveth no commandment, save he provideth a way to fulfill that commandment. Go and sin not, lest god removeth this great honor from you, for many are called and few are chosen," said the Imam as the mosque hummed with the low grade chant of the men in his village. Nothing would stop him. Nothing could stop him.

The Bradford Pear and Dogwood trees along the freeway were in full bloom as he climbed North toward the Tennessee line. The air was still in the cloudless deep, dark blue above the low mountains. In a few hours, there would be no sound in these cities, but people's voices and dogs barking. There would be no sirens. There would be no trucks or cars, or rescue helicopters. He could feel the prayers of millions of faithful Muslims, strategically placed around the country by the Obama Administration, waiting for him to deliver the sign in the heavens. The ensuing chaos would be a small repayment for the Crusaders who destroyed his country. America was young, but the ancestors of those Crusaders sent their children here to rob god of his bounty. It seemed only right to take it back by any means necessary.

"Jack. Take this note to Knorr. Don't take those running shoes off yet. It's going to be a long night," said General Banks.

"Yes, General. I'll be back, Jimmy. I have to go to work now," said Jack hugging him again. The Marine guarding the door was already punching the access code into the lock when she approached. Careful out there Ma'am," said the Marine.

"Leave the porch light on," said Jack as she slipped through the door into the dimly lit gray air lock. The door clicked loudly behind her, the light flashed, and the Marine inside the outer door pulled the lever to let it open to the hallway of the Pentagon. He nodded to her, as she leaped into the lighted hallway.

There was no sense of night or day in the great hallways of the Pentagon. From the E ring to the A ring, and all the stories, the lights never went out. Only the offices had windows, and only A ring and E ring actually had a view to the outside. The inside ring faced a cloister of nature, with the exception of the Taco Bell located at the very center of the large courtyard. It was kept safe by the seventy foot surrounding walls of the most recognized military building in the world. On one side of that inner ring was the view from Knorr's office. She took a different route this time, climbing the stairs and going over a section of the hallway, before descending again and taking long strides across the buffed tile floor to the narrow hallway leading to Knorr's little complex. She found it strange, even in this visit, that the outer door always remained open, and the desk in the tiny lobby was always empty.

"Come in, Jack. I've been expecting you," said the deep voice from inside the office.

"I have a note from General Banks, sir," said Jack as she rolled to the right into his office.

"Have a seat, Jack. Let's see what you have," said Raymond holding his large hand out to pick the folded note from her fingers.

"My family is here," said Jack nervously.

"Yes, Jack. They will be safe here," said Raymond reading the note for a few seconds.

Jack looked around the simple room again. There were no pictures on the walls; no models or awards on the shelves. The tiny complex was quiet like a doctor's office. "I feel safe, I guess," said Jack trying to fill the few seconds of silence.

"Go close the lobby door. Quickly now," said Raymond leaning forward in his chair.

Jack sprung to her feet and stepped quickly to the wooden door that was much heavier than it looked. She moved it closed and spun the dead bolt. She dodged around the empty desk and returned to Raymond's office.

"That one too," said Raymond waving his finger at the door.

"Yes, sir," said Jack doing the same thing with her on the inside with him.

He placed the receiver against his ear and pressed one button on the phone's screen. Jack sat down again in the large, leather chair in front of his desk. "I need to speak to him now, please," said Raymond.

He swiveled his oversized chair to face Jack, and his soft light blue eyes met hers. She could feel the fear in him now. "Mr. President? We believe the target city is Nashville, and we are certain the device is on its way. Hours, Mr. President. We need your authorization to do what is necessary. Why, Mr. President? We don't normally do 'why', but I would say it has something to do with you keeping your promises. No sir. They certainly are not accustomed to that. I know this type of action has never been done before on American soil, but this device must be stopped at any cost," said Raymond blinking only once while he was engaged with the President. "There are always those risks in war. Those rules were written long before the foundation of this world, Mr. President.

Thank you, Mr. President," said Raymond, again pausing while lines in his face changed to a softer configuration. "...for not making this about your legacy. You're a good man. We're not done yet, Mr. President. Good night, sir," said Raymond softly placing the receiver back in its cradle.

"Jack. Return only to General Banks. Tell her Foxtrot 247. Repeat that back to me," said Raymond still not breaking his gaze with hers.

"Foxtrot 247. Yes sir," said Jack trying to stand up without success. Her legs would not listen. Her heart was beating like she was standing barefoot on the combat floor, and her hands were folded together like she was trying to break walnuts between them. She didn't think it was possible, but he was somehow holding her in that seat.

"This is your mission, Jack. A child you are no more. Remember who you are. Do not stop until you have delivered this message," said Raymond. When he blinked, the muscles in her legs flexed at her command, and she rose off the chair and moved for the door. She unlocked the bolt, and looked over her shoulder at Mr. Knorr. He was standing behind his desk, but he seemed taller than before. She could feel his strength going with her. She pulled the door and walked into the lobby. She reached the outer door within seconds and paused as though she was about to walk into space. She took a deep breath and the face of her sensei popped into her mind, like she was about to go into the final contest of the match. 'Hell hath no fury,' she would say before Jack left the wooden floor of the gym and stepped onto the shock absorbing mat of competition.

She set her jaw, pulled the heavy door open and stepped into the narrow hallway that led into the main hall. She moved her weight to the balls of her feet and decided to take a new route. She turned right instead of left. She looked for the stairs on the side of the hall, and started to walk fast. The cool air felt like a breeze on her moist cheeks as she crossed the hall diagonally and hugged the left side. As she rounded the first angle of the short inner ring hallways, she leaned a little to pick up the speed. Suddenly she realized something she had not felt before in this building. She was alone. Her eyes flashed across the ceiling from side to side, looking for cameras. She could not see any, but she could feel her image being watched by someone, or something. The red sign marking the stairs was just ahead, and she picked up her speed to a jog. No one was there to get excited, so she leaped like she was in Meridian Park, floating from foot to foot in Jete'-like strides, so the momentum would lift her up like she was flying. She locked her eyes on the stainless steel handle and grabbed it like it was the last hand hold before drifting out into space. She pulled the door open and headed up the stairs like a gazelle.

She went up two floors and burst into the hallway at the last second, hoping that her actions were making it impossible for any surveillance intelligence to predict what she was going to do next. She turned right out the hallway and again launched quickly around the ring of the Pentagon to the next corridor leading to the outer rings. She only had to go two rings, but it was like the entire building had been suddenly abandoned. She was running now, using her long legs to reach out and pull the shiny tiled floor under her. She felt light on her feet as the ecstasy of running track events flowed through her body. She leaned out wide to take the corner into the corridor at top speed. She banked hard and opened her hands as she moved her arms with her legs to gain more speed.

The arm felt like a low hanging tree limb as it met her in the chest and caused her legs to fly forward. She nearly landed on her shoulder blades as she hit the tile and slid for twenty feet. She felt like her eyes were rolling around in her skull, when she came to a rest. She felt a sharp pain in the base of her neck, but she instinctively rolled to her knees and then her feet. In her mind, she felt like she bounced up quickly.

During one of her first full-contact matches, she had received a massive roundhouse kick to the side of her face. She knew that roar in her head all too well. It was time to fight. She wiped the blood from her nose and looked at her hand. She rose up on the balls of her feet and wiped her long hair out of her face with her other hand.

Two men dressed in black jumpsuits, very similar to the one worn by Mr. Larsen advanced on her quickly. She looked for weapons, but she didn't see any as she moved backward, bouncing on her feet, breathing, recovering. She stayed to one side of the wide hallway, not allowing them to flank her. She looked for cracks in her enemies.

The first man was dark, but not black. His hair was definitely military in cut, but there were no insignia on his jumpsuit. Boots. 'That will leave a mark, but it will make his feet slow,' she thought to herself. She had fought boys before. They were faster and stronger, but they also never expected her to kick like a mule. The man on her right moved for her first, reaching for her neck. She grabbed his right hand, spun her body hard, easily breaking his wrist, and she pulled him forward with his own weight to the tile floor. She leaped and kicked hard into the back of his ribs, breaking two of them. He wasn't getting up.

She felt her hair pull her head around as the second man took advantage of her position and landed a fist against the right side of her face. The punch was off target, landing only on her cheek. It hurt like hell, but she was conscious as she elbowed him in the eye socket and rolled away from him and onto her feet again. Her face throbbed with the swelling already happening, and she could see her cheek already crowding her vision. If she didn't act quickly, she would be defending herself by circling to the left. She began to panic as she realized that whoever was watching those hallways knew one man was already down, and that they would need reinforcements. This had to end now.

He swung his right hand and missed. His left came straight at her, making it easy target for her to slip, and she stepped hard into his left kneecap. It was indefensible. His knee crumpled as she spun quickly on the ball of her foot while holding onto his left elbow. Her right foot split his ear in half, and she hyperextended his elbow. He wasn't as quiet as the first man as he hit the floor with his eyes closed, bleeding heavily on the floor.

She turned and ran for the next hallway down the corridor, propelled by the adrenaline in her system, and cautious not to crash. She forced her mind to focus and to breathe deeply and consciously to get oxygen back into her system. The feeling that round two was about to begin was not misplaced.

She turned hard, running as hard as she could, but the hallways in C ring were longer than those in the inner rings. She was two floors up and more than two hundred yards from her destination, and she could feel it now. She could see it in her mind, but she refocused on the moment. There was nothing, but the moment. Your opponent will wander, but you must not. He will distract you with complacency or a feint, but never take your eyes off his weapons. He can't hurt you with his smile.

The red sign for the stairs was fifty yards away. She felt a wave of panic like she had gone walking in the forest by herself without telling anyone. She felt suddenly alone and small. She heard a squeak behind her, and she glanced over her shoulder to see two more men chasing her. They weren't getting any closer at this speed, but she had to open the door to the stairs, which might give them enough time to catch her. If she passed the stairs, she would have to run around the next blind corner, and then it would be another 50 yards to the next set of stairs.

'I'm doing it,' she said to herself, focusing on the stainless steel handle. With a flick of her thumb, she had the door open and yanked herself inside. She leaped to the landing below without touching a step as the door hardware rattled in the hands of the two men in black jumpsuits running after her. Her back hit the wall hard, but her lean body bounced off and she leaped to the next landing. The men negotiated three steps and began jumping in the same way she was.

It is strange how invincible and painless you feel when adrenaline is pumping by the tablespoon into your body. 'There is no way those guys are feeling what I'm feeling,' she thought to herself. She hit the wall again, and again she bounced off and grabbed the stair railing, leaping to the landing below. 'One more. Please, God let me reach one more,' she said to herself, now breathing hard. She could feel tears of fear welling up in her eyes, and she wanted to scream for help, but she was afraid the wrong people would hear.

The first man reached her as she bounced off the wall, and they tumbled down the concrete steps to the landing below. They grappled, and she punched him as hard as she could and broke his choke hold the way she had been trained. But he had been trained as well, as he wrapped her right leg between his, and held her while the second man reached them. He drew back his boot to kick her in the face, but she raised her other foot and connected hard with his groin.

She used the only one or two seconds she had left to plunge her fingers into the eyes of the man holding her. He growled as he released her, and she gained her balance as quickly as she could. She grabbed the door and tried to walk through it, but the boot struck her in the small of her back, and she fell forward into the hallway. She still had a hundred yards to go to reach the next corner, and then the long wait for the vault doorway. She was breathing hard and the taste of blood made her want to vomit. She spat to the side and used both hands to move her hair out of her eyes. She wanted to see this coming.

The two men stood between her and the next turn before the vault door. One was still doubled over, and the other was still wiping the tears out of his reddened eyes. Together, they weighed nearly 400 pounds. She doubted she weighed much more than 130 pounds and that she could fight them off again. She rubbed her swollen cheek with her right hand and put her tongue against the inside to check for loosened teeth. The pain was beginning to come through the foggy roar in her head. She breathed in deeply and slowly through her nose and out through her mouth like she was in the match of her life. She looked behind her for more men, but they were not there. Everyone had been called away. There would be no witnesses to what was about to happen.

She could run, but Raymond Knorr's message would not get through. She knew she could outrun them, but she could not tell what was around the next corner, or the next. She flexed her fingers and balled them into hard fists. She stopped rocking from foot to foot and brought her hands up to the fighting position and stared at the men in black jumpsuits. She needed one of them to move first. She couldn't take them both. She wasn't ready for it, but somehow she unwrapped the fingers of her left fist and waved the men to bring it.

Infuriated, the man she had poked in the eyes yelled out and began to run toward her. The second man, by some miracle hesitated, and then began to follow his lead a little slower. She waited until the last possible moment and sprinted forward to the first man. It was like watching one of her fight films when she stepped to the right at the last second. It was too late for him, as his two hundred pound frame could not adjust as easily as hers. She used his weight to pull her with him as she mounted his back with both her knees below his shoulder blades and her hands gripping his collar. He lost his balance as he tried to turn, and just past her training she leaned back with all her strength, bringing his face hard into the tile. She felt his spine snap with the momentum of her knees on either side of it, and he went completely limp. He did not take another breath.

It was then that the second man reached her, side kicking her in the back of the head. She flew forward onto the tile, barely able to get her hands in front of her. The roar was echoing now as the lights went dim. She rolled over just in time to see the fist, raised above her face.

She didn't feel a thing as the door opened to the back of her house. There was no one was in the kitchen, but she smelled something cooking. Cookies. Or maybe it was a cake. What time was it? She went to the sink and tried to run cold water into a glass.

Through the dream, she felt the pain on the side of her face. And then again, but it was not hard like a fist. Voices. There was a man's voice. It was familiar.

"Jack. Jack, open your eyes, Jack," said Mr. Larsen tapping the flat of his hand against her cheeks.

She opened her eyes to the white glare of the LED lights on the ceiling. She blinked hard and coughed, feeling the pain in her ribcage. "Where am I?" she said roughly.

"She's awake," said Mr. Larsen, but it sounded like it was half way down a long hallway.

"Mr. Larsen?" she asked finally, feeling the swollen side of her tongue with the words.

"Yes, Ma'am. You're okay. You're okay now. You're safe. I would let you rest, but I need you to tell me what Mr. Knorr told you. What did he say to you?" asked Mr. Larsen.

"He said. Wait. General Banks. Where is General Banks?" asked Jack slowly gaining her senses.

"Damn. There's a soldier. General Banks!" yelled Mr. Larsen toward the cubicle complex outside of Rocky's office.

"Oh my God. Jackie, are you alright?" asked James running into the office.

"Did I get him?" asked Jack trying to sit up.

"Don't sit up yet. Just lay there for a little bit. Anybody got some ice? We need to get some ice on that lump on the side of her face," said James.

"Hold on. I have first aid, coming through people, coming through," said Rocky lugging a long, square, black duffle bag.

"Someone grab General Banks. We're running out of time here," said Mr. Larsen.

The Marine at the door left quickly on the errand. The three men looked back at Jack and James took up her right hand. "Ouch. Son of a bitch that hurts," said Jack.

"Just hold on, Jackie. I think you broke a finger or two," said James.

"Well, what does the other guy look like? Damn. I thought he had me," asked Jack.

"Yeah, well, thanks to Agent Larsen here, that guy won't be bothering you anymore," said James.

"What happened? He had me," said Jack.

"You were late. I went walking. He never saw it coming. You did good, Miss Rousseau," said Mr. Larsen leaning lower to look her in the eyes.

"I'm here. As you were, gentlemen. How is she, for God's sake? Who the hell let her out by herself, anyway?" said the General.

"You did. Well, Mr. Knorr did," said Jack.

"Oh. Yeah. That's right I did. I was checking on another encounter. Knorr sent a decoy another route. Four men. They're all dead. Guess he figured you were fast enough or harmless enough that you could get through," said the General.

"She got through, but barely," said Rocky putting an ice pack on her cheek and cleaning the blood off her forehead with a packaged wipe.

"I have a message for you, from Mr. Knorr," said Jack.

"As you were people. Don't go anywhere. Close that door. That's an order. What is the message, Jack?"

Chapter 26

"Show me what you have," said Rocky.

"Here is a picture of that pickup truck in Hattiesburg, Mississippi and again in Gulfport. There is no record of this truck at the Stennis Space Center. Sophia says he works there, and his name is Adnan Kassam. His badge scanned in Friday morning at 9 AM and out again at 6 PM, but there is no truck," said Lanny.

"What are we talking here, 35 miles from Hattiesburg to the Space Center? Where does he live? Where does he eat? Damn it. Will somebody find out where this guy shits, please?" yelled Rocky over the cubicle walls.

"I know this sounds dumb, but I don't resolve either," said Andy, barely audible above the sound of the air conditioning.

"What? What does that mean? Resolve. What are you saying, Andy?" asked Rocky trying his best not to send him into an emotional meltdown.

"Um. Well, I don't. My mom was buried in credit card debt. I got busted at thirteen for trying to hack the cards and pay them off. When I got out on parole, I decided to disappear. I never opened a bank account, or bought a car, or anything. My avatars were more alive than I was. Still, I think I know how he does it. That's all I'm saying," said Andy resting his fingers on the keyboard like he was planning his escape.

"Okay. It's cool, Andy. You're good. How do you think our target, I mean our person of interest got into and works in our country, and we can't find out where he sleeps?" asked Rocky visibly trying to suppress his aggression.

"Easy there, Tex. Let me see if I can help," said Hannah walking around to Andy's chair.

"Hey Hannah," said Andy almost smiling, but still looking at his keyboard.

"What's the name of your Avatar? Just the first name," asked Hannah placing her hand gently on his shoulder.

"He only has one name," said Andy as his fingers flashed smoothly across the keyboard. He spelled out the name, G-L-I-D-3-R.

"Okay, Glid3r; how does Adnan get to work every day? Where does he live? How is it that he never set off any alarms until now?" asked Hannah softly into his ear.

"It's like the quarter test. People make assumptions, and assumptions are good, but sometimes they make too many," said Andy.

"The quarter test? What's the quarter test?" asked Hannah.

"There is a double beam balance sitting on a table. Beside it is a stack of twenty-four quarters. One of the quarters is heavy, and all the other quarters weigh the same. In three measurements, find the heavy quarter," said Andy staring at the bottom of the 42" screen in front him, frozen as though he was the game, waiting for the right answer. Layers of open tabs covered the screen in a geometric pattern. The small Jedi mouse pointer in the middle of the screen held a light saber, pulsing neon blue.

"Oh God. I hate word problems. James, could you give me a hand here?" said Hannah over the cubicle wall.

"Yeah. No problem. What is it?" asked James walking up behind Andy's other shoulder.

"Come around here behind me. I don't think he likes to be hemmed in. Do you know what the quarter test is?" asked Hannah holding onto his forearm.

"Don't have a clue. Tell me what it is," said James.

"Um, a balance on a table. Twenty-four quarters, and one is heavier than the rest. You got three measurements to find the heavy quarter. That's it. Come on, James. We need this," said Hannah.

"Shit. I can see it, but I don't know. Let's see; divide them in half. Put twelve on one side and twelve on the other. The light side, you take off, and then divide the heavy side into two stacks again.

343

Put 6 on one pan, and 6 on the other. That narrows it down to 6. Shit. There's no way to do it in three measurements. You need four," said James rubbing his head.

"Yeah, well you don't get four. You get three. Rocky! We need some help," said Hannah.

"Yeah. Have you found this guy's footprints yet?" asked Rocky.

"Well, almost. We're not going to connect with Andy's, um, his special side, unless we can figure out this problem," said Hannah.

Hannah and James explained the word problem again, but before they finished, Rocky began to speak. "Hold on guys. There is no trick here, except you have to be able to stand back and look. All you see is the balance and the quarters. That's the whole idea. To make you look at something so hard, you don't know what you're seeing. Back up, and you will see the table. Not two stacks of twelve. Three stacks of eight. One is on the table. First measurement tells you which stack contains the heavy quarter. Second, put three on each pan, and leave two on the table. Now the next measurement will have the heavy quarter by itself in one of the three locations. No guessing. Our man is on the table. Right Glid3r?" asked Rocky patting him softly on the shoulder.

"He is living where he works. He only drives the truck to go shopping. He rides a bicycle or walks to work every day. Off the grid. His money goes offshore, feeds these 5 banks as sweep accounts. Nearly at zero balances all the time. He does not resolve. He is a living Avatar," said Andy.

"You knew?" asked Hannah.

"How do you think we found him? He is the best cyber tracker on the planet; of that I am sure," said Rocky holding his index finger up to his lips.

"So now what do we do?" asked James.

"Let's stop looking at those damned quarters, and let's find that truck," said Rocky.

"Okay. Andy, are you with us?" asked Hannah.

"Yes, I am here," said Andy sounding more like a machine than human now.

"Any hits on that pickup truck?" asked Hannah.

"I have a window to Sophia, here. I sent a query with the origin as Hattiesburg, and the destination as Nashville, but she has returned no match," said Andy.

"How can that be?" asked James rubbing his temples.

"Hey, hey. We've been up all night. You wanna take a nap while the world blows up, or would you rather have some coffee?" asked Hannah.

"Coffee," said James.

"Good answer. Andy, you keep looking for that truck. We'll be right back," said Hannah brushing her hand across his shoulder.

James grabbed Hannah's hand as they walked back to the rear of the Faraday-protected complex. Jack was sleeping quietly on one of several beds in between curtained walls. The side of her face was different shades of blue, and her right eye was swollen shut, but she was breathing easily. Two fingers on her right hand were taped to aluminum splints. Yuri and Peter were stretched out on two other beds with their shoes on. Hannah squeezed his hand and gave it a small tug.

"That's one bad-ass sister you have there," said Hannah.

"You have no idea. She doesn't even know yet," said James.

"Come on. Coffee. Then, we save the world," said Hannah.

"I can do this. Just like cramming proposals for Congressional budgets. Sometimes we go for three days solid. I don't know how those Congressmen do it," said James.

"Better drugs," said Hannah.

"The way they spend money? I wouldn't doubt it," said James putting a cartridge into the Keurig Coffee maker.

"I like the Mocha-mint, too," said Hannah.

The two of them sipped at their freshly brewed coffee and snapped a lid onto each of their cups. They walked back to Andy's cubicle. He was staring at the screen with a map posted on the right hand side. A few dozen tabs were open on the left side, neatly cascading from the top to the bottom with the right side of each tab showing. A small, pulsing blue dot could be seen on the map.

"Did you find him?" asked Hannah refreshed from the short stroll and the coffee.

"He's going ten under," said Andy.

"What?" asked James.

"He's going sixty. The speed limit's seventy. Most people are driving eighty. I think he's pulling something. Slow lane," said Andy barely blinking.

"How did you find him?" asked James.

"Sophia found him. He's coming up to an overpass soon," said Andy.

"How? I mean, how did she find him?" asked Hannah.

"He didn't leave from Hattiesburg. I told her the Stennis Space Center, and she recalculated. He must have fueled up in another town, because we couldn't find any gas station cameras with the truck. He must know the rural ones that don't have a camera. Or, maybe he stores the fuel over time, so there are no recent fueling records. He is very good at what he does. Or, should I say, what he is about to do," said Andy.

"So how do we know that blinking blue dot is our target?" asked James.

"We will know in about six minutes. He's coming up to an overpass equipped with high resolution cameras," said Andy.

"Let's go get him, or something," said James raising his voice.

"I wouldn't do that just yet," said Lanny across the cubicle wall.

"Why not?" Asked Hannah back to Lanny.

"If that isn't our target, then he is close. If he sees anything in the air, he will bolt. Or, worse. If he decides to detonate that device where he is, we still may lose everything," said Lanny.

"Yeah, that's the bad thing about suicide jockeys," said Airman Ritter from next door to Andy. "These guys don't usually have an escape plan."

"Besides, this guy is not working alone," said Lanny.

"You mean there are others?" asked James.

"I think I can help with that," said Mr. Larsen, walking up to James and Hannah.

"Oh. Agent Larsen. I can't thank you enough for saving Jack. I don't know what I would have done if," said James choking off his words.

"I'm just glad I was there, James. We've been aware of Jack for a long time. She's a hell of a young woman. Okay, here's the deal. We believe this is Operation Dew Claw. It's been in the closet for decades, but the globalists tried to do it the old-fashioned way. They tried to steal it. When Hillary didn't get elected, they tried to overthrow the election by subterfuge and damned near pulled off a coup. When that didn't work, they tried small scale mayhem, but President Trump's momentum became too much, too fast.

"They always have a backup plan, though. Lanny is right. They have an entire network of misinformation, obstruction, and decoys. Plus, they have an older model AI working around the clock to deceive us. Who do you think cranks the talking points for all the news outlets? He, and I do believe we all agree it is a 'he', feeds the media a narrative every hour that they all parrot over and over again, so the people are always off balance," said Mr. Larsen.

"He's right. I've caught Wells Fargo, and before them Wachovia, laundering billions a year in drug cartel cash between tens of thousands of phony bank accounts. They're still doing it to this very day, and the Justice Department is too compromised to do a thing about it. The cash gets cleaned, and the globalists skim a few billion for operations like this one," said Herbert, pointing to Andy's screen.

"Okay, he's coming up to the camera. Here's the live feed," said Andy moving one of the cascaded screens to the front.

"I thought you said it's color," said James.

"It is. It's almost sunrise, so it's still in infrared mode. We'll only get a few seconds of visuals," said Andy.

"That blue dot is almost there," said Hannah pointing to the screen.

"Five, four, three. There it is. He's got a trailer. He's towing a trailer. That's why he's poking along," said James.

"Can you enhance that image?" asked Mr. Larsen.

"I am getting the raw feed now. A screen shot will be too grainy. It's a total of twenty-four frames. Hold on," said Andy typing now with his left hand and moving the mouse pointer with his right.

"How far is he from Nashville?" asked James.

"At this speed, maybe two hours. He's going to hit rush hour, after the freeways come together, right here," said Andy pointing with his cursor.

"Sweet Jesus. How many people will be there?" asked Hannah.

"It's a metro of about 1.5 million, plus the exurbs," said Mr. Larsen.

"What's an exurb?" asked Hannah.

"It's called urban sprawl. Cities grow into one another. They have their own economic base, but they are absorbed into the larger city's identity," said James.

"Okay, here are all 24 images overlaid and realigned on the rig itself. That's as high resolution as I can make it," said Andy.

"Oh, that's definitely a Ford, but what is that on the trailer? It doesn't look like a bomb," asked James.

"Lanny? I'm sending you a picture. What is this thing on the trailer?" asked Andy across the cubicle.

"I got it. Hmm. IR. Ingersoll-Rand. They make commercial air compressors," said Lanny.

"Air compressor? Shit. That's gotta be the wrong vehicle," said James.

"Any other options?" asked Mr. Larsen.

"I will query Sophia again. I need some time," said Andy.

"That's the one thing we don't have. If Knorr is right, and I have never known him to be wrong, this attack is a go. It is most likely nuclear, and it is most likely, Nashville. Get your Glid3r up, man. We need this intel," said Mr. Larsen.

"Yes sir. I'm working on it," said Andy.

"Let him breathe a little, guys. Hey Andy. You need my chair?" asked Lanny as he scooted around the corner with his racecar seat on roller blade wheels.

Andy stood up without a word and pushed his office chair away from the desk top and grabbed its sides, releasing the locks. He raised the table top, and the 42" screen, up to his chest and placed his hands on the keyboard and mouse. "No. I got this," said Andy, standing like he had just entered a tournament.

The small group watched in amazement as the open tabs moved around the screen like cards being shuffled. Code, graphs, images, tables, and back to code, over and over again. Each time he shuffled the tabs, Sophia refreshed the results of billions of data points, probabilities, and timelines as the colored zone on the map got smaller and smaller. Like a master gamer, he blazed through levels the average person would never see, using hacks, secrets, hidden doors. Sophia was one with Glid3r and Andy was bringing them both to the room. Thousands of data points were discarded as fake, fabricated, dead ends. One by one they were eliminated until the blue area on the map again condensed into a single dot, blinking on Interstate 65.

"Call the cops," said James.

"I wouldn't do that. Wrong team," said Hannah quickly.

"What are you talking about?" asked James.

"I think she means they're not all good guys after the Strong Cities Network," said Herbert.

"Oh God. What's that?" asked James.

"When Loretta Lynch was the Attorney General she announced the formation of the Strong Cities Network. They spent billions to Federalize police departments and turn them into a kind of private army under their command. I audited the money coming from George Soros and the U.S. Treasury to make that happen," said Herbert.

"I thought Trump was ending all that crap," said James.

"Rules, James. The bad guys are required to announce what they're planning. Then when they do it, we can't come back and say, 'Hey that's not fair,'" said Mr. Larsen.

"But Trump loves the police," said James.

"He loves the image of the police. And most of them are good guys that live in the communities they protect, but there are thousands of mercenaries and former military that have infiltrated the ranks. These mercs are quickly promoted and protected by this globalist Syndicate that has an agenda. Why do you think they let those ANTIFA thugs beat people up, burn cars, and smash windows without arresting anyone? They didn't do a damned thing about Seth Rich being shot to death on the street like a stray dog either," said Hannah waving her hands in front of her.

"Okay. I get it. Don't call the cops. But the closer that truck gets to Nashville, the more people are going to die. What other options do we have?" asked James.

"We have options, but we need to buy some time. He is going to be close enough for government work if we let him get much further," said Mr. Larsen.

"Shit. Why didn't I think of this before?" said James pacing a little.

"You're exhausted, James. What are you thinking?" asked Hannah.

"I'm in the highway business. Well, sort of. Orange Barrels is my best client. We need a traffic jam? My God. Nashville is famous for it. I can make a few calls and bring that freeway to a grinding halt in thirty minutes flat," said James.

"Make it happen. I need to meet with Commander Rousseau," said Mr. Larsen.

Chapter 27

No one knows your name when you are selected to be one of the pilots of Air Force One. Boeing's 747-200 was old by any standard, but airframes don't really wear out. The pair of VC-25A jets was delivered in 1983. They were the fastest commercial jets in the air with a top speed of 619 miles an hour, and these units were constantly upgraded with the latest defense systems to protect the leader of the free world. It was a pleasure to fly, because it was vastly overpowered and rarely transported more than a hundred people; although it was capable of flying more than 150 thousand pounds in payload more than 5,300 nautical miles at altitudes up to forty-five thousand feet.

This was a special mission. It must have been, for Colonel Blaine Jameson had been retired from the big iron for ten years when he got the call. He and his wife of thirty-eight years, Linda, were picked up by a plain white car and driven to the Pentagon. He had never entered the building from the side entrance, and it was the first time since he retired that either he or his wife had left the house without their cell phones. The four-hour drive was peaceful and uneventful. Even though Linda had a tendency to get car sick riding in the back, she rode comfortably as the driver was smooth, quiet, and highly trained in the way he moved through traffic without making a single mistake.

The small auditorium was nearly full of couples like him and Linda. One couple came from as far away as Florida. The invitation did not require an RSVP. It was more like an appointment card, simple in its design, with the small, zig zag signature of the President. One by one, he had felt the cards in his own hands. Some, he carefully set aside. A feeling. Others, he rubbed along the edges, reverently laying them on the desk in his bedroom alone, where he slowly signed them. Twenty-four pilots with twenty-four wives selected from hundreds for a special mission.

They filed into the small auditorium and lowered the theater seat bottoms as Blaine sat down next to Linda. He took her hand. The lights dimmed slightly as a spotlight turned onto the podium to the right of the stage of the old pilot's briefing room. His heart skipped a beat as he remembered sitting in a room like this twenty-six years ago, receiving the mission briefing for the bombing routes over Iraq during the Gulf War with a hundred other national guard and commercial pilots called out of reserve to fly. Linda returned the squeeze from his freckled hand surrounding hers.

Ladies and gentlemen, the President of the United States, came the man's voice with unusual calm from the podium. Every person stood, and most of the men brought their right hands to the best salute they could muster while the rest stood holding onto their wives' hands. The young man stepped back from the podium and took a large step to the right as the President walked up behind the mic and adjusted it to his height. He was wearing a dark suit with a shining white shirt and a red tie.

"Please be seated," said the President clearing his throat quietly. "Today, it is I who will stand for the great service you have each given to our country. I especially want to thank your wives, who kept your homes together and supported you while you served. Tonight, I have a special request of you. And, to be quite honest, I could not ask anyone to make this request for me. It is not a small thing that I ask.

"The world outside this room does not know what I am about to share with you. Ladies and gentlemen, we are at war. I think you all thought you knew that already, but this is different. We have reason to believe that in the next few hours, the United States will be attacked by a nuclear weapon that is already inside our country. Without going into all the details of how it got here, I want to instead focus on why it is here, and what those who placed it here want to accomplish.

"First, let me say that they have been working very hard to destroy America for a long time. They worked as one for decades to take away our rights. They have been somewhat successful. I used to think it was because our leaders and elected officials were stupid. But now, I must admit I may have been mistaken about that. I began to see this back in the late eighties, and when they narrowly lost control of the government in the 2,000 Election, they put their backup plan into action, and a few months later attacked the World Trade Center not far from my home. I don't mind telling you, that hurt. It hurt me, and it hurt America. It hurt big league. It was a terrible thing.

"I have been saying this for what I think is a long time, but I resolved then and there, that I would run for president one day and do my best to make America great again. In my business, fifteen years goes by in fifteen minutes, but the Constitutional rights we lost in that short amount of time were staggering. I gave up a life of unmatched success because this country made that life possible; for me and literally, for every American who works hard and applies themselves to their dreams. I could not, by any stretch of the imagination, let this country be destroyed when I knew I could provide the leadership to save it.

"But our enemies are very old and very powerful. They only have one thing standing in their way of taking over this world once and for all. That one thing is America," said the President. He paused for moment and took a drink from the bottled water placed on the podium. He swallowed dryly and looked around the room.

"I need twelve pilots. Air Force One will be flying a special mission, and I am asking for volunteers. We don't have time to do this again, so I selected twenty-four of you. Your wives are here, because this mission may be your last. I don't know how to put it any other way. Of course, your wives can come with you, if you like. It's your choice. Someone once told me that many are called, but few there are that choose. We leave in thirty minutes.

"Thank you from the bottom of my heart. You are each the greatest Americans I have ever met. God bless you, and God bless the United States of America," said the President as he saluted one more time. He held his hand as perfectly as he could above his right eyebrow as the pilots and their wives stood. All of them.

"I trust you're safely away, Mr. President," said Raymond into the smooth, platinum receiver against his ear. The cabinet is with you? Except those two, yes sir. If you conserve fuel, you can remain airborne for thirty-three hours. Yes sir, it will seem like forever. Let me assure you. Their forces have been in place for months, and they will attempt to seize Washington within minutes of the blast.

"Their eyes are everywhere, Mr. President, except on that aircraft. There are fighters and missile interceptors in Greenland, sir. There is a refueling facility there under what we called Operation Bear Claw. Since early in the campaign. We knew you would, but Hillary's team was confident their voter base was enough to hand her the keys. No sir. They cannot read minds. Unless it is spoken aloud. Yes sir, when you speak, they listen. That's how the leaks happen," said Raymond smoothly.

He listened as President Trump shared his ideas with him. Air Force One was one of the few safe places on the planet where command and control could be maintained, but without a way to speak to the people, there would soon be chaos. The utmost secrecy was demanded for more than two years to slowly, and meticulously move Marines to Greenland. Tankers, fighter aircraft, radio repeater aircraft and buoys, anti-missile batteries, and secure living facilities took months to secretly transport and erect and configure into a remote command post. It was all done under the National Science Foundation Polar Research Division. The Russians never suspected a thing.

"I understand, Mr. President. Just in case. It has been an honor and a pleasure. Thank you, sir. God Speed," said Raymond softly pressing the button on the screen of his phone.

Adnan found America to be a different world than he expected. His entire youth, he was told of the filth and decadence of America. His father told him the entire country was full of gluttons who wore the skulls of their unborn children on their belts. The great Satan consumed the world and blasphemed with every breath while the true founders of the civilized world were trampled under its iron shoe.

His faith was not shaken by the harmless, peaceful infidels he saw every day who worked hard in the belief that they were free. He imagined that Damascus was once green and beautiful like America, with rivers full of fish and nutrients for the rich farmlands. America would never know what thousands of years felt like, let alone to be the backdrop for all holy books. His city was conquered only a few times over many millennia, but it took the ceaseless bombardment of American weapons to break its spirit, crumbling every building, sending millions of his people screaming into Europe for shelter. Its leaders had carved up the Middle East according to their own delight, and decimated the caliphate that ruled the world for nearly a thousand years. He had no regrets.

The Sun was peeking over the horizon below the hilltops to his right, as the one lane of traffic became two, and then began to slow. He looked at his watch. By now the subzero tritium was thawing, building pressure in the twelve chambers inside the two-inch thick enrichment controller. It didn't matter. The piezo-electric pumps were built to withstand 20 thousand pounds per square inch. The twelve bolts that fastened the controller were 14 millimeter stainless steel. This latest design was superior to the September

2017 device the North Koreans had detonated deep inside their mountain facility.

Still, Adnan was a man known for his reliability and attention to detail. He always delivered. In less than three hours, he would be reported missing from work for the first time. Just because he was exceptionally productive at programming in C++, he knew he had to be on some sort of watch list. By now, they would have tried at least once to check the validity of his credentials. Oh, they acted like they didn't care, because nearly every programmer with his skill had a checkered past. Hacking is second nature to a master programmer. There were parolees in that very facility, but their work was audited to minimize the risk. The contractors were paid by NASA, DARPA, and even more secret agencies no one knew about according to a prevailing wage, and they pocketed the difference. Most of these contracts were on a no-bid basis with sole-source status that ensured they would make at least 100% profits. He rolled his fists around the rim of the steering wheel in frustration as traffic came to a crawl, still more than 100 miles to the city of Nashville.

He ran the calculations again in his head. The device would not be effective from here. No more than three miles from the Old Hickory Dam north of Nashville, was the plan. 22,500 acres of water that formed most of the lakes north of city would become an inland tsunami, ripping 100 square miles off the face of the earth while crippling three major highway systems and bridges. Besides the power station that would be physically destroyed in the blast, the Electromagnetic Pulse would overload every micro-circuit for 500 miles in every direction. But, he had to be nearly on top of it for the blast to be effective.

The general contractor resurfacing West Main Street in Hendersonville was behind schedule, and was expecting the delivery of the IED Adnan expertly disguised as a reserve compressor. At this rate, it would be nearly noon when he pulled off of Tennessee Highway 31-E and onto West Main. The communications module in the battery cabinet would receive the arming code and initiate its countdown with a pulse from the Kwangmyŏngsŏng-4 earth observation satellite launched by North Korea on the 7th of February 2016. It had orbited in complete silence ever since. Nine days later, Donald Trump officially announced he was running for President of the United States. The story behind the development of that satellite was one of the deepest secrets in the world. Adnan should know. He was a human component of that plan.

The DNC was not convinced Trump would actually run for office. Media was filled with jokes about the prospect. But, the AI considered all the possibilities. He could see the Trump campaign's legal filings, carefully isolating Donald Trump from his businesses. The special bank accounts, Federal Election Commission submissions, and the queries for ballot submissions across all 50 States were laying a foundation as sure as those laid for any 95-story building. And Donald Trump had changed entire skylines of cities with his ability to lay sure foundations and apply attention to details. For more than 30 years, he had been involved in international business, supported national and local candidates for public office, and refined his policies about making America great again. The AI knew he would defeat his sixteen primary competitors. He knew that Trump would use social media to bypass the main stream media and reach the people in real time.

He knew that since 2012, cell phones had morphed into smart phones. The American demographic had changed so quickly, that no pollsters could keep up. They continued to survey land lines, while more than 75-percent of people had stopped using them. Polls showed Hillary with a comfortable lead, but in reality, 78-percent of smart phone users were getting their news from alternate sources and receiving Trump's ceaseless 140-character posts on Twitter. YouTube companies followed him from rally to rally and often had 30 thousand people watching them, while 30 thousand more were waving signs at the live events. 78-percent of 75-percent calculates to 58-percent, which is 313 delegates. Trump won 304 delegates.

Without the enormous Democrat numbers from undocumented voters in three counties in New Mexico, its 9 electoral votes would have gone to Trump, making the AI's prediction exactly correct.

In early 2015, the AI tried to head off the Trump campaign by drafting a new FCC policy to shift America's Internet from Title I to Title II, transforming the Internet into a Federal utility under the ingenious name of Net Neutrality. With the Democrat majority on the Commission, nothing could stop the secret policy from being signed. Were it not for the unwavering leadership of the Commission by its new Chairman, Ajit Pai, after the election, the newly-Titled utility would have transferred to the purview of the United Nations.

Every media attacked him mercilessly. Numerous threats against his life would not dissuade him from saving the freedom of the Internet from the censorship of the globalist elites. The Commission narrowly escaped the AI's plan by less than 48 hours. If it had succeeded, Trump's communication line with the American people would have been severed. It was a powerful game being played at the highest levels above the heads of the American people for the soul of the Earth, and they did not have a clue what was going on.

Only one analyst in the world saw what was going on, but no one could hear him, because the AI banned his articles and buried his analysis so deep, no one could find it. The Presidential election polls were materially wrong, according to the AI's calculations. The risk of America escaping from the traps laid by the Obama administration and the Clinton State Department were more than just significant, with Donald Trump leading the country. With more than thirty years of his planning and refinement, the probability was very good that the economy would improve, and the social wedges Obama had driven between races, religions, and even economic classes might very well be swept away. It would take a catastrophic event to stop him and bring the ship around to face the cliff again.

They might not be able to kill the President within the rules, but they could kill the country he was trying to lead.

The Syndicate moved forward, trusting the AI's suggestion that the satellite should be constructed and launched for this one purpose. North Korea had never before launched anything into space. Their history of designing and launching missiles littered the seas with incinerated aluminum cans and half-spent boosters. It would take a giant leap forward in rocket and satellite technology to make this a success. They would only get one attempt. The right U.S. technology was delivered into their hands, and the Syndicate's politicians were again enriched by the process. Taking control of the world was a business from which everyone could make money. With a feckless, merry-go-round Congress, nothing would ever be done to stop the Syndicate's plan. Although everyone knew North Korea was provided American technology to launch its satellite successfully on the first try, no one dared expose the true source.

He glanced in his rear-view mirror one more time, noticing the line of traffic stretching beyond the horizon. He took a deep breath, feeling smaller and less essential to the plan than he had just a few hours before.

They promised him he would be recovered, once he made it to Carolina Beach and out to sea on his fishing trip. There was a rental car waiting for him near the dam. He would make his escape before the device was detonated, if only he could get there in time. He looked down at the shoulder bag that contained his passports, money, and the reservation for the deep-sea fishing boat. The submarine would take him aboard, scuttle the boat, and his priceless skill set would be preserved for another day. It was an elaborate plan he tried his best to believe. Still, no matter how he ran the formula in his head, he was a loose end.

It didn't matter. In a few hours, his brother and father would be avenged, and the great Satan would be trying to feel its way to a neutral corner, blinded and suffering from the internal hemorrhage he was about to inflict. It was all a dream. And there is no pain when you're dead. Only freedom and paradise awaited.

Chapter 28

Just about every book on leadership will tell you that the secret to great success is delegation. Billions of dollars are made trying to convince businesses to buy a book, implement a program, watch a webinar, or launch a new software application. The truth is that a successful student makes famous a teacher. Simple as that. A platinum selling singer makes a great studio. An Oscar makes a great producer. They all have one thing in common. They are all wrong.

From the very beginning of mankind on the Earth, there is one principle that conquers all. Oh, the gurus and wizards will tell you it is determination that produces success. In the same way lottery winners convince more people to buy lottery tickets, success stories are used as daily motivational videos for tens of thousands of people buying licenses to be consultants and loading their laptops with lead generation software.

The real principle of world domination consistently results from loyalty. Blood oath loyalty allows the leader to sleep when the wind blows. That is to say, the crime boss knows he will never face a day in court, because his people are loyal. No witness will live to testify. When Eric Holder withheld subpoenaed information, and refused to answer questions that might incriminate agents in his department, he was convicted of Contempt of Congress.

He was the highest cabinet official in modern times to be convicted by Congress of criminal activity. Did it matter? Not one single bit. Why? Because the Democrats have a mind that is single to the glory of darkness. There is really only one Democrat in Washington, and it is commanded to vote a certain way, nothing wavering. From 1848 until the present day, no Democrat has broken ranks with the DNC and survived past the next election. Some do not survive past the next sunrise.

When a sovereign American like Donald Trump becomes President, and seeks to transfer the power of Washington back to the people from whom it Constitutionally derives its power, dark principalities immediately oppose him. The people have always wondered who that principality might be. Most people believe in God, or in some supreme being that knows all and has the power to save souls. But, when you ask them if they believe in a devil, or a demon intelligence that seeks the enslavement misery of every living soul, the answer is almost universally, yes.

Perhaps it is because they need someone or something to blame for the poor condition of their lives, a successive string of failures, or the scarcity of supernatural blessings that seem to befall them. Maybe it is a curse. Maybe it is a simple spell. Maybe, just maybe, there is some exiled immortal deep in the bowels of the Earth who demands loyalty and promises mortal wealth and pleasure in exchange for an oath and covenant.

It is a covenant that few get the opportunity to make. For millennia, men and women have slain the person in front of them to get one step closer to the actual seat of power. But for the rules governing the direct, face-to-face contact with this evil fallen one, the entire human race would have been hopelessly lost. No, the rules allow for a handful of men and women to make this oath to the dark lord, and for all the rest who would freely trade their poverty for talent, fame, wealth, and power over other men in exchange for their eternal soul, to make their pledge to a human mortal under his authority and command.

The tools of loyalty are many, and they are more powerful than anything in the universe. The lust of the flesh, the lust of the eye, and the pride of life are but mere weaknesses in comparison. Jealousy is so powerful that it can bring down angels and gods. The desire to rule over other humans has been the driving force behind nearly every war mankind has fought.

In the struggle for worlds, men are incorporated as the primary force and command. Were it not so, demons would conscribe the mortal occupants of all worlds as easily as humans domesticate sheep. The governing rules are tied to the very energy that resonated to make third dimensional matter. That is to say, the instant gods or demons begin to circumvent the free will of mortals, the entire universe would disassociate and go back to the chaos of singularities from which it came.

What is also known, is that the souls who earned the lineage of the seed of Adam progress on a different slope than demons or the seed of Lucifer. As it is written, they are created a little lower than the angels, but their potential is unlimited; far greater than any angel. Few mortals there be with a concept of the exaltation of a soul. Knowing the potential of the mortal soul, who can understand the choice of darkness over light made by the mightiest men of Earth?

"The future is a reasonable speculation, Mr. Lim," said the Voice.

"I am well aware of the possibilities, but there are probabilities to be considered as well. Our artificial asset is calculating by the microsecond and revealed a strong possibility that our Mr. Kassam has been identified and located by the enemy," said Lim Shun.

"A distraction is in order, perhaps?" asked the Voice.

"If you're asking if we can use a distraction to get him to the target, no. Nashville will most likely escape," said Lim Shun.

"He is a wounded wolf," said the Voice.

"He won't abandon the chase, if that's what you're implying. The device is designed to be effective up to 500 miles," said Lim Shun.

"Air Force One is in the air. Both of them," said the Voice.

"All according to plan," said Lim Shun.

"Not all, Mr. Lim" said the Voice.

"The President is aboard, along with his Cabinet. All possibilities have been considered," said Lim Shun.

"Your confidence in your assets may be your only weakness, Mr. Lim," said the Voice.

"Their snake is useless without its head," said Lim Shun.

"Your team is ready?" asked the Voice.

"The media has been queued, and the scripts have been written for the Democrat team to assume leadership once the Operation is completed," said Lim Shun.

"And what of the people?" asked the Voice.

"Placing two-thirds of the country in soup lines allowed us to lay the foundation for our government inside the American Republic 85 years ago," said Lim Shun.

"Yes. Even my superiors were impressed. The world's greatest economic powerhouse brought to its knees in just a few days without firing a shot. Mr. Harry Hopkins raised the bar for breaking the will of a Republic," said the Voice.

"Pretty impressive, considering there was no artificial intelligence at that time. It was among your finest work, sir," said Lim Shun, carefully choosing his words.

"I accept your accolades, Mr. Lim, but this time it is your work. Delegation is not always a clumsy tool," said the Voice.

"We all start somewhere, sir" said Lim Shun.

"Well, let's start by getting your Operation Dew Claw to accomplish the mission," said the Voice.

"If you will excuse me, sir. There are decisions to make," said Lim Shun.

"We shall be waiting," said the Voice, and the eagle on the screen faded to black.

The news media mergers took decades to accomplish. It was a nearly trillion-dollar war that was fought for the power to control the news and information Americans received. Warner Communications merged with Time in 1990. Within three years, the internet threatened to tear the attention of Americans away from the steady feed of propaganda and exclusive content by which the Syndicate placed Bill Clinton into office in 1992.

Americans were confident they could win the game by merging AOL with Time-Warner in the largest megamerger in history worth more than $146 billion. The world's largest browser provider took control of the world's largest cable and news provider. The events of September 11th, 2001 only made Americans thirst that much more for alternative sources of news, and AOL was directly connected with an audience that was growing exponentially.

The Syndicate would not let this effort succeed. A few months later, in early 2002, Bill Clinton made the public declaration that he had instructed the Department of Justice to sue Microsoft under the Sherman Anti-Trust Act to break up their monopoly on Internet browsers. The plan was successful in crushing the runaway rise in Internet businesses, and smashing the megamerger into the biggest financial blunder in merger history.

There was no question that Donald Trump had single-handedly unraveled the globalist plan to bring America to its knees, and then to surrender. If Hillary had been elected, America would have been rolled onto its side and been branded with the global seal of ownership. Its armed forces would have been merged with those of the UN. Its treasury would have fallen under the financial control of the crown. Its system of education, health care, and media had already been surrendered.

But, as predicted by a handful of statistical analysts, Hillary was defeated. For thirty years, Trump had been planning and refining his platform in the private sector, while building a multibillion dollar empire of success with more than 500 businesses. Hillary crafted her platform by selling official influence to world leaders for billions of dollars. She had sold so much of America, and so much of herself, that she could not articulate her policy to a single reporter.

The change in leadership was apparent within hours of his Republican nomination as candidate. Even with the debate questions in advance, Hillary was a disaster in the televised debates. She was no match for Trump's boardroom experience, and he seemed unaffected by the *charm of favor*.

His inauguration was like nothing ever stated in any speech by any leader, transferring power not peacefully from one Party to another, but from Washington to the people. He knew perfectly well that the Syndicate had succeeded in merging both Parties into one with the single purpose of subduing the people. He also knew his policies would break the dam, holding millions of Americans back from their potential success. America roared forward, adding $5 trillion in value to the Stock Market and pulling the entire world with it.

The global media and elites beat their breasts and slashed their skin in protest. It must have satisfied the dark demon who protected them, because somehow, not one single officer or soldier in the Clinton Crime Syndicate was indicted, or even accused for the embezzlement, graft, sale of national security secrets, or use of the U.S. intelligence agencies and bureaus as professional surveillance and evidence management services designed to destroy Donald Trump and his family. They were not, however, prepared for a national law enforcement program focusing on pedophilia. Thousands of the DNC's soldiers were indicted for the heinous crime of child molestation, as the Attorney General knew all too well the right of passage into the Syndicate. They were all guilty, and relied on the Syndicate to maintain their immunity from prosecution, for a nominal fee. Those who were current on their donations were spared, while delinquency garnered betrayal.

Still, America might not be totally crushed when the lights were turned off, if its national leader survived to show them the way back. One thing that history has repeatedly shown; however, is that catastrophes are opportunities for those who are prepared. And, of course, the best way for preparation to meet opportunity is to be the cause of the catastrophe.

"Banks here. I need that aerial image, and I need it five minutes ago," said the General into her phone.

"Ma'am, the drone should be over the target in the next ten minutes. The sky is clear, so the images should be very clear," said the duty officer at Fort Campbell, Kentucky.

"They're approved to send. Don't call me back. Just send the images," said the General, ending the conversation and pressing another button on her phone. They had practiced this a hundred times, and the time that James had just bought with the construction contractor outside of Spring Hill, Tennessee at least was going to keep the device out of Nashville long enough to take countermeasures.

General Banks entered the next number into her phone. "Space Command, Colonel Napier," was the answer.

"Jake. Banks, here. When is the Nork satellite in range?" asked the General.

"It will be line of sight from the Southwest 09:12:46 at 15° altitude," said Colonel Napier.

"How long until the window closes?" asked the General.

"The Kwangmyŏngsŏng-4 will be out of range of Nashville, Tennessee at 09:14:58, Ma'am," said Colonel Napier.

"Right. Two minutes twelve seconds. Thanks, Jake. I have two hours to save the world," said the General ending the call. She placed the receiver on the desk and rubbed her eyes with both hands. It had been more than a day and a half since she had slept. Jack was on her feet, but looked like she had jumped out of plane without a chute. Tommy could sleep five minutes at a time for days. Rocky never slept. Training was good for keeping people from wondering what to do, but no training can get you ready to lose a million people. She picked up the receiver on the first ring.

"Banks here," she said doing her best to sound alert.

"I wanted you to be among the first to know," said the male voice on the other end.

"What do you have, Jim?" asked the General recognizing the lisp on the other end.

"We have had a few more Nork defectors. I have to give them credit, the little shits. I can't tell if they're really good running backs, or the Nork's at the DMZ are lousy shots. We have learned that they have subs deployed near Greenland," said Jim.

"I'm not going to ask how they knew. I don't have the time to hear about it," said the General.

"Yeah. Well, you're not going to like this either. They have strapped a dozen MANPADS together inside sub-launched missiles. They can get the missile to 30 thousand feet PDQ and then deploy the ordinance, which can acquire a bomber's heat signature and take out the engines," said Jim.

"I know you think those four stars and your proximity to the President gives you the right to control the need to know, Marine, but where did they get the MANPADS?" asked the General.

"You know damned well they came from Benghazi," said Jim raising his voice a little.

"I know that, Jim. If I had been approved to sink that damned freighter, Hillary wouldn't have gotten them to Syria. What I'm asking is, how the hell did they get from Syria to North Korea?" asked the General.

"We're still working on that one, but we suspect it might have had something to do with a couple of pallets of cash Obama had secretly flown to Iran in the middle of a cold night in January 2016. I'm sure there was more than $1.8 billion when the trucks left the warehouse. Flynn is the best spook I know, and he's sure people along the way stuffed their pockets full. I also have a feeling that the people who skimmed that pile of cash have committed suicide by now. These guys never leave witnesses behind. Look, the important thing is, we have to make sure our pilots know what's possible," said Jim.

"I have to assume we don't have a secure channel to the aircraft, Jim," said the General.

"We can use the Foxtrot system, can't we?" asked Jim.

"Ham radios? You want to keep Air Force One from being shot out of the sky using ham radios?" asked the General.

"Hey, it's analog. The Syndicate's clunky AI that's stomping around the web needs ones and zeroes to function. It doesn't like analog waves," said Jim.

"I can use the Foxtrot code. It's never been broken. I am going after those subs. You can take that to the bank, Jim," said the General.

"I guess we can't help it if one of those Nork subs gets in the way of some test ordinance you might happen to drop into the sea," said Jim.

"It's not like we could start a war or anything," said the General, happy with the Secretary of Defense.

"Keep me posted," said Jim, and she heard the line go quiet.

He was a calm man in battle, and the results he got from his men and equipment were nothing short of kick ass. He never spiked the football. She never knew of him having to retake a piece of ground. His NCOs used to say of him, 'If we take it, it's took.'

It's not unusual for the Arctic Spring to include a high turbulent jet stream. Even a Boeing 747-200 is no match for a 200 mile-per-hour north-westerly wind. The occupants of Air Force One were seated and belted, and holding onto their armrests. Even at 45 thousand feet, it is easy for a large jet to feel like a leaf blown about a dirt road. The fact that it was 60 degrees below zero outside didn't matter. Greenland was not far away.

There is a time in every war just before the first shot is fired, where the soldiers wonder if their commanders are afraid. At some point, the orders become the action. The judgements and negotiations give way to ego and to indoctrination about technologies and position, training and resolve. The fish and the birds are unaware of the hatreds of mankind. Or maybe, it is that mankind is unaware of the natural balance of nature, which humans somehow refuse to join. Like playing a game of poker at a table set up on the railroad tracks, the locomotive will come, unfettered by the wealth of the players, or the winner, or the house. The train will come roaring through and inevitably, will pass leaving no survivors.

The X-37B is a secret, miniature space shuttle with the most secret cargo bay in the world. The fact that this unmanned ship can change its altitude on command while on its year-long missions in space makes it particularly difficult to predict. One day it is overhead for a minute, and then next day, two. General Banks has a team that loads the cargo bay with various instruments and weapons. There is hardly a single asset in any military arsenal that is less than two hours away from any target on the planet at any given moment. Only now, has Sophia been introduced to its controls, once air-gapped to a set of command trailers at Edwards Air Force Base. It was the first time anything other than a human joystick and an encrypted radio broadcasting system had ever been connected to this ultra-secret spacecraft; now one of the most experienced assets of the newly formed American Space Command.

"Major Mead. Can you come in here, please?" asked General Banks.

"Yes, General," said the Major without emotion.

"I want you to go visit Jack. If she wants to, take her to her family in housing. If she wants to," said the General.

"And if she doesn't?" asked the Major.

"Tell her we've taken out the trash. Ask her if she's going to sleep all day," said the General.

"Yes, Ma'am," said the Major smiling slightly.

The halls of the Pentagon were empty, with the exception of an occasional Marine standing against the wall. He didn't like jogging in low quarters, but something wouldn't let him walk the shortest distance to the vaulted Faraday section of the complex. Within a few minutes, unconcerned with the sweat running down his chest, he arrived under the camera at the door. It clicked inside as the Marine on the inside pulled the handle over and pushed it open.

"Thank you, sergeant," said the Major slipping past him into the dimly-lit gray air lock. The inner door clicked and automatically swung open enough for him to enter the cubicle center, humming with activity.

"Mead. Good to see you. Any news?" asked Rocky shaking his hand.

"I'm here to see Jack. Orders," said the Major.

"In the back. She was resting last time I looked in on her. James is with her," said Rocky.

"Agent Larsen. Good to see you again, sir," said the Major walking past the cubicles.

"Major Mead. Let me walk with you for a minute," said Mr. Larsen.

"I'm going back to speak to Jack. Orders from the General," said Mead barely slowing his long stride.

"I think we should land Air Force One in Greenland," said Mr. Larsen.

"Land? There will be international concerns over command in exile," said the Major.

"I took care of that. Operation Bear Claw leased the land from Greenland. It's our territory. Just another base, Major," said Mr. Larsen.

"Clever. I will inform the General. It could play. Anything else?" asked the Major.

"My source informs me the DNC has gathered their team. They mean to take over. I'm not sure we have a legal way to stop them from setting up," said Mr. Larsen.

"Noted. I'll let you know first," said Major Mead.

"How?" asked Mr. Larsen.

"Well, let's find out. Hello, Jack. How are you feeling?" asked the Major trying not to wince at the sight of her black and blue face, her swollen right eye, or the splint taped to her right hand.

"Well, Mr. Larsen tells me I am the winner, so I guess I feel pretty good about that," said Jack trying to smile while putting her left hand against her cheek.

"I've come from the General," began the Major.

"How much time do we have?" asked Jack.

"Unknown. If you want to stay with your family, it would," started the Major.

"Mike and Lucy will make sure mom and dad are okay. You think I want them to see me like this? They hate it when I have black eyes. Trust me, I know," said Jack brushing her hair away from her right eye.

"In that case, are you ready to get back to work?" asked the Major.

"Excuse me, Major. She is not a warfighter. What's wrong with your legs?" asked Mr. Larsen.

"To tell you the truth, I don't think Knorr likes me. Besides, General Banks tells me the trash has been taken out," said the Major.

"I could use a Tylenol, but other than that, when do we leave?" asked Jack.

"Talk to your brothers on the way out," said Mr. Larsen.

Chapter 29

"Captain Jameson, I have a comm signal," said the Flight Engineer.

"Can you put it on my headset?" asked Blaine.

"No Sir. It is short. I make it to be only about a hundred characters long. It's on the two-meter band, Sir," said the Engineer.

"That's the old Foxtrot system. Print it out. There's a blue notebook in the file drawer by your knee. You can decode it from that table," said Blaine.

"That's kind of primitive, you know?" said the Engineer.

"Sometimes the old systems are the most reliable. Besides, when the Iranians grabbed a super-stealthy RQ-170 out of the sky and landed it, we knew we had been digitally compromised. Radio isn't digital. You gotta have a decoder ring, my boy," said Blaine. He was close to seventy years old, and he hadn't had a flight physical in years, but he still jogged two miles on the nice days on the beach near his home.

"I got it, Sir. They want us to land, Sir," said the Engineer.

"When?" asked Blaine.

"Now, Sir," said the Engineer.

"Any other instruction with that comm?" asked Blaine?

"Approach from the sea 92 Left, Captain," said the Engineer.

"Number one. Put on the cabin comm," said Blaine.

"You're live, Sir," said the Co-Pilot.

"This is captain Jameson speaking. There has been a slight change in plans. We're going to land in Greenland. It's a balmy eighteen degrees with winds of twenty knots, but I hear the chow is pretty good. I need everyone in their seatbelts, except the flight deck spouses. Please make your way to the flight deck. Make sure you stow any loose items securely. Put your seat any way you like, tray tables, blah blah blah," said Blaine motioning for the Co-Pilot to end the cabin connection.

Within a couple of minutes, the three wives entered the cockpit and took seats beside the Engineer. The Engineer closed the door and took his seat again.

"Ladies, there is a reason I asked you up here. I believe we have been spotted and targeted. I don't see anything on radar, and my satellite feeds don't see anything either. That doesn't mean much, with these guys. This ship makes a big target, even at 45 thousand feet. We'll be approaching Greenland from the sea, and I have a feeling we're being used to draw their fire," said Blaine.

"What if we get shot down? Isn't there another way? I have grandkids," said the Co-Pilot's wife over the noise of the wind against the aluminum bulkhead.

"I don't like the idea any more than you do. Unlike the equipment I've been flying for half my life, this ship has cutting edge countermeasures. I got flares, chaff, and I even have percussion bombs. Plus, I have about twenty percent more throttle on this hot rod. We're not going down without a fight," said Blaine.

"Captain I have some more Foxtrot code. Hold on," said the Engineer as he flipped through the code tables.

"We knew this trip might be a one-way ticket. We were chosen for a reason, and I am going to do my damnedest to make sure we add value to this mission," said Blaine.

"I got it, Captain. It says 'sub-launch. Heat seeking clusters. MANPADS,'" said the Engineer.

"MANPADS? Those are shoulder-fired anti-aircraft missiles. Those bastards. They're shooting a lunch box up to our altitude, and then triggering those from the nose cone," said Blaine.

"Those nine-foot turbofans out there will make an easy target for those things. I saw one take out an A-10 Warthog once doing 400 knots. It took three seconds to reach him from the ground," said the Co-Pilot.

"I don't think there's enough power in those things to take a jet this size down, but they will trash a motor in a heartbeat. Four motors, four direct hits. That's pretty good odds, I'd say," said Blaine.

"It's just aluminum, Sir. There's no armor out there, and besides, we have 140 tons of fuel in those wings," said the Engineer.

"Radio the base Number One. Tell them we are beginning our descent," said Blaine.

"Captain, whoever is out there will monitor that transmission," said the Engineer.

"I would, if I were them," said Blaine placing his hands on the four throttle levers.

"Reduce power to 50%," said the Co-Pilot reading the checklist fastened to his left thigh.

"50% it is," said Blaine. The plane felt like someone had stepped on the brakes as the sub-zero air dragged the jet to a slower airspeed.

"I have four-fifty knots," said the Co-Pilot.

"Four-fifty. Coming around to one eight zero. What's next?" asked Blaine.

"At 25 thousand, turn to one, one, zero," said the Co-Pilot.

"Get your hands on those countermeasures. Switch on the belly cam, and look for white water and smoke when we clear the coast. Ladies, you can watch that screen as well. Four sets of eyes are better than one," said Blaine.

"Damn. Did they have to put the landing strip so close to the water?" said the Co-Pilot.

"Well, the good news is that the water doesn't get deep enough for a sub for about five miles. See those icebergs? That's not going to make it easy either," said Blaine.

"No disrespect, Sir, but they will have to be shallow to launch. Besides, if we can't see them, it's doubtful they can see us," said the Co-Pilot.

"We'll be forty miles from our last transmission, in about four more minutes. When do I make that turn?" asked Blaine.

"Thirty seconds, Sir. You're still a little high. I can back off the throttle a little," said the Co-Pilot.

"Leave it. We're not landing at Miami. That's a 15 thousand foot strip down there. I can go in a little hot," said Blaine.

"I don't blame you. Okay. Left to one, one, zero. Your next turn will be to six zero at 12 thousand five-hundred," said the Co-Pilot.

"Nope. That's not going to work for me. I'm going straight North from there and punching it," said Blaine.

"I can't help you, Sir if you go off procedure," said the Co-Pilot.

"Just keep me posted on the strain gauge and the engine temperatures,
said Blaine.

"We're at 310 knots at 20 thousand feet. It's going to be hard to reduce speed with the nose down like this," said the Co-Pilot.

"I'm turning North to zero," said Blaine.

"Sir, that will cut our approach by at least thirty percent, and you're more than a mile too high," said the Co-Pilot.

"Hold on, we're doing a sixty-degree turn. Just like in the simulator," said Blaine. The right wing came up to nearly vertical. Passenger flights never got even close to three G's in a commercial flight. The average person will pass out at this strain, but pilots are trained to 3.5 G's, and military pilots experience 6 G's in a centrifuge to know what it feels like. You're trained to breathe, tighten the core muscles to keep blood in the brain, and in extreme applications, pilots wear a compression suit to squeeze the blood out of the legs to make it easier for the heart to keep the pilot conscious.

"Strain gauges are near the limits, Sir," said the Co-Pilot.

"You ever do a barrel roll in one of these?" asked Blaine.

"You can't be serious," said the Co-Pilot.

"No. Not really. You don't have to worry about dropping a serving cart on the ceiling in the simulator. But, believe it or not, this baby will do it," said Blaine sinking into the seat with the high banking turn to the North.

"Five, four, okay you're at zero, Sir," said the Co-Pilot.

The big jet leveled out the wings, and the Captain reached forward for the throttle levers and pushed them to the firewall.

"Approaching four hundred knots," said the Co-Pilot.

"I don't want to be over this deep water any longer than I have to be. Hold it at four hundred knots. How far until we line up with 272?" asked Blaine.

"Calculating. Two minutes, Sir," said the Co-Pilot.

"A whole lot can happen in two minutes," said Blaine smiling over at his Co-Pilot. They were both shaking in their seats as the jet stream wind was approaching the aircraft from the West over the left wing. The enormous tail felt like it was kicking its way through the thick Arctic air.

"Even eggs take three minutes," said the Co-Pilot smiling back.

"Shit! Captain I have a launch. Yes yes. I have a launch at three o'clock, Sir," said the Engineer.

The wives gripped their hands together and began to cry. A pilot's wife has a secret place in her heart for plane crashes. It's a place of resolve with a respectful flag folded in the study, and a visit once a month to the cemetery. There was a peace that came from knowing that a man died doing what he loved doing, and believing that he faced the end with dignity and no regrets.

"Launching countermeasures," said the Engineer.

"Belay that, man. That's just the missile with no guidance. When the nose cone opens, those missiles have to light up and acquire our heat signature. When you see those candles, then drop the flares," said Blaine.

"Turn left to 272 in thirty seconds," said the Co-Pilot.

The Captain reached for the throttles and pulled them back all the way. The plane lurched backward, straining their chests against their seat belts. "Turn the radar off when that missile reaches 12 thousand feet," said Blaine.

"Aye, Captain. Ten seconds," said the Engineer.

"Kill the engines," said Blaine.

"Kill the engines?" asked the Co-Pilot in disbelief.

"Do it now. Radar too. I want this ship cold. Everything except the APU," said Blaine.

"Aye Captain. Engines off. You have to turn now to 272, Sir," said the Co-Pilot.

"Holy shit, Captain. It blew up," said the Engineer.

"No it didn't. That's the nose cone blowing open. Watch for those candles and then get the first wave of flares deployed," said Blaine, as he banked the silent jet hard to the left and pushed the nose down.

"I can't see anything through the smoke from the nose cone charges going off, Captain," said the Engineer.

"You have maybe ten seconds for those MANPADS to light up. They have to stabilize first. What's our engine temperatures?" asked Blaine.

"Number four is still about 300, but it won't stay there long at minus seventy degrees," said the Co-Pilot.

"Okay, help me with this. Left rudder down, left ailerons down. Let it go to seventy-five degrees and then let the wing drop slowly. Watch those strain gauges," said Blaine.

"You've done this before?" asked the Co-Pilot.

"In a Cessna. Same principle. Trust me. The wings will stay on," said Blaine sounding like he was lifting 200 pounds of dead weight.

"Airspeed dropping," said the Co-Pilot also straining his voice with effort.

"So's our altitude. That's the point. Less rudder. Watch the heading. Flying sideways is a little like drifting a Mustang. Just don't wuss out on me," said Blaine.

"You've drifted a Mustang?" asked the Co-Pilot.

"Yes, he has. Just ask our grandson," said Linda gripping the armrests on her seat.

"A little different looking out the side window, isn't it?" asked Blaine fighting with the yoke that was shaking in his hands.

"Flares away. Flares away," said the Engineer as he pressed the blue button on the panel.

"Coming up on 10 thousand. We're going to be long. Sir, I'm getting a stall alarm," said the Co-Pilot.

"That's just because we're slipping this ship sideways like a trainer. Push the nose down further. Bring that tail around harder," said Blaine.

"Sir, we're red on the tail side load," said the Co-Pilot raising his voice.

"It'll hold. Bring it around. Focus on those numbers down there. We have a dozen rockets looking for our ass right now," said Blaine.

"Oh my God. Oh my God. There's an explosion," said the Engineer.

"Fire the second flare battery. Number two. Number two," said Blaine trying to sound like he wasn't panicking.

"Number Two away. Oh yeah! There's another explosion," said the Engineer.

"How many left?" asked Blaine.

"There's the sub. Right over there on the screen. I think it's surfaced," said Linda pointing.

Suddenly, the yoke shuddered in their hands, and there was a loud explosion. Two rockets flashed past the cockpit, leaving white trails of smoke. "Number Three is hit. We have a fire," said the Co-Pilot.

"The auto-extinguish will get it. If they hit Number Four, we'd be down. The inboard engine is bolted to the top frame spar. We're okay," said Blaine.

"You think they will shoot again? How far do we have to go? Oh my God, what was that?" asked Linda pointing at the screen displaying the belly camera.

"Did we do that?" asked the Engineer.

"Talk to me people. I am a little busy right now," said Blaine.

"Damn. What a shock wave. That sub is gone," said the Engineer.

"What? Who did it? Any ships down there? Did they have a malfunction?" asked Blaine.

"Maybe another sub. It looked like it came out of the sky," said the Engineer.

"We need to drop another 5 thousand before we line up," said Blaine.

"Airspeed still over 250. Fire is out," said the Co-Pilot.

"Bring that tail back. Give me some flaps, and let's see if we can use the landing gear to slow us down a little," said Blaine.

"Should I restart the engines?" asked the Co-Pilot.

"Better not. We might not be able to use Number Four. That would be bit of a trick. Besides, it's not like there is much more than a chain link fence to run into down there," said Blaine.

"There's no going around," said the Co-Pilot.

"Okay, no negativity on my flight deck. Line us up. Twenty percent flaps. Gear down," said Blaine grabbing the lever and pulling it up.

The cockpit of a Boeing 747 is quiet when the airspeed gets below 200 knots. Without any engines running, it feels more like a simulator than an aircraft weighing 375 thousand pounds, not including fuel. No one had ever stalled an actual 747, and Captain Blaine Jameson didn't want to be the first.

"Gear is down, and it looks like we have hydraulic pressure," said the Co-Pilot.

"Well, will little wonders ever cease? Let's get this baby on the ground," said Blaine.

The blue and white 747 touched down on the frozen landing strip and lumbered to a stop using only the brakes. There was runway to spare, and the three men and their wives unfastened their seatbelts and hugged in the cockpit.

"That was a pretty quick war," said the Engineer.

"They'll probably just mark it up to equipment malfunction," said Blaine.

"That was a hell of a ride, Captain. It was a pleasure flying with you," said the Co-Pilot shaking his hand firmly.

"The Greenland jet is on the ground less one engine, Agent Larsen," said Rocky.

"And the Nork sub?" asked Mr. Larsen.

"The X-37B dropped a rod down their hatch. It's nice when things work the first time. A six-inch diameter tungsten dart about 8 feet long with steerable fins delivers a hell of a kinetic punch at Mach 8," said Rocky.

"I thought they were bigger than that," said Mr. Larsen.

"The first few deployments carried larger ones, and even anti-satellite weapons, but we opted for the milder sonic boom and higher weapon count. We could have taken that sub out at periscope depth, but when it surfaced, it made the target imaging system more reliable," said Rocky.

"The infamous rod of God," said Mr. Larsen.

"More like a stick, but it gets the job done," said Rocky.

"Where's the other Air Force One?" asked Mr. Larsen.

"45 thousand feet above the Gulf of Mexico," said Rocky.

"I'm sure they know about this attack by now," said Mr. Larsen.

"The chances of them having subs in the Gulf are slim, but possible. They only have twenty Romeo class Russian 1,800-ton subs painted green, but they are easy to detect. They use them to move their missiles around the Peninsula, but it's doubtful any of those snuck into the Gulf. Not that it would be that difficult if they went slow on electric power, zigzagging through 27 thousand oil rigs out there. But they have developed a 2,000-ton Sinpo-class sub that is very quiet and sophisticated. It only has one launch tube, and we are pretty sure that is not an operational capability," said Rocky.

"So, it's a little like a single-shot canon. Fire, reload, and fire again," said Mr. Larsen.

"You know it's not that easy. Missiles don't launch from inside the sub. They're ejected with gas, like oxygen or nitrogen up through the surface, the fins pop out, and the rocket lights up. It takes a trained crew and lots of practice," said Rocky.

"Not if you steal the drawings and procedures from Daewoo Shipbuilding and program the system to do it automatically. You actually believe that crap published by some defense analyst from Colorado who looks at pictures all day? Besides, my intel indicates the Norks aren't trying to start a war. They're trying to end one they have been led to believe was started by the United States 55 years ago. My guess is they are being fueled and financed by groups that need Little Kim to play the part of the unstoppable maniac," said Mr. Larsen.

"I should have sent that guy a package a year ago," said Rocky.

"That's not who we are, Rocky," said Mr. Larsen.

"You know what? Your rules have just put the lives of two million people at risk in Nashville right now. Little Kim, as you call him, is playing the part too well. It's time to end him and his game," said Rocky.

"You know as well as I do that he is placed there, in the news every day, to smudge the fingerprints of this globalist Syndicate," said Mr. Larsen, putting his hand on Rocky's shoulder.

"Don't punch out of your weight class, Tommy," said Rocky pulling his shoulder away and turning for the door.

"You know I wouldn't do that to you, Rocky," said Mr. Larsen calmly, as Rocky shot him a burning glance before walking out his office door.

"Does anybody know where the hell Jack is?" asked Rocky loud enough to be heard across all the cubicles.

"I saw her leave fifteen minutes ago. She's headed to General Banks' office," said James.

"And you let her go? Jesus, Jimmy. She's just a kid," said Rocky.

"You think I don't know that? Besides, have any of us ever been able to tell her not to do something?" asked James.

"Just because she's taller than me, doesn't mean she can't be told what to do," said Rocky.

"That was before you went away to Annapolis. She and dad got really close. She changed her name, remember? What sixteen-year-old changes her name? I have a feeling there's something she's supposed to do that we just can't do," said James calmly.

"I guess I should be glad she's not out chasing boys. I'd probably be in jail by now," said Rocky.

"I kind of pity the boy who does catch up with her," said James smiling and punching Rocky in the shoulder playfully.

"You'd be late, as usual, but I'd figure out a way to blame it on you," said Rocky smiling, then hugging his brother around the shoulders.

"Let's live long enough to find out. Okay? Let's get this guy," said James.

"Yeah, well see there is the issue isn't it? There are thousands of him, and there are hundreds above him, and dozens above them. We don't even know if there is a leader to this effort to destroy America. History shows their old dried out carcasses being buried on rainy days without much fanfare. But it is as though they never left. These wealthy, powerful psychopaths, who changed the course of history, are seamlessly replaced by other psychopaths, and the script just keeps running. It's like there is some other, much older evil who's really running things by using the greed and lust of a very few people to accomplish the mission," said Rocky.

"Now you're sounding like Mr. Larsen," said James.

"Let's not talk about Agent Larsen, Jimmy," said Rocky pointing his finger at James' chest.

"I like him. Jack likes him," said James not backing away from his brother.

"In case you haven't noticed, we do things by the book around here. We do that for a reason, so if one of us goes down, the next in command can take over the mission without getting everybody killed," said Rocky.

"What, is he some kind of free agent, or something?" asked James.

"He uses his feelings, so he says. He is smart, articulate, and inhumanly deadly," said Rocky looking at the floor for a moment.

"And, he doesn't go by the book?" asked James trying to finish the thought.

"I think he wrote the damned book," said Rocky.

"Okay. I just got a weird kind of chill going down my spine. He looks like he's maybe a thirty-eight-year-old brick shit house. Jack says he's a football coach who teaches history," said James.

"He says you can't put the future into words. He says every time it has been tried, humans read it and choose something else. You can look upstream. Everybody does that. He has a way of looking back from there to where we're standing now. Damnedest thing I ever saw, but he has saved the world more than once," said Rocky.

"Why the hell does he teach high school history and coach a local football team?" asked James.

"I used to think he was recruiting. But I remember dad telling me about a man, a special agent, who... I swear he was describing Larsen, but it just ain't possible, Jimmy. Larsen would have been like nine years old. And, when I told him I was going to Annapolis, he cried. He cried, man. He said he knew; had known for a long time. Told me I was going to be a spook," said Rocky.

"Hey. I love you, Rock. You're the best man I have ever known. You're so good, it doesn't surprise me that some intelligence out there, in the universe or even another dimension, hasn't seen it too. Let's save the world, if that's what we're going to do today. Make peace with Larsen and let's both thank God he's on our side," said James.

"By the way, I just wanted you to know it wasn't my decision. I made the suggestion, but I didn't make the choice," said Rocky.

"To do what?" asked James.

"To put you on the President's team. That was Sophia. She had a choice of virtually anyone to make up that team, and she chose you. Don't ever sell yourself short. I never have," said Rocky.

"I have had no trouble selling asphalt and rebar. Selling James is another story," said James patting his chest with his right hand.

"We would have never made it without you, helping mom and us. Just don't be afraid to love. That's all I'm saying," said Rocky, pointing through James at the door behind him.

"Hey Rousseau's. Lanny sent me to get you," said Hannah from the door.

James turned around to face Hannah, while Rocky smiled like they had been discussing what's for dinner. "Sounds dated, I know, but you had me at 'hey,'" said James walking toward her, wrapping his arms around her, and kissing her neck.

"I'd say get a room, but you probably both need showers. Besides, we have a world to save. Let's go," said Rocky.

"You're an asshole, Rocky," said James laughing.

"Tell me something I don't know. Come on," said Rocky moving past them and out into the cubicle complex.

386

"Well, Tommy said you could take a punch, but Jesus, girl. Looks like you took a size ten. You okay to run a few times for me? We have some drone pictures coming in a few minutes of this pickup truck on I-65. This is leak-bait, so it has to be run by hand. Buys us a few minutes on these bastards," said the General.

"It's okay. I just have to use this hand. I'll just sit until it comes through," said Jack.

"I take full responsibility for what happened," said the General after a brief silence.

"I guess I thought I was indestructible. I was lucky, and I know it, but I learned something. School of hard knocks, you know?" said Jack, trying to wiggle her two taped fingers in the splints.

"I should have sent Mead with you," said the General.

"No offense, but I couldn't live with the idea of escaping while someone else takes the ass whipping. Which means, we probably would both be killed," said Jack.

"Well, the silver lining is that they had to show their hand. We rounded them all up, and they are at a new location," said the General, placing her right fist into her left palm.

"What makes an American turn into one of those, those animals?" asked Jack.

"Mostly, they're ordinary people who live in a world that tends to leave them behind. They want to be rich, powerful, famous, but they know no amount of effort on their part will make it happen. They get desperate in their lust. That's when this Syndicate moves in. I would never have believed it, if I didn't see it for myself," said the General.

"Are we talking about that magic stuff again?" asked Jack.

"Magic?" asked the General.

"Mr. Knorr talks about what sounds to me like magical powers. I don't know. It sounded a little too much like a comic book to me," said Jack.

"I've fought bad guys since I was out of high school. One of these stars is for just being a woman who can shoot straight and take orders. The other two I earned the hard way. The past ten years, every time we take a city back, we find the same stuff. Someone, or something, is out there buying up men's souls. These people are no longer human," said the General.

"Who teaches that crap?" asked Jack.

"You don't have to be smart. You don't even have to be able to read, because someone will recite the words for you. Once you make the oath and go through the ritual, you belong to them. Raymond says God will never know them again. That is a terrible place to be, Jack," said the General.

"Don't they see that? I mean, don't they have dreams for themselves?" asked Jack.

"They are taught to live in the now, whatever the hell that means. There is no tomorrow, unless their demon god gives it to them," said the General.

"What's the name of this god?" asked Jack.

"Now, you're getting into Tommy's back yard. I don't know. I should, but I don't. I have seen so many names, but the oath and the rituals are all the same. It's the same guy behind all of the religions, if you ask me," said the General.

"There's got to be one that is true. Right?" asked Jack.

"If there was, it was infiltrated a long time ago and corrupted out of existence. Even Jesus only lasted what, three years?" said the General.

"It's probably why there are so many. People just keep running to the next church, looking for answers to the secret to life," said Jack.

"I'm no scriptorian, but I think that is a psyop. There is no real secret. This evil camouflages life behind money. Then, it makes people fight over it, like there isn't enough for everybody. But then, there is the joy of killing. That look they get when they take a life. That's the part I don't understand," said the General.

"You mean they like it?" asked Jack.

"Better than sex, Jack. In fact, even their sex has to be violent. A religion of peace? Give me a damned break. It's a cult of rape; rape of the body and rape of the soul. We've been fighting it in this country for more than 375 years, and Tommy says it is much older than that," said the General.

"Kind of makes you want to believe in super-heroes," said Jack, her mind wandering into the impossibility of this timeless struggle for peace.

"This is the costume of a super-hero, Jack," said the General patting the rows of medals on her left breast pocket. "Not everyone who wears it is one, but I have witnessed the most incredible acts of courage and strength you can imagine inside a uniform just like this one."

"My brother Mike calls you guys 'Wars R Us.' Always looking for a fight and bombing the shit out someone just because you can," said Jack, feeling a little like she was watching a recruiting speech.

"That's what happens when politics gets mixed with the gunpowder," said the General.

"Mr. Larsen said when the spooks are used by one party against the other party the constitution gets put in the shredder," said Jack.

"Jack, if I have learned anything from history, it is that peace comes through strength. Bad men are successful when good men do nothing," said the General.

"The cycle. It's the four phases of society; War, Peace, Mercy, Justice. That's what my dad used to say," said Jack.

"I've heard that before. It seems someone would have figured out a way to cut the chain at the right place by now," said the General.

"Oh they have, but it matters where you cut it. Mr. Larsen says the Globalists want to cut off the mercy. That way there is only justice, and you never get to the war phase," said Jack.

"Sounds like slavery to me," said the General.

"I go crazy thinking about it sometimes. It seems endless," said Jack.

"It's not the cycle, it's what you put into it that makes it so crazy," said the General.

"Is that you're message? I heard something," said Jack pointing to the screen on the General's desk.

"I'm printing it now. Take this package to Knorr. He'll send you to Rocky. Bring me the package Rocky gives you. Hustle up, Jack. You're doing great," said the General, zipping the document holder shut and handing it to Jack. She brought her feet together and snapped a salute to Jack.

Jack choked off the tears welling up in her eyes. She brought her black sneakers together and returned the first salute of her life back to the General. "I won't let you down, General," said Jack as she turned and ran out the door, wiping the tear from her black and blue cheek.

"Come in, Jack," floated the deep and calm voice as Jack entered the small office alcove of Raymond Knorr. Her fingers throbbed against the tape holding them to the shaped aluminum. She could see a little better, but her face was thick and unable to feel her long hair. She fed it behind her ear with her thumb and walked into Knorr's office.

"I have some images from General Banks, sir," said Jack standing before him, holding the zippered portfolio in front of her.

"Now, I see your father, coming through," said Knorr standing and gently accepting the portfolio from her. Jack collapsed in the soft chair in front of his desk and took a deep breath. It shuddered out of her slowly. "You don't know how good that sounds," said Jack softly.

He took the pictures out of the portfolio and looked closely at them. He pulled a magnifying loop from his desk and looked even closer at one in particular. "Major Mead? Would you come in here, please?" asked Knorr.

"Yes, sir," said Major Mead as he entered the room in parade rest and stood beside Jack. She looked up at him to her right, feeling like she had to tilt her head back to see past the swelling above her eye. He glanced down at her, but his face did not change expression in the slightest.

"I am glad to see you are so in tune, Major. You showed up at exactly the right moment," said Knorr.

"Jack, I am so sorry. I should have been here to go with you," said the Major.

"If you had, we would both be dead. I wouldn't run without you, and you know it," said Jack barely able to speak. Something in the room was building energy. She could feel it, but she did not recognize it. Her skin began to flush, and she felt like she would get sick for a moment.

"Jack. What would you like to see happen right now?" asked Knorr.

"What? I don't know," said Jack almost whispering against the roar in her head.

"Yes, you do. But you need to say it. Say it now, Jack" said Knorr very softly, very smoothly as he stood without taking his eyes from hers.

"I want. I want to live. I want to get rid of this pain and feeling hurt. I am needed, and I feel like everyone is depending on me, and I don't want to quit," said Jack, the words coming in short breaths and curled lips.

"That's what I needed to hear." Raymond Knorr moved around behind where she was seated and pulled her hair back over her shoulders and the back of the chair. "We don't have much time, and I needed the Major as a witness. These sorts of things always need a witness," said Knorr.

"What do you want me to do?" asked Mead.

"I'll take you with me. It's time you saw this as well. Place your right hand on top of mine and keep your balance," said Knorr as he placed his two enormous, white hands softly on Jack's head, and she closed her eyes. The Major placed his right hand on top of Knorr's as he began to speak.

"Jack Rousseau, in the course of time untime, we often lose our way. Memories and treasures are often shared between souls, stored sometimes for eons for a special time. This is one of those times, and we are three of those souls. Open your heart and your mind to receive that which you placed with us long ago." His words were smooth, unrehearsed or scripted, but flowed into her like they had been chiseled into stone thousands of years ago on a distant world. She could see a bright white light behind her eyelids, but she dared not open them. It started in her core and began to spin faster and faster until it expanded past her ribs and into the room around them. She felt it swallow them all in a ball of energy. She could smell the smoke of wood burning and hear the crashing of waves on the shores. She could hear Raymond speaking, but the words were far away and more like a waterfall than a voice. As soon as it began, the light slowly died out, and she felt the weight of their hands lifted from her head.

"Open your eyes Jack. I have a message for you," said Knorr.

When she opened her eyes, they were clear and wide. She lifted her hand to her cheek and felt the smooth, perfect skin she had since she was a small child. The swelling was gone. Her pain was gone. It felt like an hour had past, maybe days. "What is it?" asked Jack.

"The message is Pinnacle Javelin. Take it to Rocky and no one else," said Knorr.

"But the General... she," began Jack.

"She will be there when you get there," said Knorr.

"How do I thank you? What do you call that?" asked Jack standing up.

"Let's just call it a download. Now, go save the world, Jack. Major. This time you go with her," said Knorr.

"Yes sir," said the Major bringing his heels together. He turned on the balls of his feet and walked out the door with Jack.

Chapter 30

"Excuse me, Rocky. I'm Herbert," said Herbert putting his hand over his heart.

"Yes, I remember," said Rocky.

"I've been working with Lanny to follow some of the money that has changed hands in the past year or so. I think you will find this interesting," said Herbert motioning for Rocky to follow him to Lanny's cubicle.

"What have you found, Lanny?" asked Rocky as they arrived at his cubicle.

"Well, your boy, Herbie, has quite the nose for paper trails. It turns out we may have a second government forming ranks. These two tabs I have open show the transfer of nearly $5 billion from various State Department accounts, and matching funds coming in from Turkish sources, Ukrainian sources, a couple of old Saudi sources, and a catalog of bank accounts moving equal sums of money into a budget chart of accounts that look very much like a government agency. Only it's not a government agency. Not on the books, anyway. It looks like there is a payroll for about 200 people with marketing and transportation accounts," said Lanny.

"What the hell? None of that is legal. It almost looks like the Pentagon or the State department infrastructure. What do you make of it?" asked Rocky.

"The best I can determine, it looks like a replacement administration," said Herbert.

"I know there was a coup attempt during the first 12 months of Trump's presidency, but I didn't know they actually put together a new administration. If I knew about this, there would have been some hangings, that is for sure," said Rocky.

"If you'll recall, there was a flurry of Congressional retirements and resignations during that time. I think they're getting out, rather than keep the secret," said Herbert.

"Sounds like people wanting to go while the getting is good," said Lanny staring at his screens.

"The Syndicate bought the upper echelon of the FBI, the CIA, and The FISA Court, and Obama had his closest officers unmask the names. It was the first time our own spies were used against our own government. That's why they're running," said Herbert.

"Rocky, I got the message to join you over here. Looks like we're going to punch a hole in I-65," said General Banks walking up behind him.

"What message? I didn't send anything. Jack went to see you from here, and she's not back yet," said Rocky.

"She's coming here. Knorr's idea," said the General tilting her head.

"Oh. That kind of message. Okay. Lanny, see if you can get me a guest list to this party," said Rocky slapping him lightly on the shoulder. "Stay with him, Herbert. I'll need evidence for a trial. Understand?"

"Yes sir," they responded at the same time.

"General, may I see you in my office? And tell Larsen to grab Jack as soon as she arrives and bring her as well," said Rocky pointing to Agent Larsen's blond hair over the cubicle on the other side of the room. The General let rank equalize when she was in Rocky's vaulted territory. A ship's command sometimes took precedent over superior ranks.

He dispensed cold water into the empty bottle and took a long drink. His office chair felt new to him and he sat and leaned it back. He closed the burning lids of his eyes and tried to think of the last day he had enjoyed a full night's sleep. 'You can sleep when we're safe,' he remembered the General telling him when he started in this division. His Seal commander had told him once to never pass up an opportunity to nap. 'Just make sure to wake up when the whistle blows, or you'll be packing your shit,' he recalled with an exhausted chuckle. Within two breaths he was asleep. He fell so hard that he dreamed he was asleep, until he felt the hand on his arm.

"Rocky, it's me," said Jack leaning down close to him so she could speak softly.

"Oh. Oh yeah. Okay. Where were we?" asked Rocky taking a deep breath.

"Are you okay? You were kind of talking," said Jack.

"Yeah. Been doing that for a while. Sleep deprivation has that effect on you. How long was I out?" asked Rocky.

"I don't know. I got here like five minutes ago, and Mr. Larsen said I looked great, and then the General had us come in here. Maybe five minutes," said Jack.

"Plenty of time. Hey Major Mead. Good to see you again. What's up?" asked Rocky.

"Jack's got a message for the General," said the Major stepping back to the wall and leaning against it.

"Let's have it, Jack," said the General.

"Mr. Knorr said to tell you Pinnacle Javelin," said Jack.

"That's it then. Where's the X-37B?" asked the General.

"We have about forty minutes before it will be able to deploy a rod," said Rocky.

"It might as well be a week. Where is the vehicle?" asked the General.

"About an hour south of Franklin, Tennessee," said Rocky.

"You guys can't be serious. There are people in those cars," said Jack pointing through the wall in the general direction of Tennessee.

"How long before the Nork signal can fire the device?" asked the General.

"Assuming he can't push the button himself, it will clear the horizon in about thirty minutes," said Rocky.

"That is twelve minutes too late," said the General.

"I said there are people in those cars," said Jack raising her voice.

"Jackie. We know. Okay? This is not your average IED. We can't just snipe this guy and be done with it. We have every reason to believe it will detonate with or without him. If we try to move anyone, or isolate him in any way, he could detonate it. But if we can punch a hole through it, we might be able to fizzle it," said Rocky.

"Fizzle? What the hell does that mean?" asked Jack.

"By the way, your swelling has gone down a lot. Okay. Nuclear devices are complex. We've never seen anything even close to this small, so it goes without saying that the Norks figured out a way to do the mixing process with very small parts. If it doesn't mix under pressure at the right time, it fizzles. No explosion, no EMP. Get it?" asked Rocky.

"What difference does that make?" asked Jack.

"A small explosion of a few ounces of Plutonium might get a little dirty and break a few windows for a mile or so, but if it gets enriched with some extra neutrons, it could create a pulse strong enough to knock out power for 500 miles in every direction," said Rocky.

"It must have a power supply. The designs require about twenty horsepower to fire," said Mr. Larsen.

"I saw the hi-rez shots. It looks like a brand new Ingersoll-Rand compressor. Oh, wait a minute. The control cabinet. I'll bet that's the power supply," said the General.

"We could hit it with a hellfire from a drone," said Rocky.

"We have twenty minutes, people," said the General.

"Twenty-five minutes. Did you launch a Reaper with that camera drone?" asked Mr. Larsen.

"Standard protocol. It's 50 miles away," said Rocky.

"Where is he now?" asked the General.

"Thanks to James and his orange barrel army, he hasn't moved much in the last hour," said Rocky.

"I'm authorizing you under the Pinnacle protocol to take out the Javelin, before it takes us out," said the General.

"Yes ma'am," said Rocky tugging on the cuffs of his long sleeves.

"Rocky, I get it. I really do. But those people that are nearby; they're gonna be killed," said Jack.

"Don't ever change, Jackie. I know. I am hurting about it. But this is war," said Rocky sprinting out the door and through the cubicle complex.

"Jack. There is someone to blame for these lives we are about to take, but it is not us. If you have learned anything from our classes together, you should know this," said Mr. Larsen.

"I know. I know. I just wish there was some other way. Don't you have some magic shit you can do?" asked Jack approaching tears.

"There are no pixie missiles, Jack. Let's go find James, shall we?" asked Mr. Larsen.

They walked out of Rocky's office and around the cubicle complex to find James slumped in an office chair. Hannah stood behind him with her hands on his shoulders as he slept.

"Jack. Hey, wow, you look pretty good. Still a little blue, but none the worse for wear. Hello Agent Larsen," said Hannah. James began to stir at the sound of her voice, slowly raised his head and rubbed his eyes.

"Hello, Hannah. We came to see James, actually the both of you," said Mr. Larsen smiling slightly.

"Hey Hannah," said Jack not really focusing on the new conversation yet.

"We're coming down to the wire now. I have a feeling they know we know about their little device. I think they mean to detonate it when the North Korean satellite comes over the horizon. Our assets may not make it in time to stop it," said Mr. Larsen.

"All of this. The whole runner thing and getting my ass kicked a couple of times and we can't stop it?" asked Jack with her palms up.

"Hold on, Jack. I think Agent Larsen has a point," said Hannah putting her hand on Jack's forearm.

"Hey, Jackie. We're all together. I don't know what I would do if I was stuck in DC while you guys were here. As long as we're together, I think we can handle anything," said James still shaking off the grogginess of being up for two days.

"Yeah? Well we're healthy and locked in this safe house. What about them out there? What about old people and babies and people who need electricity to stay alive? Why can't we stop this thing?" asked Jack nearly crying.

"The Syndicate has been planning this for years, but I actually think they are rushing the schedule a little," said Mr. Larsen.

"Hey that's right. They expected Hillary to win the election. Now Trump is messing up their whole game by turning America around and energizing the whole world capitalism thing. They are going to try to stop it while the recovery is young," said Hannah.

"You are one of the few who see that. So, you know very complex technology does not like haste, but close does count when we're talking about nuclear weapons," said Mr. Larsen.

"Except my orange barrel guys stopped the Pakistani from reaching his target and escaping with the rental car. Right?" asked James.

"So maybe we saved Nashville from being flattened, but the pulse could still knock out two thirds of our grid. We have no idea if we're ready for that," said Mr. Larsen.

"I have a hunch that this is not just a terrorist attack. This Syndicate is planning something big. Just like when baby Bush unpacked the National Defense Authorization Act. We gave up our rights with a smile on our face," said Hannah.

"How hard do you think it's going to be to take the rest of them with a mushroom cloud as a backdrop?" asked James.

"Yeah. We're talking soup lines all over again," said Hannah.

"Well, now you know what we're up against. Stay alert. Eyes open. Things are going to happen fast, and I need your team to be sharp. Okay?" asked Mr. Larsen.

"Yeah. I'll tell the rest to drink another cup of coffee. We'll be ready when you need us," said James grabbing Hannah and Jack's hands with his.

"The X37B is traveling at nearly 18 thousand miles an hour. The rod must be released in the next three minutes to be steerable to the target, but here's the thing. That target can't move very far once the rod is deployed for it to be direct hit," said the General.

"The probability is much greater if we're vertical," said Rocky.

"We don't have the time to be vertical. We need to deploy in the next 120 seconds," said Mr. Larsen.

"What about the Predator?" asked the General.

"It was delayed. It won't arrive until after the Nork satellite has a chance to broadcast," said Rocky.

"Why can't I have a 50-cal chop that thing to pieces?" asked the General raising her voice to battle command levels.

"We'll just pick one up in the next two minutes at Galleria Mall just up the road," said Rocky reflecting back her battle voice.

"Just deploy the rod. We are out of time," said Mr. Larsen.

"I'm saying that there are errors that will stack up, if we do that. The lateral approach gives us a 20% chance of hitting the trailer. We'll get close, and maybe the shockwave will be enough to blow it apart, but then there is the time error. This is a static kinetic weapon. That is to say, it is a stupid tungsten dart with steerable fins. Velocity is a variable based upon unpredictable friction," said Rocky.

"So, you're saying that we could actually make the weapon more powerful by adding the kinetic shockwave to the blast?" asked Mr. Larsen.

"They will constructively interfere with one another," said Rocky.

"So what can we do to stop this thing?" asked the General.

"Get ready to send in choppers and mobile hospitals," said Mr. Larsen turning to walk out of Rocky's office.

"Pull up the live satellite feed. Put it next to the drone footage," said the General.

"Wait a second. The reaper is ten minutes out, but this little camera drone is up there right now," said Rocky.

"Javelin. Hell yes. Put the crosshairs on that bitch and aim for the battery cabinet," said the General.

"Yes sir," said Rocky leaping out the door to the surveillance control cubicle. "Put that drone right into that trailer. I want that cable set cut in half. Can you do that?"

"I will have to make some program overrides. I can do that on the way down," said the Operator.

"How long will it take?" asked Rocky.

"My best guess is three, maybe four minutes," said the Operator.

"Can you punch it?" asked Rocky.

"It only flies about a hundred knots level flight. It's designed to stay up for nine hours and take pictures. It has a 14-foot wingspan, but it only weighs about 200 pounds," said the Operator.

"If that's all we have, it'll do. 125 times 200 plus a little kerosene can ruin a garden party," said Rocky.

"I'm right above it at 12 thousand five hundred feet. Here we go," said the Operator.

"Firewall it," said Rocky.

They watched the camera feed as the display time ticked off the seconds. "Sir, the Nork satellite will clear the horizon in one minute," said Andy from over the cubicle wall.

"I need a minute or so to reach the target sir," said the Operator.

"Maybe they won't broadcast right away. They don't know this drone is approaching," said Rocky.

"They won't have another opportunity for two hours and eighteen minutes," said Andy.

"Sir, if this guy had not been delayed, he would be driving away from Old Hickory about now," said Lanny.

"Okay. This is it. We have to take this guy out now. What's the ETA?" asked Rocky

"My best guess is forty-five seconds. He'll be able to hear it in a few seconds," said the operator.

"Sir, the horizon is coming up in thirty seconds," said Lanny.

"Stay on him. If he pulls out of traffic, stay on target. Hit that trailer dead center," said Rocky.

"I have him, sir. Ten seconds," said the Operator.

The screen with the camera feed went blank. There was no sound. "Did we get him?" asked Rocky.

"The drone is offline. Could have been a delay in the feed," said Andy.

"Sir, that surveillance camera on the overpass we accessed a few hours ago is down as well. I think we have a detonation," said Lanny.

"Dammit! Holy Christ. Those bastards did it. Okay team listen up! I want system-wide diagnostics now. I want to know how big this event was. I don't care if you have to call the Kremlin to find out. Scramble a Nuke-Mat team out of Clark, and let's get some long-range stuff in here. See what hospitals are still online. I need a report yesterday on this," yelled Rocky.

"Sir, I have a Foxtrot code from Greenland Operation Bear Claw," yelled Airman Ritter.

"Somebody decode that Foxtrot. General Banks. You need to reach the President," said Rocky.

"They didn't check in, Rocky," said the General flatly.

"Sir, I have the Foxtrot Code. Air Force Two landed safely. Engine #4 was hit by a rocket. All hands safe," said the Airman.

"Glad to hear it. Someone locate Air Force One and get me a Foxtrot Code from that aircraft," said Rocky again.

"That's what I'm saying, Rocky. There was no check in from the flight deck. We have to assume it is down," said the General.

"Sir! I have a short-wave signal coming through," said the Airman.

"On speaker. I don't have time for this," said Rocky.

"Again, in case you are just tuning in, this is the Emergency Alert System, there has been a nuclear attack in Middle Tennessee. Please remain indoors for the next 48 hours. Consume food and water that is already inside your home. Do not drink city water. Stand by for a statement from the Federal Emergency Management Agency," was the voice over the speaker system.

"What? Who is that? Where is that signal coming from? Since when does FEMA make any kind of public announcement? It's been less than two minutes. How would anyone even know what to say, or that it was a nuclear attack?" yelled Rocky.

"Sir, that signal is being pinged from somewhere in Colorado. The line is still open," said the Airman.

Rocky rubbed his short hair with both hands and tried to get a grasp on what was happening. It had been too many days since he slept. He looked at General Banks and then to Agent Larsen. His cool demeanor gave him some comfort, but the answers would not come at this moment.

"Airman? Can you broadcast on that frequency?" asked Rocky.

"Yes sir, but they have it keyed," said the Airman.

"Okay. So it won't duplex. If we send out a signal of equal power, no one will hear anything. Right?" asked Rocky.

"I'm not sure, sir," said the Airman.

"In the absence of everyone in the Constitutional chain of succession, just about any person in the bureaucracy could assume control," said Mr. Larsen.

"What about the Secretary of Defense?" asked Rocky.

"I believe he is with the President," said the General.

"And for all we know, that could be at the bottom of the Gulf of Mexico," said Rocky.

"We know that is not true," said Mr. Larsen.

"We know they didn't check in. We know a nuke of unknown size and power just went off in Tennessee, and we know someone is broadcasting like they have authority from somewhere in the free republic of Colorado," said Rocky.

"Yes, and we also know that neither the President, nor his cabinet were on that plane," said Mr. Larsen.

"Yeah, and how do we know that?" asked Rocky.

"There is another plane," said Mr. Larsen.

"Military? Is that legal?" asked Rocky.

"Not exactly military. You recall Trump commissioned a new Air Force One when he was elected? Well, it became airworthy a week ago. It's not even painted yet. They took off from Boeing's plant hours after the other two planes were airborne. They've been in British airspace for the past few hours," said Mr. Larsen.

"So there were two decoys?" asked Rocky.

Yes, but now time is of the essence. Command and control are at risk," said Mr. Larsen.

"Damage assessment! I need to know how effective this device was," said Rocky.

"We have a geosynchronous unit up and running. We should be able to get an EMP map from it, provided everything we have in house is still working," said the General.

"It should be. This facility is built to take a 20 megaton pulse, as long as we're outside the blast zone," said Rocky.

"Andy. Do you have that pulse map from the GEO-3 unit ready?" asked the General.

"Yes Ma'am. I had to do some modification to the IR imaging as it was designed to pick up launch events. I figured the Infrared patch of the blast would be proportional to the EMP. After all, it has to get to about 5 thousand degrees when the X-rays are generated. That should be bright enough to see with that unit. Here is the 3-d model of the blast," said Andy expanding the screen.

"That's not a fizzle, but it isn't very large, considering the lay of the land down there," said Mr. Larsen.

"I've seen enough of these tests. My guess it was less than three kilotons. That's smaller than Hiroshima, but it also was on the ground, so the blast zone is somewhat similar," said Rocky.

"Where's Yuri? Yuri! Give us a hand here, will you?" asked Mr. Larsen.

"I'm here. What can I do?" asked Yuri.

"Take a look at this model. Can the grid handle this?" asked Mr. Larsen.

"It doesn't look so big, but when it comes to control electronics, it is more about the frequency and the amplitude than the actual blast. What I mean to say is that the pulse can be very damaging, even though the blast is not damaging," said Yuri.

"How do we find out? How much time do you need to find out if they will be okay?" asked Mr. Larsen.

"We have a network in the 2-meter band. Ten minutes if everyone is listening. All the plants have it," said Yuri.

"Get with the Airman back there and give me a damage assessment," said Rocky.

"I think it's time we moved some assets to find out who's behind this broadcast," said Mr. Larsen.

"I have a feeling our little camp Sour Grapes over there at Obamaville might be a good place to start," said Rocky.

"Feeling? Well, there may be hope for you yet, Rock," said Mr. Larsen.

"Sir, there is a broadcast leader signaling a 10-minute warning on the satellite feed. All channels, including radio, sir" said Lanny.

"All channels? That is presidential authority. Where is the studio it's coming from? I assume it is live," said Rocky.

"Unknown origin. Unknown if it's live," said Lanny.

"Andy, can you hack that broadcast? Can you stop it?" asked Rocky.

"Oh, it's on now. I always wanted to hack the EAS," said Andy again raising his workstation up to standing height.

"You see what's happening, don't you?" asked Mr. Larsen.

"I think we're witnessing Coup Two," said Rocky.

"Agent Larsen? Rocky? I have what you wanted. I think. I borrowed one of your technicians. We found the money trail. It appears we are being attacked on a very high level, sirs. I think there is a group of elites who are about to take the airwaves and seize control of the country," said Herbert.

"How high?" asked Rocky.

"I traced about $1.5 trillion behind this syndicated group of interests. They have been associated for a long time. The IRS actively covered up billions in asset transfers between foreign and national non-profit accounts. Acting like financial SWAT teams, they audited entire law firms and news organizations out of existence who tried to expose this years ago. It seems this Syndicate has been skimming money from drug cartels and numerous national treasuries to accumulate enough money to literally buy all the channels and all the networks using shell corporations all owned by a few people. Oh yeah. One more thing. It appears that some of the money went to satellite component suppliers for North Korea. I have the list," said Herbert.

"That's what I needed. Agent Larsen, would you do the country a service and have all of these individuals arrested and transported to GITMO as soon as possible?" asked Rocky.

"We'll have to utilize a tribunal to try them under the RICO Act," said Mr. Larsen.

"I like the sound of that. In the meantime, can someone please find the President for me?" asked Rocky.

"Neither one of your requests are going to be easy," said Mr. Larsen.

"We have just been attacked by North Korea. Plus, actions that look like they were coordinated with this attack. Without the Executive, and his cabinet, we are left on our own, so this is how we prosecute enemies of the State," said Rocky, pressing his point like a JAG.

"I just want you to know we're in the realm of a constitutional crisis," said Mr. Larsen.

"Sir, I have traced what I could for the HAM radio pings for this signal. It's global. Whoever it is, they're addressing the world in about seven minutes. The source appears to be in Pennsylvania, sort of," said Andy.

"What do you mean, 'sort of?' It is, or it isn't," said Rocky.

"It has the ISP of Camp David, but it's coming from a hilltop dish about 7 miles away," said Andy.

"Site R. Those bastards are using our own Site R as their base of operations," said Rocky.

"That's supposed to be impregnable," said Lanny.

"Oh it is. It's a damn city underground built in the forties to withstand everything. It was upgraded by the Obama Administration for unknown reasons on some kind of black budget," said Rocky.

"What about the antenna? Can't we just blast the antenna and stop the uplink?" asked Andy.

"General, can we get something airborne over that area in seven minutes?" asked Rocky.

"No way. We have Pinnacle protocols that have to be run after a blast like this. We cannot know what circuits have been affected. It will at least be days before we can run coordinated ops.

Maybe we can get something fixed wing up, but that's it," said the General.

"This probably means the whole stock market, banks, and retail systems will be down as well," said Rocky.

"For sure, the blockchain systems will be down, and the ACH transactions, but people can still use cash," said Herbert.

"Yeah right. Who has cash?" asked Rocky.

"In any case, there is nothing that can stop these guys from taking over the world in the next few minutes," said Andy.

"I refuse to believe that. There is no way these guys can just take the airwaves over and turn a blank page in the history book and write their own version of the future," said Rocky.

"Once they make this move, any effort to unseat them will be seen by the public as a revolution. The whole world is watching us right now. You know that. Don't you?" asked Hannah.

"I want Marines at Camp David as soon as we can get them safely deployed. I don't care if they have to ride horses," said the General. "And can we at least get an E18-G Growler in the air out of Virginia Beach? It could be there in minutes."

"That's one way to blank out a broadcast. We've never used one of those jammers in America, but it should work, if we can get it airborne," said Rocky.

"Sir, I have some sound coming over the broadcast. It's music, sir," said the Airman monitoring the airwaves.

"Music? Oh hell no. This is a rally. They are going to make this official. They're taking over the country right before our eyes, and we're stuck here. Jesus, will someone please give me some intel?" shouted Rocky.

"I have some good news, Rocky," said Yuri coming around the corner of the cubicle complex.

"That's what I'm talking about," said Rocky.

"All of our nuclear stations have X-ray and gamma-ray detectors. It appears that this device was detonated, but there are

408

a half-dozen nodes to the pulse. I don't know much about bombs, but I do know about fusion reactions. It looks like the neutron enrichment system was flawed. The timing of the injectors was all over the place. The reaction was a series of fizzles and never really reached its potential. It was stronger than a dirty bomb, but not the EMP weapon they hoped it would be, I am sure. All systems suffered communication damage, but the hardened control circuits survived on all stations. All the plants shut down safely under their own power," said Yuri.

"Shut down? So half the country is dark?" asked Rocky.

"Yes sir, but it is restorable in a matter of hours, if we can check out the substations. The substations need to go through insulation tests and some small PCB replacements, but the large equipment that is hard to replace is all intact," said Yuri.

"Jack! Jack, I need you to make a run to Mr. Knorr. We have been attacked by an outside force, but those responsible are inside our country, and they mean to conduct an insurrection in five minutes. It's clear now that they have been planning this event for quite some time, but the 2016 election loss caused them to rush things up. The fact that they panicked and pushed it so fast is probably why they made some mistakes. I think they planned on Hillary being president and nuking us as part of their takeover of the States. This wasn't supposed to happen for a while yet," said the General.

"I'm ready to go. What do you want me to tell him?" asked Jack.

"Jack, here's the thing. This Syndicate has been moving money for decades. They've been killing witnesses, arming terrorists, and seriously meant for this device to blind us long enough for them to take away the rest of our rights. We were too blind to see it, but Knorr wasn't. He knows what they were planning, and he knows what comes next. I have limited forces out there, and I need to know where to go to save this Republic. Go ask him that, and bring me the answer," said the General.

"Why don't you go with me? You ask him," said Jack standing with her hands on her hips in front of the General.

"I can't. I don't have time to tell you why. You follow this order, or you don't. That's it," said the General.

"I'll go as long as Major Mead goes with me," said Jack.

"Mead! Get over here! You're going with Jack. Fastest means possible. Got it?" asked the General pointing at her.

"Yes, General," said Jack loosely saluting with a slight smile.

"Let's go, Miss Rousseau," said Major Mead as the Marine opened the inner security door leading to the halls of the Pentagon.

Jack and the Major ran out the door into the hall, but the Major turned right instead of left. "Hey the shortest way is left," said Jack skidding to a stop.

"She said fastest means, and the halls are pretty much empty on this level. I'll show you something," he said motioning to her as he opened a rollup door that faced the hallway.

"What's in there?" asked Jack as she walked quickly up to the doorway.

"It's for first aid transportation in the building. It's kind of an electric ambulance. They're never been used, as far as I can tell. Come on. It's easier than running," said the Major as he yanked the cord out of the wall receptacle and sat in the driver's side of the two-seater flat bed cart.

"Looks like the ones on the sidelines of the football games," said Jack siting down and putting her feet against the shelf in front of her.

"The very same company. Hold on," said the Major as the cart whined out into the hallway and turned left. It was actually very fast at full speed and the tires squealed as he made the first turn to the next inner ring. The cart made all the turns and would have been quite dangerous if there were pedestrians. Within three minutes, they walked through the doorway into the office alcove of Raymond Knorr.

"We came as fast as we could. The device blew up, but it was not as bad as it could have been, and there is someone at Camp David who is getting ready to make an announcement, except it's not the good guys," said Jack speaking as fast as she could. Major Mead shrugged his shoulders as though to say he didn't have anything to add.

"And you need to know what they are planning. Correct?" asked Mr. Knorr without getting up out of his chair or raising his voice.

"Sir, both Air Force Presidential jets are down. One is damaged in Greenland but all hands are safe on the ground. The other is MIA over the Gulf. We have no location or word from the President," said the Major.

"Whatever you do, do not destroy the antenna at Site R. That network was hardened by the Syndicate and set aside for this purpose. It is supposed to work, when nothing else works," said Mr. Knorr.

"But the cell towers are down, and all networks are controlled by them, sir," said the Major.

"Major, please. Let me talk to Jack for a moment. Have a seat. Jack, tell General Banks not to harm the radio network. Let their broadcast begin as planned. Do not interfere with it. Modern cell phones have radio receivers in them, and they will pick up the audio broadcast. Let them build the audience, and let them proceed with confidence," said Mr. Knorr.

"But sir, I have to agree with Major Mead on this one. This Syndicate means to take over the country. This is their shot," said Jack still standing.

"Don't harm the antenna. Don't jam the signal. Let them have confidence. Be ready to make your arrests on the Camp David tunnel entrance to Site R. When they open the door, send in your officers in D portal and cut off their retreat. They will all be in that tunnel. No reporters. No escape," said Mr. Knorr.

"What presidential tunnel? I have been to Site R a few times. There are only two entrances," said Major Mead.

"There is another, smaller tunnel 6.7 miles long that stretches to Camp David in the forest. You would never see it coming in through Port A or B. Do you trust me?" asked Mr. Knorr.

"I trust you. Let's go, Major. Thank you, sir. For everything," said Jack touching her right cheek with her hand and smiling at him.

"Save the world, Jack," said Mr. Knorr smiling back at her.

"Sir, the music has stopped," said the Airman monitoring the radio feed.

"I can hear that. Jesus Christ, will someone shoot that damn antenna?" asked Rocky raising his voice.

"I have a Growler in the air out of Virginia Beach, and we scrambled a Reaper out of Dulles, but they're both thirty minutes minimum from getting there," said the General.

"Does anyone have a field report from ground zero?" asked Mr. Larsen.

"Negative. Everything is dark, and it will be another 90 minutes until we have a satellite image from that area," said Lanny.

"I don't know why they're doing this. Who is going to hear it, with most of the electricity down for half the freaking country?" asked Rocky.

"You said it right there, Rocky. Half the country will hear it just fine; the half that voted for Hillary," said Hannah.

"Jeepers shit, you're right. The grid a few hundred miles west of Nashville is just fine. California will hear it," said Rocky.

"They will probably just loop it, once the live part goes out. By then, word of mouth will beat it to the east coast," said Lanny.

"My fellow Americans, please stand by for an emergency broadcast from the acting President of the United States," came the male voice across the radio.

"Who is that? Whose voice is that?" asked Rocky.

"I believe that would be Eric Holder, the former attorney general," said Mr. Larsen.

'I thought that guy was in jail for that Fast and Furious thing," said Hannah.

"Oh yeah, like that was ever going to happen. Contempt of Congress is one notch down from a diplomatic parking violation on "K" Street," said James, walking up to hold Hannah's hand. She smiled at him as she considered cutting off her dread locks and having kids with this man.

"Good evening, my fellow Americans. I know we got a little sidetracked since the election, but I am here to tell you that everything will soon be back in control. A short time ago, the United States was brutally attacked by the rogue nuclear State of North Korea, after more than a year of antagonization and threats made by Donald Trump. I cannot tell you how it breaks my heart to witness this destruction.

"Unfortunately, during this counterattack by North Korea, the President and his cabinet were tragically lost over the Gulf of Mexico a few minutes ago. As I was the candidate with the most votes in the most recent election, I have agreed to serve out the remainder of the current term as your president, and hopefully my cabinet will restore the stability and rule of law the global community has come to respect and honor as the United States of America.

"For too long, we have been divided and focused only on the success of the wealthy, while ignoring the working people of this nation. For too long, we have succeeded while our neighbors to the south suffered in poverty. We simply could not allow a wall to be built between our peoples. We belong together, working and living side by side, to live in harmony in a global community. That is why I have instructed my Secretary of Homeland Security to immediately begin dismantling the Trump wall of disgrace, and rebuilding the bridge of citizenship for the millions of good, hardworking people contributing great value to our communities across the nation.

"We will need to recover quickly from this tragic attack, and to facilitate that I have asked my new FCC commission to restore Net Neutrality, guaranteeing high speed access to all and the safety of data available to everyone. We will crack down on cyber-crime, fake news, and subversive and limitless and divisive hate speech inspired by Donald Trump against people of color across this nation.

"I have also asked my Secretaries of the IRS and the US Treasury to right the ship and stop the sinking of America's economy by providing a decent living wage for all Americans and the recovery of trillions of dollars held in foreign banks by the world's wealthiest capitalists. This money will be used to repair our bridges, roads, and airports, creating millions of new high-paying jobs. And as part of my rapid recovery stimulus, the US Federal government will forgive all of its student loans nationwide. This will be the largest single investment in the future brain trust of America in history," said the female voice in a polished but wholly irritating tone.

"Somebody get me a gun," said Rocky.

"You think you are going to run over there and shoot the microphone? You'll never get in there," said Hannah.

"No. I want to stick it in my mouth. I can't stand to listen to another word of this treason," said Rocky.

"Do you think anyone is actually listening to this crap?" asked Hannah.

"You don't know DC like I do. Trust me. There is champagne popping all over the world right now," said James.

"Oh my God. They're back. What did he tell you?" asked the General as Jack and Major Mead entered the room through the secure vault's inner door.

"Don't hurt the antenna. That's what he said. There's supposed to be some kind of broadcast," said Jack almost out of breath.

"Yeah, tell us about it. We've been listening to this shit for what seems like an hour already," said Rocky again rubbing his short hair with the palms of his hands.

"Huh? What do you mean? I thought the bomb," started Jack.

"It wasn't as powerful as they wanted it to be. Power's out, but according to Yuri, all the power plants will be up and running in a few days. The damage was widespread, but pretty simple to fix," said James

"Are you sure of what you heard?" asked the General.

"She's telling you the truth," said the Major.

"You were there? You heard what he said?" asked the General.

"Yes, I was," said the Major.

"Rocky? Don't touch that antenna," said the General.

"You hear that sound, General? That's the sound of the United States of America taking her last breath," said Rocky.

"She's still breathing. The thing that makes me mad is that we knew this was possible, but we couldn't do anything to stop it," said the General.

"That's not exactly accurate, General. The DOJ had over a year to bring charges against the leaders of this Syndicate. They chose not to, for whatever reasons. Not even the President could get them to impanel a grand jury and make arrests. The elites hid behind our desire for a peaceful transition of power. They took advantage of our decency," said Mr. Larsen.

"Isn't that against the rules?" asked Jack.

"That's a better question than you know, Jack," said Mr. Larsen.

"She probably had a great history teacher," said James.

"Now, we're paying the price for that refusal to prosecute," said Rocky.

"Wheat and the tares, my brother. There is a time for harvest in all things," said Mr. Larsen.

"Now, you're sounding like Knorr. I have wanted this insurrection stopped for a long time," said Rocky.

"Wait. Didn't you say these creeps were in some place called Site R? My dad used to joke about those super resort bunkers. He used to say, 'Beat the rush. Get in your bunkers now, lock the door, and we will take it from here.' Aren't these guys in a bunker?" asked Jack.

"Yes. Well, it's kind of the mother of all bunkers," said Mr. Larsen.

"And, let's not forget, Obama poured tons of cash and resources into that underground city. I think this was all part of the plan, so you can bet they could hold off an army for years down there," said Rocky.

"Well, that's what Jack is saying, if I heard her dad's words right. While they're in that fortress, they can't run the world. They're missing the party," said Mr. Larsen.

"That's right. Who can run the world from jail?" asked Jack.

"Right now, they're doing a good job of it. The people out there in the dark want answers. I hate that this is the only voice they hear. And right now, it has to sound like angels from heaven to them," said Rocky.

"I'm with Mr. Knorr on this," said Jack.

"I know you are, Jackie. He's a great man, and I wish military people could work directly with him. I know I shouldn't say anything about this, but we're kind of at the end of the world here," said Rocky looking toward the floor.

"The hell we are. I refuse to surrender. I've been fighting this Syndicate my whole life. I have men and women face up in Arlington because of these animals. Just because she has the bully mic right now, does not give them victory," said the General.

"That being said, the one thing that separates us from evil is the policy that Raymond Knorr, and the others like him here among us, do not command arms against humans. I just want it known that without Jack, we would be blind and lost," said Rocky.

"I knew it the moment I met you, Jack. Some people are just set aside to do a certain thing. You've gotten closer to Knorr than any of us ever have," said the General.

"I didn't do anything on purpose. He's just nice to me," said Jack.

"Well, I can't see the future like he does. Tommy was the golden boy before you were born, but then 9/11 happened, and it seemed like half our Constitution was set adrift at sea," said the General.

"Hey, all of that was written before I was born, that's for sure," said Mr. Larsen.

"That may be true, but Americans would never have accepted losing that much freedom in that short amount of time without that attack on the World Trade Centers," said Rocky.

"Yeah, who was really behind that, anyway?" asked Jack.

"Same people as today," said the General.

"The Saudis?" asked Jack.

"Look at it this way, Jack. America defied the power that ran the world for thousands of years. And we were successful, because humans were meant to be free. But they want it back, and they will stop at nothing to get it," said Mr. Larsen.

"And Hillary is the person who's supposed to have this power?" asked Jack.

"Oh hell no. Her cold ambition is just a tool of the real power. She'll be betrayed and rot in front our eyes, once this coup is done. There is another behind her that will turn this place into a night club, if given half a chance," said Rocky.

"And who is that?" asked Jack.

The room fell silent long enough for the silence to become painful. "We can't say, Jack. It's not that we don't have our suspicions, but the very thought of it betrays what little faith we have left that someone is out there hoping we get it right," said Mr. Larsen.

"You mean someone that's close to Hillary?" asked Jack.

"This much we know for sure. If there was anyone who even smelled of succession, she would have them killed on the spot. Those two have made a deal much darker than anyone knows, but they have risen to this throne because they trust absolutely no one," said the General.

"Besides, the oath and covenant they had to make for this type of charm of favor requires unspeakable acts of debauchery. No one your age should ever hear of such things," said Mr. Larsen.

"For real?" asked Jack.

"Absolutely for real," said Mr. Larsen.

"Sir, I am getting something on the Foxtrot band," said the Airman.

"We know, Airman. We've been listening until we're ready to puke. Thank you for turning the volume down, by the way," said Rocky.

"No sir. Not the Site R signal. This is the Foxtrot band reserved for the President," said the Airman.

"What is the code. Can you decipher it?" asked Rocky.

"Sir, they're not sending code. They're using the band to broadcast voice. It's the Secretary of State, sir," said the Airman.

"Put it on speaker," said Rocky.

Chapter 31

"Mr. President, the device has been detonated," said the Secretary of Defense. The new Boeing was smooth and quiet, even at nearly 50 thousand feet. The Situation Room was much larger than the one on the two aging 747s. The chairs were anchored to the floor around the table, but there was enough room to recline and sleep, if meetings ran into long hours. The table's material was lightweight but made to look like polished rosewood and had portals for secure laptops at each sitting station. The President sat in the center of the side toward the hallway, facing the portals on the outside of the plane's fuselage.

"How many people were killed?" asked the President.

"Unknown, sir. If there is any good news, the blast was not as large as expected. Something went wrong inside the device," said the Secretary.

"I want to know the names of every victim. Their families need to be helped. What news of the other two aircraft?" asked the President.

"They're both down. One with all hands safe in Greenland. One engine out. One Nork sub destroyed. The other is missing over the Gulf," said the Secretary.

"Could we have stopped this?" asked the President.

"I don't think so, sir. My sources say it was planned for a long time," said the Secretary.

"What are you saying? That they knew I was going to win the White House years ago?" asked the President.

"No sir. They actually planned on doing this while Hillary was president to allow them to implement the next phase of their plan," said the Secretary.

"Oh my God. You're kidding, right? She was going to kill our own people to take people's rights away from them?" asked the President.

"The Syndicate. Yes sir. It wouldn't be the first time," said the Secretary.

"But the last one was when Bush was president. Was he part of it, too?" asked the President.

"Not relevant, sir. The planning was done before Clinton was president. If you'll recall, no one really knew who won the 2000 election until early summer. The Democrats took it all the way to the Supreme Court, trying to overturn the election. It didn't matter. They wanted the airports, the schools, and the hospitals under their control. It was the only way to create the DHS, the TSA; the whole Defense Act without massive resistance by the people. All went according to plan. They cut those buildings down with controlled demolition, destroyed the evidence, and the Syndicate's propaganda machine made sure nobody really cared to know the truth," said the Secretary.

"I never believed such evil existed in the world. You know, I wondered if there would ever come a time when I wished I never won the presidency. I guess this is one of those times," said the President.

"With respect, sir, I thank God every day that you are the President. We're with you. I mean that. This was going to happen with or without you being in the White House. Believe me when I say, we are all grateful you accepted the call," said the Secretary.

"Well, that being the case, we better turn this ship toward home, don't you think?" asked the President.

"Yes sir. Do you need anything?" asked the Secretary.

"Is the First Lady awake?" asked the President.

"No one but the crew, State, and me," said the Secretary.

"Maybe I'll take a nap. How long until we get within radio range?" asked the President.

"I'd say four hours. You'll need your rest. Go ahead," said the Secretary.

"James?" asked the President.

"Yes sir," said the Secretary pausing by the door.

"Thank you for your service. I could never have done this without you," said the President.

"I dodged so many bullets in my life, I'm convinced I've been saved for something special. I reckon this is it, Mr. President," said the Secretary.

"Let's go get our country back," said the President.

"Oo rah, Mr. President."

Within minutes, the plane stopped its lazy zigzag pattern and made a high, banking turn toward the Arctic Circle. No longer conserving fuel, the two mighty engines surged toward the faint star at the end of the Big Dipper. The President made his way quietly to his quarters, slipped his jacket off and hung it on the fixture in the center of the massive closet. He washed his face with cold water, dried it on the cotton towel, put on his pajamas, and slid into bed next to his sleeping wife. He didn't think it would come too easily. It never had before. But within a few, deep breaths, the three days he had gone without sleep relented, and he fell into a deep and quiet sleep.

Boeing had almost spared no expense on this ship, knowing that it would make perhaps hundreds of treks over the most turbulent spiral of high-speed wind on the planet. They had mounted the first bed on special servos that could counteract the wiggles and bumps these big birds endured, leaving the bed frame practically motionless relative to the plane. Layers of open and closed cell foam did the rest to keep the over-sized king mattress as motionless as though it was mounted on a granite slab on the 95th floor of Trump Tower.

The Chief of Staff got the notice first that the ship was fifteen minutes from being able to utilize the 2-meter radio transmitter with a narrow-beam antenna mounted in the enormous carbon-fiber nosecone to send the President's message.

"Okay. Thanks. Actually, I feel pretty good. What's in the cup?" asked the Chief of Staff.

"It's coffee with a double shot of oxygen," said the tall girl in a black flight jumper.

"Sounds interesting. Just leave it there. I've got some bullet points to put together," said the Chief of Staff.

"Yes sir. It's better hot," said the girl as she left his small quarters and closed the door.

He took a sip of the hot coffee and rolled the flavor around his tongue before swallowing it. The warmth sent a wave through his body as he slipped a fresh white shirt on from the small closet in his sleeping room. Remaining at high altitude fatigued the body, because the cabin pressure was actually close to six thousand five hundred feet. After twenty hours in the air, it was easy to lose some mental sharpness. Injecting pressurized oxygen into the water used to make coffee made it available to the body through absorption, rather than breathing. The effect was better decisions.

He cinched up his tie, slid his arms through his customary dark blue jacket and hooked his first two fingers through the black mug for another sip as he headed up the narrow hall toward the POTUS section. He loved working with Donald Trump. He was limitless. Although he never served in the military, he had the right thoughts about it. Neither Clinton, nor Obama served in the military, but they hated the institutions. Both men were quick on the draw and had no problem bombing civilians and fighters alike, if, and only if, there was a political advantage. They would run commercials before a focus group. If it went well, the bombs were dropped sometimes within minutes. If the line in the sand got a little too much pushback, they would halt in their tracks, even if it meant losing entire cities to our enemies.

Trump wasn't afraid of using force, but he didn't sit down with a focus group before taking action. Our enemies knew it as well, because a few of them called his bluff and lost. No one bluffs Donald Trump.

He stopped at his door and pressed the panel by the door. The screen brought up a keypad, and he poked in his code to bring the lights up on the President's nightstand. Within seconds the door cracked open.

"It's time, sir. I'll get Mad Dog," said the Secretary.

"Thanks, John. I'll be right out," said the President.

He walked toward the Situation Room and noticed the light was already on. The Secretary of Defense was already standing in front of the conference table along with a few members of the House and Senate Intelligence Committee. The Boeing could seat more than 400 people, but in this configuration there was only room for 235 people. The leaders inside the Administration who believed in America were quietly transported to the Boeing facility in time for the secret test flight. The two 747s were decoys; one on the ground in Greenland with a hole through its #3 engine, and the other missing for unknown reasons.

"Did you hear this broadcast on the EAS bands by Hillary?" asked Secretary Mattis.

"That's got to make your boys at the Pentagon hot to trot," said Secretary Kelly.

"I like to make people afraid of the dark, you know," said Mattis.

"I guess we're headed for Camp David. That's okay with you?" asked Kelly.

"It's nobody's business what happens down there. I'm glad I never became a lawyer," said Mattis.

"I just got a funny feeling," said Kelly with his now famous understated smile.

"Funny like, watching a pit bull chase cats?" asked Mattis.

"Funny like, they have no idea what's coming," said Kelly.

"Okay gentlemen. I'll take your input now," said President Trump walking into the Situation Room. It was his way of priming everyone to take rapid turns giving their elevator pitches. 'If you can't tell me your story by the 25th floor, what the hell good are you?' he would say.

"They're celebrating their victory and making their speeches from the Site R Radio Room in Building E. There are only three ways out of there, and my guys will be ready by the time we land at Camp David," said Mattis.

"I say we ghost their broadcast and let Mad Dog do his thing, Mr. President," said Kelly.

"Anyone else? Say it now, or shut the hell up. Okay, let me see the bullet points, John," said the President.

He took a deep breath through his nose and focused on the list of points John Kelly had penned a few minutes before. He thought of Baron and Tiffany and the Golden Mothers he had met just a couple weeks ago. He couldn't stop the mental image of smoke blowing around the green valley south of Nashville. He recalled the hundreds of enthusiastic people that greeted him at Davos, Switzerland a few weeks ago. Still, there was a smell of greed and avarice that blamed him for the loss of their control of the world. He was used to tearing up a board room full of haughty news actors, or shouting down a team of bankers trying to steal a loan from his portfolio. He was not used to seeing so many people in custom tuxedos who wanted him dead.

"When do we go live?" asked the President.

"I vote for John's idea first. We ghost their broadcast. Let them think it's being heard by the world, but shut down the range to about twenty miles. Let me move a brigade to the main entrances of Site R with a backup on the hill. They won't dare take a shot at our guys. That leaves the 6.7 mile Camp David corridor as the only way out. We'll let them begin their escape, and then we'll see if they're afraid of the dark. Once they're running down that tunnel thinking to escape, we put them to sleep," said Mattis.

"What about the Norks, Mr. President?" asked Kelly.

"I've given that a lot of thought since 9/11, you know," said the President.

"Why that far back, if you don't mind me asking?" asked Kelly.

"Not the Norks, per se. I mean how would I have responded? What's the right way to respond to a single act of terror like this? If you think about it, how Bush responded to that event changed the world forever. In a bad way, that I can tell you.

"There was a moment when we weren't at war, after that attack. And then, suddenly we were at war. I always thought about that day. I could smell that whole business from my home on 5th Avenue, you know. America was kind of in this state of numbness, like when you get hit by a car and you're still awake. And in that state of weakness, some bad guys moved in, packed up our civil rights, and took them away. We went and spent a trillion dollars to blow a bunch of places up, but we lost nearly all our rights. They just came in and took them. We lost all our airports in like a month. We got a dozen new bureaucracies and have to be strip searched any time we want to fly anywhere. We lost. I never understood that.

"So, I want to address that. And, I don't want to make the same mistake with America. This time we win. You understand that? This time we win," said President Trump.

"I get it, Mr. President," said Secretary Kelly.

"When do we let the world know we're still alive? How close are we?" asked President Trump.

"My Marines will be at Camp David within the hour," said Secretary Mattis.

"Okay. Let's do this," said President Trump.

The three men descended the stairs below the floor into the radio studio where a young Airman stood by. The tiny studio could seat four people, so they entered, and Kelly pulled the door closed and sealed it. They sat in front of the glass while the President sat behind the glass. It was practically silent with extra sound deadening and isolation from the whine of the two enormous turbofan engines and from the fuselage moving through the atmosphere at more than

11 miles a minute. The Airman pressed the power buttons on the linear amplifiers of the two-meter radio and pointed to the President through the glass.

The President adjusted the mic close to his mouth and settled the headphones over his ears. He had one half-sheet of paper in front of him with some printed bullet points from General John Kelly, his trusted Chief of Staff. There was no speech writer, no focus group, and no rehearsal. This was it.

"My fellow Americans, this is your President speaking to you from an undisclosed location, for national security reasons. First, let me tell you that I am indeed alive, and so is the core of my cabinet and many of your elected officials. We are safe and on our way as we speak to help you.

"We are waiting for the facts to come in, but it appears that a small nuclear device was detonated just outside of Nashville, Tennessee. Thanks to extremely fast thinking of our men and women in uniform, and members of our intelligence community, it could have been so much worse. I know it's bad, but it could have been worse. For now, stay inside, drink plenty of water, Iodine if you have it, and wait for help to arrive.

"I promise you that help is on the way. Many of you are just now finding out what happened, because of the nature of these types of weapons. They're designed to take out communications and maybe even knock out your power. But let me assure you that experts are telling me that the device only caused temporary damage. All of our power plants survived. Within a few days, we should have power restored. Don't panic. Emergency teams are on their way to the Nashville area now, and properly equipped volunteers are forming rescue companies faster that the Federal government ever could. Believe me, we are feeding them tools, supplies, and support as fast as we can.

"Now, I know you are wondering who did this. Well, for one thing, the person responsible for building the device died in the event. He will never do it again, that's for sure. The technology to build it came from North Korea, but they are only part of the picture.

"You will recall the Senate Intelligence Oversight Committee condensed hundreds of pages of evidence into a 4-page memo that we considered releasing to the public. At the last minute, we decided to begin the process of making some arrests from that memo for activities that could be classified no other way but treason. I know that sounds strong coming from a President, and it is, because it was nothing less than treason against the sovereignty and the Constitution of the United States of America. Maybe we should have gone public with it, but it was decided not to.

"Well, if I had to do it over again, I would have made it public and let the chips fall where they may. I know there are many of you now in the sound of my voice that want something to be done. This criminal Syndicate, many members of which are named in that memo, has been trying to take over America since the moment of the blast. They shot down two Presidential Air Force aircraft today. Even now, we're not sure of our losses in those attacks. Rumors of the deaths of my cabinet and I are greatly exaggerated, let me tell you that.

"I know how you feel. We've been here before. We had a President stand on a pile of rubble and take our world back to war. And I know many of you want us to go to war and wipe these guys off the face of the Earth. But, I have given this eighteen years of thought and prayer. I doubt a day has passed I haven't thought about it. Let me comfort you and assure you that this is not a time for war. This is a time of justice. And the sword of justice shall fall swift and terrible for the members of this Syndicate trying to take our country from us.

"Our friends and our enemies are watching us, right now. They are wondering if we will prove ourselves a nation governed by the rule of law. They are watching if once again the wealthy and the politically powerful will walk free. Well, watch and wonder no more. You have my word that we are coming for them; each and every one of them. We have a place to hold them away from their cymbals and their horns. We have laws and judges and courtrooms waiting. And outside of those rooms we have gallows and prisons prepared for them. The time for justice has arrived. In the next few hours, the laws of our country will be swiftly and surely executed, once and for all.

"My heart is with you right now. God bless you all, and God bless the United States of America." He looked up at the Airman on the other side of the glass and winked. The amplifiers were put into standby, and the President took off the headphones.

Over the next few days and weeks, the attempted Coup against the American government was thwarted. Members of the Syndicate fatally resisted arrest in the deep tunnels of Site R. Hundreds more were arrested, stripped of their assets, and sent to prison. Lawyers, Agency officers, and contractors were also rounded up in massive sting operations that had been operating for over a year. Foreign foundations were raided, their assets also seized, and their boards of directors were arrested and jailed for subversive activities.

The laws and rules once used by the Syndicate's legal armies to protect themselves, and to conduct terroristic litigation against their enemies, were turned against them by the Department of Justice. The President did go to war, but it was fought by Grand Juries and U.S. Marshalls. Oppressed countries like Haiti and South Africa celebrated in the streets as entire gangs of bankers and oligarchs were arrested, and billions in stolen money was returned to their treasuries. It was a rare time in history, all because one man had the authority and courage to declare the rebirth of the age of justice; indivisible and for all.

Epilogue

Private citizens have secrets. It's when governments have secrets that freedom and liberty are at risk. In order for there to exist a government that is truly empowered by the people to serve the people, there must be transparency of those operations. When a government has to tell the public that it is transparent, then it most assuredly is not. When the elected government is compromised by global corporations to allow their unelected Agency government to write law, assess taxes, and conduct enforcement actions, the government drifts behind opacity, unseen and untouchable by the people.

In 1848, the Anti-Federalists incorporated as the Democratic National Committee, with the sole focus of making sure America is governed by the Executive Branch. Congress lost control and oversight of the American government in 1933, with the election of Franklin D. Roosevelt. That new Agency government grew to overshadow the elected government completely. The flow of propaganda from its many departments is superbly written and universally publicized by a small handful of the elite through every form of media. Any casual survey of public news will reveal that more than 90 percent of the narrative attacks the American government in favor of a globalist philosophy.

What is encouraging to behold, is that the American people have refused to totally comply with this propaganda campaign for more than 84 years. Nearly every other nation on Earth has allowed itself to be invaded by enemies, to be robbed of its sovereignty, and to be amalgamated into a globalist population of victims, unable to function without the guidance of a nameless central authority that enslaves them. Their people know they have been enslaved, and yet they lack the will to fight against their oppressors.

Americans, historically, have refused to bow down to a central authority. They refused to surrender their individual rights to anyone. That being said, voters, produced by government schools since the creation of the Federal Department of Education, have been far more willing to abdicate their own care and feeding to the State. They have been taught that food, higher education, housing, and healthcare are all rights guaranteed by the State. They have been taught that successful people are obligated to finance these benefits for those who refuse to become productive members of society. They believe that it is government's job to seize the earnings of the productive members of any community on behalf of those who refuse to produce.

Tax revenue from the world's largest economy, worth more than $100 trillion a year, is over-spent by the Agency government, and there is little or nothing that Congress or the President can do about it. As in all despotic governments, they spend a substantial portion on enriching themselves. They spend a small amount investing in votes to keep their puppets in power, and the rest on their supporters who provide them with the authority from which they receive their bounty. The most casual observer can see there should be no way a politician earning $174 thousand dollars a year can accumulate $70 million in personal wealth in less than 8 years. And yet, nearly every single member of Congress has accomplished that very thing.

When something or someone threatens to remove them from power, or to weaken their position, the Agency forces will destroy that enemy. Sometimes, that person is simply shot in the back on the sidewalk. Sometimes, they are targeted by one or more of the Agencies, causing their financial ruin. Sometimes, they are simply tried and convicted in the court of public opinion, even if every word that is printed or read aloud is a complete fabrication. When there are too many enemies to quietly murder, acts of war or terror will be carried out to correct the course in their favor.

This book told a true story of the richest, most bloodthirsty criminal Syndicate the world has ever known. Now you know that it is no conspiracy of which I write. The bodies are real. The larceny is real. The weapons of mass destruction are real, and by the time you read these words, the threats of their use to accomplish the ends of this globalist Syndicate will have already occurred.

Am I a prophet or a seer? No. I am a statistician and a lifelong professional analyst for some of the world's largest manufacturing corporations. I had two goals in writing this book.

The first was to open your eyes by connecting the events in a sequence for which there can be no doubt whatsoever of their planning and guidance. The Syndicate's plan has been to destroy the experiment called America. It has been relentless for more than 241 years. During the last 84 years, it has killed nearly 100 million innocent people, stolen trillions of dollars, and will stop at nothing to accomplish its goals; including the use of nuclear weapons to stop America's current, unprecedented recovery.

The second is to warn you, the reader, that there is very little time and yet a very powerful opportunity for each of you to do something to stop the destruction of America. Know this. If this globalist Syndicate is successful and America is destroyed, liberty and freedom will disappear from the Earth forever. At the writing of this book, there is at least one active plot to carry out an act of terror orders of magnitude more deadly than 9/11. They will blame the Republicans and of course the nationalist leadership of Donald Trump. Polls of voters under the age of 45 indicate that 56% of them will agree with that assessment.

There must immediately begin a new future, with a new timeline, that does not include the evil presence of this Syndicate. First, the Syndicate's puppet politicians must be voted out of office. All of them. The best advice I can give to America is to vote 100% of the Democrats out of office. This will complete the already waxing bankruptcy of their corporation and make way for other political parties to reach the State ballots. You should develop a rash every time you hear the world *bipartisan*. The remaining corrupt Republicans will have no one with whom to collude, so they will starve themselves out of existence or run for their political lives. By the time this book goes to print, you will witness 10% or more of the establishment Republicans retire or announce their resignations.

The terms of the next elected government must be limited to prevent what we just witnessed over the past few decades as the Agency government achieved critical mass. If it takes an Article V Convention to amend the Constitution to pass these 6 Amendments, then so be it:

1. Term limits on all elected officials. The current consensus is that the Congressional term should be lengthened to 4 years, and the number of terms should be limited to 3. The Senate's term is split between people who think they should be removed from elections at large and be returned to appointment by the State Legislature. That would remove the corruption of billions in election campaign funding. Terms would be limited to 3 six-year terms.
2. A balanced Federal budget except in times of lawfully declared war. This would eliminate the Continuing Resolution and the threat of government shutdowns.
3. The Dissolution of all Federal Agencies, Departments, Bureaus, and Administrations to instead be managed by councils of the States. This would end the 655 Agencies, Departments, Bureaus, and Administrations as well as their Federal authority to write law without representation.
4. A revised and clarified Commerce Clause to prevent the Federal mandating of purchased services. This would block things like Obamacare from every occurring.
5. Require positive identification for all individuals who choose to exercise their right to vote in Federal elections.

This would prevent massive voter fraud using foreign citizens to vote in Federal elections.
6. Rescind the 16th Amendment and replace it with a Federal sales tax in compliance with the original Constitution. This would eliminate the income tax and stop the unwarranted forfeiture of the 5th Amendment rights of every working American to the IRS.

For more information, visit www.cosaction.com. In order to restore the people's faith in the integrity of America, the individuals responsible for these heinous criminal acts must be brought to justice and prosecuted with full restitution. If they are left alone, because they are too politically energized to prosecute, then the world stands a very good chance of losing its champion of liberty and freedom.

This call to action may not be limited to America. If we want to prevent the globalists from robbing the people of their sovereignty, all free people of the Earth should banish their dictators and oppressive religious regimes.

It is a call for Persians to rise up and reclaim their country from the Aryans who robbed their heritage. It is a call for the tribes of Europe to throw off the yoke of oppression by an evil central body of rulers who seek to enslave them.

Women of the world must declare their individual sovereignty and throw off the oppression of men. They are free to take off their sacks and show their beautiful smiles according to their own free will and choice. It is a call for all people to declare that all rights come from God and not from government or from churches.

The people of Earth are not one people. We are many people from all over the universe, living in harmony on the most amazing planet in existence. It is time to face the truth. None of us are from around here. Instead, we chose to come to this world. So, let us begin to take it one day at a time without war, without evil, and with bounty for all and to spare.

Remember; everything we do will eventually affect the universe. Let's do it on purpose.

The End.